History, Abolition, and the Ever-Present Now in Antebellum American Writing

OXFORD STUDIES IN AMERICAN LITERARY HISTORY

Gordon Hutner, Series Editor

History, Abolition, and the Ever-Present Now in Antebellum American Writing

Jeffrey Insko

OXFORD
UNIVERSITY PRESS

OXFORD
UNIVERSITY PRESS

Great Clarendon Street, Oxford, OX2 6DP,
United Kingdom

Oxford University Press is a department of the University of Oxford.
It furthers the University's objective of excellence in research, scholarship,
and education by publishing worldwide. Oxford is a registered trade mark of
Oxford University Press in the UK and in certain other countries

© Jeffrey Insko 2018

The moral rights of the author have been asserted

First Edition published in 2018

Impression: 1

Published in the United States of America by Oxford University Press
198 Madison Avenue, New York, NY 10016, United States of America

British Library Cataloguing in Publication Data

Data available

Library of Congress Control Number: 2018941695

ISBN 978-0-19-882564-7

Printed and bound by
CPI Group (UK) Ltd, Croydon, CR0 4YY

For Pat and John Stephenson

{ ACKNOWLEDGMENTS }

It took me a very long time to write a book about haste and impatience. One of the happy effects of living with that form of temporal dissonance, however, has been the opportunity to engage an ever-expanding circle of intellectual companions and interlocutors. I have many people to thank.

I'd never have imagined studying literature much less attending graduate school were it not for my earliest mentors, Warren Rosenberg at Wabash College, and Andrew Levy at Butler University. They taught me how to be a student and a scholar. My teachers and advisors at the University of Massachusetts, most especially Nick Bromell, who encouraged this project from its idiosyncratic (and deeply flawed) origins, and Randall Knoper, likewise, had a transformative effect upon me. Without them, I'm not sure I'd have discovered the nineteenth century in the first place. I am grateful for their guidance then and their friendship now.

I am lucky to work and teach in an unusually congenial and supportive environment, made so by my Oakland University colleagues and our remarkable students. A University Research Fellowship, able research assistance from Christina Moore, and a graduate seminar with an extraordinary group of students, including Lisa Czapski, Jennifer McQuillan, Kelly Garnett, and Chinmayi Kattemalavadi, way back in 2007, helped me imagine what some of my longstanding interests in historical consciousness might look like as a book. My retired colleagues Jane and Bob Eberwein, Brian Connery, Ed Haworth-Hoeppner, and Gladys Cardiff provided me with models to emulate and taught me the rewards of professional generosity. I am likewise indebted to my current colleagues, who continue to maintain a vibrant environment in which to work. I am especially grateful for my friend and collaborator Andrea Knutson, a brilliant scholar and model colleague. A summer writing group with her and Joanie Lipson Freed at a key point in the life of this book helped me work out its narrative arc. The arrivals of Tim Donahue and David Shaerf have also had an energizing effect upon my work as a teacher and researcher. I thank Kevin Laam, too, whose friendship and ongoing support as department chair keep Oakland feeling like home sweet home. And from the day I arrived in Michigan, my four-fold friend Robert Anderson has been a wise and steady presence in my working life. I am lucky to have him as a teaching partner and sounding board; camerado, I give you my hand.

This project has also benefited immeasurably from the many relationships I have formed outside of Oakland. Foremost among them are those fostered by the Civil War Caucus of the Midwestern Modern Language Association, surely the ideal of an intellectual community. The warmth, generosity, and considerable intellectual firepower of that collective reflect the leadership of Kathleen Diffley, a living cynosure if there ever was one. Whenever I felt like I'd never finish this book, Kathleen reminded me otherwise by helping me not worry so much about it; that was a true gift. I have received more than my share of learning and encouragement from exchanges, formal and informal, with other members of the Caucus as well: Cody Marrs, Elizabeth Duquette, Kristen Treen, Elizabeth Young, Ian Finseth, Cristie Ellis, and Andrew Kopec among them. Other Caucus members read draft portions of this book. Gregory Laski read more than his fair share of these pages, as did Michael Stancliff and Justine Murison. Their knowledge and insight improved these pages substantially. John Levi Barnard offered conscientious advice on the book's Coda, and Julia Stern offered insightful feedback on a draft of the introduction. I am even more deeply indebted to Justine, John, and Julia for their warmth and kindness during a difficult several months I spent living in Chicago, struggling to finish these chapters in the midst of other, more pressing, duties. Their good company provided me with rejuvenation when I most needed it. Everyone should have such friends.

A portion of Chapter 1 appeared in *Early American Literature*, and portions of Chapter 2 appeared in *American Literary History* and the edited collection *John Neal and Nineteenth-Century American Literature and Culture*. I thank University of North Carolina Press, Oxford University Press, and Bucknell University Press for permission to reprint the material here. I also thank the anonymous reviewers for those publications, as well as Edward Watts and David J. Carlson for their valuable feedback. I am grateful to others who have read portions of this manuscript as well. Nick Bromell and Rachel Banner gave generous readings to Chapter 4, and John Evelev helped me clarify the argument of Chapter 5. I benefitted also from the careful consideration and constructive suggestions offered by the readers from Oxford University Press, as well as the able stewardship of the press's production team. I will also always be profoundly grateful for the early encouragement, ongoing support, and frank editorial advice of Gordon Hutner.

Over a number of years, portions of this manuscript saw their first light of day at professional conferences, notably those hosted by C19: The Society for Nineteenth-Century Americanists, the American Literature Association, and the Melville Society. I am thankful for receptive audiences in those venues and for the encouragement and comments I have received from fellow panelists, collaborators, and scholars whose work I admire, including Patricia Roylance, Melissa Gniadek, Lloyd Pratt, Thomas Allen, Dana Luciano, Hester Blum, Christopher Looby, Stephanie Foote, Jamie Jones, Matthew Rebhorn, Michelle Sizemore, Chris Castiglia, Robert S. Levine, and Cindy Weinstein.

No expression of thanks could account for the debt I owe to my bosom companion Christopher Hanlon, who not only read every word of this manuscript but lived through it with me, always there to praise, challenge, motivate, or scold, as needed. More than my friend and most trusted reader, Chris is my own inseparable twin brother; an invisible Siamese ligature unites us.

I regret that two of my greatest supporters won't see this book in print. I wrote the final two chapters while mourning the losses of my dear friend, colleague, and mentor Susan E. Hawkins and my mother Patricia Stephenson. Both great sources of strength to me, they wanted to see this project through perhaps even more than I did. For that reason, celebrating its completion has become part of the grieving process for others who also loved them and who care about me: Jay Margulies, Abigail Webb, Mike Insko, Kevin Insko, Heather Stephenson Morell, Penny Douglas, Pam Van Kurin, and Sandy and Jim Bodenmiller, among others.

Finally, my deepest gratitude will always be reserved for my best friend and partner Katy Bodenmiller, the ever-living presence in my life. Her brilliance, integrity, strength, and compassion have made this book—and me—immeasurably better. I look forward to looking back with her, forever. And Sam is a good boy.

{ CONTENTS }

Introduction

THE LIVING PRESENT

In March of 1857, William Lloyd Garrison returned to his hometown of Newburyport, Massachusetts, to deliver the final lecture of the city's Lyceum season. The local press anticipated fireworks. The *Boston Journal* noted that the announcement of Garrison's appearance had "created quite a commotion among the old fogies" and expected that Garrison would "hit some hard blows all around." The more reserved *Newburyport Herald* simply observed that many of the city's residents, "who have never seen or heard him, so much observed and listened to, will be glad to avail themselves of the opportunity to do so." The *Herald* also remarked that Garrison had not "select[ed] a subject...involving his peculiar views," but would speak instead on "The Dead Past and the Living Present."[1]

Contrary to the *Herald's* description, that subject had everything to do with Garrison's "peculiar views." It was, in fact, the very source of their peculiarity. A zealous devotion to the "living present," to acting on the exigencies and emergencies of *now*, vitalized Garrison's immediatist abolitionism from the launch of *The Liberator* in 1831. In his famous inaugural editorial, Garrison recalled his past support for "the popular but pernicious doctrine of gradual abolition" and announced that he would "seize this moment to make a full and unequivocal recantation, and thus publicly to ask pardon of my God, of my country, and of my brethren the poor slaves, for having uttered a sentiment so full of timidity, injustice, and absurdity." He dramatized the urgency of the moment and the "absurdity" of inaction with characteristic acerbity: "Tell a man whose house is on fire to give a moderate alarm; tell him to moderately rescue his wife from the hands of the ravisher; tell the mother to gradually extricate her babe from the fire into which it has fallen;— but urge me not to use moderation in a cause like the present."[2]

History, Abolition, and the Ever-Present Now in Antebellum American Writing begins with Garrison's experience of the present moment's dire intensity because for him and a number of his contemporaries, that experience exemplifies an attitude and stance toward history and one's own place in it that is this book's central focus. So, for example, when in the Newburyport lecture, Garrison concedes that a certain "reverence for the past is commendable," yet warns against the stagnation and imitation that is the result of too much worship for its great figures, he echoes a crucial element of the thought of Ralph Waldo Emerson, who, in similar language, sought for himself and his contemporaries an "original relation with the universe."[3] Garrison's view of what Emerson called "foregoing generations" is that "it is well to be inspired by their example, but we are not to make our admiration of them a finality; nor to stop where they stopped; nor to borrow their dialect; nor to wear their garb." Nor were Garrison and Emerson alone in their aversion to efforts to ossify or monumentalize the past, their resistance to historical "finality," and their embrace of the present as the sphere of action. Garrison's friend the radical abolitionist and reformer Henry Clark Wright, for instance, lectured throughout the 1850s on "The Living Present and the Dead Past." In his book of that title, published in 1865, Wright likewise emphasized action, describing the contest between living present and dead past as "a conflict of ideas and feelings, as well as of words and deeds."[4]

More famously, Frederick Douglass expressed this view in his July 5 address at Corinthian Hall in 1852. Turning away from the obligatory homage to the Revolutionary generation with which he begins the speech toward more immediate concerns, Douglass states, "My business, if I have any here to-day, is with the present," for "Now is the time, the important time."[5] For poetic emphasis, Douglass then recites the following lines:

> Trust no future howe'er pleasant!
> Let the dead past bury its dead!
> Act,—act in the living present!
> Heart within, and God o'erhead![6]

This stanza, as everyone knows, is from Henry Wadsworth Longfellow's extraordinarily popular "A Psalm of Life" (1838), the era's pithiest, but perhaps also its most saccharine, encomium for action in the present—and the poetic touchstone for the title and theme of Garrison's address. Less known than Longfellow's poem itself is this particular stanza's considerable political force in the antebellum period, visible in its wide circulation among white and black abolitionists, who employed these lines as a kind of immediatist slogan throughout the 1840s and 1850s. Douglass cited them as early as 1846 in a letter to his British friend Elizabeth Pease, after noting, "we have immediate and pressing duties to perform."[7] Two years later in *The North Star*, commenting on the Free Soil convention in Buffalo, New York, he wrote, "We feel it our duty to pursue that course which will make us in some degree a terror to evil-doers, and a praise to all that do well—to 'act in the living present'—to be a worker on the anvil now before us—that whatever influence we may possess, it shall be given in the right direction."[8] The same year, in defense of the Free Soil party's nomination of Martin Van Buren for President against charges of past capitulation to the slave power, an editorial in *The National Era* asked, "What the Past to us? We are actors in the

Present, and the evil of others in the Past, will not excuse us for not emulating their good in the Present. 'Let the Dead Past bury its Dead! Act—act in the *Living Present*, Heart within and God overhead.' "[9] Several years earlier, at a suffrage convention for free blacks in Troy, New York, in 1841, delegates passed this resolution:

> That as in looking into the past, we behold nought but chains and slavery, and as a blind trust in the future is vain and delusive, we regard it as a weighty duty imposed upon us to "Act in the *living present* Heart within, and God o'erhead.[10]

Mindful of those suffering in bondage, immediatist abolitionists didn't have the luxury of justificatory appeals to custom or cautious hand-wringing over the social and political uncertainties that would attend emancipation. They were gladly willing to break with the past and risk the dangers of an unknown future to achieve a more just present. And they found in Longfellow's seemingly unthreatening poem, widely embraced by the public, an articulation and vindication of their own radical position.

Despite the importance of "A Psalm of Life" to white and black abolitionists, modern readers have had difficulty taking the poem seriously, whether despite or because of its extraordinary and largely unprecedented popularity, a popularity that has lasted for nearly two centuries. Critical assessments of the poem long ago hardened into mockery. It is "full not only of outworn metaphor, but of superficial literary allusion" and "has spoken, as it will speak for generations more, to the hearts of simple-minded men." It is a "very bad" poem, nothing more than a "masterpiece of Yankee Unitarian agitprop," the "quintessence of facile banality," "Victorian cheerfulness at its worst."[11] To modern ears, even the line that spoke most powerfully to those who dedicated their lives to the fight for emancipation— "act in the living present"—rings hollow, like an adolescent cliché. Little more than a variation of the *carpe diem* trope, its earnest sincerity is a bit too grating for the ears of modern ironists. Longfellow's sentiment is suitable, perhaps, for *Dead Poets Society*, but is surely among the least interesting or complex elements of Romantic thought.

Yet the poem's resonance, or perhaps more accurately, its adaptability, both for the antislavery movement and for the particular conception of history that forms the main subject of this book, invites reconsideration.[12] Much of the poem's political force in the antebellum period surely resided in the way it appears to register, if not encourage, simultaneously, both the temerity and impetuosity of immediatism *and* the timidity and forbearance of more moderate gradualism; it encompasses at once multiple and disparate modes of antislavery. Just as importantly for my purposes, it also encompasses distinct modes of temporal being: the unhurried, regular pace of progressive chronology and the hastened, uneven movement of action and event. That is, while the poem's most famous lines, like "Let us be up and doing"—which Kirsten Silva Gruesz calls "the motto of the age"[13]—and "Be a

hero in the strife!" exhort action, the poem at the same time seems to counsel
passivity and patience:

> Let us then be up and doing,
> With a heart for any fate;
> Still achieving, still pursuing,
> Learn to labor and to wait.

"Fate" and "wait" are linked here by more than just rhyme: both suggest a certain
acquiescence to events beyond one's control, a passivity that is strangely at odds
with the poem's call to action. The injunction "to wait" is even subtly reinforced by
the repetition and latent signification of "still," the denotative meaning of which
in the line is redundant, since the present participles "achieving" and "pursuing"
already suggest continuing activities. Critics have accounted for this apparent
contradiction between activity and inactivity by noting the poem's ideological
compatibility with the period's emerging market logic and "rhetoric of self-made
manhood," which often separated effort from ends since "labor might not necessarily bring desired results."[14] Yet this same equation, the separation of effort from
ends, took on a very different, even frightening, tenor in antislavery debates, a
tenor that the poem also makes available. "Fate," in another of its senses, suggests
destruction or ruin, that which will become of or befall a person or thing—or a
nation—while "wait" also means to watch expectantly, *to look forward*, whether
with hopeful desire or anxious apprehension. Far from "Victorian cheerfulness,"
here is the disquieting side of Longfellow's poem: its closing stanza seeks to steel
the nerves of those who wish to "be up and doing" but know that the consequences
of their actions are entirely unknowable. That is, it takes a stout "heart" "to act"
with the understanding that the unforeseeable effects of one's causes, in both
senses of that term, might well be disastrous. In the case of the abolition movement, that meant, for many, disaster in the form of political crisis, social upheaval,
and even violent revolution.

Hence, the poem's last line, "Learn to labor and to wait," doesn't so much set up
a balanced opposition—labor/wait—as it indicates a sequence. The conjunction
"and" functions in the line additively, rather than correlatively: labor, *then* wait. Yet
this is not the sequentialism of progressive history. Rather, it is movement without
any discernible course, change without telos: one's actions might serve (yet another meaning of "wait") the emergence of any number of possible futures. So the
hard lesson the poem challenges its readers to learn is this: after you take action,
you have to await the consequences. You simply have to trust, as Douglass put it,
that your "influence" "shall be given in the right direction." That's just what it
means to "act in the living present;" you can't know in advance what your endeavors might unleash. History, the "dead past," won't help you, and the future can't be
trusted. This was a lesson much of the nation, and many abolitionists, were unpre-
pared to learn. Patient waiting, faith in the pace of slow, gradual, incremental
change, a blind trust in the progressive tide of history were for many preferable

and certainly more prudent than the rash quickening advocated by immediatists like Garrison. Nathaniel Hawthorne, for instance, countered those "who conceive that the world stands still except so far as that goes forward" by offering "another view, and probably as wise a one." This more moderate view (Franklin Pierce's view) "looks upon slavery as one of those evils which divine Providence does not leave to be remedied by human contrivances, but which, *in its own good time*, by some means impossible to be anticipated, but of the simplest and easiest operation, when all its uses shall have been fulfilled, it causes to vanish like a dream" (emphasis mine).[15] Hawthorne expresses the very opposite of the uneven, discontinuous, and, above all, *impatient* temporality of immediatism, which views the present not as the inevitable result of "divine Providence" nor of any other force. Nor does it view history as moving unidrectionally toward any particular future. As I discuss at length in my readings of Emerson and Douglass in Chapters 3 and 4, such a devotion to *now* constituted a dilemma, a peculiarly temporal dilemma, with which antebellum social reformers and literary artists alike struggled mightily. One actor's ardent, urgent devotion to a righteous cause—think: George Harris or Frederick Douglass—might well be another's irresponsible recklessness—think: Captain Ahab or John Brown.

Because of the way it brings into view distinct ways of inhabiting, experiencing, and acting within the temporality of history, the divide between gradualist and immediatist abolitionism, emblematized by "A Psalm of Life," anchors the story this book has to tell about antebellum American literature's investments in the present. In its renunciation of the "dead past" in favor of a "living present," immediatism repudiated forms of antebellum American historiography and conventional narratives of historical progress that predominated in the antebellum period and still hold great power today—the steady, though gradual, march toward social amelioration. Like other liberal reformers of the period, gradualists could look with cheer for evidence of slavery's eventual, inevitable decline by way of the general drift of history. Immediatists, by contrast, and by definition, advocated not the continuity and passivity of such slow, constant progress, but swift and sudden rupture brought on by decisive action in the present giving rise to an unknown future. Immediatism's resistance to liberal-progressive historiography—that is, its investment in a vision of history that does not stop, but advances fitfully in unforeseen directions—represents one species, certainly the most politically potent, of what in this book I call "Romantic presentism" in the literature and culture of the United States during the first half of the nineteenth century.[16] In its commitment to the immediate, to the *now*, as above and against the past and the future, Romantic presentism designates, or so I'll argue in the chapters that follow, a particular mode of historical being rooted in an understanding of the present as the fundamental sphere of human action and experience—and hence of ethics and democratic possibility. Yet the presentism this book identifies is not so much a rejection of the past as it is a distinct theory of history, an understanding of history as a form of experience, rather than a field or object of knowledge.[17] Romantic presentists imagine history as an always-unfinished activity happening *now* and remaking—as opposed to trying to know—*then*.

Although a general disposition toward the present and a concomitant antagonism toward the past have, at least since R. W. B. Lewis, long been recognized as prominent features of antebellum literature and culture, what Lewis called "the case against the past" in Romantic era writing has typically been understood as a desire on the part of American writers to escape history altogether and/or to flee from the social world into a realm of pure imagination. More recently, three or more decades of historicist inquiry, hermeneutics of suspicion, symptomatic reading, and ideological critique have decisively shown just how magnificently those attempts to flee and escape failed.[18] These days, it goes without saying that texts and the authors of texts are implicated in and determined, if not bound, by their particular historical moments. An unfortunate result of these procedures, however, especially of the impulse to place texts and ideas *in* history, to historicize or contextualize them, is that we have not taken the presentism of antebellum writers and thinkers seriously in any extended way. Our own commitment to a particular understanding of history (historicism in its various guises) has prevented us from apprehending and contending with another (presentism). Or to put this another way: we've worked so hard to see what history can teach us about American writers that we've largely failed to see what American writers can teach us about history.

The Ever-Present Now tacks in a different direction by examining the meaning and possibilities of the present and its relationship to history and historicity in a number of literary texts of the past; specifically, the writings of several familiar figures in antebellum U.S. literary history—some, but not all of whom we associate with the period's Romantic movement, whether in its nascent literary form (Irving and Sedgwick) or in its fullest flowering (Emerson and Melville). Yet in this book, I seek to recover something of the political force of romanticism, which becomes clear when we foreground time, especially the time of *now*. This focus, in turn, alters somewhat our sense of U.S. Romantic genealogy, giving greater weight, for instance, to Irving and linking his legacy, both intellectually and politically, not only to more central figures like Emerson and Melville (and even Longfellow), but to activists like Garrison, Frederick Douglass, and John Brown. These linkages are further suggested by the purview of my primary archive: the fifty-year period from 1809 to 1859, beginning with Irving's caustic historiography, the inauguration of the presentist mode of writing history, and ending with John Brown's raid on Harpers Ferry, the logical culmination of Romantic presentism's political disposition.[19] But rather than simply placing these writers and their works *in* history, this book attempts to understand what they have to say *about* history and historical experience, their shape, meaning, and value. Examining texts by figures as different as Washington Irving, John Neal, Catharine Sedgwick, Frederick Douglass, Ralph Waldo Emerson, and Herman Melville, I argue that these writers, some explicitly and others implicitly, practiced forms of literary historiography that treats the past as neither simply a reflection of present interests nor as an irretrievably distant "other," but as a complex and open-ended interaction between the two. In place of a fixed and immutable past with unidirectional movement, these writers imagine history as an experience rooted in a fluid, dynamic, ever-changing present.

Romantic presentism thus also recovers a tradition of Romantic era historiography that departs significantly from other descriptions of the period's prevailing modes of historiography, such as those examined in important works like David Levin's *History as Romantic Art* and George Dekker's *American Historical Romance*. Levin's reading of the period's great historians, George Bancroft, William Prescott, John Motley, and Francis Parkman inverts Lewis's reading of those historians' literary counterparts. Levin seeks to correct the "erroneous" assumption that Bancroft and company "sought some kind of escape from the Present into the Past." He demonstrates instead how the era's historians drew upon Romantic literary conventions in order to examine "the meaning of history." Yet as much as the writers in Levin's study may have drawn on the same intellectual resources as some of the writers I treat here, most notably Emerson, Levin's historians were all ultimately committed to a vision of teleological historical progress that Romantic presentists, including Emerson in my reading, generally challenged. Nor, for this same reason, did Romantic presentists fully accept the stadialist theory that Dekker identifies as central to so much antebellum thinking about history, although they sometimes speak its language.[20] Yet what perhaps most distinguishes the historiographical tradition I examine here from the ones taken up by Levin and Dekker is its ethical-political bent. Strikingly, slavery, abolition, and the African American literary tradition, are all but absent from both Levin's and Dekker's accounts, but are central to mine. In fact, in many ways African American readers and readings are constitutive of the tradition I describe; as we'll see, black writers like Frederick Douglass, Frances Harper, Maria Stewart, and Martin Luther King, Jr. helped to activate and unleash the political potential latent in the writings of white presentists like Irving, Longfellow, Emerson, Sedgwick, and Melville.

Uncovering this lesser-known *antebellum* tradition of literary historiography— a metahistorical discourse informing literary texts—*The Ever-Present Now* also confronts *contemporary* literary historiography, or current critical understandings of the relations between literature and the past. The "historical turn" in literary studies of the past three decades has led literary scholars to a more complex understanding of texts' embeddedness in their moments of production, a reconfiguration of the text/context relationship, a heightened awareness of the mutability of historical truth, and scrutiny of the relations between the "actual" past and modes of historical representation. However, much historicist criticism nevertheless remains bound to a linear-progressive conception of time and history that treats past and present as separate and distinct—different.[21] One of the central contentions of this book is that the theories of history developed by the writers gathered here resist, in various ways, the notion that the past, as the old saying goes, is a foreign country, that the present and the past exist in a relation of alterity, or that they are separated by an unbreachable gulf. I challenge the idea that to honor and respect that gulf—that difference—is always a historiographical virtue. At the same time, this resistance is not grounded simply in a willingness to flout conventions of history writing nor in the imaginative liberties allowed by literary, as opposed to historical, practice. Instead, I demonstrate how these authors refuse, as a matter of philosophical principle, aesthetic doctrine, or political exigency, to treat the past as irretrievably "other." They approach history instead from the point of view of Longfellow's "living present," or what Frederick Douglass, less famously, called "the ever-present now." In doing so, they help to mediate between presentism and historicism, or to use analogous terms, between experience and knowledge.

The Presentism Fallacy Fallacy

Insofar as immediatist abolitionism and Longfellow's "A Psalm of Life," together and separately, give expression to a broader Romantic orientation toward and investment in the present, that investment, while not completely unacknowledged, has not yet been taken seriously by scholars in any extended way. This is a curious fact. For while it may be easy to scoff at Longfellow's mawkish verse, it's harder to dismiss, say, Emerson's assertion that "the thought of the present moment has a greater value than all the past" or Douglass's insistence that "we have not to do with the dead, but the living; not with the past, but with the living present" or Melville's investment in the "everlasting and uncrystallizing Present" in *Pierre* or Thoreau's instruction that "you must live in the present, launch yourself on every wave, find your eternity in each moment"—even though, as I hope to show, they are all of a piece with Longfellow's dictum.[22] The problem may be that statements like these seem to suggest, especially to a generation or two of scholars trained in and committed to historicist imperatives, that these writers have no real interest in history at all, at least not in history as it is conventionally understood: as a field or sphere of knowledge (of events, actions, persons, attitudes, and beliefs) separate and distinct from the present and knowable on its own terms, through careful study of surviving documents and artifacts. This, anyway, is the historicist conception of history, which aspires to know the past "as it was." To set up the present as a bulwark against the past, to conceive of the past only in terms of its usefulness, is, according to this view, to be unhistorical.

Presentism has typically been the term that signifies such unhistorical postures. Influentially, David Hackett Fischer lists *presentism* as one in his series of "historians' fallacies," defining it as an error in chronology, a type of anachronism. In Fischer's definition, *presentism* is when "the antecedent in a narrative series is falsified by being defined or interpreted in terms of the consequent." Presentists believe that "the proper way to do history is to prune away the dead branches of the past, and to preserve the green buds and twigs which have grown into the dark forest of our contemporary world."[23] As Fischer also notes, presentism is often associated with what Herbert Butterfield, in a now-classic 1931 essay, designated as "Whig history": history writing that reads the past in terms that vindicate the present by producing historical narratives demonstrating the inevitable progress and ultimate triumph of freedom. More generally, presentism denotes the naive tendency of critics to read their own period's assumptions and values into the texts and events of the past. Presentism begins with a premise, typically characterized as partisan or political, and looks for or distorts evidence from the past to confirm that premise. The presentist judges one era using the methods, standards, and criteria of another, thus projecting modern concepts and beliefs onto the texts of the past.

We might classify these versions of presentism as *irresponsible*. They seem irresponsible, first, because they fail to adhere to normative ideas about time, to keep events, concepts, and beliefs assigned to their proper place within a chronological sequence (that is, to contextualize). Secondly, they are irresponsible because they disrespect the past insofar as they fail to view it on its own terms, in its own right. That is, they fail to properly respect historical difference. Respect for such difference, of course, has been the hallmark gesture of historicism and its contextualizing procedures. Historicism's fundamental assumption, which in turn produces its main methodological imperative, is that texts, along with ideas, beliefs, concepts, identities, the range of available subject positions, and so on, "belong" to particular moments in time, moments that historicists attempt to re-create faithfully.[24] Such procedures, therefore, preserve or produce each moment's or each period's individuality, its difference in relation to earlier or later moments in time. What it means to contextualize, then, is to attend to the particularities, the uniqueness, of discrete moments in history, to distinguish between a *now* and a *then*. Indeed, one of the most important achievements of historicism in recent American studies has been to turn this greater awareness of and attention to both historical and cultural difference toward a more complex understanding of U.S. literatures and cultures. As Valerie Rohy notes, "historicism promises respect for difference, particularity, and pluralism where the ahistorical would impose tyrannical conformity."[25] Thus, the analogue to this conception of history is the discourse of *otherness*, of racial, gender, and class difference, that has, not accidentally, developed in tandem with historicism in literary studies.[26] In that context, presentism is more than just irresponsible; it is ethically compromised because it decontextualizes and subsumes difference; it co-opts the past in the service of current (ideological) interests and thus amounts to a historiographical form of assimilation, colonization, or imperialism.[27]

However, historicism in literary studies maintains something of a paradoxical relationship to the old problem of presentism: it is at once that which historicism's contextualizing procedure is designed to avoid and, because of its frequently announced political commitments, its self-consciousness about the representational function of every act of historical (re)creation, and its engagement with the political and critical present, that of which it is sometimes accused. The result, as Rohy has argued, is a "critical discourse in which something called historicism is defended as the sole ethical possibility, and something called the ahistorical is denounced by a shaming rhetoric whose vehemence seems at times to outstrip its object." At the same time, since historiography can never "cease to transfer ideas of the present 'into the past,'" historicism's rhetoric of fidelity to the past as it was ultimately "interpellates everyone as a guilty subject of temporal self-governance and measures all against a standard none can meet."[28] Or in Jennifer Fleissner more succinct formulation, historicism tends "to beget what it most abhors: presentism."[29] Yet the presentism that dogs historicism is of a different sort than the irresponsible presentisms identified by Fischer. Instead, historicism tends to produce what we might call a kind of "complacent" presentism. Complacent because it is predicated on the critics' self-certain knowingness in relation to the authors and texts that are their objects of study. Viewing past texts from a more advanced historical position, penetrating surfaces to reveal the latent, the repressed, the ideologically veiled, or the unwitting, the present-critic understands them in ways and in terms that were unavailable and, therefore, impossible, to their contemporaries.[30] Such a view inevitably assumes the present, the critic's present, as more advanced than, not just different from, the past.[31]

Two sometimes-overlapping veins of literary scholarship have emerged recently that challenge, more or less explicitly, these methodological and ethical injunctions against presentism. The first, recognizing the extended afterlives and historical circulation of literary texts—that is, recognizing that literary texts are never really bound by the moment of their creation—cultivates deliberately presentist reading practices that attempt to compensate for some of the limitations of historicist inquiry.[32] Presentist criticism has become one of the more robust strains in twenty-first century Shakespeare scholarship, for example, as evidenced by a number of articles and volumes devoted to the subject.[33] The Shakespeare scholar Marjorie Garber proposes the "illicit" pleasures of anachronism as an antidote to what she calls "historical correctness," the entrenched historicist view "that history grounds and tells the truth about literature."[34] A number of Americanists have also advanced various kinds of self-consciously presentist styles of critical practice. To cite only a few: Phillip Barrish advocates a "critical presentism" that promises "unique interpretative and pedagogical leverage over both 'present' matters and 'past' literary works by locating unexpected, even uncanny, points of contact between them."[35] Russ Castronovo experiments with a method that displays "disrespect toward history" in favor of "far-flung and nonempirical connections that span decades and even centuries."[36] And James Dawes makes the case for a "rigorous presentism" that would motivate careful inquiry into the past by an explicit and self-conscious interest in understanding vital issues and working toward solutions to pressing problems in the present.[37]

Approaches such as these suggest promising alternatives to the historicist methods that for many of us have come to seem exhausted.[38] Yet for all their value, these approaches too often leave untouched the basic premise that presentism is fundamentally at odds with historical-mindedness, that it constitutes a transgression against the norms of history. Instead, they locate value in or demonstrate how one might make productive use of those violations. A second recent body of scholarship, however, has helped to unsettle historicism's temporal foundations.[39] Recuperating time as a category of literary and historical analysis, a number of critics have revealed the variety of temporal modes and cultures at play in nineteenth-century American culture, modes that were not always compatible with the hegemonic time of modernity and national progress.[40] An especially powerful strand of this work has emanated from queer studies, which has pursued a host of nonnormative temporal experiences that challenge the dominance of the singular understanding of time as straightforward linear chronology.[41] This latter view, as Jordan Alexander Stein helpfully notes, has long informed narratives of literary history. The "persistence of chronology in literary history," Stein argues, is the result of a "conflation between history and time," an assumption that history just *means* chronology. Yet such a view can cause us to "forget the nonlinear or nonsequential temporalities that structure some of the very ordinary but still meaningful ways that readers engage with literature—like reading a book well after it was published."[42] Calling for broader engagement with this vital and innovative body of work, Stein invites "literary historians [to] expand their notions of history beyond the normative temporal orderings of chronology."[43]

The Ever-Present Now participates both in the recuperation of presentism and in the temporal turn. I differ, however, from the methodological presentisms by refusing to concede that the kind of presentism this book describes and, to a degree, practices, constitutes a transgression against either time or history. I argue instead that Romantic presentism posits a version of history and historical experience that, to put it polemically, is *truer* than the historicist conception of history. My readings challenge historicism's proprietary regime, identifying ideas, concepts, and texts that persist over and in time, that lie dormant and recur, or that echo and reverberate across decades or centuries. Therefore, I will often be more concerned with relations of sameness than of difference, with repetition than with progressive development, and with points of cross-temporal contact than with points of departure or distinction. My guiding assumptions—that ideas and concepts are not the sole property of their historical moments, that time and history don't always move forward and progress, that the historical past is not fixed and static, and that the past does not precede or determine the present—are not simply experiments in outlaw historical thinking, but are an attempt to provide a more rigorous and more accurate account of what history *is*.

In doing so, *The Ever-Present Now* attends to alternative temporalities, but differs from other contributions to the temporal turn by focusing specific attention on the relations between time and antebellum writers' conceptions of history or, more precisely, by focusing upon those writers' modes of producing and, especially, of *experiencing* the temporality of history—relations that by definition foreground the present, the time of "now." Hence just as I will be centrally concerned with what *history* is, I will be equally concerned with what the *present* is. Few works associated with the new temporal studies have devoted sustained attention to the present as a problem in itself or as a generative site of inquiry, although three exceptions are worth mentioning briefly. In *Time, Tense, and American Literature: When is Now?* Cindy Weinstein reads a series of American novels whose fraught temporal logic, discernible at the level of grammar, leaves them without "temporal anchor," resulting in various kinds of narrative disorientation. In the absence of a clearly identifiable *now*, for instance, how does one locate a *then*?[44] For Weinstein, such *immediate* problems of time, registered in literary texts' formal designs, "resolve, reflect and/or complicate" extra-literary historical problems.[45] Another work, somewhat far afield from Weinstein's, is the medievalist Carolyn Dinshaw's *How Soon is Now?: Medieval Texts, Amateur Readers, and the Queerness of Time*, a study of medieval "asynchrony stories" (think "Rip Van Winkle") through the lens of queer theories of temporality.[46] *How Soon is Now?* seeks to "to claim the possibility of a fuller, denser, more crowded now that all sorts of theorists tell us is extant but that often eludes our temporal grasp."[47] "The present moment," Dinshaw's readings show, "is more heterogeneous and asynchronous than the everyday image of now... would allow."[48] Attending to richer, varied, more fulsome temporal experiences in the present, Dinshaw argues compellingly, can reinvigorate the historical now we currently inhabit, can "rouse us to look for other ways of world making, for other ways of knowing, doing, being."[49] Lastly, Mark Rifkin's *Beyond Settler Time: Temporal Sovereignty and Indigenous Self-Determination* challenges what he calls the "coevalness of the present" as it is ordinarily understood. Drawing upon Einsteinian relativity theory, Rifkin posits "frames of reference" as a way of understanding forms of indigenous "presentness" that are not reducible to "an inherently mutual now". Rifkin's *now* is characterized instead by "a plurality of processes of becoming that interact with each other in complex ways" and "carry their own immanent tendencies and directions."[50]

This book shares with Weinstein, Dinshaw, and Rifkin a sense of the present (whether the present of reading or of other everyday experiences) as heterogeneous, rich and varied, characterized by various forms of temporal disarray. In the present, something is always going on, experienced differently by different people in different places, the precise contours and tendency of which remains uncertain—except in retrospect. So while *The Ever-Present Now* does not share Weinstein's methodological assumption that the "temporal acrobatics" of each of the novels she reads is "inextricably linked to a historical context"—in fact, this book looks to ways that certain literary productions resist that very assumption— my readings likewise attend, often at the level of the sentence and of narrative discourse, to the intricate ways that literary texts speak the language of time. Similarly, although *The Ever-Present Now* is not, like Dinshaw's, a study of or about queer sexualities, my attention to nonnormative conceptions of time and history and to now-oriented temporal experiences in antebellum literature and culture nevertheless make this a project that is a little bit queer. Finally, while an examination of the temporal dynamics of settler colonialism in the antebellum

United States—from which conventional Romantic historiography is essentially inextricable—is beyond the scope of this study, my readings share with Rifkin a sense that a disunified *now* has liberatory potential.[51]

One final word about method: among the welcome developments that have attended the temporal turn, emerging in tandem with a revival of aesthetics, sometimes called "the new formalism," has been a renewed devotion to close reading. Weinstein's analyses, for instance, "ratchet up the pressure on close reading and… the words that get closely read, to an unusual degree."[52] Similarly, in her remarkable *Time Binds: Queer Temporalities, Queer Histories*, Elizabeth Freeman describes her "queerest commitment" as a commitment to "close reading: the decision to unfold, slowly, a small number of imaginative texts rather than amass a weighty archive of or around texts, and to treat these texts and their formal work as theories of their own, interventions upon both critical theory and historiography."[53] And Peter Coviello in his luminous *Tomorrow's Parties: Sex and the Untimely in Nineteenth-Century America* asserts that reading the untimeliness of sexuality in the nineteenth century is best "served by a practice invested in detail, particularity, and unsystematizable variousness—all the specificities that literature proffers in such abundance, *and in whose explication close textual reading specializes*" (emphasis original).[54] Along the same lines, my archive is principally comprised of a handful of literary texts that I endeavor to read closely, with as much sensitivity to language and form as I am able to muster. For me, close reading is one powerful antidote to the historicist knowingness I've described above. On this point, I subscribe to one version of "surface reading," that sensitivity to the "intricate verbal structure of literary language," advocated by Stephen Best and Sharon Marcus. As they describe it, an "embrace of the surface" can be "an affective and ethical stance," which "involves accepting texts, deferring to them instead of mastering or using them as objects."[55] My readings are first and foremost committed to just such acceptance, to the proposition that antebellum writers have much to teach us (post) moderns about what it means to live in and *do* history—if only we listen to them closely enough.

History With and Without Experience

Although the waning of and a wariness toward historicism in part motivates this book's interest in Romantic presentism and its alternative conceptions of history, neither that waning nor that wariness are unique features of our present moment. As long ago as 1874, Friedrich Nietzsche in his "untimely meditation" "On the Uses and Disadvantages of History for Life" sought "to look afresh at something of which our time is rightly proud—its cultivation of history—as being injurious to it, a defect and deficiency in it." "We are all suffering," he continued, in a sentence that might just as well have been written yesterday by a lapsed academic historicist, "from a consuming fever of history and ought at least to recognize that we are suffering from it."[56] The primary source of Nietzsche's complaint was "the demand that history should be a science" and those "knowledge-thirsty individuals whom knowledge alone will satisfy and to whom the accumulation of knowledge is itself the goal."[57] To take history as nothing more than an object of knowledge, for Nietzsche, is perilous because it neglects and fails to conserve and nurture what he calls somewhat ambiguously, although perhaps less so if we hear in it distant echoes of Longfellow, "life": the "living man," the "being who acts and strives." Feeling unhistorically, Nietzsche says, "forgetting is essential to action of any kind."[58] For Nietzsche, *doing* is at odds with knowing; life is at odds with history; experience at odds with knowledge.[59]

Such distinctions underpin historicist inquiry. As F.R. Ankersmit, in his own attempt to recover what he calls in the title of a recent book *Sublime Historical Experience*, asks, "does not historical experience aim at the union of subject and object, of present and past, whereas professionalized historical writing stakes everything on pulling them apart as much as possible?"[60] The Romantic presentism this book identifies and examines strives to navigate the tension between history as an object of knowledge and history as a kind of experience, between knowing about the past and experiencing it. What might it mean to think of the past and the present, and the relations between, them not just in terms of knowledge but of experience? What might be the alternative to the view, expressed by Nietzsche, that to study history is to banish experience, the view that history is only possible (or knowable) without experience? And how can we have a turn to experience—which, after all, typically means some sort of direct, unmediated, prediscursive encounter with the world—that is not also a rejection of representation, a disavowal of narrative, and a failure to respect historical difference?[61]

In addressing these questions, I draw upon a tradition of thinking about temporal and historical experience that runs from Aristotle and St. Augustine through the Scottish philosophers Thomas Reid and Dugald Stewart, to the American pragmatists William James, John Dewey, and (most especially) George Herbert Mead, to Edmund Husserl, Maurice Merleau-Ponty, Henri Bergson, Martin Heidegger, and, more recently, Gilles Deleuze and Jacques Derrida. The temporal turn has not fully engaged this long tradition of philosophical reflection on temporality and temporal experience.[62] Critics in search of alternative configurations of the relations between past and present, ones that fuse rather than separate them, have tended to turn instead to Walter Benjamin's powerful critique of historicism in his "Theses on the Philosophy of History" and his lesser-known but equally powerful essay "Literary History and Literary Scholarship."[63] The thinker who has most influenced my own thinking, however, is the too-often forgotten member of the "classical" American pragmatists George Herbert Mead, in my view, the most important thinker of the present moment since Emerson and Douglass. A generation older than Benjamin, Mead developed a theory of temporal and historical experience that resonates with Benjamin's in certain ways.[64] But it is Mead's ideas in *The Philosophy of the Act* and *The Philosophy of the Present*—most especially his claim that "reality exists in a present"—that most deeply inform the chapters that follow and that bear suggestive affinities with the antebellum writers that are the focus of this study.[65] For that reason, it will do to provide a brief introduction to Mead here, placing him among some of his immediate predecessors and contemporaries.

Better known among sociologists and social psychologists for his intersubjective theory of the mind and self, Mead also developed what he called a "philosophy of the act" that hinged upon the way we experience time. The classically scientific account of time describes it as a succession of punctual instants, each one uniform and divisible from the one before and the one after. This is the modern view of time upon which historicism relies, making possible both periodization and contextualization by demarcating blocks of time with terms such as *antebellum, postbellum,* or *modernity* and by assigning texts, along with their assumptions and meanings, to specific segments along a linear continuum. Yet this account of time moving along with metronomic regularity has long been at odds with experience, as anyone who has ever been bored or has had fun can tell you.

A long philosophical tradition, initiated by Aristotle, has sought to elucidate and explain this nonpunctual, irregular, and often-asynchronous human experience of time.[66] Mead's account of temporal experience is sometimes associated with this phenomenological tradition.[67] For instance, Edmund Husserl was among the first of the twenty-first century phenomenologists to examine human time-consciousness at odds with the modern scientific conception of time derived from Newton. Husserl developed a theory of what he called the "living present" to explain how we perceive objects with duration, objects that persist over successive moments. Against theories of temporal experience that posit time as a series of discrete "now" points, each of which follows the next like a string of beads, Husserl's living present possesses a certain reach, extending into both the past and the future, as in our experience of a melody. What is it, Husserl asks, for instance, that allows us to grasp and make sense of a temporal object like a sentence or a melody? If our experience of time were merely a sequence of isolated "now" points, each successive word in a sentence or note in a melody would remain distinct from the one that follows, rendering sentences unintelligible, melodies unhearable. Yet in both cases, consciousness perceives a unity in succession that allows us to take in the sentence or the melody in its entirety, as a unified whole. This unity is made possible by the unique structure of temporal consciousness, which consists not just of a "now" point, or what Husserl terms the "primal impression," but also of *retention,* in which a word or note slipping into the past remains suspended in consciousness, present as having just past, and *protention,* in which consciousness extends forward into the future to anticipate the word or note that is to come.[68]

The key point here is that for Husserl, present experience is an experience of duration, not easily plotted along a line, like a history textbook's timeline of dates. Husserl's analysis shares a number of features with the accounts of time-consciousness provided by both Henri Bergson and William James. For Bergson, for example, the standard Newtonian account of time, as a series of punctuate moments, separate instants, makes the mistake of spatializing time. To divide time into discrete mathematical units fails to account for the way we experience time's passage in the "real, concrete, live present."[69] This duration, as in Husserl's theory of time, extends to encompass portions of both past and future. In the present of perception, Bergson says—in the "live present"—I have "one foot in my past and another in my future" (177). Bergson's images for this continuous present, as in Husserl, are sentences and melodies: just as "a word is always continuous with the other words which accompany it" so "each note of a melody vaguely reflects the whole musical phrase."[70] If, by contrast, our experience of the world (or a melody) were the experience merely of bare instants, "the world at one instant would be completely wiped out by the world as it is at the next instant. There would be no connection between the two, no real duration; there would be only substitution of one instant for another."[71]

Influenced by both Husserl's and Bergson's thinking about time-consciousness, Mead's fellow pragmatist William James also sought to provide an account of temporal experience irreducible to a succession of identical, punctual instants.[72] In his chapter on "The Perception of Time" in *The Principles of Psychology*, James observes that the "complexity" of temporal experience derives from "the echo," in consciousness, "of the objects just past, and, in a lesser degree, perhaps, the foretaste of those just to arrive."[73] Hence the "sensible present" possesses a certain duration. "Let any one try," James writes, "I will not say to arrest, but to notice or attend to, the present moment of time. One of the most baffling experiences occurs. Where is it, this present? It has melted in our grasp, fled ere we could touch it, gone in the instant of becoming."[74] This ungraspable present, *now* at an instant, James terms a "knife-edge" present, which he memorably contrasts with "the specious present" of lived experience: "In short, the practically cognized present is no knife-edge, but a saddle-back, with a certain breadth of its own on which we sit perched, and from which we look in two directions into time."[75] And in another striking metaphor, this one from *A Pluralistic Universe*, James writes that "Time itself comes in drops"—an image of the present's duration as fluid cohesion that vividly challenges the mathematical conception of time as a succession of divisible units.[76]

Both Bergson and James, however, distinguish between this stretched-out present and memory. For Bergson the distinction is between pure perception and pure recollection, what, analogously, James calls "secondary" and "primary memory." For both, there is an outer limit to the present, beyond which only memory can reach. In Bergson's account, for instance, the present is characterized by one's engagement in an action. The vast bulk of one's life experiences, the entirety of one's past, is not immediately useful to the completion of the present action; therefore, those experiences appear as not present. Since consciousness is "[e]ver bent upon action, it can only materialize those of our former perceptions which can ally themselves with the present perception to take a share in the final decision" (188). However, Bergson says, it would be a mistake for one to suppose that all that appears as not present *is* not, for in that case one would simply have, in Gilles Deleuze's phrase, "confused Being with being-present" (55). The totality of the past exists simultaneously with each present; it's just that, consciously, we only access the parts of the past in general—we only make the "leap" into the past—according to some present need. Thus, the "past in general," as Bergson conceives it, is unalterable, lengthened by accretion with each new passing present, but essentially fixed, unlike the "ever renewed present" which is always changing.[77] Yet our present interests make it difficult to recognize the former, which "remains in the dark." Bergson's figure for this distinction between the present of our conscious life and the past of pure memory is of a scroll: "Our reluctance to admit the integral survival of the past has as its origin, then, in the very bent of our psychical life,—an unfolding of states wherein our interest prompts us to look at that which is unrolling, and not at that which is entirely unrolled."[78]

Although Mead valued Bergson for "taking time seriously" and was influenced by Bergson's critique of the spatialization of time, as well as his analysis of the duration that grounds temporal experience, Mead parts ways with Bergson (and James) on the question of a past that exists beyond the reach of present experience. Mead rejects what he calls Bergson's "Kantian" position. "The true view of reality" for Bergson, Mead says, "has to be got by intuition, in which you are able in some way or other to catch the something that is going on and hold to it as a reality."[79] In Bergson, the reality of conscious life, of experience, and the present is ultimately less real than the past of pure memory and intuition.[80] According to Bergson, action and utility, the interests of the moment, bind us to the now. The question for Bergson, then—and it is in many ways also the question of historicism—is how to escape the prison-house of the present and enter into the past free of burdensome present interests? Bergson's answer is to take refuge in a metaphysical flight of fancy; only by letting go of the present can we experience, transcendentally, the fullness of the past.

Mead's answer to this question, by contrast, is that a past free of present interests is not what we desire in the first place. For Bergson, the past is somehow *there*, in back of us, fixed and stable, just beyond our immediate reach. Following Longfellow and Garrison, we might call this a "dead past." Mead contests this "metaphysical assumption." "A Parmenidean reality," he says, "does not exist."[81] That is, the past does not lie behind us like "a scroll of elapsed presents, to which our constructions of the past refer, though without the possibility of ever reaching it, and without the anticipation that our continual reconstructions will approach it with increasing exactness."[82] Unlike Bergson, Mead is not preoccupied with whether such a view of the past, as having an existence beyond our capacity to know it, but serving as the measure of our historical investigations, is the correct one. Rather, the point for Mead, the pragmatist, is that, ironically, such a past turns out *not* to be the one we were looking for after all:

> If we could bring back the present that has elapsed in the reality which belonged to it, it would not serve us. It would be that present and would lack just that character which we demand in the past, that is, that construction of the conditioning nature of now present passage which enables us to interpret what is arising in the future that belongs to this present.[83]

It is the shape of our present, in other words, that motivates (or "conditions") our particular historical interests in the first place. To revisit the past in its former presentness would be, paradoxically, not to visit the past at all. In Mead's succinct formulation, "a past never was in the form in which it appears as a past."[84] Such a past, stripped of its historicity, would cease to be a past, and, therefore, "it would not serve us" since its historical character was precisely that which interested us to begin with. "The moment that we take these earlier presents as existences apart from the presentation of them as pasts," Mead says, the moment we approach them, we might say, in terms of their unique otherness, "they cease to have meaning to us."[85] So the historicist desire to capture or experience the past "as it was" would not be to experience a past at all; rather, it would simply be to experience a former present. In other words, its reality as history, as a past—its very *difference*—is a function of our experience in the *present* present.[86] This is what it means to say that the present is the precondition of the past or to say with Mead, as well as Longfellow, Garrison, Emerson, Douglass, and others, that "reality exists in a present."[87]

I revisit Mead in more detail in later chapters, but one further feature of Mead's thought, the influence of which will be felt throughout this book, bears mentioning here. In Mead's rendering of temporal experience, "The unit of existence is the act, not the moment."[88] That is to say, that what characterizes a present is action, a happening. In the present, something is always going on. In this sense, Longfellow's "act—act—in the living present" might be understood less as a command than as a sort of constative utterance. Action and the living present are simply coterminous. History, in this account, is our way of accounting, after the fact, for what happened in an elapsed present.[89] Something happens, at which point "we set about rationalizing it, that is, we undertake to show that it, or at least the conditions that determine its appearance, can be found in the past that lay behind it. Thus the earlier pasts out of which it emerged as something which did not involve it are taken up into a more comprehensive past that does lead up to it."[90] In a reversal of our ordinary understandings of cause and effect, it's the occurrence in the present that causes our reconstruction of events in such a way as to account for that occurrence. This process repeats endlessly: just as the present is ever changing, so too is the past, because each new event requires another reconstruction, a new account of the past. This is why Mead, in a statement and image that nicely captures the presiding spirit of this book, eagerly anticipates the prospect of new pasts, the renewal of history: "we look forward," he says, "with vivid interest to the reconstruction, in the world that will be, of the world that has been, for we realize that the world that will be cannot differ from the world that is without rewriting the past to which we now look back."[91]

All Advance is through Separation

This same spirit—looking forward in anticipation, if not quite hopefulness, to looking back to a not-yet-known past—helps to explain why Garrison's labor on behalf of an as yet unrealized future entails a certain irreverence toward any past that is fixed and settled, "dead." Here I'd like to return to his 1857 address, for as the most powerful statement we have of Garrison's (meta)historical vision, it brings into relief the temporality of immediatist abolition, which in the broadest and most urgent sense itself exemplifies and sets many of the terms for the literary expressions of Romantic presentism I pursue in the remainder of the book. Immediatists shared an historical sensibility with Romantic era writers that repudiated and challenged linear-chronological time and the vision of history-as-steady-progress that it served, placing trust instead in the *now* of intellectual apprehension and moral perception, in the present of ongoing experience.[92] Yet this led not to a rejection of history per se, but to revitalized conceptions of the *un*settled relations between past, present, and future.

Because of its commitment to the now, the temporality of immediatism stubbornly defies apprehension by way of familiar modes of historical understanding. Consider, for instance one of the few studies to pursue the temporal dimension of abolition, Robert Fanuzzi's *Abolition's Public Sphere*. Focusing on the movement's print culture, rather than its immediatism, Fanuzzi nevertheless helpfully foregrounds abolition's intricate relations to time. He argues that Garrisonian abolition engaged in a "politics of anachronism" by cultivating a self-consciously "untimely" campaign modeled on a "historically absent" eighteenth-century Revolutionary public sphere.[93] In Fanuzzi's account, Garrisonian abolition is a backward-looking movement, out of step with its own time but for that very reason linked to Enlightenment narratives of progress. Yet, in addition to the extent to which Garrison quite explicitly tended to cast his antagonists, as I discuss below, not his allies, as the ones who were behind the times, Fanuzzi's account itself relies upon a conception of historical time and change that assigns, rather too rigidly, beliefs and practices—or, to use his term, "idioms"—to particular periods. That is to say, Fanuzzi's argument regarding the "belatedness" of abolition is predicated upon the notion that the Revolutionary era's print culture had been rendered "obsolete" by the more fractious public sphere of the Jacksonian period that superseded it, as if the boundaries and contents of historical periods were stark and exclusionary. But how can Garrison, or anyone, speak a language that is obsolete? Isn't that an argument against its obsolescence?

Nor does Garrison's devotion to and, at times, assumption of a future without slavery fit comfortably with familiar narratives of progress, at least not by the time of "The Dead Past and the Living Present." Garrison's stated aim in the speech is to demonstrate, in a kind of inversion of modern objections to presentism, the "worthlessness of ancient...tests" as applied to actors and actions in the present. At the same time, Garrison is also at pains to vindicate his own form of radical action in the living present from charges of fanaticism and apostasy.[94] He excoriates worshippers of the past, "living sycophants of the great men of history," including clergy and the religiously pious, as well as statesmen like Daniel Webster and Edward Everett, for their "retrospective tendency" while failing to contend with the urgent demands of the present. To allow the past to set the terms for the present, for Garrison, is to ensure social stagnation. Change necessitates a conflictual counterforce. "While it is true that all dissent is not progress," he says, "it is equally true that all progress is through dissent. All separation is not advance, but all advance is through separation."[95]

The moderate antislavery unionists Everett and Webster are Garrison's primary examples of "servile idolators of the past and betrayers of the present." In both cases, Garrison condemns them for the very pronouncements that earned them their greatest public adoration. In early 1856, Everett delivered in Boston what would become the first of many speeches on "The Character of George Washington." The address proved so enormously popular that Everett delivered it in cities from New Haven down to Richmond that year and was eventually invited to deliver it as far west as St. Louis, with stops in Buffalo, Detroit, and Chicago along the way. Explicitly, the speech mostly evaded the social and political turbulence roiling the country, though its praise of the wisdom and virtue of the founding generation also sought to make reverence of Washington a source of national unity, Everett's implicit rejoinder to extremists like Garrison. But Everett's favor with his audiences appears to have caused him to shy away from controversy. He delivered the speech more than twenty times in various locations in February through late May of 1856, but when asked to speak at a Faneuil Hall gathering in protest of the caning of Charles Sumner in late May of that year, Everett declined—which must have struck Garrison as a perfect illustration of the incompatibility of reverence for the past and the vital urgencies of the present moment.[96] In Garrison's view, the fact that Everett would squander his substantial "scholarly attainment" and "eloquence" on Washington at a moment of such moral crisis marked him as a man "utterly oblivious to the demands of the present," an example of someone "serenely dwelling in the past." Everett's evasions of the exigencies of now positioned him as a kind of anachronism, a man out of step with the times: "To traverse the country for the purpose of extolling the character of Washington, at this late period," Garrison says, "is indicative of anything rather than an unselfish and brave spirit. Surely, this is an attempt to screen moral cowardice under the guise of patriotism."

Webster, if anything, fares worse. Garrison doesn't bother criticizing Webster for his famous support of the Compromise of 1850. Rather, Garrison reaches back to the shining moment in 1830 when Webster delivered his much-lauded reply to South Carolina Senator Robert Hayne, which quickly became and remains one of the most famous speeches in U.S. Senate history. Ostensibly, a debate over tariffs, the public exchange between Hayne and Webster quickly transformed into a rehashing of long-festering sectional disputes, turning on the questions of Unionism, the supremacy of the Constitution, nullification, and, behind all of those, of course, slavery. Webster was widely praised for his panegyric to the Revolutionary past, when South Carolina and Massachusetts united in a common cause. Speaking lyrically of that history, Webster uttered the most famous sentence of the speech: "The past, at least, is secure."[97] The notion of a "secure" past, fixed and settled, was anathema to Garrison. Indeed, security was the last thing the present moment called for, which in Garrison's eyes makes Webster a coward. "It costs nothing," Garrison says, "proves nothing of virtue or piety...to embrace what is respectable, to make obeisance to the illustrious dead." Yet Webster, "during his whole life... eulogized nothing but the past." With "his face directed to his dead ancestors," Webster could praise the "Pilgrim fathers at Plymouth Rock, and the Revolutionary heroes on Bunker Hill...but when, or where, did he ever show that one drop of Pilgrim or Revolutionary blood ran in his veins, in a truly heroic sense? What unpopular truth did he ever venture to enunciate?" Acknowledging Webster's intellectual and oratorical gifts, Garrison then renders a devastating historical judgment: "No man ever missed so grand an opportunity to strike a blow for the freedom of the world."

It's not an accident that Garrison here speaks so passionately ill of the dead. His denunciation of Webster's career enacts the speech's main contention: reverence for the past won't help solve problems in the present, and admiration for the heroic deeds of the dead can't substitute for action in the present. In fact, it's just the opposite. History has a way of rendering Revolutionary zeal anodyne. This is why Garrison turns, over and over in the speech, to historical examples that distinguish between the present of the past and the past in the present. The former is gone—"dead." The latter is merely the refuge of safety—security. Garrison puts the point this way: "It was a great thing to be a Lutheran in the days of Luther—a Quaker in the days of George Fox—a Puritan in the days of bloody Mary—but what is it now? What risk does a disciple of William Penn now run on making a visit to Boston?" To be sure, Garrison's argument is more than a little self-serving: its tacit prolepsis calls to mind the day when one can speak of being a Garrisonian in the days of Garrison. At the same time, however, Garrison's antagonism toward the dead past undercuts whatever honor future reverence for his own then-past acts might hold.

What Garrison extols instead of the past—and this is where his vision of history contrasts sharply with Enlightenment progress—is danger and risk. So when he says that "All separation is not an advance, but all advance is a separation," he expresses what that risk entails: both the uncertainty of what action in the present might mean for the future and the necessity of acting nevertheless.[98] Since all of the effects of an action are unforeseen—what sorts of social arrangements or social conflicts would result from immediate emancipation? Gradualists and other moderates clung to the unpredictability of the answers to a question like that—acting always entails *in*security. It's a trying out, but also a making possible, the means by which we solve problems or generate new ways of acting and being and belonging in the world. So movement, flux, experimentation, adjustment, and creation, not to mention dismantling, destruction, dismembering, and deforming: these are the defining features of the living present, and always, according to Romantic presentists, better than stasis. As Douglass put it in 1857, "If there is no struggle, there is no progress. Those who profess to favor freedom, and yet deprecate agitation, are men who want crops without plowing up the ground. They want rain without thunder and lightning. They want the ocean without the awful roar of its many waters."[99] Romantic presentists' shared commitment to action, to making sure something happens, is a recognition that the future, any future, depends upon the forces of change. Without the prospect of the new, without something that unsettles present states and past orders alike, there can be no time—and thus nothing to look forward to.

A similar temper motivates this book. Like pious regard for the founding fathers, much literary historicism has lingered too long, overstayed its welcome, outlived its usefulness; it no longer entails much risk. Why not, then, try out the present? My investigation of various iterations of Romantic presentism in the chapters that follow proceeds in two parts. The book's first section, "Deformations of the Past," examines three (un)historical fictions that together point to a direction that American historical fiction ultimately did not take. The section's two chapters center upon three early experiments in present-oriented fictional historiography that, in different but complementary ways, challenge the standard view of historical time as linear progression, the historicist contextualism that is its methodological counterpart, and even the narrative logic that distorts the experience of *now* by giving it coherent shape. Section two: "Reformations of the Present," turns from fictions of history to nonfiction genres, especially essays and speeches, likewise concerned with theorizing the relations of past and present, but in the service of more explicitly—and more immediate—political ends, before circling back, in a final chapter to one more (un)historical fiction.

I begin with Washington Irving's corrosive historiography. Chapter 1 analyzes the self-consciousness—and uncanny postmodernity—of Irving in the various works attributed to his historian alter ego Diedrich Knickerbocker, particularly *A History of New York* and "Rip Van Winkle." I argue that Irving's Knickerbocker writings inaugurated an under-recognized tradition of antebellum writing devoted less to the creation of a coherent national past than to theorizing "history" itself. Irving's *A History of New York* (1809) forms a kind of practical illustration of the dismantling of history writing in our own time. Irving's metahistorical discourse, I claim, cannot be adequately accounted for by conventional historicist contextualization, by confining his works to a particular moment in time, much less one that has been superseded by, or that is irretrievably distant and distinct from, the critical present. Working in tandem with *A History of New York*'s disquisition on the mutability of historical knowledge is the experience of history "Rip Van Winkle" offers to its readers. A story of temporal dislocation, "Rip Van Winkle" exploits and critiques Rip's—and the reader's—desire to settle upon an orienting present and to locate that present within a chronological sequence (before, during, and after the war).

Chapter 2 attends to echoes of Irving's *un*historical fiction in two early works that, I argue, resist rather than participate in the formation of the historical romance tradition in antebellum U.S. literature and in doing, so offer, like "Rip Van Winkle," an implied critique of historicist assumptions and procedures. John

Neal's *Seventy-Six* (1823) and Catharine Maria Sedgwick's *Hope Leslie* (1827) each experiments with writing (and experiencing) history through the present tense. Deploying anachronism as both narrative method and trope, *Hope Leslie's* narrative of colonial New England disrupts the unidirectional course of time, challenging fundamental conceptions of the form and shape of history that are as prevalent today as in Sedgwick's time. The novel invites its readers to experience a noncolonizing form of presentism. In *Seventy-Six*, Neal engages in an even more radical experiment. Neal's aesthetic theory prizes the immediacy of "interest"—or what he calls "incidents of themselves"—above all other qualities. His fictional account of the American Revolution—interlaced with "real" historical information—strives to render an account of history that neither refers nor means, but that simply *is*. Impossibly, Neal seeks to evacuate narrative of temporality, to circumvent the inherent tendency of narrative to shape and bestow coherence upon experience—a coherence that inevitably distorts the particular tang of *now*. Taken together, Sedgwick's and Neal's present-oriented histories indicate directions historical fiction in the United States did not take, directions that were at odds with the period's nationalist impulses, but that nevertheless offered alternative world-making possibilities.

Such alternative possibilities—for U.S. politics, social arrangements, and forms of affiliation—are taken up, I argue in the book's second section, "Reformations of the Present," by thinkers working in very different literary modes. Chapter 3 considers this question: why, when Ralph Waldo Emerson thinks of history, does he so often think of the present? Emerson's various rejections of the past—in his essay "History," for example, he insists that "All inquiry into antiquity...is the desire to do away with this wild, savage, and preposterous There or Then, and introduce in its place the Here and the Now"—seem to suggest that he had no real interest in history at all, despite the fact that a persistent engagement with the value and meaning of history provides a certain continuity to his career—from *The Philosophy of History* through *The Natural History of Intellect*—from beginning to end. Examining Emerson's writings (with particular focus on his first series of essays), this chapter argues that Emerson's subordination of the past to the present, his devotion to what in "Experience" he calls the "strong present tense," is anything but unhistorical. Rather, Emerson's presentism constitutes a mode of historical understanding rooted in a conception of history-as-experience that is of a piece both with the fiction of Sedgwick and Neal and with the impatient politics of immediatist abolitionists like Garrison and John Brown. I read Emerson's major essays of the 1840s in relation to some of his more strident antislavery addresses of the 1850s. His ruminations on history, philosophical and political, reveal that he was already an immediatist well before he was an abolitionist. For Emerson, as for immediatist abolitionists the complex, dynamic, fluid, fleeting nature of the present moment is that which gives rise to historical consciousness; it is what makes history and (historical) experience possible in the first place. The defining features of the present are movement, flux, change, adjustment, and creation; as such, it is the site of (literary and social) experimentation. Unburdened by history, it is the place where one finds not a particular hope but the precondition of hope.

Emerson's view of the world of (present) experience as in a state of constant change, and, consequently, his rejection of a past that is fixed and unchanging, and his embrace of a progressive, yet nonteleological future where one might discover hope very much resembles immediatist abolitionism's hastening toward a future that can't really be known. Abolitionists like Garrison and Frederick Douglass shared Emerson's commitment to action—to making sure that something happens—and took it as an article of faith that the future, any future, depends upon the creative forces of change and flux; without the prospect of the new, without something that happens, something that "unsettles" present states and past orders alike, there can be no time—and thus nothing to look forward to. Chapter 4 tracks Frederick Douglass's developing historical-temporal consciousness and his adoption of a presentist view of history that rhymes with Emerson's. In tandem with his embrace of political abolitionism, Douglass in his speeches and writings of the 1850s began a sweeping philosophical engagement with the relations between past, present, and future and became what I will call abolitionism's future historian—the historian of an abolitionist past that had not yet come to pass. Examining a series of recurring images—in *My Bondage and My Freedom*, *The Heroic Slave*, and most notably, in his remarkable 1857 speech on the Dred Scott decision—of Douglass gazing into the future, I argue for the centrality of a newly acquired present-oriented perspective as the animating feature of Douglass's mature pre-Civil War politics and his vision of the possibilities of social and historical transformation.

The present is social. This is the central claim of the book's final chapter, which returns to historical fiction to contend with Herman Melville's too-infrequently read novel *Israel Potter* (1855). Formally peculiar—the novel slips in and out, almost at random, of present tense narration—*Israel Potter's* narrative discourse is as unsettled as Israel himself, constantly moving, changing, shifting, and improvising. Just as Israel takes on various disguises and roles over the course of the text—farmer, whaler, soldier, ghost, scarecrow, warrior, and peasant—so does the narrator adopt a variety of stances in relation to his material—biographer, "Editor," faithful historian, and at times, mere witness of unfolding events. The novel's erratic telling of history thus mirrors Israel's wanderings. Both are, as the narrator says at one point of Israel, "repeatedly and rapidly . . . planted, torn up, transplanted, and dropped again, hither and thither." Similarly, Melville treats the historical past as unfinished business, a function of a present that is going on, that is always under way—what in *Pierre* he calls "an everlasting and uncrystallizing present"—and heading toward an uncertain future. Yet no more so than it was for Emerson and Douglass, this uncertainty is not merely pessimism for the direction of the nation, but, perhaps surprisingly, also suggests the possibility of a different, less rigid, past than those enshrined by more conventional historical romancers. My reading proceeds by way of an exploration of the novel's varying uses of narrative prolepsis, its movement away from a foreshadowing that *knows*, that is certain, and toward one that doesn't, but that hopes. Alongside its critique of nationalist posturing, *Israel Potter* imagines the conditions for a kind of hopefulness, which it glimpses in forms of sociality that reside in an unspecified, perhaps even queer, "as yet." In doing so, it anticipates the possibility of a renovated and renewed social world.

Although the readings in the chapters that follow depart from and at times critique many of the core assumptions of historicism as practiced in American literary studies over the past few decades, they do so not in order to turn away from history. Quite the contrary. One of my core assumptions is that we're not done with history yet. Following many of the writers I examine, I embrace the present, seemingly paradoxically, as a means of revivifying and revitalizing the past, not of evading or avoiding it. In doing so, I take seriously—or rather, I seek to explain and deepen as if it were a general proposition rather than a rhetorical device tied to a particular moment—Frederick Douglass's well-known claim that we have to do with the past only as we can make it useful to the present and future. The ambition of this book is to show how and why Douglass's historiographical claim is always true.

PART I

Deformations of History

Diedrich Knickerbocker, Regular Bred Historian

Washington Irving has been a casualty of chronology. More precisely, he has been a casualty of a particular way of thinking about history: the notion that history progresses through chronological, linear time.[1] For if one of the stories of the literature of the United States is the story of dawning modernity, the best that can be said about Irving is that he represents an incipient phase in the process; his writings and his career are merely harbingers of better things to come, notably, the more mature works of Cooper and then (especially) Hawthorne and Melville. This, at any rate, long constituted the standard view, which described Irving's work not as "timeless, but temporal" and cast Irving himself as "a man of his time rather than for all time," belonging "to an outdated phase of culture," "too remote to engage twentieth-century sensibilities."[2]

On this view, Irving would seem to be a victim of the very historical processes his historian alter ego Diedrich Knickerbocker attempts to forestall in Irving's first major work, *A History of New York* (1809). There, Knickerbocker embarks upon the task of rescuing the history of the Dutch settlement of New York from the "maw of oblivion."[3] If not for the toils of the patient and diligent historian, he insists, faithfully "transmit[ing] their renown to all succeeding time," empires and nations, civilizations and cities, would perish, forgotten.[4] Against the image of the reclusive chronicler pouring in solitude over dusty volumes in search of dull facts and compiling his annals, Knickerbocker describes historians as "the public almoners of fame," and likens them to the Creator—"the world—the world, is nothing without the historian!"—or crusaders in the fight against the march of time, against the inevitability of superannuation. The early history of Dutch New York, he declares, would doubtless have been passed over by the forward rush of history had Knickerbocker himself not arrived and "snatched if from obscurity, in the very nick of time."[5] Thus, the bookish antiquarian metamorphoses into a heroic figure: "little I—the progenitor ... with my book under my arm, and New York on my back, pressing forward like a gallant commander to honour and immortality."[6] But unlike Melville and Hawthorne, Irving has not had the benefit of an historian champion, a role not even filled by his early biographer Stanley T. Williams. For more than seventy years the standard authority (until the 2007 publication of Andrew Burstein's *The Original Knickerbocker*), Williams, always careful not to praise his subject, warned against measuring Irving "by the immemorial touchstones of the past, tested by which he is often trivial, or by the standards of to-day, by which he has been outmoded." For Williams, Irving "emerges as a talented writer, hardly more."[7]

So if the world is nothing without the historian who gives it life, neither is a literary reputation, which is also constantly in danger of being passed over by time. Or to put this another way, literary figures are themselves always in danger of becoming outdated, of seeming anachronistic. *Anachronism*, in one of its senses, implies the kind of superannuation that Diedrich Knickerbocker combats: the tendency of things—nations, concepts, systems of belief, and literary styles—to become "dated." As time proceeds steadily forward, or so the story goes, such things inevitably fall into disrepute and are superseded or forgotten altogether. The Ptolemaic conception of the universe, the literary form of epic poetry, and the eight-track tape are anachronistic in this sense: they are systems of belief, modes of representation, or technologies no longer in wide circulation. We know them only by their traces, only as relics. Still other creations, however, leave no trace at all: they are "lost in the maw of oblivion." Thomas Greene has called this process of supersession "pathetic anachronism," which is ultimately "the destiny of all enduring human products, including texts, since all products come into being bearing the marks of their historical moment and then, if they last, are regarded as alien during a later moment because of these marks."[8]

Or, as in the case of Irving, because of the marks they do not bear. Until quite recently, American literary history was ambivalent with regard to Irving because the vocabulary often used to describe him derived from his successors: no one, for instance, would call Hawthorne post-Irvingian, but Irving has long been labeled pre-Romantic. The tendency, on the part of early and mid-twentieth century critics was to consider Irving only in relation to later writers around whom a more vibrant critical discussion developed, to see him only by looking through the American renaissance authors.[9] Within such a narrative of progress, succession, and linear development, measured by the standards of later writers, Irving's reputation, almost by definition, didn't stand a chance.

By contrast, thanks to the historical turn in literary studies over the past two decades, twenty-first century readers of Irving have engaged in what might be called a kind of historicist corrective, one that approaches Irving not through the prism of the (later) American renaissance, but by locating him in his own time and place. Indeed, historicism's contextualizing procedure has made possible fruitful revaluations of Irving's writings by grounding them within various early nineteenth-century discourses, most notably ideologies of U.S. imperialism and constructions of masculinity.[10] In these accounts, Irving emerges as an author both shaped by and helping to give shape to the ideological conflicts and cultural anxieties of the period in which his works were produced.

Yet, even situated within his own time, Irving remains, paradoxically, out of date. David Anthony, for instance, shows how Irving's work exhibits a form of early nineteenth-century "anxious masculinity," brought about by market instability (in particular, the financial panic of 1819). Hence *The Sketch-Book*, Anthony argues, reflects "a nostalgic longing for a period predating the modern period of commerce and credit," a period in which Irving himself was "decidedly out of place." Similarly, in one of the finer recent treatments of Irving, Michael Warner attributes Irving's archaism to his famous bachelorhood, which, Warner argues, disqualified him from the "reproductive narrative" that shaped his culture's historical-temporal consciousness. Indeed, for Warner, it is the "bachelor's fall from reproductive continuity" that "lies behind Irving's preoccupation with modes of historical time." Irving thus deploys an "antihistorical rhetoric of anachronism" in order to "remediate the discontinuities of post-patriarchal sexuality." Put more simply, "Irving idealized patriarchy just at the moment when it was clearly being displaced by modernity." Thus, even for his most sensitive historicist readers, Irving remains a man behind the times, his face turned toward the past as all around him time presses steadily onward.[11]

Accounts like Warner's reproduce, rather than overturn, the charge of outdatedness advanced by earlier generations of critics—a charge, I should note, that has been with Irving almost from the beginning of his career, when, in 1825, William Hazlitt famously called Irving's writings "literary anachronisms."[12] And they do so because despite the important differences in methodology between the (more recent) synchronic analyses offered by new historicism and the (older) diachronic analyses typical of more traditional modes of literary history, both approaches remain committed to a conception of history as sequential development. Thus, rather than providing a countermeasure to narratives of historical progress, the historicist insistence on contextualization actually reinscribes historical progression by other means. To contextualize, to divide history into distinct moments (or periods) along a temporal continuum, each possessing its own unique character is to continue to labor under the assumption that Irving "belongs" to a "then" that is distinct and remote from our "now."

The unhistorical fictions that are the focus of attention in these first two chapters all challenge this standard view of time as linear progression and the historicist contextualism that is its methodological counterpart. Taken together, these works comprise a direction that historical fiction ultimately did not take, the beginnings of a countertradition that never fully matured in the nineteenth century—anticipating instead that postmodern form of historical engagement Linda Hutcheon designates as "historiographic metafiction."[13] Notwithstanding Lloyd Pratt's persuasive recent corrective reading of nineteenth-century historical romance as a genre often at odds with its own nationalizing designs, my interest here lies less in revising our understanding of that genre than with identifying within a handful of texts a set of distinct but related strategies—or experiments—for resisting conventional fictional historicizing. The experimental quality and diversity of these strategies made them disadvantageous for fashioning a unified past headed toward a discernible future, and for those reasons, they never quite coalesced into a coherent genre.[14]

Nevertheless, the experiments all call into question the new historicist idea that texts or ideas "belong" to one period rather than another. In this chapter, I attend to Irving's "rhetoric of anachronism," his metahistorical discourse, which inaugurates this discontinuous tradition. Much of Irving's best work, beginning with *A History of New York* (1809), was written in the guise of a mock historian, Diedrich Knickerbocker, the creation through which Irving engaged in a thoroughgoing critique of history writing. On the one hand, Irving's Knickerbocker writings persistently work to undermine his own era's modes of writing history. On another hand, these writings form an interrogation of the meaning of history, not easily reducible to a single determining context or ideology, a project Irving sustained throughout the various works he attributed to his historian alter ego. I proceed, first, with a consideration of the historiographical self-consciousness of *A History of New York* and turn next to the temporal intricacy and epistemological skepticism of "Rip Van Winkle." Taken together, these works form a kind of practical illustration of the dismantling of history writing in our own time, which cannot be adequately accounted for by conventional historicist contextualization, by confining them to a particular moment in time, much less to one that has been superseded by, or that is irretrievably distant and distinct from, the critical present. Paradoxically, Irving's archaism, his posture of obsolescence, amounts to an argument against the very idea of obsolescence. Far from being outmoded, I want to suggest that Irving has never been timelier than right now. Toward that end, I conclude the chapter with a brief consideration of the afterlives of *A History of New York* and "Rip Van Winkle" among nineteenth-century abolitionists and advocates of racial justice in the twentieth century. Those activists found in Irving's fictions a means by which to figure their immediatist programs, their own relationship to the historical present, and the work of social transformation.

(Anti)Nationalist Historiography

Irving became one of nineteenth-century America's most widely read authors by both participating in and lampooning the project of creating a national past—sometimes at once. His body of work includes "serious" histories (notably, biographies of George Washington and Christopher Columbus) and fictional sketches—among them "Rip Van Winkle" and "The Legend of Sleepy Hollow"— that are themselves deeply concerned with matters historiographical. Yet *A History of New York* has rarely been taken seriously in discussions of early national history writing for reasons probably best summed up by William Hedges: "The book may contain a great deal of fact," Hedges wrote, "but to call it history is simply to abuse the word."[15] However, the line separating fiction and history that underpins Hedges's assessment is surely less stark in the wake of the work of Hayden White and other poststructuralist challenges to the practice of history writing. Among literary scholars, at least, I suspect there is somewhat less concern today about considering Irving's provocative admixture of historical fact and fiction a species of history.[16]

At the time of its publication *A History of New York* was the best (in fact, the only) account of the early Dutch reign of New York that had yet been published and could thus—and was intended to—take its place among the state histories of writers like Jeremy Belknap and Benjamin Trumbull. The book was even dedicated to the New York Historical Society "as a humble and unworthy Testimony of the profound veneration and exalted esteem of the Society's Sincere Well wisher and Devoted Servant," a wry jab at the Society's "real" historians who, by the time of the bicentennial of Hendrick Hudson's founding, had been unable to produce anything approaching a comprehensive history of colonial New York.[17]

One of the functions of *A History of New York* was to deflate the high moral import of nationalist historiography.[18] As Irving put it in the "Author's Apology" included in the 1848 revised edition of the *Knickerbocker History*, he wanted "To burlesque the pedantic lore displayed in certain American works."[19] The satire and burlesque Irving deployed under the guise of his fictional mock historian captured the tensions, contradictions, and irregularities of a genre undergoing change. If nothing else, Knickerbocker's mock history provides a useful index to the transitional state of early national historiography. The book appeared between two important eras of historical writing in America, coming after the great New England colonial historians, yet preceding the Romantic historians by two decades or more.[20] *A History of New York* registers these changes in an especially perceptive way. Irving's pseudo-history provides a running self-referential commentary on its own historicity—and by extension on early national historiography. Scholars have long attributed Knickerbocker's self-reflexivity to Irving's adaptation of the narrative methods of Sterne, Swift, Cervantes, and Rabelais.[21] Yet by placing Diedrich Knickerbocker in relation to previous *fictional* narrators, critics of the *History* have tended to ignore the extent to which Irving modeled him on a tradition of *historical* narrators.

For instance, structurally, *A History of New York* moves from older to newer styles of historical narration, adopting the conventions of classical and colonial histories in the early parts of the book and gradually becoming embroiled in forms of historical discourse that are more contemporary. Book I pokes fun at early colonial chronicles, like Samuel Purchas's twenty-volume *Purchas His Pilgrimes: Contayning a History of the World in Sea Voyages and Lande Travells by Englishmen and Others* (1625)—on which Irving doubtless modeled his own outlandish chapter headings. Similarly, the pedantry of Cotton Mather's *Magnalia Christi Americana*, especially his penchant for citing the classical historians, formed a likely model for Knickerbocker's comic displays of erudition. Conceptually, too, *A History of New York* adopts conventions used by Mather (and many others), like arranging his history as a series of books organized according to the reigns of successive governors. And perhaps most notably, the "philosophical speculations" that comprise Book I have a model in another American work that Irving likely knew: Thomas Prince's influential *A Chronological History of New England in the Form of Annals* (1730). Like Knickerbocker, Prince dwells at some length on the difficulties of his researches and begins his annals with a long introduction, which runs from an account of the Creation up to the beginning of the British Empire.

Although the principal targets of ridicule in the first book are colonial historians, from the beginning Knickerbocker is a recognizably republican historian. His narrative is rife with the favored platitudes of early national history writing. As George Calcott has noted, "probably the most frequent historical cliché of the period was 'to rescue from oblivion,'"[22] which are the very first words of Knickerbocker's history: "To rescue from oblivion the memory of former incidents, and to render a just tribute of renown to the many great and wonderful transactions of our Dutch progenitors, Diedrich Knickerbocker, native of the great city of New York, produces this historical essay"[23]—variations of which are repeated throughout the text.[24] A second cliché in the early American historian's arsenal was the claim of "authenticity, honesty and accuracy."[25] For his part, Knickerbocker insists ad nauseum on his own "faithful veracity,"[26] his adherence to the "most approved and fashionable plan of modern historians," his "duty as a faithful historian," his "unimpeached character for veracity," and claims that his is a "faithful and veritable history," the "most authentic, minute and satisfactory of all histories."[27]

If truthfulness and accuracy were the "chief merits" of any authentic historian, such veracity was to be achieved principally through scrupulous research and displays of erudition, which post-Revolutionary readers expected. In fact, documentation was a particular obsession among early nationals. David Van Tassel has called the years following the War for Independence "documania," as citizens rushed to gather and preserve the materials of history, from government documents and correspondence to families' genealogical records and oral accounts of colonial life.[28] Such research was further promoted—and the findings disseminated—by the formation of state historical societies, beginning with Belknap's founding of the Massachusetts Historical Society in 1791. Connecticut and New York followed in 1799 and 1804, respectively, and by 1860, there were over a hundred such organizations, some in territories that had not yet even been admitted as states.[29] Appropriately, then, Knickerbocker, like other historians of the time—Trumbull, for instance, remarks that "The labor of collecting the materials for the history and compilement, has been almost incredible"[30]—takes pains to describe his work as an "arduous undertaking, which has been the whole business of a long and solitary life," in which he set about "carefully winnowing away the chaff of hypothesis and the tares of fable," relying on materials "carefully collected, collated and arranged" so as to produce "a history which may serve as a foundation, on which a host of worthies shall hereafter raise a noble superstructure."[31] His pages are "abounding with sound wisdom and profound erudition"[32]—so much so that, early on, he must offer his readers:

> ...fair warning, that I am about to plunge for a chapter or two, into as complete a labyrinth as ever historian was perplexed withal; therefore I advise them to take

fast hold of my skirts, and keep close at my heels, venturing neither to the right hand nor to the left, lest they get bemired in a slough of unintelligible learning, or have their brains knocked out by some of those hard Greek names which will be flying about in all directions.[33]

Once Knickerbocker turns to his subject proper, he directs his satire almost entirely at his contemporaries. A great deal of critical attention has been given, for example, to explicating Irving's political satire: his treatment of early republican factiousness, of "mobocracy," and, especially, of Thomas Jefferson, the certain model for the ineffectual governor William the Testy, whose reign is described in Book IV.[34] Less apparent, however, is Irving's historiographical satire. Products of the Enlightenment, early national historians were "anxious to disassociate their function from that of mere chroniclers," like Purchas and Prince[35] and "[leave] behind the traditional providential interpretations of history" that characterized the work of ecclesiastical historians like Mather.[36] The principal feature distinguishing early national histories from their colonial predecessors was their nationalistic tenor.[37] As one writer explained the task of the national historian in 1806:

[Independence] may indeed be considered a moral and political phenomenon, the real existence of which, after ages would find it difficult to believe, or to account for, if it were not authenticated by indubitable evidence, accompanied with correspondent illustration. To put the event upon the solid footing of undeniable historical truth, to develope the means, and to perpetuate the memory of those by whom it was effected, is the duty of the chronicler of the present day, and is the purpose of the present attempt.[38]

Nationalist histories thus performed several essential functions. Not only did they help to create a sense of a shared past among the newly republicanized former colonists, to lionize various military heroes as representative Americans, and to build a national literature, they also served more immediate political ends, like rallying support for ratification of the Constitution. And given the rancorous political environment of the early republic, historians were not unaware of this dilemma; they understood that the historian was "at the mercy" of "furious partisans" for whom "the statement of...facts will seem impertinent and the displaying of...truths appear offensive."[39] Nevertheless:

the duty of the historian, or the chronicler, remains the same...from purity, strict justice, and impartiality, he must not knowingly swerve, to please or oblige either party; he must be careful to omit no incident of moment; and he must deliver his sentiments with frankness, boldness, and impartiality.[40]

Knickerbocker registers this sentiment repeatedly. For instance, the central conflict in Knickerbocker's narrative, between the encroaching Yankees from Connecticut and the phlegmatic Dutch burghers, mirrors Knickerbocker's own struggles against both rival historians and his readers. "I have had more vexations," he writes, "in those parts of my history which treat of the transactions on the eastern border, than in any other, in consequence of the troops of historians who have infested these quarters, and have shewn the honest [Dutch colonists] no mercy." Chief among these is "Mr. Trumbull," who "arrogantly declares that 'the Dutch were always mere intruders.'"[41] In fact, Trumbull's account of the clashes between the Yankees and the Dutch in his *History of Connecticut* is a favorite target of Knickerbocker. He can barely contain his indignation—it "makes my gorge to rise while I write, he says"[42]—when telling of the alleged plot, during the reign of Peter Stuyvesant, forged by the Dutch and the Indians to unite in attacking the Yankees. At such a "wanton, wicked and unparalleled attack, upon one of the most gallant and irreproachable heroes of modern times," Knickerbocker is whipped into a paroxysm of protest and outrage:

> Oh reader it was false!—I swear to thee it was false—if the undeviating and unimpeached character for veracity, which I have hitherto borne throughout this work, has its due weight with thee, thou wilt not give thy faith to this tale of slander; for I pledge my honour and my immortal fame to thee, that the gallant Peter Stuyvesant, was…innocent of this foul conspiracy…Beshrew those caitiff scouts, that conspired to sully his honest name by such an imputation.[43]

As if battling against rival Yankee historians were not enough, Knickerbocker must also contend with a horde of "testy" readers, whom he knows are also likely to be furiously partisan. Of all the "perils and mishaps that surround your hardy historian," he notes, the one he has "no hopes of escaping" is "offend[ing] the morbid sensibilities of certain…unreasonable descendants" of the Yankees by "detailing the many misdeeds" of their ancestors. However, his duty as a faithful historian requires that he deliver the unvarnished truth: "how in heaven's name, can I help it, if your great grandfathers behaved in a scurvy manner to my great grandfathers?"[44] Here again, Knickerbocker reminds his readers of the historian's power to redress past wrongs: "I have as great a mind as ever I had for my dinner, to cut a whole host of your ancestors to mince meat, in my very next page." But his duty as an historian requires that he forebear:

> I trust when you perceive how completely I have them all in my power, and how, with one flourish of my pen I could make every mother's son of ye grandfather-less, you will not be able enough to applaud my candour and magnanimity.—To resume, then, with my accustomed calmness and impartiality, the course of my history.[45]

The obvious irony, of course, is that Knickerbocker is anything but impartial; he abuses his power as an historian to bestow honor and immortality—as did many early national historians. Knickerbocker even goes so far, at the end of history, to cast the Dutch colonists as the real progenitors of the Revolution. In the *History's* penultimate chapter, "on the decline and fall of empires," Knickerbocker explains the "subtle chain of events," beginning with the Dutch battles with the Swedes over

Fort Casimir, that have led to "the present convulsions of the globe."[46] Often cited, it is one of the *History's* richest historiographical passages:

> By the treacherous surprisal of Fort Casimer, then, did the crafty Swedes enjoy a transient triumph; but drew upon their heads the vengeance of Peter Stuyvesant, who wrested New Sweden from their hands—By the conquest of New Sweden Peter Stuyvesant aroused the claims of Lord Baltimore, who appealed to the cabinet of Great Britain, who subdued the whole province of New Netherlands—By this great achievement the whole extent of North America from Nova Scotia to the Floridas, was rendered one entire dependency upon the British crown—but mark the consequence—The hitherto scattered colonies being thus consolidated, and having no rival colonies to check or keep them in awe, waxed great and powerful, and finally becoming too strong for the mother country, were enabled to shake off its bonds, and by a glorious revolution became an independent empire—But the chain of effects stopped not here: the successful revolution in America produced the sanguinary revolution in France, which produced the puissant Bonaparte who produced the French Despotism, which has thrown the whole world in confusion![47]

Here, in a parody of historical causation, Irving's gentle satire against his historian contemporaries burgeons into a theoretical consideration of history's ways of knowing.[48] The ridiculousness—and yet strangely, the utter plausibility—of the notion that the blundering attempts of the Dutch at warfare should be responsible for "the present convolutions of the globe" illustrates the arbitrariness of determining causes.[49] Knickerbocker's procedure suggests that causes and consequences proceed not naturally, but by assertion, according to the historian's ability to construct a plausibly interconnected series of events—a narrative. In Chapter 2, I find in John Neal an attempt to turn this insight into an even more radical experiment in writing historical fiction that not only resists cause and effect relations, but that is actively hostile toward narrative per se, the representational mode upon which it nevertheless depends. Irving's skepticism didn't run quite that deep, although the implications of his extended critique of historical truth claims, as we'll see, gesture in that direction.

"An Improvement in History"

Irving's emphasis *A History of New York* on the role of narrative representation in history writing is one place where Irving seems to exceed the "context"—early national historiography—that I have thus far described. Earlier, in Book I, for instance, Knickerbocker provides an even more vivid demonstration of the preposterousness of causality. Before a single Dutch settler arrives in his narrative, Knickerbocker first, in successive chapters, "ventures a Description of the World, from the best authorities"; attempts to explain the creation of the world; establishes

the discovery of America; explains the peopling of America; and, finally, establishes
the right of the first colonists to possession of the land—all of which he deems necessary to his history. Or as he puts it, prefatory to the second chapter:

> indeed these points [how the world was created] are absolutely essential to be
> cleared up, in as much as if this world had not been formed, it is more probable,
> nay I may venture to assume it as a maxim or postulate at least, that this renowned
> island on which is situated the city of New York, would never have had an existence.
> The regular course of my history therefore, requires that I should proceed to
> notice the cosmogony or formation of this our globe.[50]

In pointing out the absurdity of historical cause and effect relations—since, appre-
hended only retrospectively, causes merely beget prior causes—Irving via Knickerbocker verges upon the kind of historical relativism typically associated with the
postmodern moment, but that, as Brook Thomas has shown, was also a concern
for American historians of the Progressive Era. As Thomas notes, Charles Beard, for
one, was led to embrace relativism because of doubts about the possibility of writing
causal history. "A search for the causes of America's entry into [World War I],"
Beard wrote in 1936, for instance, "leads into the causes of the war, into all the history that lies beyond 1914, and into the very nature of the universe of which the
history is a part; that is, unless we arbitrarily decide to cut the web and begin at
some place that pleases us" (qtd. in Thomas 92). Knickerbocker, it would seem,
provides a perfect illustration of such a causal history, beginning it just as Beard
feared a history that fully accounts for interconnectedness would need to begin:
with the "very nature of the universe of which the history is a part." By the same
token, Knickerbocker's tracing of French Despotism to the Dutch defeat at Fort
Casimir reveals his insistence upon first causes as little more than a matter of locating a pleasing point of origin—since it invests the battle for Fort Casimir with
epochal importance—to explain contemporary events.

  The point here is not to attribute to Irving some remarkable powers of prescience. Nineteenth-century writers were far more (theoretically) reflective about
historiographical practice than has often been recognized. For instance, Irving
wasn't alone in recognizing the contingency and indeterminacy of efforts to dis-
cern causes. Charles Brockden Brown began his "Annals of Europe and America"
(1807) by remarking that:

> Political transactions are connected together in so long and various a chain
> that a relater of contemporary events is frequently obliged to carry his narra-
> tion somewhat backward, in order to make himself intelligible. He generally
> finds himself placed in the midst of things, and quickly perceives that he
> cannot go forward with a firm and easy step, without previously returning to
> some commencing point. An active imagination is apt to carry us very far back-
> ward on these occasions; for in truth, the chain of successive and dependent
> causes is endless; and he may be said to be imperfectly acquainted with the

last link, who has not attentively scrutinized the very first in the series, however remote it may be.[51]

Perhaps writers of fiction, like Brown and Irving, were more sensitive to the processes of invention by which causes are deduced or constructed—more sensitive to the fictive quality of historical causation. Whatever the case, Irving and Brown were clearly attuned to the representational conundrums that confront the historian, attuned in ways that resonate with the kinds of poststructuralist challenges to historiography with which many current (literary) historians continue to grapple.[52]

For instance, unwilling to settle on one theory of the earth's formation over another—all of which Knickerbocker dismisses as "the smoke and vapours" of "heated imagination"—he settles instead on unassailable present facts. After presenting numerous competing theories for the creation of the earth, Knickerbocker concludes only that "the globe really *was created*."[53] Similarly, he demonstrates in excruciating detail how historians have established "to the satisfaction of all the world" that the New World "*has been discovered*."[54] And most pointedly, he ultimately determines that the earliest settlers of America took possession of the land by virtue of what he calls "THE RIGHT BY DETERMINATION" or "THE RIGHT BY GUNPOWDER."[55] Other critics have taken note of how in moments like these, Knickerbocker illustrates the retrospective quality of historical narrative, and Irving highlights the importance of linguistic representation in history writing.[56] Thus, for example, Knickerbocker can claim that he "make[s] it a rule, not to examine the annals of the times whereof I treat, further than exactly a page in advance of my own work."[57] And although he "cannot save the life of my favourite hero," he can "now and then make him bestow on his enemy a sturdy back stroke" or "drive his antagonist clear round the field ..."[58] Historical events are caused, then, not by explaining their connection to prior events; they are caused by the historian's narrative constructions.[59]

But, I have been suggesting, *A History of New York* seeks to undermine just such acts of (historical re-)creation in the service of nationalism, by exposing nationalist history's pretensions to truth.[60] The conclusions Knickerbocker draws from his intellectual exertions comically disrupt any claims they might make to having advanced human knowledge or understanding. So Irving's reflections upon "the relations between writing and event"[61] suggest that historical "explanations" are, at best, radically contingent—the only possible certainty regarding the earth's formation is the fact of its formation—and, at worst, utter fancies of the imagination. Relying upon tautology, rather than causation, as his preferred mode of historical explanation, Knickerbocker conceives of history as unmotivated by any pre-existing shape or design. Hence Knickerbocker presents alternative narratives not as a gradual progress toward the truth—for "all have the same title to belief"[62]—but as so many fictions, each of which has a claim to truth not on the basis of its correspondence to reality, but according to the authority that underwrites it. These Knickerbocker often takes care to mention, such as when he notes that the former "Catholic opinion" that the earth "is an immense flat pancake" was "sanctioned by a formidable *bull*, dispatched from the Vatican by a most holy and infallible pontiff."[63] Or, similarly, the "fact" of European possession of the New World "was considered as fully admitted and established" by historians in large part because "no Indian writers arose on the other side."[64] The accidents of power and transmission, not the objective uncovering of actuality nor even "reasoning from present facts to necessary preconditions," establish the "truth" about the past.

Knickerbocker's emphasis on authority as the real arbiter of historical explanation brings into relief his methodological self-consciousness. Following his explanation of the formation of the globe, Knickerbocker insists that, "like an experienced historian," he confines himself only "to such points as are absolutely essential to [his] subject," constructing it as an architect builds a theatre: "beginning with the foundation, then the body, then the roof, and at last perching our snug little island like the little cupola on the top." Pleased with his metaphor, Knickerbocker sustains it in order to "illustrate the correctness of [his] plan":

> Had not the foundation, the body, and the roof of the theatre first been built, the cupola could not have had existence as a cupola—it might have been a centry-box—or a watchman's box—or it might have been placed in the rear of the Manager's house and have formed—a temple;—but it could never have been considered a cupola. As therefore the building of the theatre was necessary to the existence of the cupola, as a cupola—so the formation of the globe and its internal construction, were first necessary to the existence of this island, as an island—and thus the necessity and importance of this part of my history, which in a manner is no part of my history; is logically proved.[65]

This illustration speaks once again to the problem of interconnectedness as it relates to causation. It also brings into focus the related question of context, that most fundamental of principles to recent forms of literary historicism. Since new historicists typically avoid diachronic analysis, they are less concerned with explaining change or continuity over time; so what provides for—or allows—their connections between literary texts and the social world is a governing context. In Louis Montrose's formulation, the new historicism "reorients the axis of inter-textuality, substituting for the diachronic text of an autonomous literary history, the synchronic text of a cultural system."[66] Where diachronic histories consider events and historical periods as following one another in a logical and determinable chain, as causes and effects that occur over time, synchronic histories treat a single historical period as a "system" of interrelated concerns, concepts, ideas, and texts. The synchronism of new historicists is evident in their readings of particular texts, which they view not as separate from and commenting upon their historical moment, but as both constituted by and constitutive of their time. In other words, new historicists substitute context for cause as their preferred mode of historical explanation.[67]

Indeed, highlighting the explanatory power of historical context is the satirical point of Knickerbocker's cupola simile, which undermines the notion of meaning as a function of context, comically asserting instead that context does not help to *explain* historical phenomena, but *determines* historical phenomena. That is, it is only after having identified the foundation as a foundation, the roof as a roof, and so forth—or more precisely, it's only after having constructed these constituent parts—that the cupola can then take on meaning as a cupola: its existence is a function of its context. Independent of that context, it could well be any number of other things—a sentry box, a watchman's box, or a temple. But the thrust of this critique is not positivist; it does not suggest that historical phenomena possess meaning independent of context. Rather, the point is that neither can context itself be taken as predetermined. It, too, is dependent, to pick up on Irving's metaphor, upon acts of construction. The key element in Knickerbocker's architectural metaphor—"As therefore the building of the theatre was necessary to the existence of the cupola, as a cupola"—is not the cupola, but the *building of the theater*, the context. The historian might well build something else, a bridge, a church, or a house, in which case, cupola would be stripped of its meaning or at least take on some other meaning.

It might be objected at this point that Irving's deployment of satire to critique the historiographical pieties of his contemporaries and, beyond that, to unsettle historical truth claims generally, might well be self-defeating. After all, it is sometimes hard to know what, if anything, lies behind or beneath the book's relentless and corrosive irony, to know whether it tends toward a useful critical awareness or merely toward a skepticism so complete as to border on cynicism. But the claim I am making for the *History* is not that the text denies truth in history writing; it is only that that truth is always made, rather than found. Hence, the irony of having Knickerbocker describe himself as a "regular bred historian"[68] has less to do with the obvious fact that his manner of presentation is so *ir*regular than it does with the way in which Knickerbocker's method turns out to be closer to the "regular" practice of history writing; closer, at least, to the ways in which late twentieth-century theorists of history have taught many of us to regard it: as a practice largely determined by what Hayden White has called "the content of the form." This Knickerbocker understands. As he says in one of his many moments of narrative self-consciousness: "...my work shall, in a manner, echo the nature of the subject, in the same manner as the sound of poetry has been found by certain shrewd critics, to echo the sense—this being an improvement in history, which I claim the merit of having invented."[69]

Nor do I mean to suggest a lack of theoretical awareness on the part of new historicists with regard to the role of linguistic representation in every act of historical (re)creation. Yet historicist methodology does, in practice, often assume a self-evident context, an assumption made possible by an understanding of historicity as bound by chronological time. In historicist literary scholarship, as Christopher Lane argues, "the date has become a fetish."[70] Along similar lines,

Wai-Chee Dimock argues that "numerical chronology" derives from Newtonian science, which converts what may simply be analytically useful—a system of numerical designations, assigning numbers to years, days, and hours—into an "absolute mathematical truth, eternally binding." Adherents of Newton in this sense, historicist critics fix texts "into a brief duration, a numbered slice of time, as if that slice were an air-tight container."[71]

Above all, it is this way of understanding the temporality of history that Irving, especially in his Knickerbocker writings, resists; indeed, it is the very numerical determinism that makes it possible to think of Irving as being behind the times (his own, as well as ours) in the first place. So however much energy Irving devoted in *A History of New York* to a critique of his historian contemporaries, his more interesting ruminations on history involve still more penetrating questions about *epistemology*, or how we arrive at historical knowledge, and *temporality*, or how we experience historical time. These are the central concerns of Irving's most famous tale, "Rip Van Winkle," which is at once a parody of the very possibility of absolute historical knowledge and a brilliant confounding of our devotion to chronological, linear time.

Rip's Now

A History of New York also addressed questions about the relations between knowledge and experience, albeit to a lesser extent. As we've seen, in his opening chapters, Knickerbocker finds himself so awash in competing theories and philosophical speculations that he accords all of them the "same title to belief," and can locate no stable ground—aside from claims of authority—from which to adjudicate among them. We have also seen briefly how Knickerbocker seeks to write history in the present tense, as it were, as if it were happening *now*. To recall Charles Brockden Brown's terms, Knickerbocker often "finds himself placed in the midst of things." This is literally the case, for instance, near the end of the book when the New Netherlanders prepare for war with the Swedes. Prior to narrating the battle, Knickerbocker asks "one small favour" of his readers:

> …which is, that when I have set both armies by the ears in the next chapter, and am hurrying about, like the very devil, in the midst—they will just stand a little on one side, out of harms way—and on no account attempt to interrupt me by a single question or remonstrance. As the whole spirit, hurry and sublimity of the battle will depend on my exertions, the moment I should stop to speak, the whole business would stand still—wherefore I shall not be able to say a word to my readers, throughout the whole of the next chapter, but I promise them in the one after, I'll listen to all they have to say, and answer any questions they may ask.[72]

This moment is just one of many, as we have seen, where Irving parodically reminds us of "the textuality of history"—the idea that our access to the "actual" past is always mediated by language and the shaping hand of the historian.

Of more particular interest to me, here, however, is this moment's representation of temporality. Knickerbocker bends time out of shape. That is, having first positioned the past as the historian's—and by extension, the reader's—present (is this not always history's aim?), Knickerbocker arrives at the scene of battle and proceeds to project a future. As they wait for the battle to commence, he writes, "historians filled their ink horns—the poets went without their dinners...antiquity scowled sulkily out of its grave, to see itself outdone—while even posterity stood mute, gazing in gaping extacy of retrospection, on the eventful field!"[73] The temporal effect here hinges upon Irving's deployment of a term that is itself perhaps the English language's most temporally ambiguous: *now*, the term with which the passage begins. *Now* registers time at its most slippery; it is never quite immediate with itself, since the very instant it is meant to capture has passed by the time it has been uttered (or read). At the same time, *now* also has a built-in temporal mechanism that allows it to catch up with itself: paradoxically, it signifies *then*, both the past and the future—as in the phrases, "now you've done it" and "now I will describe." Exploiting *now*'s peculiar semantic temporality, Irving constructs his own version of the image from George Herbert Mead, which, in the introduction, I described as capturing the presiding spirit of Romantic presentism, an image we'll encounter again: posterity, at the present time, looking forward to looking back.

"Rip Van Winkle," a story of historical dislocation, elaborates on this theme. As a number of recent critics have noted, the tale turns on its complex structure of temporality, which is thick with layers of past and present and in which time passes irregularly, alternately slowing and accelerating.[74] My reading travels alongside these astute treatments of the story, though I also wish to consider it in relation to Irving's other Knickerbocker writings, which, strangely, very few critics have done.[75] This may be because the narrative voice in "Rip" lacks the comic absurdity of that found in the *History*. Yet the tale also repeats, in compressed form, the earlier work's historiographic preoccupations with the accuracy of historical research, with the role of authority in historical explanation, and with the constructedness of narrative representation.

"Rip Van Winkle" extends those subversions by questioning what it means to have a sense of history at all, interrogating what it means to be historical, and parodying the very possibility of settled historical knowledge. Yet this fact is easily overlooked when one considers only the tale proper, interpreting it as "fable," and does not attend to the explanatory notes which frame it.[76] Those notes are an integral part of the story and a crucial narrative strategy on the part of Irving. In the prefatory note to "Rip Van Winkle," Geoffrey Crayon (the "author" of *The Sketch Book* in which the story was originally published) reintroduces the reader to Diedrich Knickerbocker, among whose papers the tale of Rip was found. Knickerbocker, we are reminded, was an historian of the Dutch settlements. However:

> his historical researches...did not lie so much among books, as among men; for the former are lamentably scanty on his favourite topics; whereas he found the

old burghers, and still more, their wives, rich in that legendary lore so invaluable to true history.[77]

The pun on the word *lie* in Crayon's note hints at the ironic attempt Crayon makes to convince the reader of the subsequent tale's historical accuracy. The "chief merit" of Knickerbocker's history, Crayon tells us in the same note, "is its scrupulous accuracy, which indeed was a little questioned on its first appearance, but has since been completely established; and it is now admitted into all historical collections as a book of unquestionable authority."[78] And again, in a note that follows the tale, Crayon appends the note Knickerbocker had originally included with the tale, in which, based upon his knowledge of similar "marvellous events and appearances" in the Dutch settlements, he gives Rip's tale his "full belief." Knickerbocker reveals further that he has even verified the story with Rip himself and "seen a certificate on the subject taken before a country justice and signed with a cross in the justice's own hand writing. The story therefore is beyond the possibility of doubt."[79]

In this way, Irving offers a parody of historical scholarship's fetishization of the source, the process of making distinctions between the levels of reliability of historical documentation. We have already seen early nationals' concern for accurate scholarship and documentation. But just as valuable to early nineteenth-century historians as state records and the papers of public figures, were oral histories and other firsthand accounts, which historical societies often recorded. Likewise, while Knickerbocker "gleaned" "many legends, letters and other documents," he also "gathered a host of well authenticated traditions from divers excellent old ladies."[80] This latter form of research lends Knickerbocker authority because, as Geoffrey Crayon implies, in "true history," the veracity of written texts is suspect; the historian's best source is someone with firsthand experience, like Rip himself. But Irving cleverly undermines any such authority by showing that Rip, ostensibly the "primary source," lacks credibility:

> [Rip] used to tell his story to every stranger that arrived at Mr. Doolittle's Hotel. He was observed at first to vary on some points, every time he told it, which was doubtless owing to his having so recently awaked. It at last settled down precisely to the tale I have related and not a man woman or child in the neighborhood but knew it by heart.[81]

Once again, we might say that Irving "deconstructs" historical truth by questioning the foundation upon which truth telling in history rests: this time, the distinction between primary and secondary sources. And he does so in two ways: first, he cleverly depicts Rip as an unreliable witness. The legal metaphor here is especially apt, not only because of Irving's early training for a career in the law, but because its rules and strictures for arriving at "truth" served as a model for early nineteenth-century historical practice.[82] As one reviewer asserted, the historian's role was to act as a judge, compelled to "examine the strength of the evidence and the character of the witness. The rules of our courts of jurisprudence are generally applicable here."[83] And indeed, it is the authority of the law that, for Knickerbocker, makes Rip's tale "beyond the possibility of doubt." That is, it is (legally) admissible into the historical record only after "a certificate" signed by "a country justice" underwrites its truthfulness.

We might pursue this legal metaphor still further. In his essay "The Practice of Historical Investigation," Mark Cousins makes a similar claim, arguing that "historical scholarship bears more than a fleeting resemblance to...jurisprudential" reasoning. In Cousins's poststructuralist account, the law establishes the "truth" or the "reality" of a past event only "in a specialised sense." It requires a truth about the past that is subject to the rules of evidence, to particular strictures of admissibility and appeal; thus, it *determines* a representation of the past that is "relevant to the law" or "definable by law." The truth of the past is not the past as it "really" happened—for surely the plenitude of a past event, all that can be said or known about it is never exhausted by forensic investigation—rather, it is a "strictly legal truth," truth only as the law defines it for itself. Or we might apply Knickerbocker's language here and say that without first building a legal foundation and constructing an evidentiary edifice, a truth could not have existence as a truth. The particular version of the past arrived at through historical investigation is similarly subject to rules and restrictions, to a determining epistemological context—accepted distinctions between primary and secondary sources, reliability and unreliability, documentation and hearsay. Hence, historical truths are likewise disciplinarily contingent. In "Rip Van Winkle," Irving undermines these distinctions and disrupts this procedure by casting doubt on even the most rigorously investigated of historical events, that linchpin of historical legitimacy, the primary source.

A second, and related, strategy he employs to cast doubt on the reliability of his "sources" is the presentation of Rip's story through a labyrinth of voices and narrators, subtly complicating our apparent direct access to the source. That is, what might be called the "tale proper"—Rip's family life, his sojourn into the mountains, and his return—is filtered not only through Rip's own many variations: it has then been transcribed by Diedrich Knickerbocker and subsequently, finally, presented in Geoffrey Crayon's miscellany. Irving employs this device in almost all of the Knickerbocker tales. "The Legend of Sleepy Hollow," for instance, is a story "found among the papers of the late Diedrich Knickerbocker."[84] There, we learn that the tale was given "*almost* in the precise words" in which Knickerbocker first heard it "related at a Corporation of the ancient city of the Manhattoes" (emphasis mine).[85] On this occasion, as Knickerbocker relates the story of his own first hearing of the story, one of the audience members expresses doubt as to the veracity of the tale. To this the storyteller, of whom we know only that he was "a pleasant, shabby, gentlemanly old fellow...with a sadly humorous face," rejoins, "Faith, sir, as to that matter, I don't believe one-half of it myself."[86] This ambiguous remark—which "half" does the speaker not believe, the ghost story? the plausible explanation of it?—is intended to cast doubt on Knickerbocker's entire historical enterprise. This is because his sources, like Rip, are usually themselves crafty storytellers, shapers of narratives.

"Dolph Heyliger" is likewise a third-hand account. In the note that frames that story, we are told that Dolph's tale was related to him by "a pleasant gossiping man whose whole life was spent in hearing and telling the news of the province."[87] For his part, Knickerbocker—ever the dutiful historian—claims to have "endeavored to give it as nearly as possible in his words," although Knickerbocker has grown old and his "memory is not over good. [He] cannot therefore vouch for the language, but [he is] always scrupulous as to facts."[88] Irving employs yet another variation of the device in "The Money Diggers" section of *Tales of a Traveller* (also found among the papers of the late Diedrich Knickerbocker), where stories are passed along a chain of narrators and thus beget more stories. So while Knickerbocker "made diligent research after the truth" of the legends he has recorded, those that follow are the only ones that "had any thing like an air of authenticity."[89] What follows, however, does not seem particularly authentic; nor is it a historian's disinterested third-person account. Instead, we find a series of voices and interrelated stories: a "Cape Cod whaler" narrates "The Devil and Tom Walker," followed by "Woolfert Webber, or Golden Dreams," told by "one of the most authentic narrators in the province"[90]—a portion of which is related in indirect discourse by yet another narrator—which gives way without resolution to yet another story, "The Adventure of the Black Fisherman"—and so on. The accumulation of these third- and fourth-hand accounts—all framed as the researches of Diedrich Knickerbocker—cast the historical enterprise not as a scientific search for reliable, or even verifiable, material evidence, but as an unruly (and perhaps unreliable) discursive practice, an elaborate game of telephone, in which a simple phrase is radically transformed as it is passed on in whispers from one ear to the next.

Yet simply to suggest that "Rip Van Winkle," like these other tales, undermines historical truth claims and raises questions about the historian's access to the past is not to do justice to the tale. Working in tandem with his disquisition on the mutability of historical knowledge is the *experience* of history the tale offers to its readers, by placing us in precisely the same position in which Rip finds himself upon his return to the village after a twenty years' nap. Or to put this another way: Rip's need to settle upon an orienting present after being removed from chronological time for two decades is duplicated in the reader's experience of the story itself, and it is this feature—the way the story acts upon the reader's sense of temporality—that is central to the story's displacement of knowledge with experience as the locus of historicity.

Rip has what amounts to the same experience twice, though in opposite temporal directions. Irving carefully constructs a parallel structure between Rip's experience in the mountain: when he steps into the past, and his experience upon returning to the village, when he leaps into (what is for him) the future, as himself a figure from the past. The marks of this structure are found in the story's details. Rip's sojourn into the mountains, rather than an escape from a particular place into a magical realm outside of history, is actually a journey deeper into history, into an estranging past. The mysterious personages he encounters bear the signs less of fancy and imagination, than of a bygone era. For example, upon meeting the stranger toiling up the mountain with a keg of liquor, Rip recognizes his clothing as being of the "antique Dutch fashion, a cloth jerkin strapped round the waist, several pair of breeches, the outer one of ample volume decorated with rows of buttons down the sides and bunches at the knees."[91] As Rip silently assists the stranger, he begins to perceive something "strange and incomprehensible about the unknown that inspired awe and checked familiarity."[92] The mysterious figures Rip encounters in the mountains are similarly "dressed in a quaint outlandish fashion" and "all had beards of various shapes and colours."[93] Initially, he only watches the grave game of ninepins, but "by degrees Rip's awe and apprehension subsided,"[94] and he eventually becomes comfortable enough to partake of the spirits. Following repeated trips to the flagon, Rip falls into a deep sleep.

Awaking from his slumber, Rip returns to the village only to find it utterly changed: his home, the village inn, the portrait of King George, bear little resemblance to Rip's memory of them. Faced yet again with the "unknown," he feels the same sense of bewilderment he felt during his first estranging experience, the language of which is repeated precisely: "all this was strange and incomprehensible."[95] Again, like the personages in the mountains, the townspeople's dress is "of a different fashion from that with which he was accustomed." Rip himself is now the antiquarian figure, and he carries the marks of his estrangement in the form of his "rusty fowling piece," his "uncouth dress,"[96] and in his most characteristic—and memorable—feature, his foot-long beard. Thus Rip's "return" to the village isn't a return at all. Rather, it is a repetition or it is a return only in the sense that he returns to his earlier bewildering experience. In both cases, Rip is a kind of "anachronistic vagrant" a "walking anachronism," a figure from an era other than that in which he finds himself.[97] He enters the future as strangely and (to him) disconcertingly as he entered the past upon meeting the crew of Hendrick Hudson. Rip, in effect, has no place in history. But, crucially, this is not the same as saying that Rip stands outside of history; instead, he is momentarily lost within it and its proliferating temporal frames. His subsequent loss of identity occurs because he can find no present that corresponds to his sense of his own. Yet just as he did previously, after an initial feeling of trepidation and confusion, Rip acclimates himself to his post-Revolutionary surroundings, gradually "assum[ing] his old walks and habits." He is ultimately able to perform as successfully in one time and place as another.

Situating and resituating Rip in historical time, the story represents Rip's dilemma as a problem of historicity, generating precisely the sorts of questions that literary scholars ask about texts: to which historical period does Rip "belong"? One way of answering this question is to say that Rip belongs to "now," a now that is both elusive and thick, crowded with temporalities. This, Carolyn Dinshaw notes, is "the very nature of the 'living present' itself."[98] "Such asynchronies as in Rip Van Winkle's world—the human body and mind striated by diverse times, spirits returning and drawing the living to them, people existing in different temporalities in the same present moment"[99] are the stuff of which historical experience in the *now* are made.

The repetitiveness of Rip's experience also bears on the feature of Irving's tale that have interested critics most: the "signs" with which Rip is confronted upon his return to the village: the portrait of King George has been replaced with George Washington, his scepter replaced with a sword, his red coat with "blue and buff," and the tree in front of the inn has been replaced by a flag pole.[100] Indeed, the interplay of the new and the old upon Rip's return is densely textured: Rip finds that his old home is new, whereas the villagers find that the new person among them is from "the old times." And, privy to both of these bewildering experiences, the reader must grapple with historical confusion. After all, while the new face above the inn strikes Rip as old and vaguely familiar, to the story's readers, the new president, George Washington, is symbolically rendered as old George III. While the replacement of one George for another is simply a joke at the expense of Rip, who confuses them, the reader, instantaneously, is able to sort out the mistake, distinguishing the monarch from the republican leader; the former belongs to the past; the latter to the present. But the very act of prying the Georges apart and returning them to their proper slots in historical chronology entails recognition of their similarities: the widespread fear among early nationals that Washington would reinstitute monarchy, the possibility that, for all the Revolutionary rhetoric, not much had changed in the lives of most Americans. Thus George the president and George the king, life after and life before, the present and the past, are asymmetrically aligned: they are at once different and the same.

One effect of this alignment, then, is that it "closes the temporal and conceptual distance between colony and nation," as Michelle Sizemore puts it.[101] At the same time, however, the tale's work of temporal compression confronts the entrenchment of normative historical time. On this point, the reader of "Rip Van Winkle" proves integral to the tale, for the manner in which the tale plays with the reader's sense of historical time, not Rip's, is its most important feature. Not surprisingly, the gap or elision produced by Rip's twenty-year nap is pivotal in this regard. As we have seen, Rip, unlike the reader, does not experience time logically or chronologically. From his point of view, time moves not along the trajectory past-present-future, but along the axis present-past-future-present. In the second half of the tale, Irving renders the disorientation of Rip's unusual temporal experience through an intricate narrative discourse in which the third-person narration is increasingly restricted to Rip's "sorely perplexed" point of view.[102] After his nap, Rip's experience is often presented in free indirect discourse, such as when Rip wakes up in the mountains to find his dog gone and his rifle rusted. "What was to be done?" the narrator asks, as if inside the mind of Rip, "The morning was passing away and Rip felt famished for want of his breakfast. He grieved to give up his dog and gun; he dreaded to meet his wife; but it would not do to starve among the mountains."[103] Similarly, upon entering the village, the narration mimics

Rip's confusion, as well as his attempt to find his bearings in a place at once familiar and unfamiliar:

> Strange names were over the doors—strange faces at the windows—everything was strange. His mind now misgave him; he began to doubt whether both he and the world around him were not bewitched. Surely this was his native village which he had left but the day before. There stood the Kaatskill mountains—there ran the silver Hudson at a distance—there was every hill and dale precisely as it had always been—.[104]

Dissolving the border between the third-person narration and the perspective of Rip, the narration in these instances attempts to place the reader inside Rip's bewildering experience. This bewilderment is compounded—or mirrored—by other moments where even direct quoted speech takes on the character of indirect discourse, such as when the orator passing out hand bills "bustled up to [Rip], and drawing him partly aside, enquired 'on which side he voted?'" As Rip looks at the man in "vacant stupidity," another "pulled him by the arm and rising on tiptoe, enquired in his ear 'whether he was Federal or Democrat?'"[105] Here, in an inversion of free indirect speech, the characters query Rip as if in the voice of the narrator, asking him about present matters (in the second instance) in the past tense. Insisting that Rip reveal "whether he *was* Federal or Democrat," the speaker appears to adopt the after-the-fact, past-tense perspective of the story's narrator—even as the narrative perspective does just the opposite by adopting Rip's point of view in order to capture with some immediacy his present dilemma. This curious exercise in point of view culminates in a final exchange—which not coincidentally occurs just before Rip's crisis is resolved. Having reached a moment of utter mystification upon seeing "a precise counterpart of himself" (his son), Rip asks a young woman (his daughter) about his wife:

> Rip had but one question more to ask, but he put it with a faltering voice—
> "Where's your mother?"—
> Oh she too had died but a short time since—she broke a blood vessel in a
>   fit of passion at a New England pedlar.—[106]

It is difficult to tell here just where dialogue ends and narration resumes. To whom are we to attribute this reply to Rip's query? If it's Judith Gardenier who speaks, did Irving simply forget to add quotation marks? Is this a mistake? Or do the dashes that demarcate the exchange imply quoted speech? If, on the other hand, we are to attribute the reply to the narrator, how are we to account for the unexpected exclamatory "Oh"?

Syntax suggests one potential answer: it would make little sense for Judith to speak of the recent death of her mother in the past-perfect tense. But it *would* make sense for the narrator to do so. It makes sense, too, in light of the present argument; for the effect of this curious moment is to register alternative temporalities, to capture the relative quality of time in the story. That is, while on the one hand, Judith's response simply conveys to Rip that her mother has recently died ("but a short time since"), on the other hand, the verb tense ("she *had* died") serves as a subtle reminder that what is a recent event to the characters in the story is an even more distant event for the narrator and the reader—and, I would add, for Rip himself. For despite the fact that in the tale, the news of his wife's death is new for Rip, in the *telling* of the tale, her death took place long ago, a fact that makes the beginning of the denouement, with its odd passive construction that immediately follows, both appropriate and multiply ironic: "Rip's story was soon told, for the whole twenty years had been to him but as one night."[107] The story is "soon told" both in the sense that it is told *in* a short time, quickly, and in the sense that it is told *after* a short time, as the implied action that immediately follows the exchange with his daughter. The irony, of course, is that by that time, the story has *already* been told—and retold: it's what we have just read—first by Rip to the villagers, then by Rip to Diedrich Knickerbocker, and then by Diedrich Knickerbocker (via Geoffrey Crayon), who tells it to us, we learn in the tale's last paragraph, "precisely" as Rip related to him.[108]

In other words, "Rip Van Winkle" ends with the telling of a story we already know. In fact, what follows "Rip's story was soon told..." amounts to little more than tidying up: corroborating evidence to explain Rip's experience supplied, fittingly enough, by "a descendant of [an] historian"; Rip returning to his family and locating his "former cronies," and, most importantly, the explanation of the War for Independence that took place while Rip slept.[109] Yet, just like Rip's telling of his own story, the sorting out of events that takes place in the tale's concluding paragraphs has also already occurred. Like the death of his wife, the Revolution may well be news to Rip, but it most certainly is not for Irving's readers. Which is precisely the point: it is the inevitable process of restoring order, of reconstituting events, that the elaborate narrative discourse I have been describing is designed to counterbalance.

Or to put this another way, "Rip Van Winkle" exploits the reader's need to experience time "naturally," as a chronological sequence, and the act of reconstruction that serves this need. The transaction that occurs as we read "Rip Van Winkle" is the replacement of Rip's experience of time with our own extra-textual experience: our role is to fill in the gaps, to recognize and supply the history that Rip himself misses. For an imaginary reader with no knowledge of the American Revolution, for a reader as closely implicated in Rip's experience of time as the narrator—and hence, unable to restore the logic of linear time, the "proper context," to the tale— "Rip Van Winkle" would, literally, make no sense. By the time Rip has his moment of crisis ("every thing's changed, and I am changed, and I can't tell what's my name or who I am!"), we as readers have restored temporal order. In doing so, we are thus implicitly aligned with the newly republicanized villagers who have experienced the passage of time that Rip has not.

But, it turns out, Rip's moment of crisis is also the pivotal moment of crisis for the reader, for it is that instant in which two distinct conceptions of time coexist in the reader's mind: Rip's anachronistic experience as provided by the tale and our own "natural" one. Although we have been "with" Rip—we have followed his movements, witnessed his strange experience—temporally, we have been with the villagers. So we are faced momentarily with a kind of epistemological crisis: do we arrive at the "truth" (of Rip's experience, of the "meaning" of the story— and metaphorically, of history) based on our retrospective knowledge of events outside the text (i.e., the history of the American Revolution, the linear move- ment of time, the fact that we already know how things turned out) or is the truth what we have "witnessed" in our sojourn with Rip into the mountains and his belated return home? The particular historical-temporal experience that reading "Rip Van Winkle" provides is this moment when we are confronted with compet- ing temporalities. We become, paradoxically, unreliable witnesses of our own (reading) experience.[110]

In this way, "Rip Van Winkle" turns out to be a kind of "temporally uncanny" gloss on historicist methodology.[111] That is to say, in the history of American lit- erary history, current historicist practice performs a function that is strikingly similar to what I have described as the reader's role in Irving's tale: it is likewise committed to the restoration of temporal order, to returning texts to their proper slots in historical chronology. Marjorie Garber has dubbed this commitment "'historical correctness,'" "the suggestion, either implicit or implicit on the part of literary scholars, that history grounds and tells the truth about literature."[112] The trouble with historical correctness, the cost of enforcing the temporal parameters within which texts can make meaning, I am suggesting, is that it can prevent us from recognizing the surprising immediacy, the *nowness*, of the texts of the past.

Remaining Awake Through a Great Revolution

The account I have given of Irving's Knickerbocker writings shares with Lloyd Pratt and Michelle Sizemore a general sense that Irving's writings—"Rip Van Winkle," in particular—worked against the nationalizing momentum that charac- terized so much of the period's historical writing (whether fictional or not) by "reject[ing] the notion of social destiny that distinguishes" the period's political rhetoric and "seek[ing] to improve upon the progressive historiography of nation- alism."[113] This view of Irving goes a long way toward rescuing him from the narra- tive of eclipse and obsolescence that has for so long shaped his place in literary history by refusing the very terms of that narrative. In Chapter 2, I explore two more experimental works of literary historiography that likewise operate aslant from both the antebellum period's prevailing forms of historical fiction and from the contextualizing procedures of historicist criticism. While not precisely com- prising a *tradition*, in the sense of a transmitted set of conventions that derived from a fixed point of origin and developed over time, my alignment of these works with Irving's Knickerbocker writings is meant to suggest at least a kind of network of affiliations, one whose evasions of the temporality of tradition perhaps accounts for its never having become one.

Before proceeding, however, I would like to linger a moment more with Irving. Specifically, I want to return briefly to my earlier discussion of immediatist abolition in order to locate Irving within it and to provide an example, perhaps a presentist one, of the sort of cross-temporal communion that the temporal involutions of "Rip Van Winkle" strives to make possible. It turns out that the discourse of abolition was one place in antebellum America where the temporo-historical dimension of Irving's writings gained purchase. The fact that Irving has rarely figured in critical discussions of the intersections between literature and race and slavery constitutes an unfortunate oversight in antebellum literary history. Of course, unlike, say, Harriet Beecher Stowe or Frederick Douglass—or even Hawthorne or Melville— Irving wasn't a prominent voice in the slavery debates. Yet he wasn't entirely absent from them either; he was present, in fact, more than one might perhaps expect. The black and white abolitionist press, for instance, took a sustained and varied interest in Irving, his life and his writings, an interest commensurate with his general fame. They printed excerpts from his writings and notices of the publication of his works, ran news of his travels, tracked his declining health, noted his support for the Liberty Party's John C. Fremont in the election of 1856, and eulogized him upon his death in 1859.[114]

Perhaps as a result of this evident affection, abolitionists also seemed eager to enlist Irving in the cause of emancipation and racial equality. The black abolitionist and intellectual James McCune Smith, for example, adopted as his pseudonym for his regular column in Frederick Douglass's paper the name "Communipaw," explaining that "I am a plain Dutch negro, with only one head, without horns or tail: I am well known in the flats, and Harsimus and Bergen, and way up to Hell Gate, and am lineal descendant from one of the folly fellows whom Washington Irving alludes to in his sketch book, as shining and laughing on our side of Buttermilk Channel."[115] As Irving explains in A History of New York, Communipaw was the Indian name for the village where the first Dutch settlers landed in North America, a village marked by racial harmony among the Dutch, Indians, and blacks. Benjamin Fagan has persuasively argued that in choosing the name, Smith "specifically aligned himself with that village's black inhabitants."[116] I would just add that because Irving described Communipaw as "the egg from whence was hatched the mighty city of New York!," Smith also perceived that Irving provided historical justification for an insistence upon the city's, and perhaps by extension the nation's, black founding and founders.

Less oblique—and more to the point at hand—is the frequency with which abolitionists referenced "Rip Van Winkle" as a way of registering the temporal disjunctions that typified their experience as agitators for social change. Indeed, Rip Van Winkle served as a convenient trope for identifying those people whom immediatists like William Lloyd Garrison believed were on the wrong side of history, out of step with the times, or whose moral and intellectual development seemed sluggish, stuck in a state of prolonged torpor.[117] This was one of *The Liberator's* favorite devices. In 1847, for instance, the paper denounced Amherst College President Heman Humphrey for advocating colonization. "One is at a loss," the paper wrote, "whether to set him down as *Rip Van Winkle*, Don Quixote de la Manchu Redivivus, or the Shorter Catechism of the Westminster Assembly of Divines incarnate."[118] Following Daniel Webster's famous speech in favor of the Compromise of 1850, *The Liberator* asked, "How long is this '*Rip Van Winkle*' of the Old Bay State to dream of the Presidency?," depicting him as mired in the past and oblivious to what is happening in the present and to the portents of the future: "He cannot see that the noble ship Abolition, breasting the fury of the waves, making her way onward, against wind and tide, in the midst of storms and the wreck of dissolving nations, is fast nearing the port of Freedom."[119]

Similar examples abound. In 1856, *The Liberator* criticized a recent lecture on slavery by New Hampshire Senator James Bell, calling him "a Rip Van Winkle" for delivering an address "suited to the state of things thirty years ago, advocating as it did gradual emancipation."[120] In 1858, *The Liberator* accused President Buchanan's failure to deal with the slavery question by saying, "He is wedded to the past, and insensible to the present. Nothing which he has done since he assumed his high office shows him to be any thing better than a Rip Van Winkle rudely awakened by his election to the Presidency."[121] The same year, the paper quotes the *New Bedford Republican* denouncing a recent speech by John S. Holmes:[122]

> The production of Mr. Holmes reads as curiously as those of the advocate of the divine rights of kings in the days of James the Second, but chronologically they are still more out of date. He appears like some political Rip Van Winkle who has been asleep for three hundred years, and finding the world has got ahead of him, imagines everything is going to wreck and ruin.

The chief problem with these Political Rip Van Winkles was not, or at least not only, that they had failed to ride the wave of historical progress along with everybody else. The force of the Rip Van Winkle trope, in keeping with Irving's tale, lay instead in pointing out how those backward looking figures—colonizationists, unionists, and gradualists—suffered from a failure of perception, an estrangement from immediate experience, an incognizance of what is going on *now*. This failing is nicely captured in *The Liberator's* phrase "insensible to the present," which locates the deficiency in the realm of affect, of emotion and bodily sensation, rather than of knowledge, understanding, or one's political position. To be insensible is to be numb, without feeling, unconscious and oblivious. To be alive to the living present, by contrast, is to feel the force of, to experience the dire intensity of, to act in and within the happenings of the moment. The Heman Humphreys and Daniel Websters and James Buchanans of the age are but somnambulists or worse: they're the walking dead.

It was precisely this sort of insensibility to the exigencies of the present, this sleeping through the vital transformations of one's own era, that the twentieth-century immediatist, Martin Luther King, Jr. in his own deployment of the Rip Van Winkle trope, warned against in his stirring address "Remaining Awake Through a Great Revolution," delivered at the Oberlin College Commencement in 1965 and again (in slightly altered form), three years later at the National Cathedral in Washington, DC—though it might just as well have been delivered in 1855 or 1858.[123] The speech channels nineteenth-century abolitionism, both explicitly and indirectly, collapsing the historical distance between two eras of turbulent social change, and transforming abolitionists like James Russell Lowell, William Cullen Bryant, Theodore Parker, and Frederick Douglass into King's contemporaries by reproducing nineteenth-century antislavery arguments.[124] In this way, the speech tacitly enacts what it describes: that to be alive in and aware of the present is to reuse time, revivify the past, and activate a hoped-for future.

King begins the address by reminding his audience of "that arresting little story from the pen of Washington Irving entitled *Rip Van Winkle*." "The most striking fact about the story," King says, "is not that he slept twenty years, but that he slept through a revolution." Like those politicians and statesmen described by Garrison, Rip was insensible to, "knew nothing about," the revolution taking place around him because "he was asleep." Admonishing against the dangers of remaining oblivious to the changes happening around us like Rip, King goes on to describe some of "the things that we must do in order to remain awake and to achieve the proper mental attitudes and responses that the new situation demands." First among these responses is to recognize what King calls the "inescapable network of mutuality" that typifies the modern world. Scientific advancements, King notes, have allowed "modern man...to dwarf distance and place time in chains...we've been able to carve highways through the stratosphere, and our jet planes have compressed into minutes distances that once took weeks and months. And so this is a small world from a geographical point of view." Here King replicates Frederick Douglass's argument at the end of his famous Fourth of July Address, in which Douglass takes as a sign of imminent sweeping historical change the fact that, thanks to modern technology, "space is comparatively annihilated."[125] For King and Douglass alike, this geographic compression promises new relations among nations and individuals, new forms of affiliation and solidarity.

Yet for King, as for Douglass (as I discuss at greater length in Chapter 4), these new spatial and human arrangements also necessitate new temporal arrangements. Douglass, for instance, concludes his speech with a recitation of a poem by Garrison, the refrain of which—"God speed the day..."—calls for a quickening of time, a hastening of the pace of historical change. King likewise repeats a call to "speed up the day" when righteousness and racial justice will prevail.[126] Yet unlike Garrison, King does not implore God for such a quickening. Rather, in terms that recall Longfellow ("Be not like dumb, driven cattle!/Be a hero in the strife!"), he exhorts his audience to become the agents of acceleration: "Never allow it to be said that you are silent onlookers, detached spectators, but that you are involved participants in the struggle to make justice a reality." King's call to action, cast in temporal terms, specifically contests the view of the gradualists of his own day, those forces that seek to stall, delay, defer, or otherwise impede social revolution, (mis)placing their trust in the slow, benign, impersonal drift of history: "Let nobody give you the impression that the problem of racial injustice will work itself out," King says in the speech's most electrifying moment:

> Let nobody give you the impression that only time will solve the problem. That is a myth, and it is a myth because time is neutral. It can be used either constructively or destructively. And I'm absolutely convinced that the people of ill will in our nation - the extreme rightists - the forces committed to negative ends - have used time much more effectively than the people of good will. It may well be that we will have to repent in this generation, not merely for the vitriolic works and violent actions of the bad people who bomb a church in Birmingham, Alabama, or shoot down a civil rights worker in Selma, but for the appalling silence and indifference of the good people who sit around and say, "Wait on time." Somewhere we must come to see that human progress never rolls in on wheels of inevitability. It comes through the tireless efforts and the persistent work of dedicated individuals. Without this hard work, time becomes an ally of the primitive forces of social stagnation. So we must help time and realize that the time is always right to do right.[127]

Emphasizing how time has been or might be "used," King's ethics of impatience here seeks to harness time as an instrument of change, rather than submitting to it as itself the (slow) force of gradual amelioration. King depicts the latter view as outmoded and anachronistic, aligned with the "primitive." Even worse, merely "to wait on time," to be a spectator to history, constitutes a moral failure demanding of repentance. Against such "stagnation," and in keeping with the Romantic presentism of the immediatists with whom he keeps company across time, King urges the present generation to be up and doing. Action in the living present constitutes the only real engine of history and social revolution because "human progress never rolls in on wheels of inevitability." The future can't be trusted simply to arrive on its own. Time, King understands, needs help.

Of course, just as King urges us to use time, to press it into immediate service, so too did he and his nineteenth-century peers press "Rip Van Winkle" into service. Irving was himself no political radical, no outspoken liberal reformer, and certainly no social revolutionary. Indeed, his satire can sometimes seem to operate without target or aim, without purpose or end. Yet more than a few radicals, reformers, and revolutionaries perceived that Irving's dismantling of history—that is, of conventional, sequential history, that fixed object of knowledge—might be a necessary first step toward recognizing that history is what is going on now, toward becoming awake and alive to the intensities and urgencies of the present. In this way, Irving's corrosive historiography helped imagine the conditions for what King calls "a creative beginning" to other ways of being in time and, therefore, other ways of reaching a hoped-for future, one that might not be inevitable, but one that human actors could make possible.

Unhistorical Fictions: Sedgwick and Neal

Although popular and influential in U.S. literary history in other ways, the renegade historiography of Washington Irving has generally been considered too idiosyncratic to have participated in the development of the historical romance genre in the United States—or more precisely, to have participated in the development of the *historicity* of the historical romance.[1] Irving's approach to history was simply too skeptical, too corrosive, to aid in the project of national pedagogy that typified so much of the history writing, both fictional and factual, produced from the 1820s onward.[2] Which is not to say that the attitude toward history Irving cultivated in his Knickerbocker writings remains altogether singular. Quite the contrary. In this chapter, I examine two more experimental works of literary historiography, both produced in the 1820s, that likewise operate aslant from the antebellum period's prevailing forms of historical fiction and from the contextualizing procedures of historicist criticism. Together, these works suggest a countertradition to the historical romance that never quite came into being in the antebellum period.[3]

John Neal's *Seventy-Six: Our Country—Right or Wrong!* (1823) and Catharine Maria Sedgwick's *Hope Leslie; or Early Times in Massachusetts* (1827) follow Irving by similarly experimenting with modes of present-oriented fictional history writing. Neglected for most of the twentieth century, both Neal and Sedgwick have benefited from a resurgence of scholarly interest in recent years.[4] Indeed, in a relatively short period, *Hope Leslie* has attained canonical status. Neal's writings, including *Seventy-Six*, a historical novel set during the American Revolution, have received less scrutiny but are also experiencing something of a revival. The mid-twentieth-century critical neglect of both authors reveals (among other things) the difficulty of assimilating them to more conventional critical paradigms, centered upon Cooper and Hawthorne, that explain the period's historical fiction. After all, Neal's and Sedgwick's texts are marred, as one critic claims, by "anachronisms" and "improbabilities."[5] This is not to say, of course, that *Seventy-Six* and *Hope Leslie* bear no relation to the historical romance, especially as that genre has been redescribed by Lloyd Pratt: as a literary mode that is "acutely time conscious and deeply committed to parsing how the new features of time relate to the past and future fortunes of the nation."[6] But what links these novels to Irving's satirical brand of fictional history, rather than to the traditional historical romance's devotion to the project of creating a national past, is their commitment to *undoing* history; that is, to challenging normative ideas about what history is or can be.[7] Accordingly, in this chapter, I examine how *Hope Leslie* and *Seventy-Six* challenge the conventional view of historical time as a straightforward linear progression, the historicist contextualism that is its methodological counterpart, and even the narrative logic that distorts the experience of *now* by giving it coherent shape. These texts' heterodox conceptions of history are rooted in distinct, but related, experiments in presentist historiography: one an attempt to bring the past and present into relation, rather than to keep them apart, and the other, even more radically, an attempt to inhabit an immediacy altogether at odds with narrative.

Hope Leslie's Challenge to Historicism

The defiance voiced by Sedgwick's seventeenth-century Indian heroine Magawisca to a tribunal of Puritan magistrates near the end of *Hope Leslie* at once distills the novel's major preoccupation with the nation's history and with historical authority, in general, and recapitulates its primary narrative strategy, the self-conscious use of anachronism, in a single utterance: "I demand of thee death or liberty!"[8] This act of ventriloquy, throwing Patrick Henry's iconic eighteenth-century voice simultaneously into the seventeenth-century world of the novel and the nineteenth-century world of her readers, performs a double service. First, the quintessential expression of the spirit of the Revolutionary moment, Henry's famous locution is recontextualized when articulated by an Indian woman, just as the figure of the Indian woman is transformed by drawing on the power of American nationalist rhetoric. That is, the fervor of the Revolutionary fathers, their oratorical authority, suddenly appears autochthonous, as if somehow "native" to the land itself, while the native Magawisca becomes a proto-nationalist, less an enemy than a source of founding principles.[9] This explains why Magawisca appears at her trial with her "national pride...manifest" in her native Indian dress and why her first words to the judges echo the political philosophy of the Declaration of Independence: "I am your prisoner and ye may slay me, but I deny your right to judge me. My people have never passed under your yoke—not one of my race has ever acknowledged your authority."[10]

Second, by evoking, simultaneously, several distinct periods in time the novel, as Walter Benjamin might say, "blast[s]" them out of the "homogeneous course of history."[11] The linearity of historical time becomes entangled, like a triple helix, a strand of DNA, as three different historical moments are woven together: within the present of the novel's colonial narrative instance, its Revolutionary future is recalled, all from the vantage point of the second decade of the nineteenth century, when Sedgwick wrote the novel. Until quite recently, critics of the novel have overlooked *Hope Leslie's* complex reimagining of historical time, treating as authoritative only one of these moments: its time of production—the context that remains fundamental to the kinds of historicism that still predominate among Americanist literary scholars.[12] Historicists treat literary characters and their creators alike as the property of the moment in history that called them into existence. In this sense, historicism is dedicated to precisely the obverse of the procedure Sedgwick here employs: dedicated not to blasting texts out of the homogeneous course of history, but to keeping them assigned to their proper place in time.[13] Consequently, while the historicist procedure of reading a text in relation to its context often yields valuable insights, it also necessarily imposes a certain conception of history on the texts of the past—even when, as in the case of *Hope Leslie*, the text itself is intent on calling into question precisely that concept. Taking seriously *Hope Leslie's* critique of conventional history's before-now-after sequence puts considerable pressure on any historicist frame (old or new) brought to bear on it.

As with my reading of Irving's Knickerbocker writings in the last chapter, here I focus upon *Hope Leslie's* meta-historical discourse, its de-formation of history. Like Lloyd Pratt and Dana Luciano, I take seriously the novel's many historical and temporal entanglements, which I view as its most salient feature. *Hope Leslie* provides an alternative conception of what history is. Additionally, I explore the way in which the novel's implied theory of history engages and challenges historicist practice. Because the novel's "historical" footing is always slippery and because it imagines history anachronistically, it seems to resist and confound that most basic of historicist moves: the attempt to place it "in context." What follows, then, is not a consideration of *Hope Leslie's* generic status, nor is it an investigation of the genre of historical fiction, although the novel does display many of the conventional characteristics of the "historical romance" as Michael Davitt Bell, George Dekker and others have described that genre.[14] But the novel also shares some important features with the writings of the other romantic presentists gathered in this book, refusing the constraints of linear chronology, imagining moments of cross-temporal contact, disrupting the historical sequence of events, or ventriloquizing voices from one historical period into another. In various ways, these writers all attempt to imagine alternatives to the sequential course of history. That is, they not only question which events properly constitute history, but whether events must be organized in just one particular way, as a chronological series. In the case of *Hope Leslie*, the novel not only questions which events precipitated the Pequot War or how particular versions of that war have been authorized, it also works strenuously to keep that war's context, its circumambient social and cultural space, to paraphrase Hayden White, from becoming irretrievably linked to a single slice of historical time. Deploying anachronism—a term I employ here to designate the deliberately nonsequential—as both method and trope, *Hope Leslie* situates its readers in an alternative configuration of past and present, offering not just knowledge of the past, but an experience that is much more attuned to what history (defined broadly as the relations among past, present, and future) has now become in everyday life: a "constellation," as Benjamin calls it, "which [our own] era has formed with a definite earlier one."[15] In so doing, it challenges fundamental conceptions of the form and shape of history that are as prevalent today as in Sedgwick's time.

My reading of *Hope Leslie* is at odds with the judgments of early critics of the novel, who viewed it as "apostasy from history," a novel that does "little more, by way of touching base with history, than invoke the Puritan era as a symbolic backdrop against which to lay out a melodrama, pitting individual against society, that belongs to no particular realm of time except the realm of romance."[16] If these critics failed to see the seriousness of the novel's engagement with history, it is because they assumed they knew what history was and where to find it in the text: history was the past, and it could be found in the novel's representation of that past. Thanks to the readings produced by a number of historicists, however, we are now in a position to appreciate how deeply engaged with history the novel is. And we are able to do so because historicist critics have looked for history in a different place: not just in the past represented in the novel but in the history of the novel's moment of production, or what we have learned to call the text's context.

Hence more recent commentators generally agree that questions of "history" are in fact central to *Hope Leslie*. So much so that it has become something of a critical commonplace to assert that the novel presents an "alternative history" to those written by the Puritan historians.[17] Phillip Gould, for instance, also concerns himself with the novel's historiographical discourse, focusing upon Sedgwick's revisionary writing of the history of the Pequot War. By "situating the novel in the context of contemporary histories written during the early republic," Gould attempts "to locate the immediate political and cultural stakes in writing revisionary history."[18] Historicizing the novel in this way, Gould finds that Sedgwick's alternative history of the Pequot War functions as a "subversion of the masculine ideologies promoted by her own era's political culture."[19] But crucially, this context reveals "two inconsistencies" in the novel.[20] First, Sedgwick's representation of the "racial 'other' reveals simultaneously a rejection of and entrapment in this classical republican ideology." And second, Sedgwick's attempt "to bestow full authority on Magawisca" is undermined by the text's argument "for historical relativism"; historical relativism, that is, "stymies [Sedgwick's] capacity to award Magawisca full narrative authority."[21]

Gould's emphasis on *Hope Leslie's* contemporary context has a great deal to teach about the politics of early national historiography and the role Sedgwick played in it, especially with regard to the cultural significance of the Pequot War among early nationals. His characteristically historicist assumption that history is found in the novel's moment of production also serves a less visible but no less important purpose: to protect the text against relativistic readings and, in particular, against presentism, the naïve tendency of critics to read their own period's assumptions and values into the texts and events of the past.[22] Presentism, as we've seen, represents the very antithesis of historicism insofar as it fails to properly contextualize. Instead, the presentist begins with a premise, typically characterized as partisan or political, and looks for—or distorts—evidence from the past to confirm that premise. Or, similarly, the presentist judges one era using the methods, standards, and criteria of another, thus projecting modern concepts and beliefs onto the texts of the past. In this sense, presentism is simply another word for *anachronism* and, as the historian Robert Berkhofer has put it, "No greater historiographic sin exists than committing anachronism, by representing something outside the supposed context of its times."[23]

The historicist emphasis on returning texts to their historical contexts has certainly been productive; it's the very move that has made the recovery of a work like *Hope Leslie* possible in the first place. Yet no less than earlier critics, historicists, too, assume to know wherein history lies: because the history of their moment of production always speaks through them, it provides a priori literary texts' historicity.[24] But what if *Hope Leslie's* engagement with history lies elsewhere as well? What if the novel demands that we question not just which events are authoritative in history, but whence derives the authority of history itself? What if it posits that events can and do exceed their containment within discrete moments in time? Or what's more, what if it questions the very notion of time—chronological succession—that makes such containment imaginable? These are questions the novel puts before us, questions we can only see if we relinquish some core historicist assumptions: in particular, the new historicist injunction to keep each historical event (and text) assigned to its proper temporal slot in the past.

To put this in slightly different terms, because new historicism depends upon the proposition that texts "belong" to particular moments in time, moments that historicists attempt to recreate, it must also posit that moment's individuality, its difference—its "otherness"—in relation to earlier or later moments in time.[25] To contextualize, in other words, is to attend to the particularities, the uniqueness, of discreet moments in history; it is to distinguish between a now and a then.[26] The analogue to this conception of history, of course, is the discourse of otherness, of racial, gender, and class difference, that has not accidentally developed in tandem with historicism in American literary studies. And indeed, one of the most important achievements of Americanist new historicism has been to turn this greater awareness of and attention to both historical and cultural difference toward a more complex understanding of U.S. literatures and cultures. Presentism, by contrast, subsumes difference; it co-opts the past in the service of current (ideological) interests and thus amounts to a historiographical form of assimilation, colonization, or imperialism.[27] At the same time, however, it's important to remember that such heightened awareness of both cultural and historical difference is itself the product of a particular historical moment (our own) and that emphasizing radical alterity also risks making the gulf between the self and the "other" unbreachable, just as a too strenuous insistence on what historians call the "otherness of the past" risks rendering the past completely unknowable.[28] *Hope Leslie's* anachronistic imagining of history attempts to negotiate this dilemma; it does not share, and, therefore, challenges, historicist assumptions about historical time; its historiographical discourse questions the very contextualizing procedure employed by new historicists. The novel thus invites its readers to experience a noncolonizing form of presentism.[29]

So let me make an unabashedly presentist claim: *Hope Leslie's* insight into the narrative character of history anticipates "postmodern" theories of history by more than a century and a half, emphasizing the mutability of historical "truth," challenging the scientific objectivity claimed by twentieth-century historians, and affirming textualist versions of historical representation. Here is one example: in the novel's remarkable preface, as rich and provocative as any in American literature, Sedgwick begins a discourse on the question "what is history?" that the remainder of her novel expatiates. The opening lines of her preface assert what her novel is not: an "historical narrative, or a relation of real events." Yet "real characters and real events are...alluded to."[30] They are employed, however, only insofar as they serve the "author's design," which was "to illustrate not the history, but the character of the times."[31] Operative at the start of the preface is this doubling of the term *character*, which Sedgwick deploys twice for its dual meaning. "Character" thus becomes both integral and opposed to "history": integral in that historical narrative transforms "real" personages (John Winthrop, Thomas Morton, and Pocahontas) into "characters;" and opposed insofar as "history" is always in danger of slipping back into chronicle when it only enumerates, or "relates," facts and does not capture the character—the spirit or moral qualities—of an age. At the same time, her deliberately slippery language suggests playfully that her work of fiction "alludes to" "real" moral qualities—as opposed to fictional ones.

It's tempting to read the preface strictly in the context of early republican historiography. History writing in the early republic was often driven by two contradictory impulses. The first is what Michael Kammen has called the "documentary" impulse—the scrupulous investigation of primary sources in the service of historical authenticity that, as we saw in the last chapter, Irving so gleefully lampoons in *A History of New York*.[32] But at the same time, both readers and writers in the early republic were often far less interested in "facts"—in history for its own sake, as we might say today—than in the uses to which history was put. For instance, a principle interest among historians and novelists alike in the early republic was the elucidation of the spirit of the American people, the characteristics and virtues that were believed to constitute that "chimerical thing" known as national character.[33] Thus the filiopietistic biographies of Revolutionary heroes like Washington did more than just praise the founders, they were also meant to provide citizens with representative portraits of "character" that would stand, synechdocically, as illustrations of the American character. In this sense, the term *character* refers not to an individual or a fictional personage, but, as Kammen describes it, to "a particular constellation of ethical qualities" deemed admirable in the republican citizen.[34] Sedgwick's interest in the character of colonial America, then, might be viewed as simply extending this investigation into national character farther back into the American past.

Yet placed in this context, Sedgwick's preface is stripped of much of the theoretical sophistication for which I am contending and becomes, instead, a somewhat more pedestrian statement, the mere expression of convention—representative of its time. It is, so to speak, put in its place. And it's a tempting move, for once having established *the* context, a reading of the rest of the preface falls neatly into place. Take, for instance, the following passage:

> The only merit claimed by the present writer, is that of a patient investigation of all the materials that could be obtained. A full delineation of these times was not even attempted; but the main solicitude has been, to exclude every thing decidedly inconsistent with them.[35]

In context, it seems obvious that Sedgwick here perfectly expresses her era's contradictions with regard to history writing. Her disclaimer serves to pre-empt criticism from her readers. Positioning herself as a "patient investigat[or]" of historical "materials," she satisfies the demand for authenticity in historical fiction. At the same time, humbly begging pardon for any potential misrepresentations by confessing that her "delineation" is inevitably incomplete, partial, she carefully distinguishes her fiction from "historical narrative." Thus, the preface might appear to be Sedgwick's attempt, at once, to show deference to history proper—the most valued genre of her time—and to claim a privilege for fiction in relation to more conventional histories. After all, as a number of critics have pointed out, fiction and history were intimately related genres in the early nineteenth century.[36] Readers demanded accuracy from historical novelists, just as they demanded narrative drama from historians. But fiction, Sedgwick seems to imply, is better equipped than history to capture "the character of the times."

This is clearly a potentially productive reading, especially for what it reveals about the development of both U.S. historiography and the genre of historical romance. However, implicating the text in ideologies proper to its historical moment risks missing the preface's more important theoretical point, which concerns not the unique historicity of fictions set in the past, but the fictive qualities of history proper. A slight shift of emphasis—attending not to the nouns ("investigation," "materials," and "delineation"), but to the verbs in this passage—brings the preface's historiographical disquisition into relief. The Sedgwick passage quoted previously first acknowledges what modern historians call the "plenitude" of the past—in this case seventeenth-century reality—emphasizing both the inadequacy of the historical record ("all the materials that could be obtained") and the difficulty of capturing the past in its totality ("a full delineation...was not even attempted"). Second, in an extraordinary admission of historiographical partisanship, it frankly draws attention to the inevitable, often willful, blindnesses that always attend historical investigations, including the present one ("exclud[ing] every thing decidedly inconsistent with them"). The passive voice in these predicates, moreover, lends these statements an ambiguity that broadens them beyond the particular case of the novel: the last two sentences may refer equally to "the materials" and "the present writer." Thus, the implication is not simply that Sedgwick avoided attempting "a full delineation" and "excluded" everything deemed "inconsistent" with her "design," but that the authors of "all the materials that could be obtained"—meaning the Puritan historians—did so as well.

It is to this last fact that the remainder of the preface—and much of the novel—pertains:

> In our histories, it was perhaps natural that [the Indians] should be represented as "surly dogs," who preferred to die rather than live, from no other motives than a stupid or malignant obstinacy. Their own historians or poets, if they had such, would as naturally, and with more justice, have extolled their high-souled courage and patriotism.[37]

Hope Leslie's narrator will thus act as a surrogate historian—or poet—to the Indians. The point, however, is not only, as most critics agree, to provide a counter-history that undermines the authority of the Puritan historians and, in particular, their representations of Native Americans. The larger point to be taken from the preface is that what historical fictions and proper histories share, inevitably, is a dependence upon representation.[38] So rather than asserting the unique possibilities of fiction as compared to history proper, the preface actually calls attention to their affinities. This is why, for instance, Sedgwick's narrator makes no distinction between Indian "historians" and Indian "poets": both employ narrative to construct worlds, worlds that are "natural[ly]" partial and interested. In other words, the "historical relativism" that Gould ultimately finds problematic is not so much an implication of Magaswisca's revisionist history of the Pequot War as it is the starting point of the novel's meta-historical discourse.

I am not ascribing to Sedgwick here some remarkable powers of prescience, casting her as a proto-poststructuralist. As we saw in Chapter 1, nineteenth-century writers of fiction were far more sophisticated about the relationship between history and fiction than they are typically given credit for. Like postmodern theorists of history, a number of early American writers challenged historical truth by calling attention to the literary qualities of history writing. And while neither Irving, Charles Brockden Brown, nor Sedgwick equate history and fiction, all of them wrestled, as do historians and literary critics in our own day, with the problem of representation common to both genres. In doing so, and in very different ways, they illustrate an important theoretical point: history and fiction aren't different because they belong to different genres; critics assign texts to distinct genres in order to establish their differences.

Which is not to say that the differences aren't important, only that the historicist insistence on the uniqueness of moments in time often prevents the recognition of certain kinds of affinities even when they are in plain sight. In the present case, this means overlooking how *Hope Leslie's* self-consciousness of its own historicity can engage current interest in the problem of representation (of the past and of "the other") common to both history and fiction. Nowhere is this more apparent than in the novel's deployment of anachronism. "The antiquarian reader will perceive," the second paragraph of the preface begins, "that...a slight variation has been allowed in the chronology of the Pequod War."[39] The variation to which Sedgwick refers concerns the events surrounding the famous Puritan attack of the Pequod Indians at Mystic, Connecticut in 1637.[40] Puritan historians (among them Hubbard, Trumbull, and Winthrop) claimed that the attack was in retaliation for the murders of the traders John Stone, John Norton, and John Oldham. Sedgwick, however, reverses this chronology, alluding to these deaths only after Magawisca— one of the few surviving members of the Pequod tribe—narrates her own version of the attack.[41]

More important than this variation as it occurs in the novel, however, is Sedgwick's admission of it in the preface. It signals *Hope Leslie's* thematic concerns with authority—those who claim it, abuse it, grant it, or resist it—by omitting the agent of that authority, even constructing authority as passive, if not altogether absent. Who, after all, has "allowed" this chronological variation—this anachronism? Sedgwick herself? Or the unnamed keepers of "official history"? Admitting to this self-conscious manipulation of the "facts" of history, and in particular their sequential ordering, Sedgwick pre-empts criticism from those who affirm the authority of "our early annals." Thus, the admission in her preface is actually critique, emphasized covertly in her grammatical structure and sustained explicitly by the narrative that is to follow. The present-perfect tense in the construction "has been allowed" serves to mitigate the liberty she takes with chronology, just as it normalizes the very practice to which she calls attention. Among historians and novelists alike, she implies, such narrativization has always been allowed.

The novel's "variation in chronology," then, speaks directly to how historians have constructed the causes and effects of the Pequot War and, in doing so, forms a remarkably clear demonstration of how historians and novelists alike employ what Hayden White calls "emplotment."[42] Sedgwick's preface effectively positions *Hope Leslie* in a kind of interstitial space between these two roles: while the novel is a fictional representation of history ("not an historical narrative")— and is thus granted license to alter the ordering of events in a way that historical writing is not—the admission in the preface forms a meta-commentary on this very issue. Such commentary becomes even clearer once the reader realizes that the "chronological variation" forms only a part of the text's deployment of anachronism. As we'll see, the novel's narrative discourse hinges on the broader notions of anachronism (or presentism) I have already discussed: judging one era according to the values, standards, and criteria of another and disrupting the unidirectional course of history.

News from the Present

But recognizing the temporal complexity of that discourse and the experience of history that emerges from it may well require dislodging historicist methodology from some of its more entrenched principles, in much the same way that historicists themselves have learned to peel the method of close reading away from the principles of the New Criticism.[43] In other words, one can continue to use careful textual analysis to explore text-context relationships, without making rigid assumptions about the historicity of texts, about which context is to be construed as the privileged site of textual meaning. After all, while the historical person named Catharine Sedgwick has long since passed, her text remains, which is only to state the obvious: *Hope Leslie* no longer occupies the same moment in historical time, the same context, that its creator did. In this section, then, I mean to shift focus away from the novel's author—the locus of its nineteenth-century context— and toward its narrator, concentrating less on the instance of the novel's writing, its moment of production, than on the instance of its narrating. Indeed, as we will see, it is through the discourse of *Hope Leslie's* narrator, which is characterized by critical irony and linguistic play, that the novel's preoccupation with historical time and the distinctive experience of history it offers to the attentive reader become clear.

Benignantly sarcastic and gently ironic, Sedgwick's narrator, rather than action (though there is much of it) or plot (which is intricate, to say the least) drives *Hope Leslie*. Yet curiously, few critics have commented on the novel's narrative voice, tone, and positioning.[44] Sedgwick's narrator strives for neither objectivity nor transparency of representation; she makes clear from the earliest chapters set in America that the reader will not be allowed direct access to the historic past. Rather, throughout the first volume of the novel, the narrator acts as a mediating presence, continually interrupting the movement of the story with news from the "present."[45] For instance, at several moments the narrator pauses to draw comparisons between "the girls of today" and her heroine Hope. At one point, realizing that Hope has yet to be "formally presented" to her readers, the narrator begins to correct this oversight by remarking that "Nothing could be more unlike the authentic, 'thoroughly educated,' and thoroughly disciplined young ladies of the present day, than Hope Leslie."[46] Now as a single instance, it might be easy to dismiss this comment as a conventional—perhaps even awkward—authorial intrusion, but as I will show the accumulation of such instances (there are many) in *Hope Leslie* works to establish both the narrative persona and the novel's complex temporal registers.

The function of these intrusions is most apparent when the novel's action shifts to Boston, seat of Puritan authority. The rebellious Hope is sent there to live with Governor Winthrop and to learn from his wife "that passiveness, that, next to godliness, is a woman's best virtue."[47] Critically ironic and laced with double meanings, the narrator's language and tone become increasingly sardonic: "We hold ourselves bound by all the laws of decorum, to give our readers a formal introduction to the governor's mansion and its inmates."[48] In a text filled with prisoners and imprisonments (the old Indian woman Nelema, Faith, Magawisca, Everell, Thomas Morton, Master Craddock, and even Roslyn, metaphorically, are all prisoners at one time or another in the novel), it is difficult not to view the narrator's choice of terms as an elaboration on this theme. The very point of sending Hope to live with the Winthrops in the first place is so that she, too, may be "bound" by the Puritan "laws of decorum." In this sense, Hope herself is a kind of "inmate" in the government-mansion.[49] Moreover, it becomes increasingly clear as the chapter proceeds that the narrator sees Mrs. Winthrop, too, as an inmate—if not worse: Mrs. Winthrop "recognized...the duty of unqualified obedience from the wife to the husband, her appointed lord and master."[50] Like most Puritan wives, the narrator continues, Mrs. Winthrop never questioned this role, "the only divine right to govern, which they acknowledged, was that vested in the husband over the wife." But in Mrs. Winthrop's case, at least, such devotion never "degenerated into the slavishness of fear, or the obsequiousness of servility." Instead, the narrator wryly notes Madam Winthrop was guided "like a horse easy on the bit" by "him who held the reins."[51]

It would not be difficult to locate the concerns of Sedgwick's culture in passages like these. In the present instance, her playfulness of language allows the narrator to comment not only upon the position of women in marriage but on the proto-nation as well. Her description, in fact, repeats but reverses Rip Van Winkle's escape from "petticoat government"[52]: here the husband is not a freedom-loving symbol of pre-Revolutionary longing, attempting to throw off the yoke of tyranny, but a tyrant himself invested with a "divine right to govern." Further, Madam Winthrop's subordinate position evokes not just colonial oppression, but the American national sin by verging on "slavishness" and "servility," insofar as she is treated as a beast of burden—a "horse easy on the bit." In this way, the narrator develops one of the novel's most powerful subtexts, rendering colonial women—rather than the Puritan fathers—as America in embryo. This is evident from the opening chapter of the novel when the tyrannical Anglican William Fletcher denigrates his nephew's Puritanism by casting freedom as female: "Liberty, what is it! Daughter of disloyalty and mother of all misrule. . ."[53]

More important for my purposes, however, is the narrative function of the news from the present that Sedgwick's narrator delivers, which is to help forge a kind of "imagined linkage" between periods in time.[54] For instance, in another comparison, the narrator remarks, "it has been seen that Hope Leslie was superior to some of the prejudices of the age."[55] But to what "age" does the narrator refer? Sedgwick's choice of the definite article here ("the age"), rather than the more precise pronoun (her age) is telling. Historical time in the novel, it suggests, is not possessive. The effect of this imprecision is a purposeful ambiguity. The readers the narrator explicitly addresses are asked to compare Hope both to her Puritan peers and to the "thoroughly disciplined" young ladies of the present age (both the narrator's and ours) at once. The result is that the reader must think both historically and presently minded about Hope; she signifies in two different temporal registers at once. Placing Hope in relation to both her fictionalized seventeenth-century world and the reader's own (future) world, the reader is asked to imagine a kind of cross-temporal community, or what Pratt describes as "diachronic simultaneity" among historical periods.[56]

In other words, the narrator's discourse should not be read as simply using Hope as a "foil" for a past age that has been superseded.[57] Again, historicist assumptions—notably, the emphasis on the novel's contemporary interests—would probably likely lead to the conclusion that what is under discussion here is historical advancement. But I am suggesting, by contrast, that what is at stake here is the meaning of history itself.[58] After all, the narrator's comparisons do not always—or at least not simply—favor the "present age." Quite the contrary: the critical irony of the narrator is often most devilish when engaged in the kinds of comparative history I've been considering. Typically, these are used as occasions to cast a skeptical eye on just how much progress has really been achieved. Or to put this another way, although Catharine Sedgwick may often seem "progressive" politically (in terms of gender relations anyway), *progressive* does not exactly describe *Hope Leslie's* implied theory of history; it does not capture the novel's variations in temporal register.

For the narrator's temporal juxtapositions work in a much more complex way, disrupting the homogeneous course of history and reminding the reader to view even the present historically:

> It must be confessed that the tendency of the [present] age is to laxity; and so rapidly is the wholesome strictness of primitive times abating, that, should some antiquary, fifty years hence, in exploring his garret rubbish, chance to cast his eye on our humble pages, he may be surprised to learn, that even now the Sabbath is observed, in the interior of New-England, with an almost judaical severity.[59]

In this instance, the narrator projects a future in relation to which her own present is past. Yet this is not an ordinary example of prolepsis, or temporal anticipation (a narrative technique I explore in much more detail in Chapter 5), for it does not refer to the story at all. Rather, it is a meta-commentary on the text itself: imagining the novel's reception "fifty years hence," the narrator projects a moment when her "antiquary" learns something not about colonial New England, but about (what is to him) some future period ("even now")—a period that the narrator's statement calls into existence.

Or consider just one more example. Here the narrator describes the temperament of the Massachusetts Bay colonists:

> The character of man, and the institutions of society, are yet very far from their possible and destined perfection. Still, how far is the present age in advance of that which drove reformers to a dreary wilderness!—of that which hanged quakers!—of

that which condemned to death, as witches, innocent, unoffending old women!—
But it is unnecessary to heighten the glory of our risen day by comparing it with
the preceding twilight.[60]

Because Sedgwick was also a writer of didactic fiction (and to be sure, *Hope Leslie*
is not without strains of didacticism), it is tempting to read such lines as moral
earnestness. Viewed in this light, this passage reveals Sedgwick's commitment, as
Michael Davitt Bell has argued, to historical progress, suggesting an incipient
Romanticism that anticipates the great nineteenth-century historians, like George
Bancroft, who came to dominate American history writing in the years just after
Hope Leslie's publication.[61] But when we take note of the narrator's characteristic
irony and her tendency to refuse to privilege "the present day," such earnestness
instead seems purposefully exaggerated by the narrator's exclamatory phrasing,
which undermines her rhetoric of advancement as it pertains to the "present
age"—whatever that age might be. The nineteenth-century reader, for example,
might immediately recognize "the glory" of her own day by thinking of the violence of indigenous disposition and slavery, while the twentieth-century reader
might make similar comparisons in light of any number of atrocities from the
Holocaust to the racial inequity of the death penalty. Thus, again, while it is
tempting—and perhaps even intuitive—to read this passage as simply a presentist
editorial intrusion on the part of the author, I am suggesting that these moments
actually create a peculiar kind of historical experience, that they are important not
simply for what they reveal about Hope or about the historical Catharine Sedgwick's
view of colonial America, but for the way they position both the novel's narrative
voice and the reader in relation to time.

   For her part, the narrator locates herself in a kind of present without clear
boundaries; she is not confined to a particular age. So while Sedgwick's story—her
narrative discourse—concerns Puritan New England, she situates her narrator
(the text's "narrating instance") at some indefinite moment in the future she merely
calls "now":

> Where there are now contiguous rows of shops, filled with the merchandise of the
> east, the manufactures of Europe, the rival fabrics of our own country, and the
> fruits of the tropics...were, at the early period of our history, a few log-houses,
> planted around a fort, defended by a slight embankment and palisade.[62]

Carefully distinguishing between the "now" of her narration and the then of her
story, the narrator emphasizes the relation between these two periods in time, a
relation that might be described as an awareness of the *present within history*. And
this awareness is central to *Hope Leslie's* imagined experience of history. After all,
what usually links a text to "its" context, what has allowed historicists to imagine a
connection between more-or-less arbitrarily selected historical artifacts (say, *Hope
Leslie* and post-Revolutionary history writing) is really nothing more than that
mode of simultaneity Benedict Anderson calls "calendrical coincidence."[63] But the

narrator of *Hope Leslie* forges a different kind of linkage by juxtaposing not coeval events, but "now" and then; or more accurately, by making "now" a part of the present of "then." As the narrator's interruptions from a future moment in time accumulate, the narrative voice gradually becomes an integral part of the experience of the text, a presence whose existence the reader remains constantly aware of even in her absence. So while on some imaginative level, we, as twenty-first century readers, conjure for ourselves the reality of a distant past, simultaneously we remain cognizant of other periods in time (Catharine Sedgwick's and our own) passing alongside of it.[64]

This rendering of the present moment of reading as replete with other times, in turn, shapes not just the reader's experience of the novel, but the novel's narrative experience of history, which is not progressive, but anachronistic, what I have already called a kind of cognitive (or imaginative) constellation of historical periods. Or to put this another way, by always positioning herself in the present as a means of imagining historical experience, the narrator also positions—or constructs—an implied reader of the novel for whom historical knowledge is not only mediated, but brought into relation with present-knowledge. What historical experience means in *Hope Leslie*, then, is not just that one is able to imagine a past that, as nineteenth-century Americans were fond of saying, has been lost to oblivion, but that one can imagine history as an experience encompassing both past and present at once, dissolving the historicist opposition between historical and present mindedness. This is why the past in the novel is always filtered through the ambiguously situated narrator, who, for her part, invites the reader continually to juxtapose "our" day and colonial America.

The peculiar way the reader experiences history in *Hope Leslie* becomes even clearer when one realizes that the narrator's news from the present typically comes at crucial moments in the narrative, often those very moments when the reader is most likely to have forgotten the present and to have entered into the seventeenth-century world of the novel, becoming imaginatively or emotionally absorbed in the novel's projected past. For instance, at the end of the fourth chapter—the chapter in which Magawisca narrates her version of the Pequod War—the narrator abruptly reminds the reader of the murders of Stone, Norton and Oldham in a voice far removed from the novel's seventeenth-century setting. Both the war and its (possible) causes, she reminds the reader, belong to "our early annals."[65] Bulletins such as these not only disrupt the story's movement, they disrupt, too, the reader's experience of it. The emotional involvement that Magawisca's story elicits—from her auditors, Everell and the reader alike—is tacitly called into question by the narrator's discourse. Readers are reminded not to lose themselves in the (narrowly historical) lives of the characters represented.[66]

These reminders occur repeatedly in the novel, such as later, when it turns out that Magawisca's moving tale has simply prepared the reader for another scene of horror. With Mr. Fletcher away in Boston, Magawisca's father Mononotto, a Pequod chief, attacks the Fletcher homestead, killing Mrs. Fletcher and taking as prisoners Everell and the young Faith Leslie, the daughter of Alice sent to America following her parents' untimely deaths. Upon learning the news of the slaughter, Mr. Fletcher receives "such moral, consoling, and pious reflections as usually poured forth from the lips of the spectators of sudden suffering." And at this dramatic point the narrator intrudes again:

> We hope our readers will not think we have wantonly sported with their feelings, by drawing a picture of calamity that only exists in the fictitious tale. No—such events, as we have feebly related, were common in our early annals, and attended by horrors that it would be impossible for the imagination to exaggerate.[67]

In this interruption, the narrator explicitly draws attention to narrative's capacity for emotional manipulation while at the same time engaging in that very practice. That is, the narrator here does not suggest that she has not "sported with [the reader's] feelings," only that she has not done so "wantonly." Readers are thus cautioned to be wary—or at least aware—of their own emotional and imaginative involvement in such tales of horror in a way that Everell, for example, is not. Similarly, what appears here to be an appeal for the reader's credulity based on a commitment to verisimilitude ("such events...were common"), the accumulation of such narrative commentary has a radically different effect. It forms not only a critique of historical representation by refusing to allow the reader entrance into an extra-linguistic seventeenth-century reality, raising the very (post)modern question of whether we can ever access the "real" past, or whether our present-day reconstructions of it, our narratives—our language—always stand between that past and ourselves. But more importantly, it provides the possibility for a way out of the representational conundrum, suggesting that "history" is not either a unique and distinct past or our present-day reconstructions of it, but a negotiation, a contact zone, an imagined experience born of the interaction between the two.

I suggested in this book's introductory chapter that this means of conceiving history derives from a recognition of the present as the fundamental sphere of human experience and, thus, of ethics and democratic possibility. Sedgwick's presentism is enlisted in a larger, non-teleological democratic project: in her case, imagining history anachronistically provided a way of dealing with both cultural and national identity in a pluralistic culture. If America, then as now, was in the process of becoming, what it would become was for Sedgwick, as for other romantic presentists like Emerson and Douglass (as we'll see in the Chapters 3 and 4), an open question. All of these writers viewed the American past as a perpetually unfinished project. In this respect, presentism served for antebellum writers as a means of working through the process of historically constituted self-realization.[68] As we will see, history, for all of these writers, as with Sedgwick, was incomplete; it was something more than knowledge of the past. Their writings present it instead as an affective experience, a palpable sensation, something approximating the paradoxical feeling of déjà vu—the memory of an experience one has not had, but a memory nonetheless real because felt.

Of course, historicist literary critics, too, link questions of historiography to questions of cultural identity. Historicist investigations into the social, cultural, and political forces that shaped, and were shaped by, American literary texts have proven a powerful weapon for revising the literary canon, recovering works by women and minority writers, and raising important questions about the role of racial and gender ideologies in the formation of disparate American cultures. But unlike *Hope Leslie*, this narrative—what might be called the historicist narrative of American literary criticism—does not reject so much as it reinstitutes history as linear progression. That is, while historicist work has effectively exposed the ideological foundations of the nineteenth-century rhetoric of historical progress, the story of the historicist enterprise itself is cast as what Brook Thomas has called a "narrative of progressive emergence"[69]—feminists loosening the stranglehold male modernist critics once held on the literary canon, African Americans and other minorities struggling to gain literary independence and emancipating themselves from Euro-centric literary values, and marginalized authors and texts being freed from oppressive ideologies and finding their way to the center.

And like all narratives of emergence, which imply a progression, the historicist narrative of American literary criticism depends upon the "homogeneous course of history;" it necessarily construes historical time possessively, as a succession of receptacles each containing certain texts (and events, discourses, beliefs, and personages). This view of history requires that each historical event and text be assigned to its proper receptacle in the past. Thus, to historicize is often to show how authors and texts are "subject to" or "constrained by" their own moment in history. For instance, commentators have generally agreed that the most problematic moment in *Hope Leslie* is the scene in which Hope is reunited with her sister Faith, who was abducted as a child during the Indian raid on the family's home. Reading this scene, a number of critics have ascribed to Sedgwick the beliefs of Hope, whose "heart die[s] within her" when she and Faith meet again several years later. Upon seeing Faith dressed "in savage attire," Hope is overcome with "a sickening feeling," "an unthought of revolting nature."[70] Judith Fetterley argues that this scene is the moment where *Hope Leslie* becomes "Hope-lessly"; it marks the limits of any radical politics one might find in the novel because "Sedgwick's narrative voice doubles Hope's" in this scene. Similarly Stephen Carl Arch asserts that "Hope's individualism is constrained by Sedgwick's culture," and Carol J. Singley argues that Faith's conversion and marriage to the Indian Oneco is finally "constrained by [Sedgwick's] own position in history." And noting that "the text is subject to the discursive materials of its own era," Douglas Ford suggests that this scene may be one place where the novel "inadvertently undercuts the progressive mission its preface has outlined."[71]

Yet all these assertions seem to me to misread the novel. Certainly, that the otherwise "progressive" Hope views her sister as transgressing against "natural" racial boundaries the scene leaves little question. That this view is shared by Sedgwick, however, is arguable. After all, in an effort to recover her sister, Hope resorts to bribery, offering Faith "jewels from head to foot" if she will return to her English family. In reply, Magawisca admonishes Hope in terms that Sedgwick's narrator (and her readers) clearly value: "Shall I ask your sister to barter truth and love, the jewels of the soul, for these poor perishing trifles?"[72] In other words, the voice that the narrator's "doubles" here, if any, is Magawisca's. Indeed, the scene is powerful precisely because it criticizes its heroine. That critique is made even more apparent when we consider that the action in the novel that most closely parallels Hope's desperate appeal is the villainous Sir Philip's equally desperate attempt to "barter" Magawisca's freedom for the life of the pathetic Roslyn.

But why would the narrator take such pains to criticize the tale's heroine? The answer to this question lies, once again, in the preface. A closer look at the grounds of Hope's disgust upon seeing her sister dressed as an Indian shows that this scene actually illustrates, rather than undercuts, the "progressive" argument set forth in the preface. Further, it effectively links the novel's racial politics to its historiographical interests; that is, the text argues not just for historical relativism, but for a brand of cultural relativism as well. In the preface, for instance, Sedgwick takes what modern critics would call a social constructionist view of racial difference. After positioning herself as a surrogate Indian poet, she further states that "difference of character among the various races of the earth, arises mainly from difference of condition."[73] The reunion scene is constructed to test this proposition. The argument there in favor of "conditions" as a marker of racial difference turns on the strangeness of the phrase used to describe Hope's reaction: "an unthought of revolting nature." The ambiguity of language and syntax in this phrase, as is so often the case in the novel, conveys disparate meanings. On the one hand, the phrase simply means that Hope's "unthought" is of a kind that might be termed revolting; in which case "revolting" is simply an adjective that describes the "nature" or type of unthought that Hope feels: Hope finds the sight of her sister repulsive. On the other hand, the grounds for that revulsion are indicated by the term *nature*, which refers not only to Hope's unthought, but to Faith's decidedly unnatural (according to Hope) appropriation of Indian clothing, manners, and speech. In this case, *revolting* also functions as a verb: Hope is revulsed because Faith seems to be revolting against nature.

Which is only to say that what so sickens Hope is that her sister is disguised as an Indian; she is, in Hope's view, passing, hiding what Hope believes is her true nature—whiteness—beneath Indian clothing. This aspect of Hope's disgust is made even more apparent when Hope tries to communicate with her sister:

Hope knew not how to address one so near to her by nature, so far removed by habit and education. She thought that if Mary's dress, which was singularly and gaudily decorated, had a less savage aspect, she might look more natural to her, and she signed to her to remove the mantle she wore, made of birds' feathers, woven together with threads of the wild nettle.[74]

Here, Hope's "unthought" has begun to take shape as a "thought": that Faith's nature is being concealed beneath Indian garb. Removing it, Hope seems to think, might restore her Faith. But as a thought, Hope's attitude with regard to Faith's passing is reversed, for what Hope actually thinks here is not that Faith's true nature as a non-Indian will be revealed by removing her Indian clothing, but only that she will "*look* more natural" [emphasis mine] to Hope. So what Hope originally (un)thought was that Faith's immutable nature has now become a matter of appearances. This explains—I think—the narrator's use of the odd term *unthought*; it refers to Hope's prelinguistic reaction to the sight of her Indianized sister. When that reaction becomes concretized, described, put into language, Hope's position— her belief in an unchangeable nature or identity—is undermined. Consequently, her strategy of restoration backfires:

The removal of the mantle, instead of the effect designed, only served to make more striking the aboriginal peculiarities; and Hope, shuddering and heart-sick, made one more effort to disguise them by taking off her silk cloak and wrapping it close around her sister.[75]

What Hope wants here, but fails to achieve, is for Faith to re-pass or to pass back to her original whiteness. But that identity is no longer available (if it ever was); instead, there are only layers of "disguise": beneath Hope's silk cloak is "Whitebird," and beneath Whitebird is "Faith," and beneath Faith is "Mary." Whom does Hope want to uncover? Yet in her failure to uncover—by re-covering—Faith's nature, Hope also activates another meaning of the pivotal term *revolting*. For in a text that makes such conspicuous use of the rhetoric of the American Revolution and in which, as we have already seen, to be "aboriginal" is to be Revolutionary: the logic of this scene holds that Faith actually becomes "natural" by becoming native. This is why Hope, in what may be the strangest gesture of all in this complex scene, attempts to "disguise" with her own silk cloak what originally she took to be Faith's disguise, her Indian dress, the removal of which does not reveal Faith's true white nature, but only her "aboriginal peculiarities."

Carolyn L. Karcher has suggested that Sedgwick, too, disapproves of Faith's passing, since the view of her as disguised links her to Rosa, the "fallen woman" in the novel, whose shameful condition is hidden beneath her disguise as Sir Philip's manservant.[76] But, again, it's only Hope who views Faith as wearing a disguise, and, as we've just seen, even that position is undercut by the narrator. Moreover, Rosa/Roslyn's is not the only other disguise in the novel: the Catholic Sir Philip is disguised as a faithful Puritan, Magawisca dresses up as Master Cradock to escape prison, and even Hope, in the chapter immediately following her reunion with Faith, "identif[ies] herself with a catholic saint" in order to escape from drunken

Italian sailors.[77] Clearly, in *Hope Leslie*, not all disguises are transgressions; in fact, the text does not pronounce on dissembling as such; disguises are neither good nor bad. Rather, they only serve good or bad ends.

The same is true of historical authority in the text. As with dissembling, the novel does not pronounce on authority (narrative or otherwise) as such; there are only good or bad authorities, like Hope's heart and Governor Winthrop's head, respectively; there are only good or bad narratives.[78] In fact, the novel actively resists the very notion of "full narrative authority" that Gould ultimately views as inconsistent with the text's historical relativism.[79] The text's relativism goes all the way down. The point of its argument for historical relativism—bringing the past into relation with ever-new presents—structurally mirrors the point of the reunion scene. That is, the narrative experience of history *Hope Leslie* offers to its readers (of whatever era), what I have called the present within history, is duplicated in the text's representation of the racial "other," in imagining what might be called a relation of sameness within difference. So just as the novel is less concerned with an objective or faithful recovery of a remote period in time than with bringing disparate periods in time into productive relation—or to borrow a phrase from Emerson that I'll return to in Chapter 3, allowing the past and the present to "meet in perception"—so is it less concerned with recovering Faith's "true" cultural identity than with the negotiation that results from the meeting between disparately situated individual subjects.[80] What the reunion scene is about, in other words, is Hope—and, by extension, because she is our heroine, the reader—struggling to cope with "otherness." In racial and cultural terms, Hope sees her sister as at once different from and the same as herself. And the reader not only witnesses this struggle and sees Hope duly reprimanded for her particular method of coping, but experiences something like it as well: for not only does the reader sympathize and thus imaginatively identify with Hope, the novel's heroine; the scene simultaneously asks the reader to identify with the Indian Magawisca, the scene's voice of moral authority.

Of course, Sedgwick finally is left with the problem of resolution—both novelistic and cultural—which is anathema to the open-endedness of the (historical) process the bulk of her text embodies. And to be sure, despite Everell's feeble and naïve assertion that "the present difference of the English with the Indians, is but a vapour that has, even now, nearly passed away," the Indians in the novel are banished to "the deep, voiceless obscurity" of the "western forests" at the end of the novel. Or rather, they choose obscurity over assimilation; as Magawisca puts it, "the Indian and the white man can no more mingle, and become one, than day and night."[81] But as unsatisfactory as this denouement may appear to the modern reader, its reliance on the myth of the vanishing American may have less to do with the "constraints" of Sedgwick's culture than with the formal constraints of the novel itself; unlike the movement of history or the formation of personal, national, and cultural identity, it has to end.

John Neal's American Revolution

The formal constraints of the novel are precisely what John Neal, as brash, unruly, and reckless a writer as any in the period, seeks to break free from in *Seventy-Six*, his novel of the American Revolution. It's an impossible task, of course, but recognizing it as one of the central dilemmas Neal's brand of literary historiography confronts is crucial to making sense of the novel, its formal disarray, and the chaotic reading experience it invariably produces. The peculiar challenge posed by *Seventy-Six* is this: how do we read a work of historical fiction that seems largely uninterested in the relation between the historical and the fictional? Although little known and infrequently read by modern critics, *Seventy-Six* was the novel of which Neal himself, never shy about rendering a literary judgment upon himself or anyone else, was proudest. He considered it "the best novel I have written," "one of the best romances of the age," and "quite a faithful history of the old American War—told with astonishing vivacity."[82] Literary history has not been as kind. As with so much of Neal's fiction, readers of *Seventy-Six* have found it to be an undisciplined work, rife with excesses, extravagances, and incoherencies. Where, on the one hand, the novel is notable for its graphic depictions of battle, numerous passages of vigorous prose, and its experimentation with colloquial language (its attempt, as the narrator puts it, to "*talk on paper*"—it is marred, on the other hand, by a lack of formal unity, an apparent disregard for thematic coherence, and a convoluted and awkwardly rendered romantic plot—many of the same deficiencies, incidentally, early reviewers of *Hope Leslie* complained about.[83] Thus, Edgar Allan Poe's general assessment of Neal's fiction, as Robert A. Bain has pointed out, remains the consensus view: Poe found himself unable "to account for the repeated failure of John Neal as regards the *construction* of his works." One always finishes a Neal novel, Poe wrote, "with dissatisfaction... in no mood to give the author credit for the vivid sensations which have been aroused *during the progress* of perusal".[84]

Poe's difficulty with Neal, endorsed by modern critics almost without exception, rests on a distinction between the formal design of Neal's works—their "construction"—and the experience of reading them—the "vivid sensations" they provoke "during the progress of perusal." It is not my aim to challenge the dominant view, expressed here by Poe, of Neal as a writer who failed to produce tightly controlled, unified works of art. After all, Neal himself, as we'll see, didn't dispute that fact. Rather, taking *Seventy-Six* as a particularly revealing example of Neal's aesthetic commitments, I want to question the distinction upon which Poe's and later critics' negative assessments of Neal's work rest. That is to say, just as Sedgwick's novel resists the historicist frameworks critics have imposed upon it, so too does Neal resist the terms upon which his novel has been judged. Specifically, for Neal, there is no distinction between the novel's "construction" and the experience it seeks to engender in its readers. That which happens "during the progress of perusal," in other words, *is* the novel's principle of construction. In the case of *Seventy-Six*, for example, the measure of its success, according to Neal, was that when reading it, "The reader becomes an eye-witness in spite of himself."[85]

Although *Seventy-Six* has garnered very little critical attention, those scholars who have discussed it, whether glancingly or in more extended readings, have generally accepted Poe's framework, foregrounding the question of how one harmonizes, or how Neal harmonized, the text's interest in U.S. history and the romantic entanglements of its plot.[86] What is the relationship, these critics ask, between the "historical and nonhistorical" elements of the novel? Donald Ringe, for instance, praises Cooper, Kennedy, and Simms in almost precisely those terms upon which Letter's reading of *Seventy-Six* relies. Each "writer's handling of the family conflicts," Ringe claims, "reveals...his attitude toward the social" conflicts the text sets out to explore.[87] A common trope in this regard is "the divided family," which provided historical romancers with "the best and most economical means for depicting the American Revolution as a civil war."[88] But while *Seventy-Six* is striking, in part, precisely for the *absence* of divided families—there are virtually no Tories at all in Neal's novel—such an absence does not prevent critics from finding other ways of reading familial relations as depictions (or personifications) of national or historical conditions. In his reading, allegory helps supply the integration of the historical and nonhistorical that Ringe finds wanting.[89]

But what if we considered the possibility that Neal might be interesting, not *despite*, but precisely *because* of his incoherencies? In my examination of *Seventy-Six*, I attempt neither to find coherence in the novel's disparate strains nor fault it for failing to integrate them. Rather than dismissing Neal's unruliness, I strive to take it seriously by considering the lack of coherence or unity of his fiction not as a problem to be overcome (or forgiven) in order to arrive at his texts' meaning, but instead as itself the meaning of his fiction. The peculiar challenge Neal poses in *Seventy-Six*—a challenge both to the discourse of Revolutionary history, and historiography, and to the conventions of historical fiction—is its keeping of the historical and the fictional more-or-less distinct, its resistance to assimilating them into some coherent meaning. Neal's American Revolution in *Seventy-Six*, in other words, is his insight that the war—and beyond it, history and human experience—does not in itself possess coherent meaning. Neal's fictional narrative is radical—revolutionary—insofar as it attempts to undo, to circumvent, the inherent tendency of narrative to shape and bestow coherence upon experience.[90] It endeavors instead to do what *re*presentation, by definition, can't: to present—if we can read that verb, phonically, speaking it as a noun. What Neal is after in *Seventy-Six*, in other words, is what we might call historical immediatism.

Like Poe, Neal was a shrewd critic. He developed and articulated a clear, if idiosyncratic, theory of fiction.[91] Indeed, Neal was often remarkably candid in his assessments of his own work, at times anticipating or pre-empting the views of critics and scholars who, as we've already seen, have criticized his novels for their formlessness, their bewildering plots and implausible conclusions, his "lack of any idea when to stop." Neal himself described his novel *Logan* as "incoherent" and admitted that another novel, *Errata,* is "loaded with rubbish." Writing about himself anonymously, in the third person in his series on *American Writers* Neal claimed that "he overdoes everything," writing "volume after volume, to the tune of three or four a-month; hardly one of which it is possible to read through."[92] He even acknowledged the excesses and waywardness of *Seventy-Six,* writing that "With a little care—some pruning: a few alterations, it might be made an admirable book of."[93]

The fact that Neal did *not* take such care suggests that "admirable" books were not exactly what he set out to produce. This is evident to anyone who has made it through the two volumes that comprise *Seventy-Six,* which, because it is relatively unknown, I'll briefly describe. The outlandish plot of the novel defies easy summary. Narrated by an aging veteran of the Revolution, Jonathan Oadley, to his children, the novel begins in late 1776, and follows Oadley and his younger brother Archibald almost to the conclusion of the war. The action begins as Jonathan, Archibald, and their cousin Arthur Rodman prepare to join Washington's army. Before their departure, Hessian raiders descend on the Oadley home, burn it to the ground, ravish Mrs. Oadley, and run away with Mary Austin, a young woman whose identity remains unexplained. At the house of their neighbor, Robert Arnauld, we are introduced to Arnauld's two daughters, Clara and Lucia, the respective love interests of Jonathan and Archibald, as well as a Colonel Clinton, a mysterious figure who has close ties to George Washington and an eye for Lucia Arnauld. Jonathan and Archibald, along with their father, Mr. Arnauld, and Clinton go off to battle, fighting at Trenton, Brandywine, and Valley Forge. Mr. Oadley dies in battle early on, but the valiant Archibald, reckless and brooding in the Byronic mold, quickly distinguishes himself in battle and is given an officer's commission. Soon enough, Archibald and Clinton quarrel over Lucia and Archibald kills his rival in a duel. Meanwhile, it is revealed that Mary Austin, whom everyone has given up for dead, is alive and well in Philadelphia, although it is revealed that she had nearly been seduced by Robert Arnauld, who confesses and is forgiven for his behavior. Mary is then reunited in Philadelphia with her lover Arthur Rodman.

Meanwhile, the war continues, providing Oadley with the opportunity to offer a number of vivid, brutal, and bloody descriptions of skirmishes large and small. Archibald broods over his killing of Clinton and becomes increasingly gloomy over the violence of the war and his love for Lucia. He also befriends another officer, Chester Copely, who, like Archibald, fights a duel and kills his adversary. Jonathan, meanwhile, makes love both to Clara and to a feisty young girl named Ellen Sampson, whom he meets in Philadelphia. But eventually, Jonathan is wounded in battle, loses a leg, and returns to the Arnauld house, where the remainder of the novel is set. On furlough, Copely, Arthur, and Archibald visit, at which point the novel's several lovers square off and avow their devotion, resulting in the marriages, in a joint ceremony, of Copely to Ellen Sampson, Jonathan to Clara, and Arthur to Mary Austin. Archibald and Lucia reconcile, but for undisclosed reasons, refuse to marry, and we learn that Archibald is dying of consumption, a fact he has tried to keep secret. In the novel's climax, Lucia reveals that Clinton had seduced her, and Jonathan learns the source of Archibald's shame and guilt: the night before the Hessian raid on the house, Archibald had killed another young man in a duel, burying the body at the site of their contest. The sources of their guilt thus partially expiated, Lucia and Archibald finally agree to marry. The novel concludes at their wedding, where, at the instant they are pronounced husband and wife, Archibald dies.

As this brief summary, which scarcely begins to do justice to the plot's intricacy, suggests, *Seventy-Six* is, as Jonathan Oadley concedes near the end, "a disorderly story at best."[94] Indeed, more than just a description of the narrative, disorderliness proves one of the novel's primary topics of interest. The novel is quite explicit about its incoherence, the signs of which penetrate every level of the text: from Neal's reference in the preface to the "rambling incoherency, passion and extravagance of [his earlier novel] *Logan*" to Oadley's own references to the "rambling incoherent journeying of my thoughts," his "disordered memory," his "troubled, disorderly dreaming," the "disordered dreaming of my brain," and late in the novel, "the wild, incoherent, disordered language" of a letter from Archibald to Lucia that Oadley transcribed.[95] Moreover, characters in the novel are frequently described as "disordered" or they refer to the "disordered wandering of my mind" or "disorderly dreaming."[96] The battle scenes are, likewise, frequently and aptly characterized as disorderly.[97] Even the material status of the text reflects this fundamental disorderliness and incoherence: it is rife with typographical errors, misspellings, and other printer's mistakes, including, at one point, a missing manuscript page for which the publisher inserts, in the middle of a character's speech, an apology.

The disjointed quality of the text extends to its awkward handling of shifts from scenes of battle in which the novel's characters participate to retrospective discussions of the military campaign and political maneuvering, and scenes at the Arnauld house and elsewhere that advance its intricate romantic plot. For two-thirds of the novel, these three elements seem to vie for primacy in the novel so that it's not quite clear whether Oadley's (or Neal's or the reader's, for that matter) principal interest lies in depicting the brutal experience of war, providing an accurate account of the Revolution's progress in military and political terms, or in exploring affairs of the heart. The narrative of the Oadleys' experience in the war is frequently interrupted, for instance, with digressions that address the politics of the war from an historian's perspective. For these discussions, Neal drew heavily upon Paul Allen's *History of the American Revolution* (1819), large portions of which Neal had written himself. Rather than seamlessly incorporating this material into the action of the novel, however, Oadley explicitly presents it digressively. Early on, for example, as the characters prepare with Washington for the campaign in New Jersey, Oadley writes, "My children! I must pause. I would have you realize the tremendous peril in which your father and uncle—all his family and friends— nay! All the hopes of America were placed at this hour."[98] What follows is a consideration—nearly identical to the one found in Allen's *History*—of why the British army chose not to pursue Washington across the Delaware, a pursuit, according to Oadley, that could have decided the war in Britain's favor. At the conclusion of this discussion, Oadley merely states, "But let me return," at which point the novel's fictional characters are reintroduced.[99]

This pattern repeats frequently in *Seventy-Six*. Following a discussion of the Battle of Trenton, Oadley writes: "There, my dear Children—I have been willing to forget the battle, and the subject for awhile, and amuse you, for I know your taste and that of our people, with a few rockets,—and—but let me return—."[100] Later in the first volume, Oadley takes up the actions of the American Congress, introducing the digression by saying:

> And here my children, you will allow me to pause awhile, remarking, that no matter of importance took place for several weeks in our little camp, till Archibald was restored, and Clinton, rejoined us—for the purpose of carrying your thought abroad, to the more distant operations of our country, in the field and council.[101]

What follows is an account of Washington's appointment by the Continental Congress as the supreme commander of the American army (which Oadley views as a terrible mistake, salvaged only owing to the great virtue of Washington), a brief mention of the appearance of Benedict Arnold, and a discussion of the vulnerable weakness of the Continental troops. Yet beyond the function of marking the chronological advancement of the war, these "more distant operations" have little, if any, bearing on the activities of the novel's principal characters. Hence when the discussion concludes, once again with the statement, "So—let us return to our story—."[102] Oadley picks up his narrative at a seemingly random point: "I shall take it up, at the time that I first saw Clinton, face to face" following his return to camp.[103] Later, in what may be the novel's strangest digression, Oadley tells the story of how, after the war, "the artful, terrible" Aaron Burr attempted to enlist Oadley and Copely in his secessionist conspiracy.[104] Copely violently resists, accusing Burr of treason, at which point Oadley concludes the tale by saying, "But let me return—to the Revolution."[105]

Eventually, even these intermittent attempts to track the Revolution's progress cease entirely. At the beginning of the novel's final chapter, Oadley admits, "My heart fails me. I never shall be able to carry you through the whole war, as I intended to do, when I began. It is out of the question." He begins a final update on the status of the war, but aborts it just as quickly: "Intelligence from the south— no—I will have done with the war."[106] "The war, and the men of the revolution," he continues, "my own sufferings, and those of my family; the army—my country; all are forgotten or remembered, as a matter subordinate to the sorrow, of Archibald and Lucia."[107] It's tempting to explain this abandonment of the war by saying that Oadley or, more likely, Neal himself, has simply run out of steam (in Neal's case, because he has nearly reached the requisite page count for his second volume)—a plausible conclusion given Neal's habits of composition, about which, more in a moment—and hence, to view it as a clear sign of Neal's shortcomings as a novelist. But we shouldn't too quickly dismiss Oadley's answer as to why "it is out of the question" to make it through "the whole war": because his interest is absorbed by the story of Archibald and Lucia. It has "taken such possession" of him that he "can see nothing, hear nothing, think of nothing, but him and her."[108]

On one level, this explanation might suggest that if, as I have claimed, the historical and the fictional elements of the novel vie for primacy for most of the narrative, in the end, fiction trumps history. On another level, however, Oadley here aptly demonstrates a central tenet of Neal's theory of art: that what is paramount is *interest*.[109] Indeed, Oadley's absorption in his own story—disorderly though it may be—provides a figure for the compositional habits of Neal himself. Neal prided himself not only on his ability to write quickly—in his memoir *Wandering Recollections*, for instance, he boasts of the "wonderful rapidity" with which he wrote *Seventy-Six* over the course of just twenty-seven days in February and March of 1822—but on the explosive power with which he did so.[110] For instance, in *Wandering Recollections*, he describes writing his earlier work, the narrative poem "Battle of Niagara," as "a clear case of spontaneous combustion," the outpouring of an inflamed imagination.[111] "I was carried away," Neal writes, "with a sense of hidden wings, in the contemplation of what I saw and heard, as the picture began to shape itself with appalling distinctness, to my imagination. It was a revelation: I felt as if I had become an eye-witness of the great transaction."[112] Neal described the creation of *Seventy-Six* in similar terms, as a kind of explosion of pent-up energy: "I had got charged to the muzzle with the doings of our Revolutionary fathers, while writing my portion of 'Allen's History,'" Neal recalls in *Wandering Recollections*, "and wanted…to go off like a Leyden jar, and empty myself at once of all the hoarded enthusiasm I had been bottling up, for three or four years."[113] The result, as Neal describes it in his series on *American Writers* is that: "The reader becomes an eye-witness in spite of himself."[114]

Incidents in Themselves

It's not just that Neal was willing to sacrifice coherence and polish for emotional power and "vivacity." Rather, it's that coherence and polish, for Neal, are actually inimical to vivacity. At the end of his novel *The Down-Easters*, Neal responds to the concern of his publisher that he did not provide a full accounting of the novel's characters:

It is in vain for me to tell him, that incidents of themselves are interesting in real life, unconnected though they are, with a story before and a story after them, that if a fine girl for instance, were to destroy herself, it would be the fault of the narrator, if people were not interested, without knowing all the causes, all the circumstances, and all the consequences. But all in vain: a plot there must be with a regular development...[115]

The claim Neal makes for "real life" here comes close to expressing a phenomenology of pure experience that is fundamentally at odds with narrative. Narrative seeks the meaning of experiences in causes, circumstances, and consequences, rather than in the experience itself. The function of a narrator (or author) is thus not to explain, but simply to present incidents with such vividness of interest that the reader becomes "an eye-witness." Thus the controlling idea of what we might call Neal's aesthetic of incoherence is that narrative is not immanent in our experience, but merely a structure that is imposed upon it retrospectively.[116]

The same principle holds for history, where experience and knowledge are likewise at odds. To know the history of the American Revolution, to know its major battles, its turning points, its principal players, indeed, to know its causes, circumstances, and consequences, is one thing; to experience the heat of battle is quite another. This is why Neal's discussions of the former come in the form of digressions, only loosely connected to the latter. The two are, in a very important sense (for Neal) simply unrelated. And both are unrelated to the other incidents the novel depicts: the affairs of Archibald, Clinton, and Lucia; Copely and Ellen; Jonathan and Clara; and the rest. What makes *Seventy-Six* so unsatisfying (apparently), or simply bewildering, as a work of art is the fact that Neal *laments* the idea that "a plot there must be"—an unusual reservation, to say the least, for a novelist to hold.

Yet on another level, Neal's view possesses a certain logic, in terms of both the kind of "history" Oadley sets out to write and, relatedly, the paradoxical conception of history that Oadley, and Neal himself, appears to advance. Oadley explains the former in the novel's opening chapter, where he instructs his children on how to read the story he has to tell. Recognizing that the Revolutionary generation is quickly passing away, Oadley reminds his children that they'll soon ask, "Our Fathers!—the men of the Revolution—where *are* they?" Having left behind his narrative as a "record," his children will merely have to open his book, which will "call up his apparition before" them, allowing them to "see his aged and worn forehead—his white hair in the wind."[117] His book will encourage them to "travel in imagination, with your father, barefooted, over the frozen ground, leaving his blood at every step, as he went" and make their "thought go in pilgrimage, over the same ground, remembering that the old men who travelled it, in the revolution, doing battle at every step, for your inheritance, were an army journeying, deliberately, to martyrdom."[118] Even more, Oadley vows to conjure forth his fellow veterans: "at my bidding, they will appear! And harness and array themselves—and stand before you, as I have seen them stand before GEORGE WASHINGTON—a battalion of immoveable, impregnable, and unconquerable old men."[119] Oadley's insistence here upon immediacy and presence is a desire for his children, stand-ins for readers of the novel, not just to *remember* the men of the Revolution, the scenes of their suffering, and the sites of battle, but to *witness* them. His wish is not that they'll *know* about the war—for that they could turn to "the blundering, tedious compilations, which, are called the Histories of our Revolution"— but that they'll *experience* it.[120]

Of course, the paradox of such a rendering of history—making it present—is that it ceases to be historical. To return to the past, to become an "eye-witness" to historical events, would be to have a present experience—the only kind of experience there is. The dilemma, then, with which Neal is faced—and the central problem, I would suggest, of the unique brand of historical fiction Neal practices in *Seventy-Six*—is this: how to get the past into one's present experience? By this, I don't mean how to represent the past or how to understand it, or even to remember it. I mean—and this is the unique problem Neal's aesthetic creates—how to render it "interesting," in Neal's understanding of that term. Neal's way of negotiating this dilemma is through a curious temporal sleight of hand. Consider, in the passages cited previously, the most striking feature of the future memories Oadley projects: he would have his children recall the Revolutionary veterans, himself included, not in their youthful vigor at the time of the war, but in their dotage, as "old men." Indeed, those who did battle at every step, those who were arrayed in front of Washington, were, at the time, not "old" at all. Oadley's image of the men of the Revolution calls to mind the images of decrepit Revolutionary-era specters summoned by Whitman in his satirical poem "A Boston Ballad" (which I analyze in more detail in Chapter 3), and, as in Whitman, they help to figure a generational divide. Oadley's soldiers will appear, he says, as "shadowy sovereigns coming back to a degenerate people."[121] Just as in "A Boston Ballad," the present generation—Oadley's children's generation—has lost the spirit of liberty embodied by their forefathers; they've become, Oadley says, "base and showy," "a fettered people—fettered too, by manacles that would have fallen from the limbs of your fathers like rain."[122]

But while Oadley certainly shares Whitman's sense of generational declension, it's less clear that Neal does. Rather, the image of aged soldiers at the start of *Seventy-Six* is Neal's way of locating Revolutionary history itself not in a distant past, but in a living present on the verge of passing away. In this regard, a more apt point of comparison than "A Boston Ballad" is Emerson's famous "Concord Hymn" (1836):

> The foe long since in silence slept,
> Alike the Conqueror silent sleeps,
> And Time the ruined bridge has swept
> Down the dark stream which seaward creeps.[123]

Emerson's poem betrays an anxiety about remembering not unlike that expressed by Oadley. The poem appears to mourn the fact that the "bridge" that would connect the past to the present has been "swept" away by "Time" into the sea. Yet at the same time, the poem, paradoxically, casts time itself as a ruined bridge. As such, it *always* fails as a means of traversing history. Emerson's poem, of course, was written to commemorate the completion of the Concord Monument, and so by the end it registers hope that the "set[ting] of a 'votive stone'" will aid memory in performing the function that time's ruined bridge cannot.[124]

The difference between Emerson and Neal here, however, is that Emerson's solution is to substitute memory for time, to cast memory (potentially) in the role of an *un*ruined bridge establishing "concord"—a relation of harmony—between present and future citizens of Concord and the Revolutionary past. Neal, by contrast, simply attempts to do away with both time—that is, time as a sequential unfolding, time in the form of explanatory causes, circumstances, consequences, and memory (in the form of commemorative monuments). Instead, he locates history in the soldiers themselves. "Look at the men of our revolution," Oadley says in an apostrophe to his children near the end of volume I:

> where do you find such faces now? Why are not their children's written over, and sculptured so deeply? Why! Because the impress of relationship the hand of nature, never yet operated upon the countenance of man, and never will, with aught of that terrible distinctness, with which political convulsion chissels [sic] out the head and the faces of her chosen ones. Look at the men of our revolution—their very countenances are the history of the time.[125]

At first glance, Neal's metaphors of inscription here might suggest that Neal is simply participating in what Russ Castronovo has identified as the antebellum U.S. "culture of monumentalism," a particular "historical mode of articulating national culture" that "underscores the interstices between the fabrication of historical consciousness and civic being"—a reading that would accord with Neal's well-known promotion of U.S. literary nationalism.[126] Yet, Oadley's insistence that the faces of the Revolutionary veterans "are the history of the time" differs in crucial ways from the monumental impulse. Devoted to "magnificent narrative[s] of homogeneity and unity," monumentalism effaces the particular in favor of the mythical, the local in favor of the national, and the individual in favor of the collective. As Castronovo puts it, "Hardly worth memorialization, the people are not the stuff of history. Instead, history resides solely in the national."[127] By contrast, for Neal, the people—the faces of Revolutionary veterans—are *literally* the stuff of history, which is why Neal extols a form of history "written by men acquainted by participation therein" and delivered in "the style of a soldier, plain and direct."[128]

However, in arguing that Neal refuses the monumental impulse that so many antebellum American writers and others found congenial to the work of consolidating a timeless national identity, I, likewise, do not wish to align Neal with the kind of "countermonumentalism" that, as Dana Luciano has insightfully shown, informs some nineteenth-century critiques of nationalist commemoration. Luciano describes the countermonument as "deliberately untimely." Like Emerson's ruined bridge, it "marks out spaces in which damaged time becomes visible."[129] But where Emerson's poem imagines the healing of such "damaged time" through the unifying power of the monument:

> the countermonument supplants the timeless symbolic appeal of the traditional monument with the destabilizing effects of both irony and allegory. The turn to allegory in countermonuments, in particular, reflects a desire to find ways of negotiating the relationship between past and present that depend neither on linear emplotments of time nor on its collapse into timelessness.[130]

Because it "exposes the incompleteness of objects, gesturing toward a referential relationship that is both arbitrary and necessary," allegory "emphasizes the necessity of making meaning of (rather than receiving meaning *from*) the coutnermonument, a process that will, like allegory itself, necessarily be dispersed across time."[131] In this, allegory—as Walter Benjamin notes—is related to the ruin, which because it only becomes commemorative over time and derives its variable meanings from later periods, commemorates nothing more than the passage of time itself.

However, *Seventy-Six*, I am arguing, refuses both the timelessness of the monument and the untimeliness of the countermonument, and, in doing so, it refuses both the symbolism of the former and the allegorizing of the latter. To read *Seventy-Six* allegorically is to treat the novel itself as a ruin, to assume the necessity of the text's referentiality. Yet this assumption, I am suggesting, is at odds with Neal's devotion to "incidents of themselves," his attempt to convert readers into eyewitnesses, his desire to produce a novel in which "plot" is little more than an unfortunate side-effect, his experiment in constructing a narrative that neither refers nor means, but that simply *is*. Of course, such a project could not *not* fail, given that both writing and reading inevitably unfold in time and given that the historical past is irretrievably past. Yet a large part of the interest and exhilaration—and oddity—of reading *Seventy-Six* is watching Neal make the attempt nevertheless. Consider one of the novel's more vivid passages: Oadley's first experience in battle. Robert Bain praises this passage for its "psychological perceptions," but it is equally notable for its comparative lack of interest in the battle itself or its historical meaning:

> For myself, I can hardly tell what my feelings were. First, there was a rush of fierce, terrible delight—and then, a brief alarum in my heart; followed by a sort of religious fervour, exceeding wrath and indignation, tranquilized and subdued, as if God and his angels were fighting with us. Nay, at the very onset; when the word had been given to *charge!*—and all the hills round, rung with the melody of trumpets—the neighing of horses, and the shouting of their riders—when we had joined battle, and I heard nothing but the shriek of women—saw nothing but the pale, wasted face of my poor mother—and the dead body of Mary, under the hoof of trampling horses—there was no feeling of terrour, in all this—none!—but there was a sublimity, that distended my whole heart, as with fire, and flood, and

tempest—and when, in the thick of the battle, our ranks were broken, and each was wrestling, man to man, with his adversary, on foot, or on horseback—the face of my father and brother, and that of the death struck Arthur, went by me, in one rank, as I thought—and all fled before them! After all this, I know not what happened, until my horse stumbled among the dead bodies, and threw me into a mass of human blood and trodden snow. God! how the field looked. But stay!—I am anticipating. Is it not wonderful. I had stood, and gazed upon my brother, not a minute before, after the blood of one man was upon him—and listened to his composed voice, and fancied that there was something preternatural in it—but now, I was dripping with it, from head to foot—and I felt no other emotion than a little loathing and sickness.[132]

To the extent that this passage depicts a sequence of events, those events are not what happens in the fight, but are instead Oadley's "feelings," which come in succession: "terrible delight," then "alarum," followed by "religious fervor." Yet the passage never makes clear what induces these sensations, but only that each of them "was." Distinctions between present and past, outside and inside, collapse. The sensations of the battle itself, its sounds, for example—from the melody of trumpets to the "neighing of horses—and its sights—dead bodies, the 'mass of human blood'"—are no more real, no more present, than the sensations drawn from Oadley's past: the face of his mother, the body of Mary Austin. Everything dissolves into an undifferentiated, affective "now." Indeed, at the one moment when this account begins to slip into a conventional representation—"God! how the field looked," Oadley begins to say, as if to take an external, retrospective view of the battle and its aftermath—he fights against the impulse, saying "But stay!—I am anticipating." To anticipate, in this context, is to narrativize, to think of events as connected "with a story before and a story after."

Thus when Oadley reminds himself to "stay"—to arrest the inevitable movement of narrative, to resist placing events in sequential relation to other events—he gives expression to Neal's own resistance to plot and his devotion instead to affective experience, to the incident as it happens: without the benefit of an immanent direction or meaning, without cause or consequence. As we'll see in Chapter 5, Melville attempts something quite similar, though perhaps slightly less audaciously, in his own unhistorical fiction, *Israel Potter*. At any rate, the temporality of the Neal passage in the previous paragraph, I am arguing, is the duration of experience, rather than the cause-and-effect relations between successive historical events. Incidents of themselves may possess a certain temporal spread (or duration), but as they are experienced, they do not possess continuity. To the contrary, the principle characteristic of the incident is in fact its novelty. Only in retrospect, after its occurrence, do we set about reconstructing events to account for it, to give (narrative) shape and meaning to the incident in relation to that which we experienced before and that which is yet to come. This retrospective act of reconstruction is what it means, conventionally, both to narrativize and to historicize.[133]

Neal's attempt to reproduce for the reader experiences and incidents in them-selves, in their autonomous discontinuity, is illustrated in yet another way in the novel's penultimate chapter. All of the principal characters, now (with the excep-tion of Archibald and Lucia) married with children, enjoy a "warm, sultry day" outdoors. As they watch the children, with their hands full of flowers, playing near the woods, Archibald recalls a painting he had once seen. The picture, he says:

> "represented a mother and her babe. The story was this...The child had crept to the brink of a precipice, before the mother had missed it: when she turned her face, she discovered her babe upon the very verge. God touched her heart—she tore away the covering from her bosom; and the little nestling turned, saw the place of beauty, and remained immoveable, til she had crept near enough to catch him, and faint."[134]

Archibald goes on to explain why the painting "troubled" him. "The painter ought to have seen these children," he says, because they demonstrate why the painting's rendering of a similar scene is "wrong." First, the child in the painting "held the flowers, just as a grown person would, by the stems; but these children do not." Rather, they catch at that part which attracts their eye: "the light of a candle—the coloured leaf, or the blossom. It is the flower, that they seize and tear up." A second fault of the painting, Archibald continues, is that the child in it "is sitting upon the precipice":

> "That was wrong. When the child had gone so far, as to sit upon it, and let its little feet hang over, the danger was already past; the extreme danger I mean...Now, my notion is, that the child should not be sitting, but creeping; nay, I would have it so, that the spectator should start, and hold his breath, and put out his hand to save it, if he came suddenly into the room, where the picture was."[135]

Archibald's alternative version of the painting, which he describes in minute detail, would, he remarks, "make your blood run cold."[136]

What Archibald objects to in the painting is not just its lack of precise verisi-militude (evident in the way in which the child holds the flowers), but its narrative completeness. The picture presents danger averted ("already past"), rather than danger itself. In doing so, it appeals to the viewer's understanding or intellect, not the viewer's emotion.[137] Or more precisely, it only reproduces the *knowledge* of a moment of "extreme danger," rather than producing in the viewer the *experience* of that danger. Archibald's painting, by contrast, would make of the reader an "eye-witness," pulling him so powerfully into the moment that he would act, "put[ting] out his hand to save" the child, as if there. The difference between Archibald's ver-sion of the painting and the original, then, is that Archibald's would resist narrativ-izing the scene, would resist *representing* fear, danger averted, potential loss—or whatever else the painting might be said to depict or mean. Instead, it would merely produce a particular sensation or induce a certain affective state in the viewer; it would present (not *re*present) an experience—an experience whose chief characteristic, as Archibald's scenario of the viewer who suddenly enters the room where the painting hangs suggests, is that it is disruptive.

Of course, the scene does not just make its point by analogy. It is itself disruptive and discontinuous in relation to the disparate threads of the novel's plot. Indeed, nothing up to that point in the novel has prepared the reader for Archibald-turned-art-critic and nothing that follows helps to make any sort of sense of the scene at the level of plot or even character development. Like so many other episodes in the novel—whether a depiction of war's ferocity, the facts of Revolutionary history, or love's vicissitudes—its significance is entirely self-contained; it refers only to itself. Yet for Neal, this discontinuity is not that which prevents him from arriving at some coherent meaning of the Revolution. Rather, it *is* the "truth" of history.[138]

In *Hope Leslie* and *Seventy-Six*, Sedgwick and Neal continued and extended the project of preemptively dismantling nationalist history begun by Irving in *A History of New York*. Embracing anachronism, eschewing the causal logic of narrative, their respective early experiments in presentist history writing refuse the terms and assumptions—especially progressive teleology—that later came to typify both the dominant tradition of historical fiction in the United States and the modes of historical understanding through which that tradition would be understood.[139] But while the heterodox conceptions of history and history writing of these three writers never coalesced into a recognizable and reproducible generic shape or fictional tradition, neither did it simply wither and fade. As we'll see, it helped set some of the terms and establish many of the prerogatives of the various immediatisms—philosophical, political, and aesthetic—I will examine in the second half of this book. Those terms and prerogatives found their most potent—and contentious—expression in Emersonian transcendentalism and in immediatist abolitionism, movements that produced their own present-oriented theories of history.

Of course, *Seventy-Six* and *Hope Leslie* were both written before the advent of Garrisonian immediatism—or at least before that immediatism became a public doctrine and social demand, rather than a disposition or unarticulated moral imperative. Nor were Sedgwick and Neal, even in the 1830s after Garrison launched *The Liberator*, themselves immediatists. But both writers were ardently antislavery. Sedgwick's family members labored in the legal arena for the cause of emancipation—her father, for instance, represented Elizabeth Freeman in her successful suit for freedom in Massachusetts court—but remained antislavery moderates. Like many old guard New England liberals, the Sedgwicks, including Catharine, were chary of what she, like others, referred to as the "ultraism" of radicals like Garrison who advocated for immediate emancipation.[140] Neal, too, was a committed social reformer and an early advocate for antislavery (and women's rights). He participated actively, for example, in the Maine Antislavery Society and attended meetings of the American Antislavery Society. Yet he was also a unionist and like

Sedgwick, he expressed misgivings about the more radical doctrines of Garrisonian abolitionism, even though by temperament—in his series on American writers he describes himself as "audacious, whimsical [and] obstinate" (Sedgwick, by contrast, he calls "simple, chaste, and very sensible")—one might think him ideally suited to the impetuosity of zealous immediatism.[141] He even criticized Garrison publicly, although this may well have had to do in part with Garrison's criticisms of his *American Writers* series. Later, however, Neal appears to have had a change of heart: at the end of the Civil War, he conceded that on the question of slavery, "I was wrong…and Mr. Garrison was right."[142]

In 1853, Sedgwick contributed a (rather unfortunate) short essay to Julia Griffith's *Autographs for Freedom*, but neither Sedgwick nor Neal ever published any antislavery fiction, although Sedgwick made an attempt, which she eventually abandoned and never published.[143] Nor did either writer provide abolitionists with a figure quite as powerful, adaptable, and enduring as Irving's "Rip Van Winkle." However, the broad readership of *Hope Leslie* did include African Americans, who recognized in Magawisca a kindred symbol of resistance to oppression. The black poet and abolitionist Sarah Forten, for instance, adopted Magawisca as a pseudonym for her article "The Abuse of Liberty," published in *The Liberator* in 1831. The essay is a passionate denunciation of white supremacy in the United States as Forten observes that "those who cannot shew a fair exterior, (no matter what be the noble qualities of their mind,) are to be robbed of the rights by which they were endowed by an all-wise and merciful Creator."[144] Then, in rhetoric that, as we'll soon see, typified immediatist discourse, Forten projects a future that will witness destructive natural forces unleashed and calls for Americans to rouse from their slumber and become sensible to the urgency of the moment:

> Oh, that the scales of error might fall from their eyes, that they might clearly behold with what rapidity that little stream they first introduced into their country has spread itself! It will soon expand into a mighty river, that will ere long overwhelm them in its dark abyss. Awake from your lethargy; exert every nerve; cast off the yoke from the oppressed; let the bondmen go free; and cry unto your offended God to send freedom with its strong battlements to impede the progress of this raging flood.[145]

Neal's novel seems to have had no similar resonance. But the impetuous quality of *Seventy-Six* and especially its investments in immediate sensations and history as an affective experience rhyme with the temporal disposition adopted by immediatists, as Chapters 3 and 4 will show. Thus both writers produced fiction that helped demonstrate some of the possibilities of romantic presentism as a mode of thinking about history, a mode that ultimately informs, or at least gets recapitulated and gains political force in, the writings of later romantic presentists who turned their energy and attention more explicitly toward the problem of slavery.

Or put another way, the formal experiments in Sedgwick's and Neal's historical fictions helped to identify and promote ways of being in history that, whether influentially or simply coincidentally, came to be adopted by abolitionists and activists in the next few decades: in their irreverent attitudes toward the past, their emphasis on affective experience over knowledge or understanding, their refusal of the logic of teleology, their skepticism toward historical progress, and their embrace of futural uncertainty.

PART II

Reformations of the Present

Emerson's Strong Present Tense

Why, when Emerson thinks of history, does he so often think of the present? As he prepared his lecture series on "The Philosophy of History," for instance, which he delivered beginning in December 1836, he wrote in his journal that October: "History's best use is to enhance our estimate of the present hour"—a statement evidently of such lasting importance to him that he recycled it more than twenty years later in only slightly altered form in his lecture "Works and Days," first given in 1857: "The use of history is to give value to the present hour and its duty."[1] Related statements suffuse his notebooks, lectures, and essays throughout his long career. In his lecture, "The Present Age," given in 1840, he says, "In the present moment, all the past is ever represented."[2] Twenty years after that, in *The Conduct of Life* published in 1860, he writes, "the thought of the present moment has a greater value than all the past."[3] And the first entry, titled "History," in his first book of *Essays* (1841) advances the perhaps startling claim that "All inquiry into antiquity—all curiosity respecting the Pyramids, the excavated cities, Stonehenge, the Ohio Circles, Mexico, and Memphis—is the desire to do away with this wild, savage, and preposterous There or Then, and introduce in its place the Here and the Now."[4]

All of this, of course, might seem to suggest that Emerson has no real interest in history at all, at least not in history as it is conventionally understood—as a field or sphere of knowledge of events, actions, persons, attitudes, and beliefs separate and distinct from the present and knowable on its own terms through careful study of surviving documents and artifacts.[5] This, as the Chapters 1 and 2 have likewise discussed, is the historicist conception of history, which aspires to know the past "as it was"—a view that Emerson called the "pedantic way of writing history."[6] From the historicist perspective, Emerson can hardly be seen as anything but unhistorical, a hopeless presentist who fails to respect the uniqueness of the past. He is, hence, not someone to be taken seriously as either an historian or a philosopher of history, despite the fact that a persistent engagement with the value and meaning of history provides a certain continuity to his career—from "The Philosophy of History" through "Natural History of Intellect"—from beginning to end.

Yet with only a few exceptions critics interested in Emerson's relation to history have sought mainly to place him and his writings within the various currents of his time, to position him as a writer not disengaged from the political, scientific, and social questions of the day, as earlier generations of scholars described him, but as deeply immersed in and shaped by them.[7] Or to put this another way, Emerson, like so many other nineteenth-century American writers, has been thoroughly "historicized" in recent years, subjected to historicist criticism's relentless contextualizing procedures. Neal Dolan, for instance, argues that another recent strain of Emerson scholarship, efforts that seek to align him with the pragmatist tradition in American philosophical thought, "is starkly anachronistic" because it fails to account for the "historical distinctness" of Emerson's own era and is inappropriately wary "of imposing our own ideas and assumptions" upon him.[8] Indeed, Dolan conjures up those specters that, as we saw in the last chapter, typically attend critiques of perceived presentism: the tendency to "assimilate" past figures to present-day values, a maneuver tantamount to a kind of "colonization." Dolan seeks instead to demonstrate how and why Emerson "may be interesting and valuable to us precisely to the extent that he does not exactly share our contemporary views."[9]

As productive as historicist readings such as Dolan's have been, however, the assumptions that inform them might themselves be seen as presentist insofar as they assume that, with the benefit of historical hindsight, we can see Emerson in his time more clearly, more "rightly," than he himself could. Or at the very least, they take for granted the notion that we can understand him in ways that he, like any other product in history, inevitably bound and determined by its particular historical moment, simply could not have understood himself. But what if the historicist critic's knowingness is fundamentally at odds with Emerson's thinking about history? What if Emerson, as Lawrence Buell has put it, "doesn't want to be historicized?"[10] What if, in the rush to place Emerson *in* history, critics have tended to brush past Emerson's ideas *about* history—not just about its shape and value, but his conception of what history *is*? What if what we have here is the misrecognition of one understanding of history (Emerson's) by another (historicism)? How might we approach Emerson's relation to history differently if we abandon some of our historicist assumptions?

These questions, and an effort to take Emerson's presentism seriously, motivate this chapter. Like Irving's, Sedgwick's, and Neal's, Emerson's conception of history is at odds both with the prevailing romantic historiography of his day and with the historicism of our own. In this chapter, I mean to try out Emerson's present-oriented understanding of history—or what, borrowing a phrase from the essay "Experience," I will call his "strong present tense"—as much as to explain it. This means that, following Emerson, I will at times risk running afoul of historicist conventions: I will be more concerned with relations of sameness than of difference, with repetition or uneven movement than with progressive development, and with points of cross-temporal contact than with points of departure or distinction. In doing so, I hope to bring into relief some of Emerson's core assumptions about history: that ideas and concepts are not the sole property of their historical moments, that time and history don't always move forward and progress, that the historical past is not fixed and static, and that the past does not precede or determine the present.

More specifically, I want to align Emerson's conception of history not just with the antihistoricist tradition I have described in chapters one and two, but with the implied theory of history proffered by immediatist abolitionism, a subject of central importance in Chapter 4. Emerson thus forms a bridge between the deformations of history I have explored in Chapters 1 and 2, and the more politically and socially charged reformations of the present epitomized by, but by no means the sole province of, William Lloyd Garrison and Frederick Douglass, between the abstract questions posed by romantic presentism (what is history? what does it mean to be historical?) and its political imperatives (social justice and the abolition of slavery). Of course, whether and how Emerson bridged the divide between philosophical abstractions and political exigencies has been a defining problem in Emerson studies for a long time now. And while important recovery work by Len Gougeon, David Robinson, T. Gregory Garvey, Albert J. von Frank, and others has at least vindicated Emerson from the charges of political apathy and inaction levied by earlier generations of scholars, it remains an open question whether, as Maurice Lee has put it, "Emerson's philosophy and his social activism...get along."[11] While I make no general claims in response to that question, other than to suggest that it may be by now overdetermined, I do want to suggest that Emerson's conception of history marks one place where his transcendentalism and his social activism converge.

Soon after the passage of the Compromise of 1850, Emerson became, rhetorically at least, precisely the sort of reckless immediatist, akin to Garrison, Douglass, John Brown, or Captain Ahab, that more cautious gradualists viewed as dangerous and fanatical. His antislavery addresses display many of the terms and distinctive features of Garrison's brand of immediatist abolitionism: its investments in the hasty and quickened time of now, its accent on affective experience, and its commitment to extemporaneity and experimentation. Yet these are terms and features likewise apparent in Emerson's thought well before his public embrace of immediatist abolitionism; they animate, especially, his first series of *Essays*, and, in particular, those essays that most keenly articulate his view of history. Focusing, like Martha Schoolman, on Emerson's "Garrisonian engagements," in this chapter I argue that Emerson's ruminations on history reveal that he was already an immediatist well before he was an abolitionist. Indeed, the movement from the one to the other was less a "conversion," as Gougeon has described it, than simply the concrete application of an abstract principle.[12] Moreover, Emerson's path to a passionate engagement with antislavery politics, his journey from a state of sleepy insomnia to a state of total wakefulness, did not occur along a straight line of development, as the conversion narrative might imply. For that reason, my analysis eschews chronology and mainly works backward and recursively, from his full-throated immediatist abolitionism after the Compromise of 1850 to his first series of essays' theorizations of history and then back again.[13] If Garrison was immediatism's most vocal crusader within abolition's public sphere, Emerson was its most sensitive philosophical exponent.

Rashly Do

Emerson concludes his 1853 poem "On Freedom" aphoristically, with an echo of Longfellow's "A Psalm of Life": "Right thou feelest rashly do." Prescriptive rather than descriptive—by this time, Emerson had spent more than a decade reminding readers and audiences of just how infrequently their convictions drove their actions—Emerson's exhortation exceeds Longfellow's "Act—act, in the living present" in both eloquence and urgency. While both poems encourage action rooted in one's personal sense of moral rightness, Emerson's adverb "rashly" makes explicit that toward which Longfellow's poem only hints: the uncertainty of acting on one's spontaneous, affective impulses and the potential dangers of acting impetuously, without sufficient caution or concern for consequences. To act "rashly" is to act precipitately, hurriedly—too soon.

While they are among the defining features of romantic presentism, impatience, haste, and a certain reckless disregard for outcomes, ends, and effects are not things ordinarily associated with Emerson, especially in the context of the politics of slavery. Quite the contrary. When it comes to political action, Emerson can seem, at least early in his career, rather too prudent, even somewhat behind the times. Indeed, critical assessments of Emerson's public entrance into antislavery politics have typically turned on the question of timing: his reluctance to speak out on matters of immediate public concern, his willingness to wait on the slow forces of ameliorative progress, and his failure to take up the cause of abolition as quickly as others within and without his circle. By now, the consensus, even among the most ardent champions of his political activism, is that Emerson was a kind of slow-footed laggard, his arrival to abolitionism belated. Not until the mid-1840s did the pace of his activism begin to accelerate until he finally caught up, however tardily, to his fellow abolitionists during and after the crisis of 1850. Maurice Lee, for instance, has shown how in the three essays, "Lecture on the Times," "The Conservative," and "The Transcendentalist," published (in 1849) from his 1841–2 lecture series "The Times," Emerson emphasized the importance of patience to social reform, aligning him with moderate antislavery figures like William Ellery Channing. At this period, Lee concludes, Emerson "takes his political waking slow."[14]

Lee's metaphor is particularly apt, for that may have been the judgment of Emerson's contemporaries as well. In a phrase that echoes Garrison's charge that backward looking politicians like James Buchanan were "insensible to the present," Emerson's early biographer James Eliot Cabot reports that abolitionists in the 1830s thought that Emerson was "insufficiently alive" to the problem of slavery. As a result, Cabot notes, "some of his friends tried to rouse him to a fuller sense of the occasion," to awaken him, that is, to "the fierce urgency of now."[15] Yet however much Emerson was slow to action, he was hardly a slumbering Rip Van Winkle—though he may have wished he were. In a telling journal entry from November 1849, just weeks before Henry Clay would introduce his Compromise bill in the hopes of averting sectional catastrophe, Emerson recorded an experience from his day on the train:

> I envied a young man in the cars who when his companion told him they had arrived at Waltham…was asleep, & his friend shook him, lifted him up, & called in his ear, in vain, he could not wake him, & the cars went on again to the next station before he could be fully aroused. Then I came home & counted every hour the clock struck all night.[16]

Himself an insomniac, Emerson envies the sort of young man who can sleep so soundly, remaining unaffected by events and by his compatriots' attempts to awaken him. Of course, it's doubtful that Emerson had slavery or politics in mind when he reported this episode to his journal; he just wishes for a good night's rest. But one is nevertheless tempted to see in it a metaphor for Emerson's own lethargy, at least early in his career, in the face of the era's most urgent problem, especially given the entry's timing. Just three months earlier, Emerson had delivered brief remarks to a large crowd in Worcester, assembled by the Massachusetts Antislavery Society, in which, perhaps to the dismay of some of the more impatient immediatists in attendance, he leaned cheerfully on the "course of history" as a "constant progress of amelioration," even while recognizing that "this progress of amelioration is very slow."[17] Because his remarks in Worcester were delivered extemporaneously and, according to reports, rather awkwardly, uncomfortably, and falteringly, it's not altogether clear whether Emerson meant to celebrate or lament the sluggish rate of progress.[18] Yet his account of his insomnia, those wasted hours watching the clock and counting every hour, perhaps registers his growing restiveness with waiting patiently for the impersonal forces of progress to effect social change.

Whatever the case, just a few months later, the disastrous Compromise bill would speed the pace of antislavery agitation, including Emerson's, considerably (Frederick Douglass, for instance, as I'll discuss in the Chapter 4, spoke memorably about this *hastening* of the course of history toward emancipation). The bill's most controversial provision, the new Fugitive Slave Law, certainly lent new urgency to Emerson's own sense of and response to current affairs. So when he did begin to speak about slavery with greater exigency, as in his 1851 address on the Fugitive Slave Law in Concord, he did so fully alive—fully sensible—to the dire intensities of the moment, to which he responds, echoing the injunction of "On Freedom," affectively. "I have a new experience," Emerson tells his audience, "I wake in the morning with a painful sensation, which I carry about all day."[19] Emerson feels the injustice of the Fugitive Slave Law somatically and immediately, as a "painful sensation" he cannot shake. No longer merely something known or understood from a distance, the law has "now" entered into his "experience." And he perceives a "like sensibility" in his neighbors. The outrage of the Fugitive Slave Law has produced such a quickening that "the whole population will in a short time be as painfully affected."[20]

Or to put this another way, the body politic will find itself "painfully affected" only insofar as it is awakened and attuned to the living present, the time, the *only* time, of experience. By contrast, Daniel Webster, the primary target of Emerson's indignation in the speech, is incapable of such feeling, suffering as he does from a monstrous defect of "blood and constitution." He is, Emerson says, "a man who lives by his memory, a man of the past."[21] In a withering denunciation of Webster strikingly similar to Garrison's in "The Dead Past and the Living Present," Emerson accuses Webster of revering only that which is settled and dead. "What he finds already written," such as the Constitution, "he will defend," Emerson writes, adding wryly, "Lucky that so much had got well written when he came."[22] So while Webster might praise the nation's founders and its founding documents, he has "no faith" in "extemporising a government"; nothing "new ... would receive his sanction." Hence, Webster "praises Adams and Jefferson; but it is a past Adams and Jefferson that his mind can entertain. A present Adams and Jefferson he would denounce."[23]

Emerson's unsparing condemnation of Webster displays all of the features that typified the most strident forms of immediatist abolitionism: its presentism, its affective register, its aggressive impatience, its emphasis on experience and insistence on action, its unsettling of the past and hostility to letting the dead rest in peace. "The powers of invention," "the readiness for reforms," and "the eagerness for novelty" lie at the heart of Emerson's conception of self-government, for "as the people have made a government, they can make another."[24] Emerson thus commits himself to mutability, impermanence, and unmaking, all those elements that bear with them the kinds of unforeseen dangers and potential risks that men of the past like Webster most fear and seek to curtail. Indeed, if anything affronted antislavery antiabolitionists more than immediatists' intemperate rhetoric, it was what Channing, for example, bemoaned as "precipitate measures ... violent changes." "Precipitate action," he wrote, is "inconsistent with the well-being of the slave and the order of the state." Only a trust in God, he insisted, can save us from "human impatience" and "rashness."[25] Catherine Beecher in her *Essay on Slavery and Abolition* (1837), written in reply to Angeline Grimké's *Appeal to the Christian Women of the South* (1836), expressed a similar concern for "men of ardent and impulsive temperament."[26] Not to be outdone in her concern for the dangers such men posed, she then prophesied the inevitable results of precipitate action, imagining a sequence of events in a not-so-distant future so terrifying it warrants quoting at length. Abolitionist agitation in the South will only spur iron-fisted southern reactions:

They will make laws so unjust and oppressive, not only to slaves, but to their Abolitionist advocates, that by degrees such men will withdraw from their bounds. Laws will be made expressly to harass them, and to render them so uncomfortable that they must withdraw. Then gradually the righteous will flee from the devoted city. Then the numerical proportion of whites will decrease, and the cruelty and unrestrained wickedness of the system will increase, till a period will come when the physical power will be so much with the blacks, their sense of suffering so increased, that the volcano will burst,—insurrection and servile wars will begin. Oh, the countless horrors of such a day! And will the South stand alone in that burning hour? When she sends forth the wailing of her agonies, shall not the North and the West hear, and lift up together the voice of wo? Will not fathers hear the cries of children, and brothers the cries of sisters? Will the terrors of insurrection sweep over the South, and no Northern and Western blood be shed? Will the slaves be cut down, in such a strife, when they raise the same pæan song of liberty and human rights, that was the watchword of our redemption from far less dreadful tyranny, and which is now thrilling the nations and shaking monarchs on their thrones—will this be heard, and none of the sons of liberty be found to appear on their side?[27]

In an anxious future tense, Beecher recounts a chain of events governed by a process of cause and effect that seems almost mathematical in its ineluctably: this, "*then*" this. What Beecher fears most—more even than intensified oppression—is swift and sudden slave rebellion, which she figures in terms of powerful natural forces unleashed: "the volcano will burst." Immediatists like Douglass, as we'll see in Chapter 4, deployed the same trope to express emancipatory hope, rather than apprehensive terror. And Emerson, as I'll discuss next, used similar imagery to figure welcome historical change. But where Douglass and Emerson can hardly wait for such seismic events, Beecher worries that they are already too near at hand:

> This is no picture of fancied dangers, which are not near. The day has come, when already the feelings are so excited on both sides, that I have heard intelligent men, good men, benevolent and pious men, in moments of excitement, declare themselves ready to take up the sword—some for the defence of the master, some for the protection and right of the slave. It is my full conviction, that if insurrection does burst forth, and there be the least prospect of success to the cause of the slave, there will be men from the North and West, standing breast to breast, with murderous weapons, in opposing ranks.[28]

Overcome with apprehensions about the future, Beecher all but forgets the present. Her program of antislavery reform is premised on forestalling contingency, on seeking foreknowledge of the consequences of one's actions. Indeed, the likelihood of an outcome is, for Beecher, the best guide to conduct. For her, perceived effects dictate causes. As she puts it (repeatedly): "the wisdom and rectitude of a given course, depend entirely on the *probabilities of success*," or a bit later, "the propriety and duty of a given course is to be decided by *probabilities as to its results*" italics original).[29] Of course, from another point of view—the view of and from the present—"wisdom" and "propriety" simply look like complacency and quietism.[30]

In the 1851 Fugitive Slave Law address, Emerson explicitly dismisses the misplaced criticisms of abolitionist agitation by moderates like Beecher. "It is absurd," he says, "to accuse the friends of freedom in the north with being the occasion of the new stringency of the southern slave-laws. If you starve or beat the orphan, in my presence, and I accuse your cruelty, can I help it?" Such a reaction, Emerson says, is as inexorable as the laws of the physical universe: "Will you blame the ball for rebounding from the floor; blame the air for rushing where a vacuum is made or the boiler for exploding under pressure of steam?"[31] Emerson here reassigns culpability: abolitionists ought not to be blamed since it's the slaveholders' actions that cause the abolitionists' responses in the first place. He also reveals the groundlessness of the kind of conjectural fearmongering upon which Beecher's position rests. Unlike the causal relations Beecher describes in what is ultimately a speculative exercise, guessing after probabilities, Emerson presents "facts" that are "after the laws of the world," just as it is law that "when justice is violated, anger begins."[32] For Beecher, the way to prevent mayhem is to display cautious self-control, to think through and calculate probabilities before embarking upon a course of action. But for Emerson, such prudence amounts to a denial of one's own humanity insofar as it suppresses one's natural, involuntary, affective responses: "the very defence which the God of Nature has provided for the innocent against cruelty," he says, "is the sentiment of indignation and pity in the bosom of the beholder."[33]

Emerson thus gives voice to a vision of social justice that is affective, experiential, and immediate, defined by the here and now of stimuli-response, while Beecher's vision is (conventionally) historical and futural, defined by the sequential relations of cause and effect. But as Longfellow's poem teaches, the future, whether cataclysmic or liberatory, can't be trusted; accepting that uncertainty is just what it means to act according to one's sentiments. Angelina Grimké says as much in her response to Beecher. Adducing Biblical examples ("What probability of success was there that [Moses] could move the heart of Pharaoh?"), Grimké states succinctly the immediatist position with regard to results: "All who see the path of duty plain before them, are bound to walk in that path, *end where it may*" (italics mine).[34] In other words, right thou feelest rashly do. Grimké calls this condition of unknowing "walking by faith, not by sight." "The *result* of our labors is hidden from our eyes," she writes, "whether the preaching of Anti-Slavery truth is to be a savor of life unto life, or of death unto death to this nation, we know not."[35] Beecher and Grimké thus differ in their attitudes toward futurity: whereas Beecher seeks and insists upon a visible and knowable future, for Grimké the future is obscured and inscrutable. Yet for Grimké, that not knowing in no way relieves us of the obligation to act.

Beecher's paralyzing concern for the future is the flipside of Webster's fidelity to the past. Both are numb to the pressing demands of *now*. This is why in the 1851 Fugitive Slave Law address Emerson insists that Adams and Jefferson are only worth honoring insofar as they are alive, present. In the same way, the only country worth healing is the one that exists *now*. As Emerson puts it, the nation "is to be administered according to what is, and is to be, and not according to what is dead and gone."[36] Emerson's careful verb construction here, underlined by the repetition of "is to be" indicates not, like Beecher, a particular future toward which this present is inevitably headed, but a present state of affairs that always obtains: we can only ever administer that which *is*. The point is further reinforced by

Emerson's playful exploitation of "administer," the apparent meaning of which (to manage the affairs of government) is undercut by the more vital meaning Emerson intends: to attend or minister to. After all, Emerson insists, "the union is a real thing"—living, breathing, and in need of healing and spiritual restoration— "not a statute union" or a mere set of written laws to be executed rigidly according to fixed and settled procedures.[37]

The opposite of this latter kind of administration is what Emerson calls "extemporising": improvisation, spontaneity, and experimentation; terms instantly recognizable to students of Emerson's transcendentalism and his elliptical prose style, but perhaps less commonly associated with his abolitionism. This may be why readers of "On Freedom," despite its concluding line's seeming affirmation of immediatist abolitionism and Emerson's nearly total embrace of immediatist tenets by 1851, such that he could produce some of its most artfully compelling articulations, have typically described the poem as yet another example of Emerson's much-discussed "fumbling" or "hesitation" toward acting on behalf of the cause of emancipation, rather than a call to precipitate action.[38] To present the poem in full:

> "On Freedom"
> Once I wished I might rehearse
> Freedom's paean in my verse,
> That the slave who caught the strain
> Should throb until he snapt his chain.
> But the Spirit said, "Not so;
> Speak it not, or speak it low;
> Name not lightly to be said,
> Gift too precious to be prayed,
> Passion not to be exprest
> But by heaving of the breast;
> Yet,—would'st thou the mountain find
> Where this deity is shrined,
> Who gives the seas and sunset-skies
> Their unspent beauty of surprise,
> And, when it lists him, waken can
> Brute and savage into man;
> Or, if in thy heart he shine,
> Blends the starry fates with thine,
> Draws angels nigh to dwell with thee,
> And makes thy thought archangels be;
> Freedom's secret would'st thou know?—
> Right thou feelest rashly do.

The poem's opening lines do seem to register the speaker's inability, and perhaps even his belief in the futility of trying, to "rehearse/Freedom's paean in my verse" in such a way "That the slave that caught the strain/ Should throb until he snapt his chain." Yet this seems an oddly despairing sentiment for the forum in which "On Freedom" was first published in 1854: the second volume of Julia Griffiths' *Autographs for Freedom*, a compendium of short antislavery writings, in poetry and prose, accompanied by their authors' signatures, sold to raise funds for the Rochester Ladies' Antislavery Society. Emerson's poem appeared alongside contributions from Theodore Parker, William Wells Brown, Thomas Wentworth Higginson, William Julius Wilson, Geritt Smith, Frederick Douglass, James McCune Smith, Harriet Beecher Stowe, and others. Given such company, one might expect a more emphatic statement than critics, accustomed to identifying the signs of Emerson's irresolution toward abolition, have found in the poem.[39]

In fact, immediatist imperatives motivate the poem. Shifting from a past tense when the speaker thought, perhaps naively, that writing poems *about* freedom might help to bring about emancipation, to a present tense in which one *feels* (among the places freedom resides is in "the heaving of the breast") and *acts*, the poem doesn't so much capture Emerson's ongoing ambivalence as it charts his new-found presentist-immediatist perspective. To "rehearse/Freedom's paean" is to approach the problem of slavery from precisely the opposite direction, since rehearsal suggests a retrospective bearing, wherein one repeats mechanically that which has been done before. Yet that is not the attitude of the poem's speaker *now*; rather, he "once," at some time in the past, imagined a causal narrative with a clear sequence of events leading to a determinate outcome in an imagined future: the poetic equivalent of counting hours or clocking a carefully planned scheme of gradual emancipation. But "Spirit" disabused him of such a notion. Writing a poem that precisely identifies and locates freedom, Spirit tells the speaker by way of a cluster of more or less conventional poetic images—"mountains," "seas and sunset-skies," "starry fates" and "angels" near—won't get you any closer to freedom's secret. Or if it does, so the arch rhetorical question in the poem's penultimate line suggests, it won't much help because it will offer you only something to "know," not something to "do"—a key distinction in the poem, formally reinforced by the off-rhyme, the only one in the poem, of the concluding couplet.[40]

In his astute reading of the poem as one of the period's rare expressions of "antifreedom," Russ Castronovo has highlighted this dichotomy, noting how in the poem "freedom consists not in knowing but in the sensuousness of doing."[41] Refusing to provide an abstract "theory of freedom," Castronovo argues, Emerson "instead offers a strategy responsive to context, emerging from passions of the local and momentary"—that is, the immediate. "Freedom" thus "ceases to be both immanent and imminent...knowing must be forsaken in preference to the uncertain results of doing."[42] Yet Castronovo balks at the implications of the poem's emphasis on action's "uncertain results." Although Emerson's poem "depart[s] from nationalized definitions that respond to, rather than sublimate, historical context," ultimately, Castronovo asserts, "the poet stops short, lounging in the comfort of a hypothetical posture that hesitates to consider exactly how sensuous commitment to action will flesh out a liberatory agenda."[43] Castronovo's otherwise penetrating reading errs here by attributing the poem's final line to the speaker, not to Spirit, who imparts it to the speaker as both admonishment and command.[44] Even more importantly, Castronovo seems to forget his own emphasis on the poem's key term "rashly," which by definition precludes the kind of consideration and fleshing out that might otherwise dictate and direct action by way of an "agenda."[45] That is to say, as both Catherine Beecher and Angelina Grimké recognized, the point—and power—of acting rashly resides in the fact that it is "uncertain," unplanned, and spontaneous—*extemporized*.

Extemporization is the province of the impatient. If you're going to act on impulse, without forethought, you'll need to be willing to adjust to swiftly changing circumstances. Of course, a want of forethought, or worse, an aversion to planning, is hardly the stuff of which political programs are made. Still, critics have made much, too much, I would suggest, of Emerson's political cold feet, and not enough of his restiveness, a possible source of his insomnia. By 1854, Emerson, like so many others, had clearly had his fill of carefully designed political programs, with their endless delays and deferrals. In his second Fugitive Slave Law speech, delivered in New York on the by-then infamous seventh of March, Emerson expresses growing frustration with the centuries-old view, which he traces back to the ancient Greeks, that justice will arrive in due time. "These delays," he says, "you see them now in the temper of the times. The national spirit of this country is so drowsy, preoccupied with interest, deaf to principle."[46] Contrasting the "drowsy" national spirit with the vigor that produced the European revolutions of 1848, he laments, "torpor exists here throughout the active classes on the subject of domestic slavery and its appalling aggressions." And he seems scornful of, or at least irritated and no longer willing to abide by, "the stern edict of Providence, that liberty shall be no hasty fruit."[47] "While the inconsistency of slavery with the principles on which the world is built guarantees its downfall," he says," I own that the patience it requires is almost too sublime for mortals, and seems to demand of us more than mere hoping."[48] Emerson might well have substituted "waiting" for "hoping," for both suggest a passivity and anticipation that no one can endure. Thus, like Martin Luther King, Jr., Emerson came to realize that the time for waiting on time had long passed. Emily Dickinson expressed this view compactly in her 1863 poem "They say that 'time assuages.'" Often taken as an instance of Dickinson's tough-minded deflation of conventional truisms (in this case, the old consolatory bromide), the poem also hints at a more pointed political meaning, effectively expressing an attitude toward time held by immediatists, something she may have learned from, or at least witnessed in, her friend Thomas Wentworth Higginson:

> They say that "time assuages",—
> Time never did assuage;
> An actual suffering strengthens,

As sinews do, with age.
Time is a test of trouble,
But not a remedy.
If such it prove, it prove too
There was no malady.[49]

A "test" not a "remedy," time reveals problems, rather than solves them. Waiting, in fact, only makes things worse. The image Emerson deploys to make this point— "one sees how fast the rot spreads"—is not so distant from Dickinson's own metaphor of disease. Emerson, however, suggests an antidote: that "we demand of superior men" to "accelerate the progress of civilization."[50] Such an impatient temper, a readiness or desire for rapid change, come what may, likewise constitutes a significant, albeit overlooked, element of Emerson's less explicitly political writings.

Dying Lately

When a full decade before his second Fugitive Slave Law speech Emerson writes in "Experience," "We must set up the strong present tense against all the rumors of wrath, past or to come,"[51] he responds, if only obliquely, to the assurances of the unnamed "they" in Dickinson's poem and to the warnings of antislavery gradual-ists like Catherine Beecher. Abolitionists, Beecher charges, "promote wrath and strife."[52] Yet Beecher's nightmare vision of the future, of the "results" of abolitionist actions, is no more certain than any other outcome. Her dire portents thus amount to little more than rumor, circulating widely, repeated and passed on, but finally unverifiable. The spread of such rumors serves mainly to delay, defer, and deceler-ate the pace of social change, and to promote instead slow, cautious deliberation and careful calculation of probabilities. "Experience" is an essay about learning to divest oneself of such prudence: "we should not postpone and refer and wish," Emerson writes, "but do broad justice where we are."[53] "Objections and criticism we have had our fill of," he says, for "there are objections to every course of life and action."[54] And he claims that "nature hates calculators" for the "results of life are uncalculated and uncalculable."[55] Postponement, objection, calculation—these are the things that keep people in a state of torpor, passively waiting to act until the time is right, whenever that might be. Once again echoing Longfellow, Emerson encourages us instead to be up and doing: "So many things are unsettled which it is of the first importance to settle," he writes, recasting a crucial statement from his earlier essay "Circles" that I will take up later, "and, pending their settlement, we will do as we do."[56] Learn to labor *and* to wait, Emerson counsels.

Although "Experience" appeared in print the same year that Emerson delivered his first major antislavery address in Concord, at the invitation of the Women's Anti-Slavery Society to commemorate the tenth anniversary of West Indian eman-cipation, only recently have critics attempted to integrate the essay into what Lee calls "the story of Emerson's hesitant abolitionism."[57] Yet what makes "Experience" particularly interesting in relation to that story is not that it provides further evidence of that hesitation, but that, as I've already begun to suggest, it takes the impulse to hesitate as one of its main subjects. In fact, the terms and figures with which Emerson works his way through that problem mirror the terms and figures of the debates between gradualist and immediatist abolitionists so strikingly that the essay might be read profitably as an anticipatory allegory of the political awakening that so many northerners, Emerson included, experienced after 1850. Here I concentrate mainly on the essay's principal figure for slow hesitation—"lethargy"—and the essay's antidote to that somnambulant state of unresponsiveness—"to set up the strong present tense;" that is, to counter the passive bewilderment of what he calls "succession" by acting in the living present. "Experience" speaks the language of immediatist abolitionism in its urgent concern for what it means to be awake and alive.

Garrison was far from the only critic of slavery to view his fellow citizens, complacent on this most pressing of issues, as asleep or dead. That same indictment is the basic conceit of Whitman's "A Boston Ballad," the one explicitly topical and unambiguously political poem in the first edition of *Leaves of Grass*. Garrison launched *The Liberator* by saying that "the apathy of the people is enough to make every statue leap from its pedestal and to hasten the resurrection of the dead."[58] In "A Boston Ballad," the dead are already walking. Distraught over the spectacle that is the rendition of the slave Anthony Burns, soldiers from the American Revolution rise from their graves and limp along the streets of Boston, their limbs convulsing and bare gums chattering. Despite being long dead, these Yankee phantoms are nevertheless alive to the urgencies of the moment. Roused to action, they raise their crutches like rifles. Emotionally affected by the scene unfolding before them, they weep and groan. By contrast, the "smart" living citizens of Boston stand by, idle, passive, and evidently benumbed. "Well-dressed" and "orderly," they "gape" and "gaze," stupidly, insensibly—like zombies. When the phantom soldiers begin to leave the scene, having failed to reanimate their lifeless grandsons and granddaughters, the speaker of the poem asks after them, stating the poem's central irony in the form of a rhetorical question: "Can't you stand it?" he asks, "Are you retreating?/ Is this hour with the living too dead for you?"[59]

In its depiction of the stupefaction of the public body, "A Boston Ballad" provides a poetic variation of what Castronovo calls "necro citizenship," the desire of U.S. democracy to render citizens into abstract, disembodied, passive subjects—social corpses not unlike the well-dressed and passive citizens in "A Boston Ballad," unmoved by the scene of injustice right in front of them.[60] White and black abolitionists, according to Castronovo, participated in the formation of such citizens, consenting to the period's "necro ideology" that abstracted freedom from historical and material existence and "represent[ed] passivity and somnolence as democratic virtues."[61] The reversal at the heart of Whitman's poem—that the living are the real walking dead—indicates that there was a degree of recognition, even at the time, of the operations of necro ideology; or if not quite that, at least a sense that many citizens seemed barely alive, their senses deadened ("deaf to principle," as Emerson says). Indeed, some antislavery advocates, not unlike Whitman, produced their own critiques of necrocitizenship.

Henry David Thoreau, for example, provides an even more caustic description than Whitman of a deadened citizenry in his 1859 address "A Plea for Captain John Brown." The period's very paragon of precipitancy and rash action—he was routinely described as "reckless" and "impatient"[62]—Brown's fusing of sentiment with deed provides Thoreau a fit occasion to deride, by way of contrast, the "want of vitality" in those who fail to properly estimate Brown's "character and actions."[63] Five years earlier in *Walden*, Thoreau had insisted, "We must learn to reawaken and keep ourselves awake."[64] Since that time, the bulk of his fellow citizens had failed to rouse, remaining virtually benumbed. In "A Plea," Thoreau laments what he calls "the all but universal woodenness of both head and heart" in his neighbors.[65] Contrasting the true religious spirit of Brown with the average "modern Christian," Thoreau says that the latter would prefer not to be awake: "All his prayers begin, 'Now I lay me down to sleep,' and he is forever looking forward to the time when he shall go to his 'long rest.'"[66] And in a statement that echoes Emerson's description of Daniel Webster as afflicted by a defect of "blood and constitution," Thoreau says that the modern Christian suffers "not merely from a stagnation of blood, but a stagnation of spirit."[67]

Which is to say that, compared with John Brown, most American citizens are all but dead. So it's ironic that for most of the address, Thoreau purposefully speaks of Brown as if in eulogy, even though at the time of the lecture on October 30, 1859, Brown was still very much alive, awaiting execution in a Virginia prison and helping to create the conditions for his own public sanctification. Thoreau himself at one point notes this fact: "I am aware that I anticipate a little," he says, "that [Brown] was still, at the last accounts, alive in the hands of his foes, but that being the case, I have all along found myself thinking and speaking of him as physically dead."[68] Thoreau's premature burial of Brown is more than just a recognition of the inevitable (Brown would be hanged a month later); treating Brown as proleptically dead is a crucial part of the conditions of Thoreau's praise, since in his view, Brown is one of a very few men who *can* die. Brown's heroic attempt, which Thoreau calls a "sublime spectacle," demonstrated "the possibility of a man's dying." Thoreau explains the point, mordantly, in one of the speech's best moments:

> It seems as if no man had ever died in America before, for in order to die you must first have lived. I don't believe in the hearses, the palls, and funerals that they have had. There was no death in the case, because there had been no life; they merely rotted or sloughed off, pretty much as they had rotted or sloughed along... Let the dead bury their dead. The best of them fairly ran down like a clock.[69]

A moment later, he reiterates that most men "haven't got enough life in them to die," adding drolly, "They'll deliquesce like fungi, and keep a hundred eulogists mopping the spot where they left off."[70] Humor aside, Thoreau's sense of Americans' general lifelessness might form a kind of rejoinder to Emerson's remark about the listless state he finds himself in at the opening of "Experience": "Nothing is left us now but death. We look to that with a grim satisfaction, saying, there at least is reality that will not dodge us."[71] But to look forward to death while in such a condition, Thoreau asserts, is folly; from there, as if by definition, one can't die.

So "the possibility of a man's dying" depends upon his having lived in the first place. But what does it mean to have lived? The answer to that question is suggested by Thoreau's allusion to Longfellow's "A Psalm of Life" ("Let the dead bury their dead"), the succeeding lines of which Thoreau could expect his audience to know by heart. Thoreau glosses the poem, obliquely, anyway. In response to his own assertion that "we've wholly forgotten how to die," he counsels, "But be sure you do die, nevertheless. Do your work, and finish it. If you know how to begin, you will know when to end."[72] This, for Thoreau, is the lesson of Brown's "acts and words," which he expects will "create a revival" and reanimate a torpid populace. Already, Thoreau observes, news of Brown's venture has "quickened the feeble pulse of the North, and infused more and more generous blood into her veins and heart."[73]

The news is of particular importance to Thoreau in the address; it marks the point of departure for his defense of Brown.[74] After Brown's raid, Thoreau, presumably not unlike many in his audience, "read all the newspapers I could get within a week...." Indeed, in recognition of the fact that even before gathering together at the First Parish Meetinghouse those assembled had already participated in a communal ritual by way of the shared experience of reading the papers, Thoreau promises from the outset to "omit, as much as possible, what you have already read." Throughout the speech, then, he quotes from and quibbles with various recently printed accounts in order to vindicate Brown from oft-repeated characterizations of him as "a dangerous man," "undoubtedly insane." (It's no leap to read Thoreau's address as a prose rendering of Dickinson's well-known poem "Much madness is Divinest Sense": "Assent—and you are sane—/Demur—you're straightway dangerous—".) Made timid by a fear of alienating subscribers, editors, according to Thoreau, including Garrison at *The Liberator*, cannot "print truth." Of course, newspapers, as Elisa Tamarkin has pointed out, were a particular *bête noire* for Thoreau.[75] "Most men," Thoreau writes in *Walden*, "vegetate and dissipate their faculties in what is called easy reading," such as the daily papers. To a philosopher, he says memorably, "all news, as it is called, is gossip, and they who edit and read it are old women over their tea."[76] Yet Thoreau's disapproval of the news as a medium of truth and his unfortunately gendered metaphor for editorial pusillanimity are both complicated by the particular kind of event that was Brown's attempt on Harpers Ferry. Far from being mere gossip, to Thoreau it is "pregnant news," the kind of event that brings forth life, possessing a lasting meaning and significance that exceeds the ephemerality of, say, base politics. Indeed, extending the metaphor of parturition in a peculiarly gender-bending way, Thoreau says that "office-seekers and speech-makers...do not so much as lay an honest egg," for most of what counts as "news" is unlikely to hatch anything at all. By contrast, Thoreau thinks that Brown's raid "is the best news America has ever heard."[77] He, therefore, urges editors to "exclude the [sterile, lifeless] reports of religious and political conventions, and publish the words of a *living* man" (emphasis mine).[78]

As Tamarkin shows, the rise and predominance of daily newspapers in the United States, beginning around 1830—roughly coinciding with the advent of Garrisonian immediatism, I might add—marked an important new site of presentism in U.S. culture, one that exerted pressure on writers of fiction, poetry, and essays, who were forced to contend with "impatient audiences" demanding a "recency" and novelty often at odds with "the more layered and synthetic attitude toward time that literature sustains."[79] Such readerly expectations bear a strong resemblance to romantic presentism to the extent that both "embraced the tempo-rality of a particular and fleeting present as the most meaningful horizon of his-torical experience."[80] In this regard, it's no surprise that Emerson would be among the most ardent champions of the new temporal modes generated by the age of news. "Newspapers," he said, "are the proper literature of America."[81] Nor is it a surprise, given Tamarkin's investment in the basic historicist notion that literature "must inescapably refer to the immediacy of its contexts," that she would describe such "faith in the primacy of the present" as essentially a- or antihistorical, linked both to "a culture of liberal individualism that depends on a pervasive disregard for precedent and prior attachments" and to familiar "American narratives of progress."[82] However, what Tamarkin calls "the temporal logic of the news" diverges from romantic presentism insofar as the investments of the former are ahistorical and straightforwardly progressive. Neither Thoreau nor Emerson, whether derisive or in praise of the news, is easily assimilable to such an analysis, for both under-stood the present as a far more dynamic, replete, and asynchronous domain than the ephemeral "self-sufficient present that the newspaper produces."[83]

For Thoreau, for example, the news of Brown's raid isn't just linked to a (re)pro-ductive future unmindful of the past. Instead, Thoreau repeatedly emphasizes Brown's untimeliness, describing him in dizzyingly asynchronous terms. Unlike those who "ran down like a clock," expiring as if on schedule, Brown's death resists intercalation. He is, paradoxically, both the man of the moment and a figure from another time, both a "living man" and already dead. So on the one hand, Thoreau can "rejoice that I live in this age—that I am his contemporary," while on the other, he says that Brown "was an old-fashioned man."[84] He was "one of that class of whom we hear a great deal, but...see nothing at all—the Puritans." "It would be vain to kill him," Thoreau continues, for he "died lately in the time of Cromwell, but he reappeared here."[85] Thoreau does not just anticipate a death that is inevitable and very close at hand (a mere matter of weeks; or even "this morning, perchance"); he also dates that yet-to-occur death both two centuries in the past ("the time of Cromwell") and very recently ("lately"). All of which is to say that the "pregnant news" of Brown's raid is so temporally fecund that it leaves conventional linear chronology, the forward-marching time of the news and national progress, with its series of rigidly distinct self-contained now-points, in complete disarray.

It may well be, too, that the future Brown portends—a future that "veils its face," as Melville would put it in his discomfiting poem about Brown—is similarly in disarray, perhaps even in precisely the way that Catherine Beecher imagined it would be almost a quarter century earlier. That is, while the news of Harpers Ferry does indeed herald a future, the lineaments of that future remain disquietingly, or perhaps terrifyingly, if you are a cautious moderate, hidden from view. In this regard, the "slowly swaying" Brown of Melville's "The Portent" duplicates in more historically pressing terms the general philosophical situation Ahab thunders against in "The Quarter-Deck" chapter of *Moby-Dick*: "in each event," Ahab tells Starbuck, "in the living act, the undoubted deed—there, some unknown but still unreasoning thing puts forth the mouldings of its features...." Similarly, in "The Portent," all that can be seen of Brown's features is his "streaming beard," which, like a meteor, augurs who knows what? As if following that trailing tail, at the end of "A Plea" Thoreau turns *his* face toward the unknown future. He quotes Brown's own words, drawn from an interview with Brown conducted in Charlestown prison on October 18 and widely printed in newspapers all over the country. The people of the South, Brown says, should:

> prepare yourselves for a settlement of [the slavery] question, that must come up for settlement sooner than you are prepared for it. The sooner you are prepared the better. You may dispose of me very easily, I am nearly disposed of now; but this question is still to be settled—this negro question, I mean; the end of that is not yet.[86]

Looking forward to his own death and its aftereffects, Brown emphasizes that the "settlement" of the slavery debates is, above all, a matter of time—a matter, that is, of conflicting attitudes toward the workings of time: the sedate, protracted time of cautious political and economic calculation or the impetuous hastening that Brown himself incites. Justice, Brown warns, is bound to outpace preparation. Brown's words prompt Thoreau to look forward to looking back, to envisage a future when "Slavery shall be no more here": "I foresee the time when the painter will paint that scene," Thoreau says, and when "the historian record it." Whether that time is near or far, however, Thoreau doesn't say, even though he is clearly impatient for it, so much so that his concluding expression of sorrow ("We shall then be at liberty to weep for Captain Brown") gives way to an unspecified threat that feigns a kind of patient waiting until the moment is right, but in fact conveys the restive, anticipatory tension of one who *can't* wait to act: "Then, and not till then, we will take our revenge."[87]

Thoreau appears to have recycled this sentence, altering its terms only slightly while retaining its structure, from one that Emerson writes near the end of "Experience": "Patience and patience, we shall win at last."[88] The hint of violence in Thoreau's version marks the difference between 1844 and 1859, before and after

Harpers Ferry, but otherwise the rhyme is hard to miss. Both advise patience as a way of registering a kind of hopeful *im*patience, as a way of reminding themselves that one ought not to be paralyzed by the fact that one cannot know outcomes, neither the what nor the when, in advance. Yet, "there never was a right endeavor," Emerson says, "but that succeeded."[89] This is Thoreau and Emerson's version of Grimké's "walking by faith, not by sight," or what Emerson in "Experience" calls *"the universal impulse to believe."*[90] The accent in that phrase, prefiguring the final line of "On Freedom," belongs at least as much on "impulse" as it does on belief. An impulse is a desire or urge to act unreflectively, the very opposite of premeditation. Physiologically, impulses are electrical currents, signs of life and vitality: "Man lives by pulses,"[91] Emerson says. These two senses of impulse provide "Experience" with its narrative drama, like the defibrillation of a cardiac patient— "up again, old heart!" Emerson says at the essay's end—as Emerson goes from a state of near-death at the essay's opening to renewed life at its conclusion.[92]

That reanimation depends upon Emerson extricating himself from linear chronology and accepting the conditions of the dynamic present. The essay's famous opening image identifies a specifically temporal dilemma where we, along with Emerson, find ourselves "in a series of which we do not know the extremes":

> We wake and find ourselves on a stair; there are stairs below us, which we seem to have ascended; there are stairs above us, many a one, which go upward and out of sight. But the Genius which according to the old belief stands at the door by which we enter, and gives us the lethe to drink, that we may tell no tales, mixed the cup too strongly, and we cannot shake off the lethargy now at noonday.[93]

A basic image of progress and straightforward linear chronology, the stair implies both a past behind us and a determinate future toward which we are headed. But the destination, the termination of the staircase, remains "out of sight," just as the lethe, over-concocted, induces a complete loss of memory, leaving us stuck in the middle ("noonday") with neither history nor prospect. The result is a state of somnolence, as "Sleep lingers all our lifetime about our eyes, as night hovers all day in the boughs of the fir-tree."[94]

To rouse himself from the state of lethargy he describes in the essay's opening, Emerson strives throughout the bulk of the remaining pages "to set up the strong present tense," that is, to learn how to rightly perceive and inhabit *now*. In the essay's opening image, Emerson misapprehends the present, viewing it as the cause, rather than the potential solution to, his lethargy. The staircase provides a figure for sequential time, in which one moment follows another with dull, plodding, mind-numbing regularity, each step, each moment, identical in form to the one before and the one that follows. The stair is thus the architecture of sleepwalking. This is what we might call a "weak" present tense, a present that is, as Sharon Cameron has argued, "dissociated from all other moments."[95] The present that Emerson comes to celebrate in the essay, however, is not one that is distinct from that which comes before and that which follows, thereby arresting time. Indeed, it can't be "dissociated from all other moments" because it is what produces them.

Rather than an isolated point in a series or a single bead along a string, to use another of the essay's temporal images, the present moment, the "strong" present tense, is characterized by movement, change, flux, and novelty. In the present, as George Herbert Mead reminds us, something is always going on. Emerson's term for this defining feature of the present is surprise. "Life is a series of surprises," he says,

> and would not be worth taking or keeping if it were not. God delights to isolate us every day, and hide from us the past and the future. We would look about us, but with grand politeness he draws down before us an impenetrable screen of purest sky, and another behind us of purest sky. "You will not remember," he seems to say, "and you will not expect."[96]

Here Emerson returns, in a very different tenor, to the essay's opening image of a past and a future veiled from sight. But the bewilderment and despondency of finding oneself lost in a "series" has given way to another, more buoyant mood, as Emerson begins to revel in what might be called the joys of unknowing. Susceptibility to such joys, however, becomes possible only when we relinquish our ordinary understanding of succession and the movement of history, when we let go of our desire to "adjust ourselves...to the perfect calculation of the kingdom of known cause and effect."[97] Emerson recognizes the appeal of such calculations, which, as Neal Dolan explains, provide experience with "a sense of structure, order, and intelligibility."[98] Yet it is the upending of such order that Emerson welcomes: "But, ah! *presently* comes a day, or is it only a half-hour, with its angel-whispering,—which discomfits the conclusions of nations and years!" (emphasis mine).[99]

Obviously, in 1844, Emerson could not have been thinking of John Brown and Harpers Ferry, even though I can't also help but note the (perhaps) uncanny fact that Thoreau describes Brown as "an angel of light" or that, dislodged from its numerical context, Emerson's statement effectively captures the widespread sense, in the North and South, that Brown's raid had unsettled an already fragile order in some uncertain but epochal way, that the Union and its history had been altered in some fundamental but not-yet-apparent manner. Notwithstanding his seeming prescience, the more important point here is that in "Experience" Emerson models a vision of history as "surprise." That is, he articulates a view of history that locates "power" and "genius," two of the key terms of the essay, in "spontaneity" and "newness" and "sudden discoveries" and the "unlooked-for result."[100] This present-oriented vision aligns with the vision of social justice and social change promoted by immediatist abolitionists whose willingness to act on impulse and their immediate perception of right discomfited those devoted to "nations and years," to the slow, ameliorative time of national progress.

Knowing Not

Emerson's immediatism, in both its philosophical and its abolitionist guises, lies at the heart of his conception of history. Although admittedly intricate and at times seemingly contradictory, Emerson's historical vision has received relatively little focused attention, at least as compared, say, to his politics, his epistemology, or his theories of individualism and democracy. And those scholars who have examined it have typically linked Emerson's hostility to the past to various notions of linear progress, whether by way of Hegelian dialectics, evolutionary racial theory, or the classic Whig interpretation of history.[101] Emerson certainly did at times express faith in the notion that in its broadest sweep, history tends toward liberty, or, in Martin Luther King, Jr's words, that "the arc of the moral universe bends toward justice."[102] However, as my discussion of Emerson's immediatism to this point has sought to demonstrate, neither the pace, the precise trajectory, nor the mechanisms of that hoped-for liberty could be discerned in advance. For that reason, Emerson challenged, rather than accepted, as Dolan claims, the idea that history is a "linear narrative of gradual emancipatory ascent."[103] Emerson was far too restless and eager for change to find gradualism in any form very satisfying. "The soul is impatient of masters and eager for change," he wrote in 1850.[104] Moreover, as James R. Guthrie has shown persuasively, Emerson had a longstanding "aversion to linear time," an aversion, as I've shown, discernible in "Experience."[105] The patience, passivity, and willingness to wait necessitated by acceding to slow, straightforward, chronological progress Emerson found both unendurable and unenviable. So however much Emerson's emancipatory hope and faith derived from his transcendental belief that "the sentiment of right...is the voice of the universe," it did not follow from that belief that one ought to rest, that one has nothing to do *now*.[106] As he put it in his own praise of John Brown, the old man "was an idealist. He believed in his ideas to that extent, that he existed to put them all into action. He did not believe in moral suasion;—he believed in putting the thing through."[107] Brown thus embodied the "true romance" that Emerson describes in the famous closing sentence of "Experience": "the transformation of genius into practical power."[108]

The basis of Emerson's praise of Brown—"putting the thing through"—as well as the terms of his abolitionism after 1850 not only reveal, although in retrospect, some of the political force of "Experience." They also recapitulate the presentist theory of history Emerson developed in his first series of essays, most emphatically in "History" and "Circles."[109] Together those two essays delineate a heterodox view of history that might be described as Emerson's preabolitionist immediatism, which just so happens to coincide with what many scholars describe as the period of his preimmediatist abolitionism—that is, the moment that marks his tentative, reluctant entrance into the antislavery movement. Aside from some early journal entries criticizing the zealotry of abolitionists, the primary locus of this latter strain of Emerson's thinking is his first major public utterance on the question of slavery, his "An Address...on...the Emancipation of the Negroes in the West

Indies," delivered in Concord on August 1, 1844, the ten-year anniversary of West Indian emancipation. Seemingly tepid in comparison to his more strident post-1850 speeches, the West Indies address appears to advocate a gradualist approach to emancipation, providing, according to some critics, yet another example of Emerson's "patient politics" and his "relatively conservative abolitionist position."[110] The address takes on a different and more urgent cast, however, when read in relation to his earlier musings on history, not just in relation to his later pronouncements on slavery; when read, that is, as much for its historiography as for its abolitionism.

Among Emerson's most direct statements of his philosophy of history is the essay appropriately titled "History," which he placed at the start of *Essays* (1841), underscoring the importance of his conception of history to the collection as a whole. Significant portions of the essay are drawn from the first and last lectures in his series "The Philosophy of History," the former delivered in 1836 and the latter in 1837.[111] Although more concerned with the reading, rather than the writing, of history, the essay seeks to reorient readers' relationship to the past by keeping them mindful of the present. Hostile toward the materials out of which conventional histories are made—chronology, facts, names, places—"History" argues passionately against the pastness of the past, staking out a position that might easily be misconstrued as antihistorical.[112] In fact, the essay is as aggressive an attack upon historicist norms as has ever been written. Yet conventional history writing, Emerson says in the 1836 lecture, is "barren and wearisome" because it blunts lived experience. "The student...reads history as he would read the tables of a Life Assurance Company," he says sardonically, "which affirmed that the births were ten thousand and the deaths were eight thousand."[113] In a variation of the distinction at work in "On Freedom," Emerson objects to treating history as merely an object of knowledge, the dull and lifeless compilation of data, rather than as a type of action or experience.

Thus "History" calls for history's revivification. The past, he insists, is no foreign country but is directly, immediately accessible: "There is one mind common to all individual men," he writes in "History," "Every man is an inlet to the same and to all of the same...What Plato has thought, he may think; what a saint has felt; he may feel; what at any time has befallen any man, he can understand."[114] These claims are unapologetically, aggressively presentist: "The fact narrated," Emerson continues, "must correspond to something in me to be credible or intelligible. We, as we read, must become Greeks, Romans, Turks, priest and king, martyr and executioner; must fasten these images to some reality in our secret experience, or we shall learn nothing rightly."[115] Rather than respecting the otherness of the past, Emerson seeks to dislodge things—deeds, feelings, and experiences—from their particular contexts and to insist upon their availability across time, rather than embedding them ever more deeply within a single moment in time. That is, rather than insisting upon their distinctness and remoteness, which risks rendering them unavailable or unintelligible to us, Emerson insists upon their nearness and immediacy: "the moral sentiment," he says, "speaks one and the same voice in all ages," and "I have no expectation that any man will read history aright who thinks that what was done in a remote age, by men whose names have resounded far, has any deeper sense than what he is doing today."[116]

This perception of the identity and nearness of things is antichronological insofar as it refuses to assign (or consign) things to specific segments in time. For Emerson, the value of the productions of the past is their availability *now*, their immediacy. "The student is to read history actively," he writes, "and not passively"; he is "to esteem his own life the text and books the commentary."[117] Such statements might appear to promote the very assimilationist mindset that haunts the historicist. But, in fact, Emerson makes almost precisely the inverse point, casting the actions and actors of the past as the encroachers: the reader of history "should see that he can live all history in his own person. He must sit solidly at home, and not suffer himself to be bullied by kings or empires, but know that he is greater than all the geography and all the government of the world."[118] Here Emerson calls not for an assimilation of the past to the present, but a resistance to the *past's* colonizing power. This resistance is accomplished by way of a perspectival shift, one that entails a refusal of chronology's and contextualism's proprietary regime: "he must transfer the point of view from which history is commonly read, from Rome and Athens and London, to himself, and not deny his conviction that he is the court, and if England or Egypt have anything to say to him he will try the case."[119]

This irreverently antihistoricist claim—that in the present we *should* judge the past—is the point of Emerson's playful characterization in "History" of the "There or Then" as "preposterous," a term that recalls the original, temporal dimension of the term—placing what should appear later (the *posterus*) before (*pre*).[120] That which is "preposterous" in other words "inverts in position or order." Historical inquiry's ordinary sequence, in which the present follows from the past as if it were the (later) effect of a (prior) cause, reverses what for Emerson is the truth of history—that the past follows from the present, that chronological time and the knowingness it enables (or produces) thwarts historical experience. By contrast, Emerson seeks a relationship with the past in which things "live again to the mind, or are now."[121]

The insistence upon *living* here echoes both Emerson's later critique of Webster's adoration of dead Adams's and Jefferson's over living ones and the process of reanimation that drives "Experience." To emphasize the living present is to extol experience over knowledge. True history, for Emerson, which resides in sameness, not difference, can't be had by way of knowledge, it must be experienced. "The grossest ignorance does not disgust like this impudent knowingness," he says in "Experience." In "History," he is likewise hostile to the stuff of knowledge: "I hold our actual knowledge very cheap," he says; facts only "encumber" and "tyrannize."[122] Instead, Emerson grounds his historical sensibility in experience and feeling, as in his reading of Sophocles:

> I admire the love of nature in the Philoctetes. In reading those fine apostrophes to sleep, to the stars, rocks, mountains, and waves, I feel time passing away as an ebbing sea. I feel the eternity of man, the identity of his thought. The Greek had,

it seems, the same fellow-beings as I. The sun and moon, water and fire, met his heart precisely as they meet mine. Then the vaunted distinction between Greek and English, between Classic and Romantic schools, seems superficial and pedantic. When a thought of Plato becomes a thought to me,—when a truth that fired the soul of Pindar fires mine, time is no more. When I feel that we two meet in a perception, that our two souls are tinged with the same hue, and do, as it were, run into one, why should I measure degrees of latitude, why should I count Egyptian years?[123]

The counting of Egyptian years here is analogous to Emerson's counting of hours in the journal entry on his insomnia. Both leave him beholden to the dull, plodding uniformity of chronological succession, which is inimical to the firings of the soul that vanquish time's measurements and quantifications. The "identity," the sameness, that is so crucial to Emerson's antihistoricist conception of history, rendering the "distinctions" of traditional historical understanding "superficial and pedantic," is not something one comes to know; it is something one "feels."

Measured against such an unconventional conception of history, Emerson's West Indies address, which finds him taking on the role of historian, might seem a failure by his own standards. After all, Emerson devotes roughly two-thirds of his remarks to a more or less straightforward recounting of the available facts surrounding the decades-long efforts by which the British eliminated first the slave trade and finally slavery throughout the Empire. Emerson's version of that story relies heavily on Thomas Clarkson's *The History of the Rise, Progress, and Accomplishment of the Abolition of the African Slave Trade by the British Parliament*, first published in 1808 and updated in 1839, and it accepts both the linear-chronological narrative shape and the thematic emphasis on legislative processes that Clarkson's title announces with so little subtlety. It's possible that Emerson also read and drew upon Catherine Beecher's *Essay on Slavery and Abolitionism*, if not specifically in preparation for the West Indies address, then perhaps some time earlier as it circulated among his family and circle of friends after its publication in 1837. In any case, Beecher likewise drew heavily on Clarkson, treating him and his fellow British abolitionists with the same kind of deference and reverence that Emerson displays. British emancipation, Emerson writes, "was a stately spectacle" in which "the cause of human rights" was pursued "with so much patience and generosity."[124] "All was achieved," Emerson says, "by plain means of plain men."[125] Similarly, Beecher notes that the British campaign was "conducted by some of the wisest and most talented statesmen, as well as the most pious men, in the British nation" and was "conducted slowly, peaceably, and by eminently judicious influences."[126] Rather than the dangerous intemperance of U.S. abolitionists like Garrison, Beecher admires and advocates for the "patience and magnanimity" that typified British emancipation.

Just as Emerson's history of British emancipation seems at odds with Emerson's sense of history, so might it seem to be at odds with his abolitionism. That is, given his post-Compromise radicalism, his exasperation after 1850 with the administration of legislative affairs, and his contemptuousness in 1844's "Experience" toward the prudent calculations that leave one paralyzed and in a state of lethargy, his echoes of Beecher's conservatism and his celebration of such a protracted, dully procedural route toward emancipation might strike one as comparatively meek. It might also appear to confirm Dolan's assertion that the speech adheres to a conventionally liberal "progressive sense of history."[127] Yet the legislative history of British emancipation is not the only, nor even the most vital, history Emerson has to tell in the address; it's just that, ten years after its culmination, its events, facts, dates, and actors documented, gathered together, and assembled into orderly form, it's the story more easily told. What gives the address its edge, organizing both its dramatic movement and its vacillation between commendation and rage, is the second, more urgent and less settled history Emerson invokes to perturb the triumphal narrative the address foregrounds. Unlike the history of emancipation, the history of slavery remains both hidden and unfinished, a fact that attenuates the praise Emerson lavishes upon the heroes of the British cause. Before commencing his rehearsal of their campaign, for instance, Emerson laments his inability to provide an account of this other history. "Language must be raked," he says, "the secrets of slaughter-houses and infamous holes that cannot front the day, must be ransacked, to tell what negro-slavery has been."[128] Because I cannot tell *that* history, Emerson seems to suggest, because I have neither the language with which to adequately convey its abominations nor access to its most terrible "secrets," I will make do with this other history.[129] Yet unlike West Indian emancipation, slavery's history continues into the present, as Emerson's present-perfect tense— "what negro-slavery *has been*"—makes clear. The enslavement of Africans extends "from the earliest time…down to the day that has just dawned on the world," Emerson notes, deploying an image that, uncharacteristically, is no metaphor, but that calls attention to this day, *right now*, the first of August 1844.

But because slavery's hidden history is concealed away in obscure places that hoard its dark truths, it remains less accessible to narrative recounting. Emerson punctuates his narrative with what glimpses of this hidden history are available to him from his own reading, but recognizes that no verbal representation can produce the same kind of affective response as direct experience. For that reason, Emerson goes out of his way to underscore that his own accounts of slavery's atrocities are themselves retellings, as in the graphic, anaphoric passage that precedes his account of the British antislavery movement:

> …if we saw the whip applied to old men, to tender women; and, undeniably, though I shrink to say so,—pregnant women set in the treadmill for refusing to work, when, not they, but the external law of animal nature refused to work;—if we saw men's backs flayed with cowhides, and 'hot rum poured on, superinduced with brine or pickle, rubbed in with a cornhusk, in the scorching heat of the sun;'—if we saw the runaways hunted with blood-hounds into swamps and hills; and, in cases of passion, a planter throwing his negro into a copper of boiling cane-juice,—if we saw these things with eyes, we too should wince.[130]

Unable to convey the immediacy of such atrocities, Emerson places them instead in a conditional past tense ("if we saw") that evokes the possibility of a future witnessing. Evidently unable to generate any expression of outrage adequate to such scenes, past or to come, he resorts to understatement—"They are not pleasant sights," he says—and then turns his attention to the circulation of such tales. "Well, so it happened," he says, "a good man or woman, a country-boy or girl, it would so fall out, once in a while saw these injuries, and had the indiscretion to tell of them. The horrid story ran and flew; the winds blew it all over the world."[131] Here, in a reversal of his stand against rumors of wrath in "Experience," Emerson likens the dissemination of the "horrid" truths of slavery to the spread of gossip, the indiscreet loose-talk of country schoolchildren. Blown by the winds, this information spreads rapidly ("it ran and flew") and irregularly, its sources obscured and its effects uncertain.

That Emerson would cast this more vital history in terms of the diffuse circulations of rumor is all the more ironic given his critique in "History": "I am ashamed," he writes near the end of the essay, "to see what a shallow village tale our so-called History is. How many times we must say Rome, and Paris, and Constantinople!"[132] Such a statement undercuts the importance of grand, epoch-making histories—the rise and fall of empires—and reduces them to provincial gossip. The statement might seem to mitigate, too, Emerson's extravagant praise of British emancipation, which he describes as an event "signal in the history of civilization," "a moral revolution."[133] But as Emerson describes them, moral revolutions, unlike political ones, are peculiar events, unfolding according to their own historical logic: "All the facts in history are fables, and untrustworthy," he says in his second address celebrating emancipation in the West Indies, this one in 1845, "beside the dictates of the moral sentiment which speaks one and the same voice in all ages."[134] It's a sentence that might just as well have been taken from "History." There Emerson also insists on the "one mind common to all individual men" across history: "Every revolution," he says, "was first a thought in one man's mind, and when the same thought occurs to another man, it is the key to that era."[135]

What's most striking about the 1844 West Indies address is the way that Emerson registers, alongside the more conventional (fabular and, by comparison, perhaps even "untrustworthy") history he tells, the kinds of spontaneous meetings of mind, firings, and occurrences that "History" so cherishes. Gossip and rumor provide an apt figure for such happenings insofar as their underground, indirect, anonymous, and tantalizing modes of circulation defy history writing's ordinary, orderly explanatory schemes. This is to say that while Emerson provides a reasonably detailed, factual account of the *administration* of emancipation—the actions of the principal figures, the political organizing, the legislative maneuvering, and the implementation of laws and economic policies—a second, far less scrutable process of change proves to be the more powerful force driving the movement. In relation to that force, Clarkson, Parliament, planters, the colonial governors, and Wilberforce and Lord Brougham are merely instruments.

However, this other, unofficial history can only be glimpsed by way of affective states, emotions, and bodily sensations that belong, at once, to no one in particular and to everyone. "Conscience rolled on its pillow and could not sleep," Emerson says as a way of beginning his history of emancipation, suggesting that a general awakening was the crucial first step to the pursuit of any scheme.[136] The image is a slightly more vivid rendering of the "painful sensation" he describes waking up with in the 1851 Fugitive Slave Law address. "The blood is moral," Emerson continues, describing the somatic responses slavery's brutalities induce, "the blood is antislavery: it runs cold in the veins: the stomach rises with disgust, and curses slavery."[137] As the "tragic anecdotes" spread and fly, carried by the winds, more and more people experience these sensations: "the nation was aroused to enthusiasm," the "outrages kindled the flame of British indignation," man's sense of justice "ripened," "flashing out," suddenly and spontaneously and "open[ing] the eyes of the dullest in Britain."[138] These heightened states contrast sharply with the equanimity and the peaceable, cool-headed deliberations that characterize the efforts of the British abolitionists.

The importance of this alternative, affective history becomes clear when Emerson interrupts his historical narrative and fixes his gaze upon the present. At that moment he adopts not the stately composure of the heroes of British emancipation, but the hot-blooded urgency of one recently aroused: "Forgive me, fellow citizens, if I own to you that in the last few days that my attention has been occupied with this history, I have not been able to read a page of it without the most painful comparisons. Whilst I have read of England, I have thought of New England."[139] Then, having brought his audience back to the here and now, Emerson returns to scenes of slavery's atrocities in a passage that parallels his earlier list, but this time in a present-tense that positions him as an eye witness. Instead of the "patriots and senators who have adopted the slave's cause," Emerson says:

> I see other pictures—of mean men: I see very poor, very ill-clothed, very ignorant men, not surrounded by happy friends,—to be plain,—poor black men of obscure employment as mariners, cooks, or stewards, in ships, yet citizens of this our Commonwealth of Massachusetts,—freeborn as we,—whom the slave laws of the States of South Carolina, Georgia, and Louisiana, have arrested in the vessels in which they visited those ports, and shut up in jails so long as the vessel remained in port...these men, I see, and no law to save them.[140]

The scandal of kidnapping free blacks in Massachusetts leads Emerson, in what may be the address's most heated moment, to call for Congress and the President to take immediate action—"forthwith," he says—using force if necessary, to release those taken into slavery under such circumstances. As for potential objections to such a rash move, Emerson brushes them away like a true Garrisonian disunionist: "As for dangers to the Union, from such demands!—the Union is already at an end, when the first citizen of Massachusetts is thus outraged."[141]

My reading of the impassioned undercurrent that disturbs the more "process-oriented" history Emerson foregrounds in the West Indies address parallels, and in some ways is indebted to, Schoolman's trenchant reading of the "dialectic of love and hate" that constituted Emerson's pre-1850s abolitionism and, in particular, his "engagement with the Garrisonian politics of affront."[142] For Schoolman, this dialectic accounts for what she describes as Emerson's "mixed representation of civility" in the address, in which he "compensates analytically for the distinctions between British and American governance by emphasizing the importance of extra-governmental antislavery agitation to the British emancipation process" while also "criticiz[ing] the politesse of American legislators who would avoid discussion about slavery."[143] Instead, Schoolman notes, Emerson praises another collection of emancipators: "Toussaint, and the Haytian heroes... [and] the leaders of their race in Barbadoes and Jamaica."[144] The brief reference to the Haitian revolution marks an important culminating point in Emerson's performance, one that links the West Indies address to the most unsettling (a term I use here deliberately) elements of his abolitionist and historiographical immediatism. Yet it's on this point that my reading deviates slightly from Schoolman's insofar as she too depicts Emerson's historiography as shaped by a familiar "progressive narrative" rooted in "a typically romantic belief in a general evolution from brutality to enlightenment."[145] In this chapter's final section I want to push back against that characterization—and further specify the terms of Emerson's historical vision—by looking at one more of Emerson's essays, the radical and unnerving "Circles," in order to distinguish between such familiar narratives of progress and what Emerson in the West Indies address calls "the tendency of things."[146]

Unsettling Things

The theory of history Emerson articulates in "Circles" draws on language inextricable from the moral and political debates over slavery, and deploys imagery broadly resonant with descriptions of the violence and social upheaval many moderates believed would surely be wrought by the actions and rhetoric of irresponsibly reckless abolitionist radicals like Garrison. Obversely, I suggest, Emerson's view of abolition in the West Indies emancipation address is ultimately informed by the sense of history—as unsettled, fitful, and tending in unforeseen directions, rather than the gradual, incremental teleology of progressive amelioration—enunciated in "Circles." West Indian emancipation represents, for Emerson, the sort of emergent event that is apt, to borrow an image from "Circles," to shake and rattle all that is reckoned settled. "The First of August marks the entrance of a *new element* into modern politics," he says as he nears the end of the address, "namely, the civilization of the negro... Not the least affecting part of this history of abolition, is, the annihilation of the old indecent nonsense about the nature of the negro" (emphasis mine).[147]

Emerson's alignment of emancipated "negroes" with newness is the culminating move of the address, as he turns from his rehearsal of the past to gaze toward the future. Appropriately, given the occasion, he concludes on a note of tentative hopefulness, although he concedes that there remains "room for the infusions of a skeptical philosophy." His optimism derives from a sense that "the time [has] arrived when [blacks] can strike in with effect and take a master's part in the music...now, let them emerge and clothed in their own form."[148] Precisely what that "form" will be Emerson doesn't, or can't, specify, only that it won't resemble anything seen before. As he puts it in one of the address's best-known passages:

> When at last in a race, a new principle appears, an idea;—that conserves it; ideas only save races. If the black man is feeble, and not important to the existing races not on a parity with the best race, the black man must serve, and be exterminated. But if the black man carries in his bosom an indispensable element of a new and coming civilization, for the sake of that element, no wrong, nor strength, nor circumstance, can hurt him: he will survive and play his part.[149]

It's hard to disentangle these sentences from the theories of race, racial hierarchy, and racial developmentalism that preoccupied Emerson in vexing ways throughout his career; and the hint of "biological determinism" in these remarks has, understandably, struck readers as "disturbing."[150] There are echoes here, as well—especially in the possibility of the black race as the harbinger of a "new and coming civilization"—of the kind of romantic racialism widespread among antislavery northerners and rendered so vividly in *Uncle Tom's Cabin*, especially in its encomiums to Africa's glorious future.[151] Yet those aren't the only conversations in which the passage is involved. Emerson's concluding gestures also position him in relation to the more radical immediatists for whom the protracted and carefully planned history of British emancipation provided, perhaps, a measure of inspiration, but hardly a model path toward emancipation in the United States.[152]

For instance, Emerson recalls the remarks of his brother Charles, when he hails "the arrival in the world of such men as Toussaint, and the Haytian heroes, or of the leaders of their race in Barbadoes and Jamaica."[153] Their arrival, Emerson continues, "outweighs in good omen all the English and American humanity." Similarly, in his 1835 lecture in support of immediate emancipation, Charles also turned to Toussaint and the Haitian Revolution as harbingers of an untried future. As Colleen O'Brien notes in her perceptive reading of Charles's lecture, "retelling the story of the Haitian Revolution," Charles suggested, "would change the way people thought about race. He believed this retelling was characteristic of a new age."[154] Of course, neither Emerson could describe with any degree of certainty the precise contours of that new era. Rather, both men simply apprehend an "omen" or a "tendency." Yet it is the Emersons' attitude toward that uncertainty that distinguishes their immediatism from the gradualism of so many of their contemporaries who, as we've already seen, feared the unknown future and therefore sought to slow movement toward it. However, as Charles argued, "the evil is not in prospect." Rather, it is "seated & rioting in the bowels of the country" right now.[155] If for no other reason than that, the Emersons considered it a moral imperative to welcome, not to delay, the new. Indeed, "the moral sentiment," Waldo says in "Experience" "is called 'the newness.'"[156]

Although it was written three years earlier, "Circles," is an essay that picks up where "Experience" leaves off. Or to put the point less preposterously, "Circles" is the essay Emerson recalls in "Experience" in order to fight his way out of lethargy. "Step by step we scale this mysterious ladder," he writes near the beginning of "Circles," the image an only slightly modified version of the one that opens "Experience," "the steps are actions, the new prospect is power."[157] Where the later essay begins by describing a state of bewildered stasis and only arrives at the prospect of power in the essay's concluding sentence, "Circles" is from its opening sentence a manifesto for the power of ongoing action in a world of experience that is itself always in motion, undergoing continual transformation. "There are no fixtures to nature," Emerson says, "the universe is fluid and volatile," "every action admits of being outdone."[158] "every thing is medial" on the verge of "tumbling into the inevitable pit which the creation of new thought opens for all that is old."[159] Even the crucial sentence from "Experience"—"Life is a series of surprises"—appears verbatim in "Circles," although in the earlier essay, it's not "the past and the future" that God hides, but "the total growths and universal movements of the soul"; these, Emerson says, are "incalculable."[160] "Circles" thus celebrates the movements, the processes of recreation, readjustment, revisioning, and extemporizing, that are required to live in a world that is itself always in motion, whose "surface" (yet another image that turns up in "Experience") "is not fixed, but sliding."[161]

"Circles" also shares with "Experience" an idiom recognizable in debates over the temporality of abolitionism. As I've argued, "Experience" is an essay in which the speaker learns to divest himself of a certain kind of prudence, the sort of circumspection associated with political and philosophical conservatism and moderate forms of antislavery. The speaker of "Circles" has long since learned that same lesson. "The great man will not be prudent in the popular sense," Emerson writes, "all his prudence will be so much deduction from his grandeur."[162] Here Emerson returns, as if in refrain, to a theme in *Essays* established by another piece in the collection: the infrequently remarked-upon "Prudence." "Who is prudent?" Emerson asks there, "The men we call greatest are least in this kingdom."[163] He aligns prudence instead with the sensual world, calling it "the science of appearances"[164] and "the art of securing a present well-being."[165] The province of administrators and proceduralists, planners, and calculators, all those concerned with what Emerson calls, dismissively, "the inventing of means and methods...adroit steering...gentle repairing," prudence inhabits and promotes the slow time of postponement, delay, and deferral. "Life wastes itself whilst we are preparing to live," he says, sounding a Thoreauvian note.[166] In "Circles," which Emerson placed after "Prudence" in the collection, he identifies yet another stifling feature of prudence: that it can never release you from the very things it is meant to guard against. As he puts it, "it seems to me that with every precaution you take against... evil you put yourself into the power of the evil." Therefore, paradoxically, "the highest prudence is the lowest prudence."[167] Adopting, for a moment, the voice of one who might worry about haste or precipitancy, he asks, "Is this too sudden a rushing from the centre to the verge of our orbit?"[168] He answers that question in the essay's concluding paragraph, where he declares that "The way of life…is by abandonment," by which he means both relinquishing or letting go (of old ways of thinking and acting, conventions, and acquired habits) and acting with a certain heedless impetuosity, a sudden rushing unconcerned with what he calls prudence's "pitiful calculations."[169] "Circles" might thus be seen as an extended meditation on the maxim "right thou feelest rashly do."

But as much as "Circles" echoes "On Freedom" and "A Psalm of Life" in its commitment to rash action, the essay confronts more squarely the dangers that the poems for the most part suppress. Insofar as "Circles" devotes itself to recreation, readjustment, and revisioning, it must, by definition, devote itself to the preconditions of those activities: destruction, undoing, and unmaking—all those things that the cautiously prudent most fear. "The terror of reform," Emerson writes in acknowledgment of those fears, "is the discovery that we must cast away our virtues, or what we have always esteemed such, into the same pit that has consumed our grosser vices."[170] Emerson also deploys the word "terror" in "Self-Reliance," to describe the socially imposed demand for "consistency," or what he specifies as the "reverence for our past act or word."[171] In both instances, the term can seem somewhat out of proportion to the matter at hand, insofar as it tends to conjure up images of, say, the French Revolution or, as in Catherine Beecher, slave insurrection.[172] But the term's extremist connotations, and perhaps even those very images, are precisely the point: we cling to the old, Emerson asserts, because of an outsized fear of the new. That sort of disposition, the sort that sees subversive dangers and threats to moral and social stability around every corner, Emerson in "Circles" associates with "rest, conservatism, appropriation, inertia; not newness, not the way onward."[173] He advances another version of this critique in his 1855 "Lecture on Slavery," an address prompted by the rendition of the slave Anthony Burns in the spring of 1854 and delivered in Boston the following January. In it, Emerson assailed those who "wish their age should be absolutely like the last."[174] "There is no confession of destitution like this fierce conservatism," he continues, "What means this desperate grasp on the past, if not that they find no principle, no hope, no future in their mind? Some foundation we must have, and, if we can see nothing, we cling desperately to those whom we believe can see."[175] For Emerson in 1841 and 1855 alike, imagining a future, any future, inevitably entails accepting and responding to change in the present. Therefore, as an antidote to so desperately clinging to the past, Emerson advocates upsetting, rather than stabilizing "foundations." In doing so, he embraces and revels in the very terrors that beleaguer conservatives of all kinds: "Fear not the new generalization," he counsels insouciantly in "Circles."

Nowhere can the parallel tracks of Emerson's conception of history and his ethical commitment to abolition be seen as clearly as in his enthusiasm for the new. "New" is the pivotal term in "Circles." Emerson uses it more than thirty times in the essay, significantly more times than in any other essay in the collection, more even than in the entirety of *Nature*. To cite only a handful of instances: "New arts destroy the old"; "Every ultimate fact is only the first of a new series"; "The new statement is always hated by the old"; "A new degree of culture would instantly revolutionize the entire system of human pursuits"; "Why should we import rags and relics into the new hour?"; and "I cast away in this new moment all my once hoarded knowledge, as vacant and vain."[176] Of course, newness is also among the defining features of the present. As Emerson says, "In Nature every moment is new; the past is always swallowed and forgotten; the coming only is sacred. Nothing is secure but life, transition, the energizing spirit."[177] Here Emerson recasts a statement from "Self-Reliance": "Life only avails, not the having lived. Power ceases in the instant of repose; it resides in the moment of transition from a past to a new state, in the shooting of the gulf, in the darting to an aim. This one fact the world hates: that the soul *becomes*..."[178] To a certain extent, in these remarks Emerson joins in a long tradition of thinking about time—from Aristotle and St. Augustine to the phenomenologists and later theorists of temporal experience like Deleuze—that takes evanescence as the constitutive feature of the present; because it is by definition fleeting, a moment of transition, the present always, at every instant, escapes our apprehension.[179] George Herbert Mead, for instance, echoes Emerson when he asserts that what "marks a present is its becoming and its disappearing."[180]

Because his conception of the present and his devotion to the new bear such striking affinities with Emerson's, it's worth turning briefly again to Mead here to help elucidate this feature of Emerson's thought. For one thing, both depart from conventional depictions of the present as merely a series of discrete instants, each one identical to the last. Mead, for instance, seeks to recover the present of lived experience—or what he calls "the functional present"—which is defined by the ongoing activity in which we are engaged—"the darting to an aim," as Emerson puts it. "The functional boundaries of the present," Mead says, "are those of its undertaking—of what we are doing...we seldom have the sense of a set of isolated presents."[181] Emerson, too, defines the present in terms of doing: "every action admits of being outdone," he says, "around every circle another can be drawn... there is no end in nature, but every end is a beginning; that there is always another dawn risen on midnoon, and under every deep a lower deep opens."[182] In fact, it is remarkable just how closely Mead's philosophy of the present echoes Emerson's sense of "incessant movement."[183] Employing the same figure that commences "Circles," Mead writes:

> The presents...within which we live are provided with margins, and fitting them into a larger independent chronicle is again a matter of some more extended present which calls for a wider horizon. But the widest horizon belongs to some undertaking, whose past and future refer back to it. For instance, the present history of the sun is relevant to the undertaking of unravelling the atom and, given another analysis of the atom, the sun will have another history and the universe will be launched into a new future.[184]

Here Mead explains what might seem paradoxical: the theory of history that attends his own and Emerson's devotion to "newness." For both thinkers, the present is the precondition of the past; "novelty," "emergence," and "passage"— terms analogous to Emerson's "surprise," newness," and "transition"—generate history and historical consciousness.[185] Because in the present something always happens, each new event requires a new rendering of the past in order to account for its appearance. Mead again:

> Given an emergent event, its relations to antecedent processes become conditions or causes. Such a situation is a present. It marks out and in a sense selects what has made its peculiarity possible. It creates with its uniqueness a past and a future. As soon as we view it, it becomes a history and a prophecy.[186]

History, in other words, along with its conceptual vocabulary of cause and effect, continuity, and sequence, is a matter of constant adjustment and readjustment in order to integrate and incorporate the appearance of that which is novel, in order to heal the rift in (temporal) experience caused by new events. Our accounts of the past are our ways of explaining to ourselves, retrospectively, our arrival at the present; history thus lends temporal continuity to our experience. But because of emergence or newness, there are always disruptions, breaks in that continuity, at which point we once again set about reconstructing events in order to account for novel events. This is why the past, unlike the present, is provisional: it is produced as a way of reestablishing a continuity of experience disrupted by the emergence of something new. As Mead puts it in his essay "The Nature of the Past," "The past which we construct from the standpoint of the new problem of today is based upon continuities which we discover in that which has arisen, and it serves us until the rising novelty of tomorrow necessitates a new history which interprets the new future."[187]

These new histories we reconstruct, according to Mead, are not just serial additions, additional points along an ever-extending timeline; rather, they are complete renovations of the significance of the past order in its entirety, since the novel or new cannot be understood according to the old system—that's what makes it new. This ongoing process of reconstruction helps to explain why, in "Circles," Emerson so blissfully celebrates disruptive forces and displays, in stark contrast to worried gradualists, moderates, and unionists, such a surprising zeal for mayhem. "Beware when the great God lets loose a thinker on this planet," he writes, for example:

> Then all things are at risk. It is as when a conflagration has broken out in a great city, and no man knows what is safe, or where it will end. There is not a piece of science but its flank may be turned tomorrow; there is not any literary reputation, not the so-called eternal names of fame, that may not be revised and condemned.[188]

And later:

> When each new speaker strikes a new light, emancipates us from the oppression of the last speaker, to oppress us with the greatness and exclusiveness of his own

thought, then yields us to another redeemer, we seem to recover our rights, to become men...The facts which loomed so large in the fogs of yesterday,—property, climate, breeding, personal beauty and the like, have strangely changed their proportions. All that we reckoned settled shakes and rattles; and literatures, cities, climates, religions, leave their foundations and dance before our eyes.[189]

Instability, conflagration, and seismic events—these are Emerson's images for the powerful effects of the arrival of the new, which he describes in language ("emancipate," "oppression," and "rights") inextricable from the politics of slavery. Yet despite the violent imagery, of cities burning and foundations shaking, and the admonitory rhetoric, Emerson meets the prospect of such radical change not with apprehension and trepidation but with exultation. He even adopts the role of agent of such change, describing himself as an "experimenter." "I unsettle all things," he says, "No facts are to me sacred, none are profane; I simply experiment, an endless seeker with no Past at my back."[190] The kind of experimentation Emerson embraces—or embodies—in "Circles" entails adopting a course of action without any assurances or certainties with regard to consequences or results.

Such a process requires, or sparks, creativity. Indeed, because "the present is that which is going on," because its defining feature is passage, novelty, emergence, arrival, and newness, nature itself is, for Mead and Emerson alike, a creative, productive force. Our readjustments and reconstructions, our recreation of the world that was in order to account for emergence in the world that is are the means by which we solve problems, by which we generate new ways of acting and being in the world. This is something a past that is fixed and settled—dead—cannot accomplish. Hence, rather than viewing presentism as an attitude toward history that is ethically compromised, Mead sees presentism as a kind of ethical imperative: "We cannot interpret the meaning of our present through the history of the past because we must reconstruct that history through the study of the present...We cannot find the meaning of human life on earth in the present-day history of the earth." Like Emerson, Mead thinks that history as tradition, a past that is finished and stable, embodied in our customs and institutions, can never be the source of a new future.

This helps to explain Emerson's commitment in "Circles" to forms of thinking and action, (terms often synonymous for Emerson) that "unsettle." It helps to explain, too, why Emerson can augur emancipation—in Haiti, in the West Indies, and in a U.S. future that can't arrive soon enough—largely free of the trepidation and terror that bedeviled so many of his contemporaries: experimenting and unsettling identify a condition necessary for hope. For as Mead explains, there is no future, literally, without change and the adjustments and reconstructions it necessitates. Something must happen, Mead says "to and in the thing which affects the nature of the thing in order that one moment may be distinguishable from another, in order that there may be time."[191] Emerson, in "Circles," makes the same point more eloquently: "People wish to be settled," he says, "only as far as they are unsettled is there any hope for them."[192] Although playful, Emerson's statement here ought not to be taken as entirely figurative. It states, perhaps as directly and certainly as succinctly as anything he ever wrote, his view of time and history: the future, any future, depends upon the disruptive forces of change and flux; without the prospect of the new, without something that happens, something that "unsettles" present and past alike, there can be no time—and thus nothing to look forward to.

Frederick Douglass's Historical Turn

Early in his second autobiography, *My Bondage and My Freedom*, Frederick Douglass describes a lesson he learned as a child during the frightening journey he made with his grandmother from Tuckahoe to the Great House plantation on Wye River. Making their way through the woods, the young Douglass spies in the distance "old logs and stumps," which he takes for "wild beasts." He could "see their legs, eyes, and ears" until he "got close enough to them to see that the eyes were knots, washed white with rain, and the legs were broken limbs, and the ears, only ears owing to the point from which they were seen." Thus, early, Douglass concludes, "I learned that the point from which a thing is viewed is of some importance."[1]

At first glance, this seems a simple enough lesson: objects appear different from afar than from up close. A distant view, this experience teaches, might well be an inaccurate view and, therefore, ought not to prevent one from proceeding. But Douglass's tone here rather understates the importance of the point. In a penetrating exploration of the origins of Douglass's political philosophy, Nick Bromell has shown just how crucial this lesson was "to the persepectivalism . . . that emerges as a core principle of [Douglass's] life and work," his adoption of a "philosophical outlook" that embraced historical contingency.[2] In this chapter, I'd like to walk alongside Bromell, similarly emphasizing the importance of Douglass's hard-earned persepectivalism, but supplementing it by attending to its critically important temporal dimension. As the child Douglass moves closer and closer to the trees and stumps, his view of them changes. The alteration of the objects presented to his field of perception is not simply a function of space or distance, however; his movement toward these objects also occurs in time. For one thing, his initial view of the trees and stumps as wild beasts possesses the character of a frightening future; yet when that future becomes present, as he comes directly upon them, they lose their menacing character and provide him with a useful insight. Second, the story itself is a function of Douglass's memory. He begins the story by saying that he remembers it "as if it were yesterday." The lesson, in other words, has meaning only in retrospect; it is a function of Douglass's present understanding of his past. As such, the insight belongs not to the past to which Douglass attributes it, but to the present moment within which he constructs that past. The lesson, then, is as much about *historical* perspective, about one's particular attitude or bearing toward the "ongoingness" of events and the uncertainty of the future, as it is about spatial perspective.

In this chapter, I track Douglass's developing historical-temporal consciousness as it advances toward and beyond this moment in *My Bondage and My Freedom*, arriving eventually at a presentist view of history, predicated, to borrow a phrase from Dana Luciano, on "the time of the 'now,'" but also looking forward toward an unknown future.[3] Building upon the insights of critics like Luciano, Lloyd Pratt, Valerie Rohy, Gregory Laski, and Cody Marrs into the temporal intricacies and complexities of Douglass's writings, my task here is to map what I will describe as Douglass's historical turn of the early to mid 1850s. My contribution to this recent vein of inquiry will be to show that Douglass's philosophical engagement with history and temporal experience extends well beyond the autobiographies and his famous Fourth of July address (with its well-known emphasis on what is "useful to the present"). Developing a distinct theory of history formed one of the central preoccupations of his intellectual career during the 1850s.

The key element of Douglass's conception of and attitude toward history and historicity during this period is the movement from apprehension (fear of the future) to expectation (looking forward to the future become present). Rather than locating and explicating this turn by way of a sustained reading of a single text, however, I trace its arc across Douglass's speeches and writings during the ten-year period roughly between his return in 1847 from his first trip to England to his extraordinary response to the Dred Scott decision in 1857—the period, most critics agree, during which Douglass produced his most important literary work: *The Heroic Slave*, *My Bondage and My Freedom*, and his Fourth of July oratorical masterpiece. This was also a formative period in Douglass's life and thought, encompassing the founding of *The North Star*, his break with Garrison and embrace of political abolitionism, and his change of mind on the question of the Constitutionality of slavery. In addition to this list of important transformations, Douglass, also during this period, began a sweeping meta-historical engagement with the relations between past, present, and future, adopting the role of abolitionism's future historian—the historian of an abolitionist past that had not yet come to pass.[4] Eventually, Douglass accepted a present-oriented view of historical transformation, one that was forward looking, but neither steadily progressive nor teleological, hopeful but never certain.[5]

Over the Chapters 1 through 3, I have argued that romantic presentism in its various guises and sites helped to position antebellum writers in relation to versions of history not determined by the sequentialism of cause-and-effect, by linear chronology, by straightforward development, nor even by the notion that the past and present are separate and distinct. This experiential and experimental conception of history unsettled the past, freeing both it and the writers who sought to orient themselves to it from the kinds of fixity or unidirectional numerical determinism that gives the past power over the present, that provides certainty about the direction toward which the present tends, or that assigns things (texts, ideas, and phenomena) to their "proper" place in time. Douglass, a writer and thinker who is not ordinarily associated with the development of historical consciousness or even historical writing in the antebellum United States, occupies a pivotal place in this story, but not solely—nor even primarily—because of his role as one of the era's most influential and eloquent spokespersons for immediatist abolitionism, romantic presentism's most socially vital iteration. Rather, Douglass's vision of history rhymes at least as much with Emerson's and George Herbert Mead's as it does with Garrison's. More to the point, Douglass reveals some of the ways that romantic presentism disposed, adjusted, and addressed itself to the future as much as to the past.

Douglass's futural disposition and the importance of "the point from which a thing is viewed" provide the methodological scaffold and framework for the examination that follows. Each section of my analysis centers on an image of Douglass gazing into the future, one of the most striking recurring figures of the period that interests me here. These images function as revealing touchstones for the development of Douglass's historical consciousness, his ambivalences and perplexities, and his mature theory of history. As with Emerson's embrace of immediatist abolitionism, Douglass's development did not move precisely along a straight line, and for that reason I narrate it partially, but not strictly, chronologically, and focus primarily on Douglass's pre-Civil War thinking.[6] I begin with an examination of the incipient proleptic historiography in a number of Douglass's speeches and writings, moving toward the intellectual impasse—centered on the question of the Constitution—that gave rise to Douglass's full commitment to the unsettled present, looking briefly toward *The Heroic Slave* and *My Bondage and My Freedom*, and arriving finally at Douglass's most forceful expression of his newly acquired present-oriented perspective: his remarkable and underappreciated 1857 speech on the Dred Scott decision.

The Watchtower of Human Freedom

The defining feature of Douglass's historical sensibility was always anticipation, one of the asynchronous experiences that are a common feature of ordinary life, yet all the more urgent for a former slave whose early existence was defined in no small part by the anticipation of the very possibility of anticipation. As he puts it, famously, in *My Bondage and My Freedom*, "I longed to have a future—a future with hope in it."[7] An affective, rather than an analytical mode, anticipation suggests a complex of feelings, experiences, or even bodily sensations one can have toward and of the future: from prepossession (in the sense of being favorably disposed toward something), to presentiment (an intuition about what is to come, whether a good omen or a foreboding), apprehension (both a cognitive-temporal action, such as the forming of an idea, and a feeling of dread or anxiety about the future), and expectation (waiting, looking for something to occur or arrive, and, of course, hope). These varying senses of anticipation guide my investigation of this emergent phase of Douglass's historical turn. Although forward looking, anticipation always takes place in a now that is not so much fleeting and evanescent as it is *early*, drawing otherwise distant or remote futures nearer to hand. Its analogous representational techniques are prolepsis and foreshadowing, modes in which we already know (or perceive), in the present, that which has not yet happened.

An anticipatory bearing is a recurrent feature of Douglass's addresses of the late 1840s, one that becomes even more prominent in his writings of the 1850s. In the earlier addresses, Douglass begins to foretell the history of abolitionism, approaching that history as if he possessed knowledge of the future. This rhetorical strategy is akin to the one that Valerie Rohy identifies in Douglass's 1845 *Narrative*, which she describes in terms of the "future perfect" tense. In narrating their lives, both Douglass and Harriet Jacobs, Rohy argues, "anticipate the moment when they *will have been* slaves, and in the act of authorship that necessarily looks backward from that moment, then retroactively constructs the impulse of anticipation" (italics original).[8] The circularity of this procedure produces a state, an anachronistic enfolding of time, in which causes become effects and effects become causes. An important difference between the speeches and writings I examine here and the autobiographies, however, is that in the former we see Douglass's anticipations in real time, as it were. In this, they are the inverse of what Rohy examines in the *Narrative*: not retrospective anticipations, but anticipations of retrospection. That is, in the *Narrative*, as Rohy describes it, Douglass looks back to the moment when he looked forward to freedom. The temporal stance I examine here is of Douglass *looking forward to looking back*.

For example, in his 1847 farewell address to the British people, the culminating speech of his English tour, Douglass describes the history of the movement in which he is presently involved as though he possesses foreknowledge of how future generations will view its present work. "When the history of the emancipation movement shall have been fairly written," Douglass says, "it will be found that the abolitionists of the nineteenth century were the only men who dared to defend the Bible from the blasphemous charge of sanctioning and sanctifying Negro slavery." He continues:

> *It will be found* that [the abolitionists] were the only men who dared to stand up and demand, that the churches calling themselves by the name of Christ, should entirely, and for ever, purify themselves from all contact, connection, and fellowship with men who gain their fortunes by the blood of souls. *It will be found* that they were the men who, "cried aloud and spared not" [who] "lifted their voices like trumpets," against the giant iniquity by which they were surrounded. *It will then be seen* that they were the men who planted themselves on the immutable, eternal, and all-comprehensive of the sacred New Testament—"All things whatsoever ye would that men should do unto you, do ye even so unto them" (emphasis mine).[9]

Douglass here invites his audience to imagine how their present will look from the vantage of a future that sees it as past. The shift from the future-perfect to the simple-future tense projects a moment beyond emancipation's realization to a moment when its history has already been written—a moment that, in Douglass's dizzying rendering, also happens to be *now*, the moment of Douglass's enumeration of the findings of his prospective historians. This anticipation of the history of abolition appears as a kind of presentiment informed by biblical certainty and the inevitability of the coming of a new dispensation.[10] Or perhaps it is just wishful thinking.[11]

In other moods, however, Douglass seems more prepossessing, as in a May 5, 1848, piece for the *The North Star* titled "What of the Night?" In it, Douglass insists that the "moral and religious, no less than the political firmaments, North and South, at home and abroad, are studded with brilliant and most significant indications, pointing directly to a settlement" of the slavery question." "Slavery," he pronounces flatly, "is doomed to destruction."[12] Abolitionism "has attained a point of progress when its devoted advocates may press its claims in the full assurance that success" is at hand. "At present," he states, we feel hopeful." As I'll discuss later in my examination of his response to the *Dred Scott* decision, "settlement" and "hope" eventually become key terms in Douglass's theory of history. And as in that speech, the hope that Douglass expresses here seems in many ways completely unfounded. The "perfidious annexation of Texas," the support of slavery from "a corrupt church and degenerate priesthood," and a "slaveholding President," would all seem to provide more than enough reason for despair. What keeps such despair at bay, transforming it instead into certitude about the future—or what I am describing here as a kind of prepossession; that is, the possession of something (like historical knowledge) beforehand—is Douglass's long view, the extension of his present vision into a distant future, now pulled near. The unique position Douglass occupies as an abolitionist reformer affords him this perspective. In an article published two months later in *The North Star*, imagining himself and his fellow reformers, he describes this vantage as "Standing... upon the watch-tower of human freedom."[13] A watchtower provides the lookout with an advantageous view, a widened field of vision from which to anticipate approaching threats and dangers. For Douglass, "the watch-tower of human freedom" allows him a broad survey of the tendency and direction of events. From his watch-tower view in 1848, Douglass espies the "Spirit of Liberty... sweeping in majesty over the whole European continent."[14] "These stupendous overturnings throughout the world," he writes, "proclaim in the ear of American slaveholders, with all the terrible energy of an earthquake, the downfall of slavery."[15]

As his seismic analogy suggests, the European "overturnings" of 1848 provided Douglass with an especially vivid means of apprehension that informed his sense of history's direction. In "The Revolution of 1848," a speech Douglass gave in Rochester, New York, in celebration of the tenth anniversary of West Indian emancipation, Douglass uses the occasion not to look back upon the past that the event is meant to celebrate, but to turn his audience toward an historical view of the dynamic present: "We live in stirring times," Douglass says, "and amid thrilling events. There is no telling what a day may bring forth. The human mind is everywhere filled with expectation."[16] "Expectation" here suggests not the dread or anxiety of apprehension, in the sense of apprehensiveness, but a kind of exhilaration, the thrill of that affective state, as we saw in Chapter 2, that John Neal calls *interest*. Douglass's excitement builds in a series of images of upheaval that also echo the seismic shaking and rattling, like an earthquake, that he associates with "the downfall of slavery" and that, as we saw in Chapter 3, characterize the foundation-shaking happenings that Emerson welcomes and celebrates in "Circles." "We live in times which have no parallel in the history of the world," Douglass says:

> The grand commotion is universal and all-pervading. Kingdoms, realms, empires, and republics, roll to and fro like ships upon a stormy sea. The long pent up energies of human rights and sympathies, are at last let loose upon the world. The grand conflict of the angel Liberty with the monster Slavery, has at last come. The globe shakes with the contest.—I thank God that I am permitted, with you, to live in these days, and to participate in this struggle. We are, Mr. President, parties to what is going on around us. We are more than spectators of the scenes that pass before us. Our interest, sympathies, and destiny compel us to be parties to what is passing around us.[17]

In a rewarding reading of Douglass's "chronopolitics" and "capacious philosophy of history" that runs parallel to mine, Cody Marrs notes how in this speech "the present becomes a point of release, an elastic moment of unburdening."[18] Yet what Marrs identifies persuasively as Douglass's chronopolitics of European revolution, I am suggesting, is an instance of a more general—or more extensive—investment in the "living present," a present or "now-time" not only tied to Douglass's sense of the era's political revolutions. Defined by the fact that "something is going on," in which one finds oneself "in the midst of things" (to recall Mead and Washington Irving, as well as Longfellow), Douglass stresses that this dynamic present, as in Longfellow's poem, is the sphere of action. Three times in this passage, he insists upon the participation of abolitionists in that which is "going on" or "passing around."

Douglass's devotion to activity, to happenings in the living present, is likewise on display in his 1848 "Address to the Colored People of the United States," delivered two months after the "Revolution" speech. Once again, taking an historical view, Douglass considers the advancements made by free blacks like himself: "The time was, when we trembled in the presence of a white man," Douglass writes," and dared not assert, or even ask for our rights, but would be guided, directed, and governed, in any way we were demanded, without ever stopping to enquire whether we were right or wrong."[19] Today, however, "this sentiment has nearly ceased to reign in the dark abodes of our hearts; we begin to see our wrongs as clearly, and comprehend our rights as full, and as well as our white countrymen.

This is a sign of progress; and evidence which cannot be gainsayed."[20] But it's at this point that Douglass warns his readers to resist the complacency of a settled view of the present: "It would be easy to present in this connection, a glowing comparison of our past with our present condition, showing that while the former was dark and dreary, the present is full of light and hope. It would be easy to draw a picture of our present achievements, and erect upon it a glorious future."[21] The pictorial metaphor here provides an apt image of stasis and containment, of the isolation of a moment in time, a kind of historicist snapshot, we might say. For it is just such a view of the present that Douglass sees as dangerous, a recipe for *in*activity. Thus his historiographical bottom line: "We have done much, but there is more to be done."[22] Or, as he puts it near the close of the address: "As wise men it becomes us *to look forward* to a state of things, which *appears* inevitable" (emphasis mine).[23] Douglass puns cleverly here on the word "becomes." He reminds his fellow abolitionists that their work is prospective, that it is appropriate that they continue to look ahead toward a world without slavery and race prejudice. At the same time, the pun also suggests that "to look ahead" is to transform the looker: the one who looks ahead *becomes*, begins (anew) to be, even though doing so entails a high degree of uncertainty, which Douglass emphasizes by refusing to specify, as I have just done, the precise character of the "state of things" that only "appears"—and, therefore, may not be—inevitable.[24]

Marks, Traces, "Possibles," and Probabilities

That Douglass seems sometimes prepossessing about the future and at other times apprehensive, sometimes emphatically certain and other times happily unsure, might be explained in terms of his ambivalence, or perhaps simply his wavering, between a providential view of history (and of his own life) and historical contingency, between what Maurice Lee has described as teleology and chance, or what Bromell sees as the "tension," in Douglass's thought, "between the universal and the contingent, the abstract and the particular, the eternal and the historical."[25] Rather than a contradiction or inconsistency, Bromell views Douglass's ability to "hold opposites in tension with each other" as one of the signal achievements of Douglass's thought, a function of his "embodied knowing."[26] Or to put this another way, if Douglass could, at times, largely as a result of his Christian millennialist beliefs, seem a providentialist, he was so primarily in *other*worldly terms. When it came to *this* world, at least in the near term, Douglass more often appears to embrace contingency. One might think here of the "virtuous expediency" advocated by Plotinus Plinlimmon in Melville's *Pierre* as a way to reconcile—or at least live with—the disparity between heavenly "chronometricals" and earthly "horologicals." Immediatists, as we have seen, had no choice but to learn to live with such friction since nothing could guarantee the precise contours of the future toward which they wished to hasten. Douglass expresses this uncertainty at the opening of "The Destiny of Colored Americans" in 1849: "It is impossible to settle, by any light of the present, and by the experience of the past, any thing, definitely and absolutely...." And he might just as well have stopped there, without the sentence's final clause—"as to the future condition of the colored people of this country"—which is not so much a qualifier, or so I am suggesting, as it is a particular instance of a more general proposition: that the past is not an unalterable guide to any particular future and that the present, any present, points in any number of directions at once.[27]

An image that encapsulates the variability of this unclear if not entirely unforeseeable future can be found, fittingly, at the beginning of Douglass's one work of historical fiction, *The Heroic Slave*, first published in 1853. After invoking the great statesmen of Virginia from the past—George Washington and Thomas Jefferson—the narrator then turns to his novel's hero, the black Revolutionary Madison Washington:

> Glimpses of this great character are all that can now be presented. He is brought to view only by a few transient incidents, and these afford but partial satisfaction. Like a guiding star on a stormy night, he is seen through the parted clouds and the howling tempests; or, like the gray peak of a menacing rock on a perilous coast, he is seen by the quivering flash of angry lightning, and he again disappears covered with mystery.[28]

The passive voice here works oddly against the paragraph's present tense. "Now" would seem to suggest the now of narration, the particular presentation at hand: *this* view of Madison Washington will be partial, fragmentary, indecisive. But if so, why the distancing effect of "is brought to view" and "is seen"? The consequent ambiguity there suggests that this is as much history's view of Washington—after all, unlike George Washington and Jefferson, there are no accounts, written or pictorial of Madison—as it is the view that Douglass's narrator *will* present. If these sentences are meant as a description of the narrative that is to follow, shouldn't they be rendered, as I have just done, in the future tense? He *will be* brought to view and *will be* seen? The present tense suggests instead an unfolding state of affairs: this is where history has left us.

If this reading seems overly fastidious, consider the paragraph that follows, which marks a significant shift in grammatical subject:

> Curiously, earnestly, anxiously we peer into the dark, and wish even for the blinding flash, or the light of northern skies to reveal him. But alas! he is still enveloped in darkness, and we return from the pursuit like a wearied and disheartened mother, (after a tedious and unsuccessful search for a lost child,) who returns weighed down with disappointment and sorrow. Speaking of marks, traces, possibles, and probabilities, we come before our readers.[29]

Here, Douglass's narrator, speaking in the conventional first-person plural, steps forward unequivocally. This unambiguous image of Douglass, as fictional narrator, looking-but-not-seeing contrasts sharply with the earlier image of Douglass on the watchtower of human freedom. There, Douglass took an expansive view, espying apprehensively the general temporal landscape. But now his particular view of Washington, and of the meaning or truth of Washington, is obscured; all he sees are marks and traces, which, the sequence of listed items implies, suggest only possibles and probabilities. What Madison Washington means—or more precisely, what black Revolutionary action in the present might unleash—can't be seen at present; it remains a matter only for an as yet unrealized, and perhaps unreachable, future.[30]

At issue here are the attitudes and expectations of Douglass's audience, as much as his own, toward the potential havoc that decisive Revolutionary action in the living present might wreak. In a different context, Millette Shamir has described this passage as Douglass's "disclaimer that the truth must remain unknown."[31] I would state this slightly differently: what is unknown here may not be "truth"— unless by truth we mean something closer to fruition or attainment—so much as it is outcomes or consequences, that which Madison Washington's heroic actions make, or could make, possible or probable. Douglass refuses to provide his readers with any comforting assurances, any sense of security about *that*; he certainly offers none of the consolations that one encounters, say, in *Uncle Tom's Cabin*, with its panegyrics to the glorious Christianized future of Africa which must "some time" come.[32]

Or, to draw out this contrast with another example—surprisingly apt in this context in more ways than one—Douglass resists offering assurances of the kind presented in one of Emily Dickinson's best known poems:

> Tell all the truth but tell it slant—
> Success in Circuit lies
> Too bright for our infirm Delight
> The Truth's superb surprise
> As Lightning to the Children eased
> With explanation kind
> The Truth must dazzle gradually
> Or every man be blind—[33]

Although written in 1872, Dickinson's poem about the necessity of indirection and the dangers of abrupt, sudden, *immediate* flashes of light is in harmony with Stowe, providing perhaps as apt a metaphorical statement of the gradualist position as the nineteenth century could possibly devise.[34] "Man" requires sympathetic protection, like a mother's "explanation kind," from the shock of the truth if it arrives at once, in an instant like lightning. Therefore, gradual, not immediate, apprehension is safest. Of course, this poem has typically been read as a poem about poetry, not politics, a statement on Dickinson's own oblique poetic method. Yet having witnessed the turbulence of the 1840s and 1850s, followed by the unimaginable violence of the Civil War, it's not implausible that she could have had immediatist abolition or other forms of radical social reform in mind, especially considering her long friendship with Thomas Wentworth Higginson, one of the period's most militantly zealous immediatists, as well as her father's long career in antebellum politics. Regardless, the resonances in her poem with the opening paragraphs of *The Heroic Slave* are remarkably striking, if quite different in tenor. Whereas the speaker of Dickinson's poem represents lightning as a danger—because people just can't handle the truth—Douglass's narrator "wish[es] for the blinding flash" of lightning, which will "reveal" Washington and (perhaps) disclose the sort of future his heroism makes possible. For Douglass, it's not that the truth is "too bright;" it's not bright enough. As he puts it in the Fourth of July address, "it is not light that is needed, but fire; it is not the gentle shower, but thunder. We need the storm, the whirlwind, and the earthquake."[35] So in *The Heroic Slave*, the flash of lightning in Douglass is not that about or from which the parental figure needs to reassure or protect her child, but that which will help her to locate her child; lightning's *absence* leaves her, like Rachel, disappointed and sorrowful.

Which isn't to say that Dickinson didn't have a point about the culture's ill-preparedness for the truth's sudden jolts and what they might reveal. Speaking in Concord in 1851 in response to the Fugitive Slave Law, Emerson told his auditors that the debate over the Compromise bill "had the illuminating power of a sheet of lightning at midnight. It showed truth."[36] But the details of the truth that it revealed probably weren't anything most citizens much wanted to see: "the slightness and unreliableness of our social fabric... what straws we dignify by office and title... the shallowness of leaders... that men would not stick to what they had said" and worse.[37] But if the lightning flash of 1850, as Emerson described it, showed cowardice, corruption, and moral failure, at least it didn't lead—at least not yet—to total disaster. The same can't be said for Herman Melville's tale of reckless immediatism *Moby-Dick*. Unlike Emerson and Douglass, Melville appears to have felt more than a little trepidation at what John Stauffer describes as Ahab's "monomaniacal, immediatist vision"—a vision, I would add, that possesses all the transformative meteorological and seismic power I've been observing: Ahab describes himself as "Old Thunder," living an "earthquake life."[38] Yet if Stauffer is right in casting Melville as a gradualist, he wasn't the sort of timid gradualist depicted in Dickinson's poem, afraid to look the truth clearly and urgently in the face. Quite the contrary, through Ahab, Melville courts it, despite its potentially disastrous implications. This difference is evident in Melville's deployment of the same figures employed by Douglass, Dickinson, and Emerson. Before *Moby-Dick*, Melville had meditated fictively on the prospective dangers of immediatism in *Mardi* (1849), when his travelers visit the South of Vivenza, the novel's thinly allegorized version of the southern United States. There they encounter forced laborers "toiling in trenches" and continuously whipped by overseers, including one named Nulli (obviously John C. Calhoun), whose "wondrous eyes" are "bright [and] nimble, as the twin Corposant balls, playing about the ends of ships' royalyards in gales."[39] Babbalanja and Yoomy query the "thralls" on their condition, wondering at the apparent lack of rebellious energy among them. "Do no thunders roll,—no lightnings flash in this accursed land!" Yoomy exclaims, at which point ensues a brief discussion on the dangers of immediate Revolutionary action versus the wisdom of more prudent gradualism. Babbalanja gives voice to the latter position: "Better present woes for some, than future woes for all," he counsels. When Yoomy muses that "a way may be found, and no irretrievable evil ensue," Babbalanja demagogues consensus—even if agreeing means that they must "weeping all but echo hard-hearted Nulli"—in a speech that strains so hard for apparently fair-minded cross-sectional understanding that it leaves us, as Robert S Levine aptly if understatedly puts it, with "an uncomfortable lack of direction on the practical matter of action."[40] Babbalanja leans instead on the solace afforded by liberal-progressive history, the same slow but steady forward-moving temporality upon which gradualists always relied. "The future is all hieroglyphics," Babbalanja says:

> Who may read? But, methinks the great laggard Time must now march up apace, and somehow befriend these thralls. It can not be, that misery is perpetually entailed...Yes. Time—all-healing Time—Time, great Philanthropist!—Time must befriend these thralls![41]

The modal here, echoing Stowe's "must some time," controverts the future's apparent unreadability. Time may be slow, a "laggard," but it is also ameliorative and benevolent—"kind," to recall Dickinson's gradualism. In *Moby-Dick*, Melville imagines the opposite of Babbalanja's patiently cautious statesman: the very sort of rash "firebrand," to cite Nulli's language, who seeks to "wreak some dreadful vengeance." But whereas the speaker of Dickinson's poem and Melville's Babbalanja are both wary of lightning, and whereas Emerson and the narrator of *The Heroic Slave* welcome its flash, Melville's Ahab *is* lightning.

In "The Candles," one of *Moby-Dick's* most vivid and vividly baffling chapters, Melville revamps this strangely braided discursive network—of corposants, thunder and lightning, impetuous immediatism, and slow, benevolent kindness—and twists and winds it into an inextricable knot. In the midst of a fierce, lightning-filled storm, the *Pequod's* three masts suddenly begin to blaze with the light of St. Elmo's Fire, burning like "three spermaceti candles." Heedless of the danger, Ahab refuses to allow Starbuck and the crew to employ the lightning rods. Instead, transfixed by the burning corposants—which hearken back to Calhoun's eyeballs in *Mardi*, but here calling to mind Calhoun's monomaniacal verso Garrison[42]—he attempts to merge with them himself, or at least to "feel [their] pulse, and let mine beat against it; blood against fire!" Amid "repeated flashes of lightning," Ahab proceeds to address the atmospheric force in what is surely the most deliriously peculiar of all the novel's soliloquies. "Oh! thou clear spirit of clear fire," Abab says, "I now know thee and I now know that thy right worship is defiance." Holding tight to the chains, he attempts to join with the electrical force: "I own thy speechless, placeless power," he repeats, as "the lightning flashes through my skull." It's at this point that Ahab's speech takes a curious temporal turn, generated by a strange, missing lineage:

> Oh, thou magnanimous! now I do glory in my genealogy. But thou art but my fiery father; my sweet mother, I know not. Oh, cruel! what hast thou done with her? There lies my puzzle; but thine is greater. Thou knowest not how came ye, hence callest thyself unbegotten; certainly knowest not thy beginning, hence callest thyself unbegun. I know that of me, which thou knowest not of thyself, oh, thou omnipotent. There is some unsuffusing thing beyond thee, thou clear spirit, to whom all thy eternity is but time, all thy creativeness mechanical. Through thee, thy flaming self, my scorched eyes do dimly see it. Oh, thou foundling fire, thou hermit immemorial, thou too hast thy incommunicable riddle, thy unparticipated grief. Here again with haughty agony, I read my sire.[43]

Himself a motherless child of the lightning, Ahab here speaks to his "fiery father" of the latter's absent parentage.[44] Without lineage or history, the spirit of fire exists outside the linear time of biological reproduction—he is "unbegotten." It inhabits instead what we might describe as a queer moment not organized by sequence and succession—it is "unbegun," neither initiating nor the result of some other action or event. This, to Ahab, is precisely the source of the spirit's power and wonder. Whatever the "unsuffusing" thing is (suffusing, it's worth noting, is a slow, gradual process of spreading) that generates this spirit does so according to some other, incalculable order of time, a time in which "eternity" and creativity are measured clock-like—an impossible quantification suggested here by the subtle parallelism of eternity/creativeness, time/mechanical. Ahab's shallow genealogy, the unbegotten and unbegun power of lightning, provides a frenzied rendering of a pure, nonsequential immediatism, without antecedent or successor, an immediateness that Ahab "defyingly" worships.

The strange power, arresting imagery, and manic rhetorical exuberance of "The Candles" all suggest that Melville was drawn to the vigorous, insurgent intensity of Revolutionary action. Notwithstanding Stauffer's reading, this would seem to align Melville in certain ways with Douglass and to put him at odds with some of the period's prevailing logics of social change. Ahab's motherlessness and his firefather's absent parentage, for example, place him outside the "maternalist temporality" that Dana Luciano identifies as characteristic of the sentimental tradition, exemplified by *Uncle Tom's Cabin*. Stowe, Luciano shows, "links affective reform to a *slow* process of change" brought about through reproduction and childrearing (emphasis added). In a vision of "social change as a (re)generational process," Stowe imagines the problems of slavery solved gradually over time by generations of children born of and raised by right-feeling women.[45] Such a vision necessarily excludes Ahab, who is *unregenerate* in more ways than one: both stubbornly defiant in his ungodliness (he'd strike the sun, after all) and proudly resistant to conventional heterosexual reproductive logic: at once "the child-bride and offspring of pure power," in David Leverenz's phrase, glorying in the genealogy of his "unbegotten" father.[46] Ahab both inhabits and represents *now*, the moment of "each event," as he terms it in "The Quarter-Deck" chapter, the time of "the living act, the undoubted deed."[47] Yet, Melville also appears to have been unable to shake a certain anxiety over the unforeseeable consequences of such spontaneous action. The novel's cataclysmic ending seems to register a deep fear that abrupt social transformation, revolutionary action lodged in a figure like Ahab, would lead only to "future woes for all," that "irretrievable evil" might "ensue," or as Stauffer puts it, that the immediate abolition of slavery will lead to "social revolution, chaos, and death."[48]

Melville's misgivings aside, Ahab and Frederick Douglass are kin. Both are *irregularly* descended, to use a phrase Douglass coins at a pivotal moment in his celebrated July 5, 1852, speech now called "What to the Slave is the Fourth of July?"[49] At the moment that marks the crucial shift in the speech from the Revolutionary past to the political present, Douglass delivers what may be its most cutting remark: "I leave, therefore, the great deeds of your fathers to other gentlemen whose claim to have been regularly descended will be less likely to be disputed than mine"—a wry reminder to his audience that black Americans like himself are both excluded from the national genealogy and, as a result of slavery's brutal and racist sexual economy, cast as "illegitimate."[50] Just as importantly, Douglass here refutes the "rhetoric of the nation-as-family...through which his audience has come to understand freedom, synonymous with Americanness, as their inheritance."[51] Like Ahab in "The Candles," Douglass rejects the temporal "logic of reproductive generationality" in favor of the perspective afforded by his position as someone of irregular descent: the perspective of the "living present" of action and event, where he is beholden to neither patrimony nor progeny.[52] Fittingly, Douglass invokes this "ever-living now" by way of a recitation of the familiar stanza from Longfellow's "A Psalm of Life":

> Trust no Future, howe'er pleasant!
> Let the dead Past bury its dead!
> Act,—act in the living Present!
> Heart within, and God o'erhead![53]

This alternative viewpoint, this inhabitation of *now*, corresponds to the other perspectival shift in the speech that Douglass soon after effects. "I shall see this day and its popular characteristics," he says, "from the slave's point of view."[54] From that vantage, the nation's sequential history appears as "hideous and revolting" as it does fixed and inexorable: "America is false to the past, false to the present, and solemnly binds herself to be false to the future."[55] America, in other words, is in thrall to sequential time. By contrast, chronological history is no more important to Douglass than is lineal descent. Rather, "Now is the time, the important time," he says. The present within which Douglass situates himself is not settled, not bound by any particular chronology and for that reason, no more tied to any particular past than to any particular future.[56] The living present is instead, as with Emerson, experiential and experimental, what Luciano describes as "a moment of radical eventfulness," full of "possibles and probabilities"—to once again recall *The Heroic Slave*—and, therefore, potentially transformative, but also, for many of Douglass's contemporaries, potentially dangerous.

What Is in the Distance, Rather Than What Is Near or Behind

What I have presented in this brief look at a handful of writers speaking the same language as Douglass in *The Heroic Slave* is a partial index of the range of responses to the abrupt change, figured by earthquakes and lightning, advocated by immediatist abolitionists like Douglass: Dickinson's poem counsels protective caution, Emerson sees it as a kind of ghastly mirror, and Melville, at least in his presentation of Ahab, renders it as a form of madness at once compelling and terrifying. What keeps Douglass so seemingly sanguine by comparison? What distinguishes Douglass's version of immediatism, his faith in action in the living present, from Ahab's madness? It's tempting to answer this question in a single word: hope. After all, Douglass closes his Fourth of July address, despite all its searing denunciations, with "hope" and "encouragement." But hope, for Douglass, is no simple matter. In fact, in his 1853 lecture on "The Present Condition and Future Prospects of the Negro People" he "confess[ed]" that he is "not a hopeful man...apt even to undercalculate the benefits of the future."[57] Nevertheless, throughout the 1850s, Douglass applied the lesson of perspective learned from his early years and his newly acquired presentist orientation in an attempt to see the "bright side."[58] The hopefulness Douglass displays, then, is mainly a matter of "possibles and probabilities," a necessary willingness to take an alternative view and, from that vantage, to make a bet on the future.[59]

In this section, I suggest that Douglass learned how to bright side during his intellectual crisis over slavery and the Constitution. Scholars generally agree that Douglass's thinking about the Constitution, which led to his break with Garrison and his embrace of political abolitionism, marks a decisive turning point in his career.[60] It is not my intention to challenge that narrative. Rather, I hope to show how this pivotal moment in Douglass's career, in which he turned away from the past and toward the future, a future understood as a promise though not a guarantee, also centrally informed his developing philosophy of history in the mid-1850s. Douglass gestures toward the debate over the Constitutionality of slavery in the Fourth of July speech, calling the Constitution "a glorious liberty document," insisting, as Marrs insightfully puts it, that it is "defined not by the context of its inception but, instead, by its nonsynchronic potentials, by its capacity to articulate...'LIBERTY' across disparate historical moments."[61] But it's elsewhere that Douglass pursues this question in detail. What concerns me specifically is not just the view he eventually acquired, but the means by which he came to it.

By 1851, Douglass faced a serious conceptual dilemma. For years, as an agent of the American Anti-Slavery Society, he had promoted the Garrisonian view, which argued that the Constitution was a proslavery instrument and was, therefore, in Garrison's famous phrase, "a covenant with death and an agreement with hell." But soon after moving to Rochester, New York to establish *The North Star*, Douglass began to weary of this argument. Hence his dilemma. He hadn't changed his mind; he was simply—as he put it in a letter to his new friend and patron Gerrit Smith in early 1851—"sick and tired of arguing on the slaveholders' side of [the] question," in search of another vantage from which to argue the point. Yet despite his desire to take a different view of the question, Douglass still expresses astonishment at Smith's position: slaveholders, Douglass maintains, "are doubtless right as far as the intentions of the framers of the Constitution are concerned. But," he writes, "these intentions you fling to the winds."[62] Douglass's tone here is more envious than accusatory, expressing more wonderment than disapproval; and for me, it's just about the most beguiling moment in all of Douglass's writings. He feels the pull of Smith's position, can almost taste the exhilaration he might experience from a similarly impetuous disregard for "intentions." Yet he can't quite bring himself to it. He is both bewitched by Smith's position and hindered from adopting it; it is both within Douglass's reach and just beyond his grasp. So while Douglass seems to find Smith's disregard of intentions an appealing, even liberating, prospect, his own understanding of the historicity of the Constitution prevents him from adopting it. For Douglass in 1851, the Constitution is a document that is anchored to the past, bound by the context of its time of production, the meaning of which is to be sought by way of careful historical investigation of the most traditional sort. Douglass had not yet learned to view the Constitution as a document that breathes in the present—what we now call, participially, a *living* Constitution.

As a result, this anxious enchantment with Smith's attitude toward the Constitution and his cavalier gesture of flinging intentions and historical and interpretive protocols to the winds precipitated in Douglass a crisis over his own intellectual integrity. He writes to Smith:

> There is a consideration which is of much importance between us. It is this: may we avail ourselves of legal rules which enable us to defeat even the wicked intentions of our Constitution makers? It is this question which puzzles me more than all others involved in the subject. Is it good morality to take advantage of a legal flaw and put a meaning upon a legal instrument the very opposite of what we have good reason to believe was the intention of the men who framed it?[63]

As a matter of "morality," Douglas feels himself bound both by the sound rules of legal interpretation and by the facts of history. This state of affairs is complicated by the fact that he can clearly see the alternative to his own legal-historical position. Two years earlier, in *The North Star*, Douglass had stated that view—the one he would eventually adopt—quite plainly: "if strictly construed according to its reading," the Constitution "is not a pro-slavery instrument."[64] Yet Douglass has no choice but to reject this view, as he makes clear in an article published a few weeks later. Once again acknowledging the possibility of a reading of the Constitution divorced from the intent of its framers, Douglass nevertheless considers the matter a question of what he calls "truth and duty." "How a document would appear under one construction, is one thing," Douglass writes, "but whether the construction be the right one is quite another and a very different thing."[65] Thus Douglass finds himself confronted with a kind of historicist dilemma: his sense of how he might read the Constitution *now* is constrained by a sense of obligation, a kind of fealty, to how it was meant to be read *then*. Is it good morality, Douglass wonders, to be presentist?

So even though he was unwilling, in 1849, to accept the Constitution as anything but "a most cunningly devised and wicked compact," in these articles Douglass lays the cornerstone both for what would eventually become his antislavery view of the Constitution, and, I want to suggest, his conception of history. The pivotal moment occurs at the second article's outset, when Douglass proclaims himself "perfectly free to change [his] opinion in any direction, and at any time which may be indicated by our *immediate apprehension* of truth" (emphasis mine).[66] The temporality of the phrase "immediate apprehension," which yokes the present to an anxiously awaited future—if we take apprehension here to mean more than just "understanding"—nicely captures the felt intensity of being in history, of living in the living present, that Douglass was learning to accept. Following this statement, Douglass strikes an Emersonian note, declaring, "The only truly consistent man is he who will, for the sake of being right today, contradict what he said wrong yesterday." "True stability," he continues, consists only "in a fixed principle of honesty, even urging us to the adoption or rejection of that which may seem to us true or false at the *ever-present now*" (emphasis mine).[67]

So what finally allows Douglass to keep his intellectual integrity intact and still change his view—to change, that is, his opinion on the question of the Constitution and slavery—is *a change of view*—a change in the place from which he looks at the matter. That is, Douglass adopts a perspective on the Constitution that is rooted, not in legal traditions, the facts of the past, or the framers' intentions, but one rooted in the "ever-present now" of the antislavery movement. What I am suggesting, then, is that Douglass's turn away from the original intentions of the framers and toward a Constitutional argument rooted in "immediate apprehension," in "now," represents not, as it might at first glance appear, a rejection of history in favor of political expediency. Rather, it represents a major realignment of Douglass's understanding of history and his own orientation within history's temporal movement. Instead of traveling back into the past in search of the answer to his interpretive dilemma, Douglass positions himself firmly in the present with an eye toward the future. This vantage affords Douglass a way out of his impasse.

This largely overlooked chronopolitical dimension of Douglass's new method of Constitutional interpretation and embrace of political abolitionism reveals another way in which Douglass departed from Garrisonian abolitionist doctrines. Douglass's particular mode of immediate apprehension reveals what Cristin Ellis, in an insightful reading, describes as Douglass's "growing impatience with moral suasion."[68] It's not just that Douglass was "sick and tired"—impatient—of arguing the slaveholders' side of the Constitutional question. More generally, he was increasingly concerned about whether "the slow pace of moral reformation" could be "calibrated to the ticking clock of imminent danger."[69] Garrison's brand of immediatism, in other words, just wasn't immediate enough for Douglass.[70] As a result, he sought after, as we'll see later, signs of history's acceleration. That inquiry required revisiting the project of writing the history of abolition he began a decade earlier and refashioning the antislavery past to comport with his newly acquired presentist vision.[71]

On March 19, 1855, Douglass delivered an address on "The Anti-Slavery Movement" to the Rochester Ladies' Anti-Slavery Society, announcing his subject as "the nature, character, and history of the anti-slavery movement." It's arguably the most extensive—and the most theoretically rich—rumination on the history of antislavery that Douglass wrote during his long career, important enough to Douglass that he published extracts from it in the Appendix to *My Bondage and My Freedom*, although those extracts also leave out Douglass's fascinating rehearsal of antislavery history. He begins his inquiry into the movement's history stating that he will avoid philosophical questions, leaving them, he archly notes, "to the abolitionists of the superior class to answer"—a shot at Garrisonians like John Collins who condescendingly encouraged Douglass to "stick to the facts" while they "take care of the philosophy." With ironic self-deprecation, Douglass promises to "avoid water in which I cannot swim, and deal with anti-slavery as fact."[72] Yet Douglass has no intention of avoiding philosophical waters. These remarks— like others at various points in the speech—are mainly cracking wise, subtle jabs laced with no small traces of bitterness at the Garrisonians. Indeed, his sardonic claims to humility aside, much of the speech, as Maurice Lee observes, "aspires to grand metaphysical heights."[73]

The central assertion of "The Anti-Slavery Movement" is that abolition, and especially immediatist abolition, is not "a new thing under the sun." This otherwise historiographical claim is driven in part, as I've indicated, by more settling of scores, as Douglass labors to deny Garrison the honor of abolition's founder. "Some who write and speak on the subject, seem to regard the anti-slavery movement as a recent discovery," Douglass says, "brought out for the first time less than a quarter century ago," alluding to the founding of *The Liberator*. "I cannot consent to view it thus," Douglass continues:

> This movement is older and weightier than that. I would deprive William Lloyd Garrison of no honor justly his. All credit must forever redound to him as the man whose earnest eloquence—more than to any other living man—we owe the revival of the antislavery movement of this country; but it is due truth to say, he neither discovered its principles, originated its ideas, nor framed its arguments. These are all older than the preacher. It is an error to speak of this venerable movement as a new thing under the sun.[74]

But it's not just an effort to take Garrison down a peg that motivates Douglass's historical narrative. The key term in the previous Douglass quote is "revival." For Douglass, antislavery exists in an "ever-present now," latent and awaiting its activation, or reactivation. The "causes producing" antislavery, according to Douglass, "have slumbered in the bosom of nature since the world began" only to be discovered and re-discovered again and again. Thus the history of antislavery proceeds not in a straight line, but recursively, in a kind of feedback loop that both repeats and alters, or revivifies, the past. The history of antislavery in this sense is both immanent (it already exists) and imminent (always set to happen again)—but it is also aleatory, occurring according to no fixed or discernible direction, design, or telos. Douglass describes it instead in language that echoes the opening passage of *The Heroic Slave* discussed previously:

> Occasional glimpses of these important principles have gladdened the eyes of good men, at different stages of the world's progress, who have wisely written down, to be read by after coming generations, their apprehensions of them.[75]

History here is a kind of affective state, registered by present-tense experiences, "glimpses" and "apprehensions," immediate sensations that are then recorded for "after coming generations," who presumably will catch their own glimpses and have their own apprehensions.

Such a vision of history and historical movement, as a written record of immediate apprehensions and a nonconsecutive series of rediscoveries, helps to explain why Douglass can describe, as he subsequently does, Garrisonian immediatism in terms that at first appear contradictory: he concedes that it is "new," but insists that it is not "original." Reviewing the antislavery movement in colonial America (to follow Douglass, one has to resist calling it *nascent* or *early*, for he asserts, "antislavery sentiment was national at the very beginning of the Republic"), Douglass asks how that movement differed "from the present one." His answer is "in this only, *as to time*. The first looked for the gradual abolition of slavery; and the other looks for immediate emancipation" (italics original).[76] Douglass then states, "the only new idea brought to the anti-slavery movement, by Mr. Garrison, is the doctrine of immediatism." But just two sentences later, Douglass says, "The doctrine of immediatism was not, however, original with Mr. Garrison." The distinction is subtle but crucial. "New" for Douglass does not connote that which has not previously existed, as if to align the new with temporal progress or sequential advancement. Rather, it means something more like reanimation, "a resumption or repetition . . . resurgent" or "restored after demolition, decay, disappearance," or as Douglass puts it, as that "which an age had lost sight of or discarded."[77]

One way to describe and explain Douglass's newfound understanding of history as a present-tense experience is to say that he came to accept the present as the locus of reality. Here I return again to George Herbert Mead's formulation because his notion of the past as constantly in flux, along with the idea that the present is the necessary condition for the existence of the past, provides a way of framing

Douglass's embrace of a presentist view of history, not to mention his career-long autobiographical project. The later versions of his life story, in *My Bondage and My Freedom* and *The Life and Times*, for example, are not simply serial additions to the 1845 *Narrative* of events in his life as they accrued over time; rather, each version also entails a repetition and substantial reconstruction of his early life.[78] In an analogy that resonates strikingly with Douglass's literary career, Mead puts it this way:

> When one recalls his boyhood days he cannot get into them as he then was, without their relationship to what he has become; and if he could, that is if he could reproduce the experience as it then took place, he could not use it, for this would involve his not being in the present within which that use must take place.[79]

Douglass understood that "who he was," even as a slave, was a function of who he later became, a fact that necessitates rethinking his personal history in light of the "living present" within which he writes.[80] In terms of the trajectory of his career, this means his move away from Garrisonian abolitionism and toward political abolitionism, as well as the series of tumultuous political events related to slavery that roiled the nation during the 1850s. *My Bondage and My Freedom*, then, is more than simply the desire, as William Andrews describes it, "to tell a free story."[81] It is also the desire—or the imperative—to reconstruct a past that accounts for Douglass's understanding of the present. And not just the present: Douglass also agrees with Mead that what motivates our interest in the past in the first place is its value for "interpreting our present and determining our future"—what Douglass in 1848 described as the wisdom of "looking forward." He states this most memorably in the well-known statement in the Fourth of July address: "We have to do with the past only as we can make it useful to the present and the future."

But for Mead (and Emerson, as we saw in the Chapter 3), it's not simply the past that is always in flux. So, too, is the present. Mead rejects the notion of what he calls a "knife-edge present," an isolated, or even isolatable, moment or instant, distinct from the past and the future. The knife-edge present is a "specious present." In the *actual* present, "something is going on." "Now" has temporal breadth. For instance, in his account of "distance experience," Mead posits that when we experience objects at a distance, we adopt toward them what he calls a "terminal attitude."[82] Terminal attitudes are "beginnings of the contact response that will be made to the object when the object is reached."[83] Perception (we could also say "apprehension"), for Mead, presupposes action, so even though the *object* of perception—the percept—may lie far in the distance, we experience it in terms of "manipulation" or what we will do with it. I see a hammer on the table across the room, and the experience of seeing it implies picking it up and driving a nail. Or, I see a colleague at a distance as one with whom I will shake hands when she is near to me. Thus, as Mead says, "the percept is there as a promise."[84] Actual manipulation or contact lies in the future, but that futurity is there in the beginning, in the terminal attitude; it is a future that has been pulled into the present of experience.

Another way of putting this is to say that while the distant object is "there," it is *not* altogether "then." We abstract time from space, thereby "endowing [the futurity] of objects with the temporal character of the 'now,' rendering them simultaneous" with the seer.[85]

So when Douglass, as a child, mistakes trees and stumps for wild beasts, and learns that "the point from which a thing is viewed is of some importance," he begins to learn how to wrench the future for the present, to view it as a promise. This lesson, I have been arguing, proves a crucial part of his intellectual development in the 1850s and forms the basis for his wary—his apprehensive—hopefulness. Douglass figures this in yet another striking image of gazing forward, which nicely illustrates his developing temporal consciousness, his turn away from fixed or settled notions of the past in favor of the uncertainties of the future as promise. Upon leaving the Lloyd plantation for Baltimore for the first time in *My Bondage and My Freedom*, Douglass describes boarding a sloop. Once aboard, he first walks aft to take one final look at the plantation, after which, he writes, "I made my way to the bow...and spent the remainder of the day in looking ahead; interesting myself in what was in the distance, rather than what was near or behind."[86] Gazing forward as a way of understanding the past, as Mead describes and Douglass learned, is crucial to historical understanding. So when Douglass reconstructs his past in such a way that explains how he has arrived at his present position, he replaces the plodding succession of "specious presents," devoid of future, that characterizes the temporality of slavery, with a reorientation of perspective within a dynamic present, a present with temporal extent, the present of *ongoing experience*.[87]

Looking Out Upon the Boundless Sea of the Future

"We have to do not with the dead, but the living; not with the past, but with the living present," Douglass says in the remarkable, though surprisingly little remarked upon, speech he delivered to the American Abolition Society in New York on May 14, 1857, in response to the Supreme Court ruling in *Dred Scott v. Sanford*. Curiously underexplored by Douglass scholars, the *Dred Scott* speech in many ways marks the culmination of his historical turn as I have thus far described it. The *Dred Scott* speech is also his most playfully sophisticated and rhetorically audacious rendering of antislavery history. It is audacious if for no other reason than his pronouncement in the face of the Supreme Court's devastating ruling—Douglass calls it a "judicial incarnation of wolfishness"—that "my hopes were never brighter than now." What could possibly warrant such a startling claim?

Douglass's turn to hope was hard won and cautious. Longfellow's poem, after all, had taught him to "trust no future/ howe'er pleasant." Two years before that in "The Present Condition and Future Prospects of the Negro," he claimed that he is "not a hopeful man," and in "The Anti-Slavery Movement," he admits to taking only "a sober view of the present anti-slavery movement...sober, but not hopeless."[88] Yet one might also view Douglass's earlier claims of a lack of hope as a rhetorical strategy he would later refine in the Dred Scott speech—or the early stages of learning how to adopt a terminal attitude toward events barely perceptible on the horizon. In the "Present Condition" address, Douglass declares his lack of hope in the midst of a description of the current state of affairs with regard to antislavery, stating, "I confess the case looks black enough."[89] Similarly, a central theme of *My Bondage and My Freedom* is Douglass's attempt to find and maintain hope. In fact, the moments of his greatest despondency involve his future prospects, which he sums up in the phrase "to be a slave for life": "It was not my enslavement, at the then present time, that most affected me," Douglass writes, "the being a slave *for life*, was the saddest thought" (emphasis original).[90] Indeed, this Douglass later describes as an "ever-gnawing and soul devouring thought," which "rendered me a living embodiment of mental and physical wretchedness."[91]

Yet as he claims in the "Present Condition" speech, Douglass also realizes—and this, as we'll see, is the crucial point—"There is a bright side to almost every picture of this kind, and ours is no exception to the general rule."[92] What Douglass was trying out here, in other words, was *how to look* at events, how and from what vantage to view past, present, and future. (This is why, in *My Bondage*, he takes care to note that his lack of hope is a function of "the *then* present time," as opposed to the time of his writing.) In other words, what is involved in these earlier instances—and what warrants Douglass's hope in the face of *Dred*—is both his developing sense of antislavery historiography, which forms the heart of the *Dred Scott* speech, and his new commitment to presentism as a guide to action and to social and historical transformation.

Thus Douglass begins the *Dred* speech, fittingly, by placing his auditors in the midst of a crowded living present, not speciously knife-edge, but densely populated; a present in which, to recall Mead, "something is going on." That this present is a time of action and event is signaled by Douglass's repetition in the speech of the temporally loaded adverb "while." A term of duration as well as simultaneity— as a noun it denotes both an unspecified interval of time and *at the same time*—it indicates in its adverbial form a relative time in which there is a happening: "While four millions of our fellow countrymen are in chains—while men, women and, children are bought and sold on the auction block...while the remorseless slave-whip draws the warm blood of our common humanity—it is meet that we assemble as we have done to-day...."[93] The present tense that Douglass establishes then turns immediately to a look toward the uncertain future. "It is natural on occasions like this," Douglass writes, "to survey the position of the great struggle which is going on between slavery and freedom...it is a fitting time to take an observation to ascertain where we are, and what our prospects are." "To many," Douglass continues, "the prospects of the struggle against slavery seem far from cheering." Yet at this point, gazing forward, Douglass places himself in a position not unlike that of the young slave he describes in *My Bondage and My Freedom* or like the historian seeking a glimpse of Madison Washington at the start of *The Heroic Slave*:

> Standing, as it were, barefoot, and treading upon the sharp and flinty rocks of the present, and looking out upon the boundless sea of the future, I have sought, in my humble way, to penetrate the intervening mists and clouds, and perchance to descry, in the dim and shadowy distance, the white flag of freedom, the precise speck of time at which the cruel bondage of my people should end and the long entombed millions rise from the foul grave of slavery and death.[94]

Douglass's present perfect tense recalls his prior attempts to catch "glimpses" through "the parted clouds and howling tempests," to see "what is in the distance," while also emphasizing that the action continues in the present, in anticipation or expectation of the moment slavery "should end." For the time being, however, Douglass concedes, "of that time I can know nothing, and you can know nothing. All is uncertain at that point." He even acknowledges that "in one view," the pro-slavery forces "have a decided advantage over all opposition." The states' and the federal government, the church, "the pen, the purse, and the sword," and now even the Supreme Court, he says, are all arrayed against the cause of abolition, against "the simple truth, preached by humble men in obscure places."[95]

Yet unlike the child in *My Bondage and My Freedom*, frightened of what lies in the distance, Douglass here has long since absorbed that lesson of perspective, which he now applies, adopting, we might say, a "terminal attitude" toward emancipation: "This is one view," he says, "It is, thank God, only one view; there is another, and a brighter view ... [so] let us look at the other side, and see if there are not some things to cheer our heart and nerve us up anew in the good work of emancipation."[96] At this point, Douglass notes the growth of the antislavery movement, the fact that "other subjects of much interest come and go, expand and contract, blaze and vanish, but the huge question of American Slavery, comprehending, as it does, not merely the weal or the woe of four millions, and their countless posterity, but the weal or the woe of this entire nation, must increase in magnitude and in majesty with every hour of its history."[97] Indeed, Douglass notes, "Politicians who cursed it *now* defend it; ministers, once dumb *now* speak its praise, and presses, which once flamed with hot denunciations against it, *now* surround the sacred cause as by a wall of living fire" (emphasis mine).[98] The prospects implied by the state of affairs "now"—which Douglass repeats both to emphasize "the important time" and to highlight the transformations wrought by antislavery—lead him to declare that "I, for one, will not despair of our cause."[99]

To bolster his argument—and to justify his lack of despair, his hope—Douglass then turns historian, engaging in an extraordinary bit of temporal analysis. He provides a thumbnail sketch of the political history of slavery over the past thirty-seven years, a series of legislative acts each designed to "settle" the question of slavery—the Missouri Compromise, the Gag Rule, War with Mexico, the Compromise of 1850, and finally the Kansas-Nebraska Act, in which, Douglass observes drolly, "the whole question [of slavery] was once more settled, and settled by a settlement which unsettled all the former settlements." To "settle," of course, is to bring to an end, to stop or conclude. But Douglass also punningly refers to the fact that each of the accords he cites were, quite literally, attempts to regulate or legalize the resettlement of slaves to the west. Continuing this verbal play, Douglass says, "The fact is, the more the question has been settled, the more it has needed settling."[100] Such wordplay helps distinguish between a conception of history that tends toward completion and finality—"the voice of the Taney court" would say "peace, be still"—and an alternative conception of history as in a permanently fluid state. Like Emerson, Douglass understands that history is *always* "unsettled."

This truth of history's unsettled character, for Douglass, requires a certain distance from recent events; it requires the perspective he finds in what we might call the quickening or acceleration of historical time. Douglass cleverly observes, "the space between the different settlements has been strikingly on the decrease. The first stood longer than any of its successors."[101] And so, in Douglass's reading "There is a lesson in these decreasing spaces." That is, "the first [settlement] stood fifteen years—the second, ten years—the third, five years, the fourth stood four years—, and the fifth has stood the brief space of two years."[102] The spatio-temporal metaphor Douglass employs here—an echo and reversal of his childhood experience—renders the decreasing returns of so-called national settlements signs of slavery's inevitable collapse, in a kind of satirical version of Zeno's paradox in which Achilles finally *does* close the gap on that tortoise. Douglass thus directs his audience to see in the present what they can't see in the future: the moment at which emancipation is immediately at hand. Douglass terms this vision the "hastening of the triumph of righteousness."[103]

This view of slavery's end may well be made possible, Douglass says, by the same violent natural forces that reveal fleeting glimpses of the insurrectionist hero Madison Washington. If political solutions fail, "The lightning, whirlwind, and earthquake may come." Douglass warns, "The time may come when even the crushed worm may turn under the tyrant's feet."[104] He then reminds his audience of a recent series of conspiracies planned and plotted by slaves all across the south that were discovered and violently suppressed—"some were shot, some hanged, some burned, and some died under the lash," Douglass notes—in November and December of 1856. While those attempts may have been thwarted, more carefully planned revolts with greater chances of success "may break out at any time." To reinforce this point, Douglass then recites the last two stanzas of a long poem of his own composition, published in his newspaper in January of 1857 under the title "The Tyrant's Jubilee":

> The fire thus kindled, may be revived again;
> The flames are extinguished, but the embers remain;
> One terrible blast may produce an ignition,
> Which shall wrap the whole south in wild conflagration.

The pathway of tyrants lies over volcanoes;
The very air they breathe is heavy with sorrows;
Agonizing heart-throbs convulse them while sleeping,
And the wind whispers Death as over them sweeping.

William Gleason, who first identified this poem, places it in the context of Douglass's career-long engagement with and promotion of antislavery poetry, speculating persuasively that Douglass produced "The Tyrant's Jubilee" as a kind of corrective, since "abolitionist poetry had done so poor a job of representing black rebellion."[105] The imagery in these lines—transformative geological power held in reserve, waiting to be "revived"—resonates both with tropes employed by Douglass elsewhere of natural forces unleashed and with his description of the immanence/imminence of historical change in "The Anti-Slavery Movement." But, here, that dormant state of social reform temporarily obscured, has become the latent energy of violent black insurrection.

Notwithstanding Gleason's observation about most antislavery poetry's evasions of black rebellion, the lines from "The Tyrant's Jubilee" as they appear in the Dred Scott speech constitute an extension, rather than a counterpoint, to the lines from "A Psalm of Life" that Douglass recites in the Fourth of July address. And in more ways than one: in place of Longfellow's conventional, though slightly modified, hymnal form (he adds an extra beat to the expected trimeter of the second and fourth lines of each quatrain), Douglass employs the much longer, and relatively rare, Alexandrine line, which can often feel like lines of trimeter stitched together. The effect, pointedly ironic in the present context of Douglass's quickening of the pace of history, is a poetic line that can seem *too* long, and that slows the pace of the poem, as if to extend, torturously, the "heart-throbs" that haunt slaveholders' dreams. "The Tyrant's Jubilee" also extends Longfellow's poem insofar as it takes seriously—or takes *literally*—Longfellow's call to action, which "Psalm" leaves deliberately unspecified and abstract and, therefore, endlessly portable, adaptable to virtually any circumstance.[106] So while "A Psalm of Life" does not explicitly encourage violent rebellion generally or slave uprising specifically, it also can't be said that it doesn't—which, for immediatists like Douglass, was surely no small part of the poem's appeal. Indeed, among black writers that appeal lasted for more than a century. For instance, the twentieth-century immediatist Amiri Baraka alludes to and revises Longfellow in his poem "It's Nation Time" (1970):

Time to get
together
time to be one strong fast black enrgy space
one pulsating positive magnetism, rising
time to get up and
be.[107]

An example of what Daylanne English calls "strategic presentism," Baraka's poem emphasizes "urgency [and] action," modifying and truncating Longfellow's line, omitting the word "doing" which Baraka renders redundant in his call to be "strong fast black enrgy [sic]."[108]

Just as Douglass's citation of the Longfellow stanza signals a shift in the Fourth of July speech, so does the recitation from "The Tyrant's Jubilee" help him turn a corner in the *Dred Scott* address. Having invoked his own sort of "strong fast black enrgy"—in the form of the (very real) possibility of a violent overthrow of the slaveocracy—Douglass pivots back to politics; specifically, to the U.S. Constitution. First, he criticizes disunionists like Garrison for "fighting a dead form [the Union] instead of a living and powerful reality [slavery]." The Constitution isn't responsible for slavery, Douglass argues, the American people are. What's more, "dissolution of the Union" would only serve to preserve slavery by "shut[ting] up the system in its own congenial barbarism."[109] Further, Douglass rehearses in more detail than in the Fourth of July speech his argument that the Constitution is *not* proslavery according to the "plain and common sense reading" of it; that is, according to a reading that "refuse[s] to see slavery where slavery is not, and only to see slavery where it is."[110] Those who see it otherwise, "delight in supposed intentions—intentions nowhere expressed in the Constitution." Lastly, Douglass takes Justice Taney to task on a narrowly specific point: his historical claim that a belief in the inferiority of blacks at the time of the adoption of the Constitution was, in Taney's words, "fixed and universal with the civilized portion of the white race...an axiom of morals which no one thought of disputing."[111]

Each of these arguments—about disunion, about Constitutional interpretation, and about the facts of late-eighteenth-century antislavery sentiment—follows from Douglass's insistence that "we have to do not with the dead, but the living, not with the past, but the living present." Garrisonian disunionism, Douglass points out, fails to abide by Garrison's own oft-stated commitment to the "living present." The Union, Douglass argues, is but a form, "a mere human arrangement," contingent and mutable. Yet disunionists treat it as if it were fixed and static, as if the Union's past character or "arrangement" possesses the power to bind present generations to an earlier period in history. At the same time, Garrison's mistake— which is also Taney's mistake—is to view the Constitution as if it were bound to the era of its adoption (or, as literary historicists say about literary texts, its moment of production), as if its historicity could be constrained by the time of its creation. In the same way, the proslavery interpretation of the Constitution, Douglass asserts, depends upon "showing that the Constitution does not mean what it says, and says what it does not mean" and assuming that it "is to be interpreted in the light of a secret and unwritten understanding of its framers."[112] Douglas calls this a "contemptible, underhand method" of interpretation. It is "underhand" because it relies upon things *other than* what is available to immediate apprehension; specifically, upon knowledge—historical knowledge—of the non-public debates at the Constitutional Convention. (We might say that Douglass rejects symptomatic reading and the hermeneutics of suspicion!) That knowledge, however, is available only to the few, not to the many, which is why Douglass leans heavily on "common sense" and rules of legal interpretation that are, like the causes of antislavery, derived not from any particular moment in time or point of origin, but that are "as old as law" itself. Such rules are not the province of judges, lawyers, and other specialists, but are apparent and available to everyone, which is why Douglass asks "*any* man to read the Constitution" (emphasis mine).[113] Douglass advocates an *amateur* reading of the Constitution: creative, heterodox, and rooted principally in the passions and exigencies of *now*, rather than in the imperative to preserve a continuity of readings, loyal to the "dead past," stable and consistent across time.[114]

Which makes Douglass's final argument that he mounts with particular outrage, somewhat surprising. Having established, for purposes of Constitutional interpretation in the present that the eighteenth-century context is beside the point, why does Douglass contend so fiercely for historical accuracy on the question of antislavery sentiment at the time of the framing? After quoting Taney at length on this point, Douglass says, in one of the most impassioned moments of the speech:

> As a man, an American, a citizen, a colored man of both Anglo-Saxon and African descent, I denounce this representation as a most scandalous and devilish perversion of the Constitution, and a brazen misstatement of the facts of history.[115]

To correct this "perversion" of history, Douglass provides concrete historical evidence of antislavery sentiment in the 1780s and 1790s, focusing primarily on the church, which he claims "is often a better index of the state of opinion and feeling than is even the government itself."[116] He quotes documents from the Methodist and Presbyterian churches, then from a letter written by George Washington, notes the presence of abolition societies in slaveholding states, asserts that a number of the framers "looked for the gradual but certain abolition of slavery," and cites William Goodell on the free-black franchise in eleven of the thirteen colonies. Thus Douglass, however much his new view of the Constitutional interpretation might disregard the past, nevertheless, demonstrates his own sense of respect for historical fact and proves himself—in contrast to Taney—a conscientious student of history.

But what interests me here more than the care Douglass takes to show that to be presentist need not make one a- or antihistorical are the grounds upon which he denounces Taney's "false" and irresponsible rendering of history. He takes Taney's misrepresentation of this historical record as an affront to his own sense of identity, variously construed. In fact, it's striking that Douglass describes himself as both "American" and a "citizen"—first, as if those two things are separate and distinct, and second, in direct defiance of Taney's ruling that Douglass (and every other person in the United States of "African descent") is neither an American nor a citizen.[117] In the Fourth of July address, Douglass had hinted slyly at both the nation's vexed definitions of citizenship (repeatedly referring to his audience, as many scholars have noted, as "fellow citizens") and his equally vexed lineage (in his jab about irregular descent). But, here, Douglass doesn't employ subtle irony to comment upon the nation's injustices, exclusions, and prejudices. Rather, he positions his American citizenship and biracial identity—or more precisely, the convergence of the two—as the place from which his denunciation issues. That place is both near and far, both present and future. In a gesture that is more than just anticipation, Douglass speaks from a moment in time that has not yet come to pass, but that the *Dred Scott* decision, as a harbinger of antislavery history's acceleration, has helped to make visible as a percept, a promise about to be fulfilled. Douglass speaks, then, from a moment of *transition*, a moment of becoming, or what Mead would call "emergence," and at this moment, it is not, to recall Priscilla Wald's important reading, that Douglass is "neither citizen nor alien," but rather, he is *both* citizen *and* alien and a stranger, just as he is—and the list is important here—a man and an American (and not an American) and a citizen (and not a citizen) and an African and an Anglo-Saxon.[118] On this point, Mead is once again useful, since just such a "capacity of being several things at once" is Mead's definition of "sociality," one of the key features of the present being its "social nature." But, here, *I* anticipate, for the sociality of the present is the subject of Chapter 5.

Israel Potter; or, Hither and Thither History

"Everything is lost through this shillyshallying, timidity called prudence," the fictionalized John Paul Jones exclaims during his initial swaggering appearance in Herman Melville's remarkable *Israel Potter: His Fifty Years of Exile* (1855). "To be effectual," he continues, channeling Captain Ahab, "war should be carried on like a monsoon; one changeless determination of every particle toward one unalterable aim. But in vacillating councils, statesmen idle about like the cats' paws in calms."[1] The third in a succession of Melville's novels featuring reckless, impetuous characters—Ahab, Pierre Glendinning, and Paul Jones—the comparatively neglected *Israel Potter*, even more than *Moby-Dick* or *Pierre*, captures something of Melville's own impatient temper during the first half of the 1850s. Dogged by financial difficulties and commercial failures, Melville's career at this period seems marked by a particularly acute sense of urgency and haste, a state of mind registered in Ishmael's expression, part apostrophe and part lament, near the end of the "Cetology" chapter of *Moby-Dick*: "Oh Time, Strength, Cash, and Patience!"[2]

Yet if time and strength and cash and patience were all limited resources for Melville personally in the early 1850s, the first and the last of them, at least, nevertheless proved to be generative literary affordances, animating some of his most charismatic characters and providing him, conceptually and formally, with a powerful mode of engagement with the most pressing moral and political issues of his day. Or so this chapter will argue. Of course, time and im/patience also, as Chapters 3 and 4 have shown, figured prominently in the politics of slavery, increasingly so after the Compromise of 1850. Temporal questions framed public debate and structured individuals' attitudes and affective responses to the persistence of slavery as a social reality and a moral stain. With varying degrees of explicitness, Melville's fiction of the period registers and at times reflects the restless and seemingly reckless temper displayed by immediatist abolitionists and other citizens who found themselves weary, like Paul Jones, of waiting for the "idle" statesmen of the nation's "vacillating councils" to finally devise a permanent solution to the problem, rather than forestalling real resolution with yet another temporary "settlement" (to recall Frederick Douglass's apt description). By the mid-1850s, particularly after the outbreak of violence in Kansas and Nebraska, more and more citizens—among them Romantics like Emerson, Douglass, and John Brown—seemed eager for the arrival of monsoon season. As Emerson put it, waiting for time to put an end to slavery requires a "patience . . . almost too sublime for mortals."[3]

Locating Melville along the spectrum of responses to antislavery—from outright aversion to cautious prudence to reckless, even violent, impetuosity—has proven an often perplexing critical task, even though a significant body of scholarship has clearly established the involvement of his 1850s fiction, most notably "Benito Cereno," in the politics of race and slavery more generally. In this chapter, I enlist one of Melville's least-read novels, *Israel Potter*, in that ongoing scholarly project. *Israel Potter* is an especially apt subject for my final chapter because it brings together this book's two primary threads: the undoing of history in the antebellum period, exemplified by the wayward unhistorical fictions of Chapters 1 and 2, works that comprise an alternative tradition of historical fiction that never quite came into being in the nineteenth-century (but that reappeared in the twentieth); and the reconstitution of the present and its possibilities epitomized by some of the antebellum period's most potent nonfiction, the essays and speeches examined in Chapters 3 and 4, writings that derive their force from their deep investment in *now* as the time of experience, action, and ethical reform.

Israel Potter, brief yet capacious, braids these threads together. Like the works of Irving, Sedgwick, and Neal, Melville's third-hand tale of a forgotten Revolutionary patriot displays an irreverence toward history writing that likewise contests the prevailing Romantic historiography and progressive nationalism of the antebellum period.[4] Melville experiments with a style of history writing that, paradoxically, is devoted less to the past than to the present, one that attempts to render not what we know about history, but to capture the experience of living and acting in it. Or to put this another way, Melville's brand of unhistorical fiction seeks to invent a form that captures a particular kind of temporal experience: the experience of an improvisatory, extemporized, multidirectional *now*. This, I hope to show, is what accounts for the novel's formal peculiarities, most evident in its almost obsessive preoccupation with time and its variabilities. In *Israel Potter*, Melville tries to write a history as if he doesn't know its outcome.

The historical experience rendered in *Israel Potter* thus rhymes with the attitude toward history displayed by immediatists and other Romantic presentists. Its narrative strategies share an historical sensibility that bears strong affinities with the modes of temporal being associated with the embrace of the present I have explored in the last two chapters: most significantly, the immediatist abolitionism that was such a socially disruptive force in the 1850s when the novel was published, but also the particular disposition toward history and historical change, sometimes political (as in Garrisonian abolitionism), sometimes philosophical (as in Emerson's writings), and sometimes aesthetic (as in Neal's *Seventy-Six*) that I have been calling Romantic presentism. These forms of immediatism all share a distrust of the slow, uniform time of linear chronology, national progress, and social amelioration in favor of the potentially threatening uneven tempos demanded, and the uncertainties generated, by impatience, haste, and reckless precipitancy—the defining features, I hope to show, of *Israel Potter's* formal design.

Anticipation once again provides the organizational schema for my inquiry. Fear and hope, as Chapters 1 through 4 have shown, formed two of the most powerful "affective structures" through which antebellum Americans experienced the period's politics.[5] In this chapter, I once again describe the difference between them as a difference between knowing and unknowing, between a disposition that calculates the certainties of calamity and one that gambles on the uncertainties generated by the impetuous embrace of novelty, or, to recall Angelina Grimké's pithy phrase, between walking by sight and walking by faith. But with *Israel Potter*, that story takes some new turns. One is a shift in focus toward *literary* forms of anticipation; specifically, that anticipatory narrative mode called foreshadowing or prolepsis. Prolepsis is central to *Israel Potter's* formal design and its temporal anatomy and my reading proceeds by way of an exploration of the novel's differing uses of foreshadowing, its movement away from a foreshadowing that *knows*, that is certain, and toward one that doesn't, but that hopes. Another turn is a queer one; specifically, a turn toward new forms of sociability and world making promised by what I identify as the novel's queer temporalities and spectralities. Toward these ends, I begin not with *Israel Potter* but with a coeval companion piece, the short story "The Lightning-Rod Man," a text that takes cautious prudence (and the fear-mongering that often attends it) and its rejection, as its central subject. That reading prepares us to turn to *Israel Potter*, a novel that, while it is unable, finally, to choose hope over fear, at least contains the conditions for a kind of hopefulness, which it glimpses in forms of sociality that reside in an unspecified "as yet." Thus despite its abiding cynicism, *Israel Potter*, nevertheless, perhaps more than any other text in this study, imagines, or at least anticipates, the possibility of a renovated and renewed social world.

Lightning-Rod Men

"The Lightning-Rod Man" first appeared in the August 1854 issue of *Putnam's Monthly Magazine*, the same issue that ran Chapters IV through VII of *Israel Potter*. Short and enigmatic, the story recounts the visit, on a stormy night, of a bumptious peddler of copper lightning rods to the home of the narrator, who refuses to fall for the salesman's manipulative tactics. Because nothing much happens in the tale—the storm rages, lessens, and then increases again in intensity as the exchange between the lightning-rod man and the narrator becomes increasingly heated—it tends to invite allegorical readings.[6] Yet critics in pursuit of its allegorical meanings have not considered that the tale might gesture toward slavery politics, a curious fact, perhaps, given both the strongly antislavery editorial position of *Putnam's* and the fact that so much of the rest of Melville's *Putnam's* fiction during the same period ("Benito Cereno," "The Bell-Tower," "The Encantadas," and "I and My Chimney") *does* address the politics of slavery, either directly or obliquely.[7] Moreover, as we saw in the last chapter, Melville had already participated, quite explicitly, in the period's meteorological figurations of debates over slavery and the fate of the nation. "The Lightning-Rod Man" revisits the questions taken up in the Vivenza section of *Mardi* and "The Candles" chapter of *Moby-Dick*—but with what appears to be much less ambivalence. Whereas Babbalanja's brief for gradualism may or may not be seen to voice Melville's own position and whereas Ahab's madcap playing with fire might seem almost impossible to endorse, there is little doubt as to which side "The Lightning-Rod Man" takes: the story emphatically rejects the kind of fearmongering masquerading as prudence that typified so much antiabolitionist and gradualist discourse.[8]

One night during a thunderstorm, a stranger selling lightning rods appears at the house of the narrator. Taking advantage of the tempest outside, the peddler attempts to play upon the assumed fears of his potential customer. But in the narrator, the salesman has met his match. Melville signals the opposition between them at the story's outset by contrasting their attitudes toward the storm. While the narrator views it, with its "grand irregular thunder" and "zig-zag irradiations" of lightning as "a fine thunder-storm," the salesman considers it "awful!"[9] Invited into the house, the salesman commences his routine. He carefully situates himself in the center of the room, resisting the narrator's entreaties to join him near the hearth to warm himself by the fire. Instead, the salesman implores the narrator to join *him* in the middle of the room, explaining, with melodramatic concern, that "by far the most dangerous part of a house during such a terrific tempest... is the fireplace" (119). He goes on to point out the many other dangerous features of the house: the iron window bars, bell-pulls, chimney, and walls, all of which conduct electricity. Playing along, for a time, the narrator soon asks why the room in which they are standing is the safest. To which the salesman replies:

> Your house is a one-storied house, with an attic and a cellar; this room is between. Hence its comparative safety. Because lightning sometimes passes from the clouds to the earth, and sometimes from the earth to the clouds. Do you comprehend?—and I choose the middle of the room, because, if the lightning should strike the house at all, it would come down the chimney or walls; so obviously, the further you are from them the better.[10]

This description signals the story's political concerns. Figuratively, the image suggests careful moderation; it enforces the "middle" way as safest and suggests that danger and calamity are best avoided by occupying a position that is "between"—in this case, between the upper and lower portions of the house (between, perhaps, North and South?). The salesman cautions against occupying the peripheries or extremes.

At the same time, the salesman's plea for prudence features a certainty about future events, a foreknowledge that echoes the rhetorical position of more moderate antislavery advocates like Catherine Beecher, who, as we saw in Chapter 3, worried that more radical abolitionists like Grimké were dangerously precipitate. For Beecher, as for Melville's salesman, danger is not just possible or probable, but nearly *inevitable*. Both of them, in their way, foreshadow calamity. "Think," the salesman says to conclude his pitch, "of being a heap of charred offal like a haltered horse burnt in his stall;—and all in one flash!"[11] It's this point—the salesman's certainty toward future events—that causes the already irritated narrator to finally lose his cool. On what authority, he asks, becoming heated, is the salesman able "to peddle round [his] indulgences from divine ordinations?"[12] As the storm outside wanes, the narrator continues, insisting that what is to come is beyond anyone's ability to know:

> The hairs of our heads are numbered, and the days of our lives. In thunder as in sunshine, I stand at ease in the hands of my God. False negotiator, away! See the scroll of the storm is rolled back; the house is unharmed; and in the blue heavens I read in the rainbow, that the Deity will not, of purpose, make war on man's earth."[13]

"War" is the unexpected term here; nothing else in the story prepares us for that particular metaphor—a sign that therefore gestures, I am suggesting, toward political conditions outside the purview of the story itself: sectional division and the looming threat of sectional violence. Indeed, this allegorical signaling is further reinforced by the salesman's infuriated—and baffling—reply: "'Impious wretch,' foamed the stranger... 'I will publish your infidel notions!'"[14]

Most readers, understandably, have found this the story's most perplexing moment.[15] After all, what is "infidel" about the narrator's response to the lightning-rod man? And why does the salesman threaten to "publish" those notions? One answer is suggested by the intersection of abolition and print culture, which a number of critics have explored generatively.[16] William Lloyd Garrison and *The Liberator*, of course, occupied a pivotal position within abolition's print culture. And one prominent feature of the print discourse of abolition were widespread and longstanding references to Garrison as "impious" and an "infidel," accusations leveled at him because of his heterodox notions on any number of issues in addition to his immediatism (such as his view of northern clergy, his position on the public roles of women in social movements, his anti-Sabbatarianism). Garrison embraced and reveled in these characterizations, reprinting and repeating such imprecations both in the pages of his newspaper and in his public speeches. Examples are so abundant as to hardly need rehearsing. An 1850 notice in *The Liberator* reprints an article from the *Cincinnati Gazette* describing the proceedings of the New England Anti-Slavery Convention, "wherein the Bible, the churches, ministers of the gospel, Christianity, and great and good men were assailed with impious execrations by Abby Kelley, Wendell Phillips, Garrison, Wright, Foster, and their fanatical associates."[17] In another reprint, this one from 1853, an article from the *Boston Bee* about the Hartford Bible Convention appears under the headline "The Late Infidel Convention." In it, Garrison is described as "the bold leader of the infidels" while his friend Parker Pillsbury is accused of "belch[ing] out…fearful impiousness."[18] Remarks such as these were so common that Garrison often made them the starting point of the subject of his own addresses. A speech he gave at Faneuil Hall in Boston on December 30, 1846, for example, begins: "The 'infidel anti-slavery movement!' The 'infidel abolitionists' of the United States! How and why infidel? What do the abolitionists aim to accomplish?"[19]

In this context, what is "infidel" is the narrator's blithe disregard for the dangers of the (metaphorical) storm, his willingness to risk even death—both the "hairs of our head" and the "days of our lives" are numbered anyway, he says—rather than invest in precautionary measures to protect himself against it. As his exclamation in the story's opening paragraph—"a fine thunder-storm"—indicates, the narrator *welcomes* the thunder and the lightning. That this attitude is an essentially political one is made clear by the narrator's response to the salesman's brief disquisition on the safety of the "middle" of the house. The narrator does not find the salesman's description of the many dangers the house presents "alarming." Rather, the narrator notes that something the salesman said "strangely inspired confidence." Specifically, the narrator finds himself drawn to the idea that "sometimes lightning flashes from the earth to the clouds." This the salesman calls "the returning-stroke," a phrase the narrator repeats: "The returning-stroke; that is, from earth to sky. Better and better."[20] One might view the "returning-stroke" as suggestive of either revolution—a power from below striking at something above—or of blasphemy (reminiscent of Ahab's willingness to strike the sun); perhaps it is both.[21] In his reading, Joshua Matthews argues for the former, asserting, "the egalitarian narrator appreciates the idea because of the symbolic anti-authoritarianism of the rod's function. The rod is potentially a tool of political revolution."[22] But while I agree that the returning-stroke provides a figure for political revolution, Matthews is mistaken in attributing that power to the rod. The rod's function is simply to direct the electrical charge along a preferred path (the ground). Return strokes, the dramatic bolts we typically see when lightning strikes, occur even in the absence of lightning rods. The return stroke is a *natural* phenomenon.

In other words, it's not the rod that figures revolutionary power. Quite the opposite: the rod helps to contain powerful electrical currents, to render them harmless and safe. In rejecting the rod, then, the narrator rejects attempts to attenuate revolutionary energy. So the conflict between the narrator and the lightning-rod man, I am suggesting, is the difference between those who welcomed what Melville in *Battle-Pieces* would call "the coming-storm"—radicals like Frederick Douglass, William Lloyd Garrison, and Captain Ahab—and those who sought to protect themselves from its dangers—slaveholders, unionists, and Starbuck. Indeed, the former wanted to feel the lightning's shock—"would fain feel [its] pulse," as Ahab puts it in "The Candles"—and to channel its power, not to conduct it harmlessly to the earth, but to transmit it outwardly toward the agents of injustice. Recall, for example, Douglass's criticism of "those who profess freedom" but "deprecate agitation": "they want rain without thunder and lightning,"[23] For his part,

Garrison famously described himself as "all on fire" for the cause of abolition. Even more to the point, he also described himself, on more than one occasion, as "storm-proof."[24] Garrison's ability to absorb the shock and withstand the storm is echoed by his fellow abolitionist Thoreau, who, in 1852, quipped to Emerson, while "talking of lightning-rods, that the only rod of safety was in the vertebrae of his own spine."[25] In his own fearless attitude toward the storm (he jokingly thanks the lightning-rod man for bringing "this noble storm" to his cottage) the narrator of Melville's story aligns with these *other* lightning-rod men—Ahab, Douglass, Garrison, and Thoreau—not charlatans playing on the fears of the anxious and prudent, but figures who wished to harness atmospheric power and direct it toward their cause. "O that I had a voice louder than a thousand thunders," Garrison said, "that it might shake the land and electrify the dead."[26]

"The Lightning-Rod Man" concludes with the narrator physically accosting the salesman, breaking his rod, and forcibly throwing him from his house. He then adds, ruefully, "But spite of my treatment, and spite of my dissuasive talk of him to my neighbors, the Lightning-rod man still dwells in the land ... and drives a brave trade with the fears of man." Almost as if to illustrate the story's final point, just a few months later in December 1854, *Putnam's* ran a lengthy article by William Gilmore Simms titled "Our Parties and Politics: A Southerner's View of the Subject."[27] (Chapters VXII–XIX of *Israel Potter* ran in the same issue.) Trading on "the fears of men" by invoking peril and cataclysm as the result of imprudence, the essay exemplifies the rhetorical chronopolitics that "The Lightning-Rod Man" allegorizes. That kind of gradualist politics values hesitation and sober deliberation over impulsiveness and passionate action and views history as a slow process of amelioration. Indeed, Simms begins by situating "the present aspect of American politics," within just this kind of historical continuum. Now is a moment in time, he says, that "invites reflection and calm discussion." "We have arrived at a standpoint in history," he continues, "when it behooves every patriot man to pause and reflect. The living present imposes the weightiest responsibilities; the past is teeming with instruction; and the future is radiant with hope."[28] But Simms's "living present," unlike Garrison's or Longfellow's, is hardly alive at all. Rather, it is characterized by its lack of movement, the arrival at what he calls a "stand-point" in history, a time given to "pause." Simms thus advises his readers to "trust" that "*in His own good time* ... God will move above the troubled waters with creative power, evolving light from darkness" (emphasis mine).[29]

Despite its attempt to assume the mantle of "deliberate and calculated purpose" and to approach matters "seriously and calmly," the essay soon becomes an antiabolitionists screed, one that, echoing the tactics of Melville's lightning-rod salesman, trades on fear but presents itself as thoughtful prudence. Simms's basic thesis is that intemperate "New England fanaticism ... makes war against" the South. To make this case, Simms aligns "abolitionism" with "Jacobinism," in which "blood and carnage, fraternal discord, and civil war are ... *rashly* courted" (emphasis mine).[30] Abolitionism's "infidel spirit," he warns, "will yet awaken in all sections of our country a public sentiment that will sweep the God-defying empiricism from among us with the bosom of destruction."[31] Then, in what reads almost like the historiographical obverse of Frederick Douglass's quickened history of antislavery in his Dred Scott speech, Simms provides an account of the recent political history of slavery: in his version a tale of slow, steady progress periodically arrested by the "mad haste" of fanatical abolitionists who "arouse the passions" and thwart the forward movement of history. The Missouri Compromise, for example, despite is violations of Southern sovereignty, nevertheless "disposed of" the controversy for a time so that "the public mind settled down into quiet acquiescence." However, the Virginia legislature's response to Nat Turner's rebellion "infused new life into the abolitionists." The "renewed…agitation" that ensued hampered the efforts of the "calmest and ablest" of Virginia's citizens, many of whom "were open and avowed advocates of prospective emancipation," gradualism by another name. Thus, had it not been for the counterproductive efforts of "fanatics of the North," the Virginians' plans for emancipation might have been realized "in a few years."[32]

Continuing this history, Simms describes the Gag Rule (conceding that it may not have been good policy—or even constitutional), the annexation of Texas, debates over the Wilmot Proviso, the organization of the Oregon territory, and then the Compromise of 1850. The last of these, Simms says, saw the entire nation "lashed into a state of intense excitement." But despite the "mad haste" of the abolitionists which led the county "blindfold to the brink of the precipice," the country was saved when the "Northern masses" "affrighted and horror-struck at the blackness of darkness before them," "shrunk back" at the last moment.[33] The Compromise, Simms claims, especially its fugitive slave provision, affirmed the principle of state rights and with that "a controverted question was settled, and it was settled for all coming time upon the principles of the Constitution and of equal right."[34] Simms ends his tour through this political history with the Kansas-Nebraska Act, only recently introduced and still under consideration at the time of his essay's publication, and expresses confidence that time will do its architect Stephen A. Douglas "ample justice." "The present storm is but temporary in duration," Simms assures his readers, "there is more of thunder than of lightning in its clouds."[35]

Simms's weather forecast was ultimately even less accurate than his history, of course. Kansas would soon be bleeding; the coming storm would rage. But the more important point here is that Simms deploys a set of figures—and speaks a language of caution, danger, and "infidel notions," figured by thunderstorms and the prospect of war—that, just as they do in "The Lightning-Rod Man," help mark distinct attitudes toward events to come, toward the prospect of social and historical change, the very attitudes that often distinguished moderate antislavery advocates from radical abolitionists.[36] Those attitudes might be described, to recall John Paul Jones's terms, as the "shillyshallying timidity" of prudence, on the one hand, and the "monsoon"-like "determination" toward a single given aim, on the other.

Melville's Paul Jones, even more so than the narrator of "The Lightning-Rod Man," embodies the latter disposition. Like Garrison, Jones, the animating spirit of *Israel Potter*, is associated with fire; he is "flaming with wild enterprises." And like *Moby-Dick's* "Old Thunder," he is the storm incarnate, "hovering like a thunder-cloud off the crowded harbors...discharging his lightnings" (see 109). Recalling Ahab in "The Candles," he flies in battle "hither and thither like the meteoric corposant-ball, which shiftingly dances on the tips and verges of ships' rigging in storms." But the resonances between "The Lightning-Rod Man" and *Israel Potter* extend beyond their shared thematic interest in the conflict between prudence and precipitancy. They also share a formal method, one whose primary imperative is haste. This accounts, for instance, for the brevity of the two texts: "The Lightning-Rod Man" is by far the shortest of the *The Piazza Tales* just as *Israel Potter* is the shortest of Melville's novels. Though basic, this is no superficial observation; their compactness bespeaks a narrative impatience, a sense of urgency that manifests in an often-dizzying reading experience. That experience derives from Melville's experiments with a somewhat uncharacteristic narrative style that eschews his usual discursive prolixity in favor of narrative economy. Here for example is part of the opening paragraph of "The Lightning-Rod Man," which rushes the salesman into the scene through monologue, free of narrative conjunctions:

> Hark!—some one at the door. Who is this that chooses a time of thunder for making calls? And why don't he, man-fashion, use the knocker, instead of making that doleful undertaker's clatter with his fist against the hollow panel? But let him in. Ah, here he comes. "Good day, sir;" an entire stranger. "Pray be seated." What is that strange-looking walking-stick he carries:—"A fine thunder-storm, sir."[37]

Staccato sentences and phrases—"some one at the door," "But let him in," "here he comes," "an entire stranger"—hurry the action along, unhindered by exposition's decelerations. In fact, for most of the story, a few short paragraphs excepted, passages, even sentences, of narration are absent; the story consists almost entirely of dialogue and nearly achieves what the narrative theorist Gerard Genette calls "isochrony": a perfect congruence between the time of the narrative and the time of the story.[38]

Israel Potter: His Fifty Years of Exile is even more briskly paced than "The Lightning-Rod Man"—and even more explicitly concerned with time. I draw upon Genette's method and vocabulary for analyzing narrative speed to help make sense of this feature of the novel. *Israel Potter* both represents haste—as in the behavior of the impetuous Paul Jones, or of Israel himself, who, as we'll see, spends a great deal of time in the novel running, fleeing, and taking to his heels—and is itself a rather hasty production, what Walter Bezanson has aptly described as Melville's "hurry-up history."[39] But the novel's precipitancy derives less from its swift action and extemporaneous, improvisatory quality than from its narrator's preoccupation with and attitude toward time. Temporal concerns overload the novel. We are constantly reminded of the time of day, of how much time has elapsed, or how long an action will take. The text is replete with terms that indicate rapidity—"instantly," "shortly," and "presently." For much of the story's telling, the narrator seems oddly impatient to just get on with it. Repeatedly, he sweeps away long stretches of time with what seems like a dismissive wave of the hand: "Let us pass on to a less immature period," "other rovings ensued," "and so six months elapsed," "to be brief," "without more ado," and "to be short."

The novel's uneven tempos and its disrespect for the uniform passing of time even bothered some contemporary reviewers who seemed especially piqued by Melville's apparent disregard for anything even remotely resembling an equitable narrative distribution of the "fifty years" announced in the novel's subtitle. One reviewer, for example, wrote:

> Mr. Melville follows his hero's fortunes, from the time of his being taken prisoner by the English, with great minuteness in the beginning and middle of the book, and then suddenly generalises towards the end for the sake of getting to the death of "Israel Potter," without exceeding the compass of one small volume.

Another complained that while the novel is "A downright good book...*five years*, in place of *fifty*, would have been a more appropriate title, seeing that forty five of them are shuffled off in a few pages at the close."[40] It may well be surprising, in the wake of *Pierre*, that Melville could still leave readers wanting more; perhaps that was even part of his aim. But I think the novel's peculiar and persistent haste still begs the question: what's the big rush? To approach this question, I concentrate upon the novel's telling of time, devoting particular attention to the sorts of temporal markers I've already begun to describe—verb tenses and adverbs, words that indicate time or tempo, references to dates or the time of day.[41] Such a granular focus, I hope, can help make sense of the rather disorienting experience of reading *Israel Potter*, which has often been deemed a failure, despite occasional flashes of brilliance.[42]

What Might Yet Be

Very late in *Israel Potter*, just before the novel turns from its comical, headlong account, twenty-two chapters long, of Israel's (mis)adventures as a soldier, an envoy, a captive, and a seaman during the American Revolution and toward its final four chapters depicting Israel's forty years of labor and poverty in London, Melville ends a chapter with this one sentence paragraph: "But here we anticipate a page."[43] The sentence is worth pausing over for a number of reasons. First, it is one of only two moments in the novel where Melville's narrator employs the conventional third person plural pronoun. Second, the sentence marks a return to the present tense—though a very different present tense—that characterizes, albeit unevenly, the novel's early chapters, but then disappears for most of the rest of the book. And third, and perhaps most interestingly, the sentence constitutes a very peculiar way of marking the passage of time, transferring its measurement in the novel from the diegetic to the extradiegetic level. That is to say, the narrator does not "anticipate" a future moment in the life of Israel (as in what Genette would call prolepsis), having skipped over some interval of time that might be more or less accurately measured by days, weeks, months, or years. Rather, the narrator anticipates the next page of his book, having skipped only that interval of time measured by the distance between this moment of narration and the one that begins on the next page. But what sort of unit of temporal measurement is "a page"? Is it a self-conscious reference to Melville's composition of the text? In that case we might want to know, say, when he completed Chapter 22 and when he began to write Chapter 23. Or maybe we're to take "a page," literally, as a reference to the material properties of the text. But if so, which text? In the novel's first edition, the end of Chapter 22 and the beginning of Chapter 23 appear on facing pages; the reader doesn't even have to flip a leaf. The interval is even shorter in the novel's original serial publication, where the beginning of Chapter 23 is printed on the same page as the end of Chapter 22—a distance of just a column inch or two. Or perhaps "a page" is not meant to be taken literally at all, but metaphorically, as a reference to the reader's experience of the text. In which case "a page" indicates the period of time—anywhere from a few seconds to never—between the reader's completion of one chapter and her commencement of the next.

Of course, all of this might seem to be overly punctilious, making too much out of very little, if it weren't for the fact that for most of the novel, the narrator is himself especially fastidious about the time: what time of day it is, how swiftly or slowly time passes, the length of time spent on recounting or *not* recounting some event or events. The narrator is especially aware of the clock, for example. He frequently registers the precise hour at which some event, typically of minor importance, occurs: Israel escapes from prison "about three o'clock in the morning;" he labors in the fields "till four o'clock;" the chambermaid knocks on his door "about half past ten o'clock"; and the ship of Paul Jones is seen off the coast of Scotland "about five o'clock." Just as frequently, the narrator will provide the duration of time between events or the amount of time it takes to accomplish a task: Israel sails aboard a whaleship "for sixteen months;" "in five minutes' time" he is on his way to London; he speaks with King George at Kew Gardens "for some ten minutes;" St. James' Park is "but a three minutes' walk" from the Old Brewery of the Palace; Benjamin Franklin looks over the papers Israel has brought to him "in half an hour's time"—and so forth. One could go on.

Other recurring words and phrases in the novel register the felt quality of time's movement or characters' particular temporal bearings. In almost every case, the experience is of urgency or haste: Israel "hastened to the woods," he was willing "to fly to battle at an instant's notice," he put "speed into his feet," he acts "quick as a flash," he "hurried on," he "bolted down" a loaf of bread, he moves "quick as lightning." Most outlandishly, at one point Melville has Israel take flight, "one dare say, at the rate of something less than thirty miles an hour"—a world-record pace. Other phrases and terms in the text, adverbs in particular, indicate rapid responses, immediate reactions, or time passing swiftly: "next moment" (which occurs in the novel eight times), "instantly," "instantaneously," or "in an instant" (versions of which occur some thirty times), "shortly" (twelve times), and what may be the novel's favorite and most important term "presently" (twenty-two times). In fact, "presently" performs multiple functions. It can mean *soon* (as in "Presently he came to hilly land in meadow") or it can mean *right now* (as in "Presently, passing the large mirror over the mantel, Paul caught a glimpse of his person") or it can mean *quickly* (as in "fortitude now presently left him"—because otherwise "now" renders "presently" redundant). The repeated use of "presently," which persistently reinforces time's brisk passage, helps lend the novel its "breathless" quality, to borrow Robert S. Levine's apt term, and reinforces the immediacy or present-ness that the novel works so hard to sustain in other ways, such as in its intermittent use of present-tense narration.[44]

It is worth noting at this point that none of these features of the novel's narrative discourse can be accounted for by Melville's source text, the 1824 *Life and Remarkable Adventures of Israel R. Potter*, which—as close as Melville sticks to it in his early chapters, and he sticks *very* close—features very few, if any, of these temporal markers, making their addition one of Melville's more significant deviations from the original text.[45] The former notes clock time only once, mentions intervals of time on only a very few occasions, and never uses, for instance, the terms *shortly* or *presently*. Nor can the recurrence of these temporal markers in Melville's *Israel Potter* be accounted for by any particular stylistic idiosyncrasy of Melville's. Specific references to the time of day and the use of the term *presently*, for example, occur far fewer times in more than twice the pages in both *Moby-Dick* and *Pierre*, two novels that are themselves, in their own ways, preoccupied with time.[46]

The cumulative effect of all of this timekeeping, this hustling and hastening, is a narrative discourse that seems to be racing against the clock and feels therefore as unsettled as Israel himself—constantly moving, changing, shifting, and improvising. Just as Israel takes on various disguises and roles over the course of the text—farmer, whaler, soldier, ghost, scarecrow, warrior, and peasant—so does the narrator adopt a variety of stances in relation to his material—biographer, "Editor," faithful historian, and at times mere witness of unfolding events. It's the difference between the last of these roles and the others that helps explain the novel's key terms "anticipate" and "presently." Together, these two terms organize *Israel Potter's* main historiographic and aesthetic principles. On the one hand, the novel strives to render history *presently*, to hastily pull it into a now that is happening, soon to pass away, and headed in unforeseen directions. In this, *Israel Potter* resembles John Neal's *Seventy-Six* and its aspiration to register the affective immediacy of historical experience. On the other hand, the novel displays an historical sensibility that recalls Frederick Douglass's investments in various forms of anticipation. This is best seen in the text's multiple instances of prolepsis or foreshadowing.[47] Ordinarily in a work of fiction, prolepsis is predicated on knowing, already, that which has not yet happened. But the narrator of *Israel Potter* tries to relinquish that knowledge. Or to put this another way, Melville tries to write a history as if he doesn't know its outcome, so it feels heedless, and precipitate, and improvised; but it doesn't quite succeed because he *does* know and because he has to bring it to a conclusion.

The early chapters of the novel repeatedly feature rather conventional, even heavy-handed, instances of foreshadowing, in which the narrator views all of Israel's youthful adventures before the war as preparation for his eventual role first as a revolutionary soldier and later as a fugitive in England. The novel's opening chapter, for instance, "The Birthplace of Israel," concludes, "How little he thought, when, as a boy, hunting after his father's stray cattle among these New England hills, he himself like a beast should be hunted through half of Old England, as a runaway rebel."[48] In the next chapter, when Israel becomes a chain-bearer for a surveying team, the narrator notes that Israel accepted the job "little thinking that the day was to come when he should clank the king's chain in a dungeon."[49] Soon after, Israel becomes a hunter of deer and beaver, causing the narrator to remark, in the novel's only use of the narrative first-person singular, "I suppose it never entered his mind that he was thus qualifying himself for a marksman of men."[50] Similarly, when Israel ships aboard a whaler, the narrator says that he "further intensified his aim by darting the whale-lance; still, unwittingly preparing himself for the Bunker hill rifle."[51]

These instances emphasize the gap—or what Peter Bellis describes as the "distance"—between the narrator and Israel, between the former's knowledge of future events and Israel's thoughtless unconcern, reinforced with very little subtlety by the narrator's language: "little thinking," "it never entered his mind," "unwittingly," for the past as prologue. The effect is to induce in the reader a sense of anticipation, or eager expectancy, for events yet to come. But one of the things that makes the novel's use of foreshadowing peculiar is the fact that when that later moment finally arrives—that is, when Israel finally does join the rebel army in Chapter 3, for example—the narrator refuses to satisfy those readerly expectations; he refuses to narrate. "But every one knows all about the battle," he says insouciantly, before devoting barely one paragraph to the famous skirmish.[52] In his analysis of prolepsis, Genette distinguishes between what he calls "advance notices"—explicit foreshadowings of events to come, like the instances listed above—and "advance mentions," which he describes as "insignificant seed[s]" whose importance only becomes recognizable in retrospect. Advance mentions, Genette explains, raise questions about the narrative competence of readers; it takes practice and skill, a familiarity with genre conventions and codes, to recognize advance mentions. But that competence also makes available "false snares," advance mentions that turn out not to be advance mentions at all, the ferreting out of which by readers, in turn, makes possible *false* false snares, and so on. The narrator of *Israel Potter* plays a kind of inverted version of this game with his advance notices: announcing them with so much obviousness that by the time the narrative present catches up to what it had earlier anticipated the now-present event hardly seems worth recounting anymore. Take, for instance, another scene in Chapter 3, after Israel is captured by the British navy, escapes, and finds himself on the run in England. To evade detection he offers to switch clothes with an old ditch digger. "Little did [Israel] ween," the narrator says, "that these wretched rags he now wore, were but suitable to that long career of destitution before him; one brief career of adventurous wanderings; and then, forty torpid years of pauperism."[53] But, as the reviewers mentioned above, feeling cheated, complained, those "forty torpid years" are compressed into just a few chapters.

Nor is this the only way in which the narrator undercuts the function of his narrative prolepsis. It is undermined, too, by the text's shifting verb tenses and by the narrator's self-defined role as faithful "recorder" of the events of Israel's life. The early chapters of the novel, as I've said, slip in and out of present-tense narration. The shifts often happen so quickly and so apparently randomly that it's sometimes hard to know whether the past or the present tense is the default mode from which the narrative occasionally lapses. Here is just one example, from Chapter 3, when Israel, newly landed in England as a prisoner of war and attempting to flee his captors "lets grow his wings... flying one dare say, at the rate of something less than thirtymiles an hour":

> "Stop thief!" is now the cry. Numbers rushed from the road-side houses. After a mile's chase, the poor panting deer is caught.

> Finding it was no use now to prevaricate, Israel boldly confesses himself a prisoner-of-war. The officer, a good fellow as it turned out, had him escorted back to the inn; where, observing to the landlord, that this must needs be a true-blooded Yankee, he calls for liquors to refresh Israel after his run. Two soldiers are then appointed to guard him for the present. This was towards evening; and up to a late hour at night, the inn was filled with strangers crowding to see the Yankee rebel, as they politely termed him. These honest rustics seemed to think that Yankees were a sort of wild creatures, a species of a 'possum or kangaroo. But Israel is very affable with them. That liquor he drank from the hand of his foe, has perhaps warmed his heart towards all the rest of his enemies"[54]

Both of these paragraphs feature a number of abrupt shifts in tense. They happen from sentence to sentence, sometimes even within a sentence. The second paragraph, for instance, moves from the simple present to the past tense, with a present participle thrown in for good measure, back to the present, then to the past tense, before returning, finally, to the present tense again. Such oscillations can make it difficult to gain one's temporal bearings. When, for instance, did it "turn out" that the officer was a good fellow? Before or after he had Israel escorted to the inn? And what to make of the perplexing construction "are then appointed to guard him for the present"? If we are witnessing events as they unfold, in the present tense, shouldn't they be appointed to guard Israel "now"? And while "for the present" apparently indicates that this guardianship will be of limited duration, the phrase seems unnecessary and serves mainly to add further to the passage's temporal confusion; after all, "then" suggests later and "for the present" suggests now.

More to the point, however, is that these shifts sometimes make it difficult to locate the *narrator* in time. It is almost as if Melville can't decide which temporal perspective to take: that of an observer watching events as they transpire or that of one recounting events that have already occurred. The former sort of narrator would be unaware of how things turn out and would, therefore, be incapable of prolepsis (but not, as we'll see, of anticipation), while the latter knows how things turned out and can therefore hardly resist understanding present events in relation to later ones. One might think of these as two different forms of presentism: the first devoted to immediacy, to the apprehension of and response to things as they happen, to what is going on without regard to where things are headed or from whence they have come. The second imposes a shape and a meaning on past events after the fact, viewing them from a now-present perspective that no longer apprehends the former present in its "then-presentness."

Melville's narrator alternates between these two positions, which correspond roughly to what Genette calls "story time" and "discourse time," but that might also be understood as the difference between knowing and not knowing. Immediately following the suggestion, quoted above, that liquor may have warmed Israel's heart toward his captors, the narrator adds, "Yet this may not be wholly so. We shall see."[55] This remark might seem to be closer to Genette's "advance mentions." It is certainly not the kind of overt foreshadowing we've already seen; it does not refer to a specific event yet to come, but only wryly hints at something. To read "we shall see" as a sly hint is to posit a knowing narrator, winking at his readers, one with access to what comes next. But what if we take "may not be" and "we shall see" at face value? What if we take them literally? To do so is to posit an *un*knowing narrator, one who anticipates the possibility that Israel's heart may not be warmed at all, but that can't say so with any degree of certainty. This sort of narrator, one whose temporal horizon is limited by what is happening right now—limited, that is, by the present tense—merely wonders, hazards a guess, considers alternatives, all the while realizing, as the old saying goes, that only time will tell. Hence, "we shall see."

It's not just the text's use of the present tense that recommends this latter reading. (After all, as anyone who has watched an historical documentary on PBS can tell you, there is nothing particularly unusual, or even interesting, about narrating the past in the present tense.) It's also that the narrator often adopts, quite explicitly, a role that suggests he is as subject to the vicissitudes of action and event as Israel himself. For example, following Israel's brief, humorous encounter with King George at Kew Gardens, the narrator says that "it must still be narrated" that Israel came away from the interview "with very favorable views of that monarch."[56] The narrator then speculates that were it not for Israel's genuine American patriotism, he might well have joined the British army, adding "Nor in that case would we have had to follow him, as at last we shall, through long, long years of obscure and penurious wandering."[57] The tangled temporal grammar here obscures the narrator's relation to the events he describes. On the one hand, the present perfect tense expresses an action that has already occurred—or more precisely, couched as it is in Melville's negatives and conditionals, an action that might not have occurred under a certain condition; the narrator had to follow Israel. On the other hand, the narrator suggests that that same action—following Israel—has yet to take place; "we shall," at some point in the future (i.e., "at last.") follow him through his long years of wandering.

Setting aside the fact that, as I've already noted, the narrator never really does, by novel's end, fulfill that command to trace those "long years" of Israel's life, what interests me about this moment in the novel is its rendering of what we might call the contingency of the text's narrative prolepsis, a contingency expressed through Melville's tricky deployment of modal verbs: "it may not be," "it must be narrated," "nor . . . would we have had." Modal verbs, as any grammar guide will tell you, behave irregularly with regard to time. Melville harnesses that latent ambiguity. It's not just that, as the novel continues, the narrator seems to know less and less about the future, about where the story is headed. It's also that he foreshadows events and experiences that do not (or did not) come to pass; his anticipations points to the possible as well as to the actual. Yet those possibilities do not always reside in the future, the what might yet be, but just as often reside in the past, the what might have been. Or sometimes, they seem to be both at once. Later in the novel, for example, when Israel once again finds himself impressed into Her Majesty's navy, the narrator says:

> And now, we might shortly have to record our adventurer's part in the famous engagement off the coast of Coromandel, between Admiral Suffren's fleet and the English squadron, were it not that fate snatched him on the threshold of events, and, turning him short round whether he had come, sent him back congenially to war against England instead of on her behalf.[58]

Whereas in the earlier example Melville refers to a past-that-never-was in which he would have had to narrate Israel's experience as a British soldier, here his grammatical construction points to a possible future moment (indicated by "shortly," which in this context denotes either "soon" or "next") in which he could find himself narrating Israel's adventures as a sailor in Admiral Suffren's fleet. The effect is a convergence of the narrator's "now" and Israel's, a collapse of prolepsis as the time of narration and the time of the story coincide. It is as if the narrator is present, waiting for events to unfold, ready to "record" Israel's movement in whichever direction events propel him.[59]

In this way, we might say, Melville modalizes *now*. The present, figured aptly in the previous passage as a "threshold of events," is marked by contingency and unpredictability; it tends in multiple direction at once, no one of them any more certain or even likely than any other. This is why, as often as he has his narrator foreshadow, indicating that he does know which way events turned, Melville nevertheless repeatedly registers the prospect that Israel's life might have taken any number of different trajectories. In doing so, he recognizes that he might just as likely have had some other story to tell, that this one is accidental, not determinate, not inevitable, and certainly not providential. "Thus repeatedly and rapidly," Melville writes to conclude the passage above, "were the fortunes of our wanderer planted, torn up, transplanted, and dropped again, hither and thither, according as the Supreme Disposer of sailors and soldiers saw fit to appoint."[60] This statement encapsulates Melville's sense of the movement of history in *Israel Potter*. "All human affairs," he says, "are subject to organic disorder." They are "created in, and sustained by a sort of half-disciplined chaos."[61] Accordingly, since human affairs— history—possess no immanent shape or design, he tries to write history "presently," as if he doesn't know where it is headed (this attempt resembles John Neal's effort, discussed in chapter two, to render "incidents in themselves"). Inhabiting that kind of immediacy, entails a kind of unknowing, a willingness to relinquish the certainties and comforts provided by, say, providence, or progress, or normative ideas about time as a steady, unidirectional, and ameliorative force. (On this point, Melville also echoes Emerson's affirmation of the joys of unknowing that I discussed in Chapter 3.) It entails not knowing where you are headed more than "a page" in advance and accepting the possibility that, like Israel, you are liable to being "repeatedly and rapidly…planted, torn up, transplanted, and dropped again, hither and thither."

A Character as Yet Unfathomed

Such a view of the movement of history might seem harmless enough in a work of fiction—although Melville's critique of nationalist, progressive history, as critics have demonstrated persuasively, is not without its power. But as Chapters 1 through 4 have shown, as a style of social reform, acting rashly, responding impulsively to the urgencies of the moment, has long remained a source of danger and fear and anxiety; "The Lightning-Rod Man," I have suggested, registers that anxiety. Which returns me to the "interepid, unprincipled, reckless, predatory" Paul Jones, "civilized in externals but a savage at heart."[62] More than any other character in the book, Jones represents the principle of human affairs as "organic disorder," just as he represents for my argument, as we've seen, the stormy political impatience that animated immediatist abolitionists and other radical reformers. Readers of *Israel Potter* have generally taken a negative view of Jones, seeing him as a symbol of what the novel calls "primeval savageness," or worse, of "man's capacity to perpetrate evil through violence," or somewhat more generously, of the self-aggrandizing desire for glory, "mighty ego," his own "barbaric egotism."[63] My reading departs from this consensus and locates in Melville's portrayal of Jones, a beguiling admixture of Queequeg, Ahab, and Johnny Depp in those pirate movies, a source of futural possibility in an otherwise bleak and cynical, novel. This note of tentative hopefulness is important, in part, because Melville identifies Jones explicitly with the nation. "America is, or may yet be," Melville says cryptically at one point, employing yet another of his many conditionals "the Paul Jones of nations."[64]

Hence my interest in taking a closer look at Melville's depiction of Jones ultimately has less to do with tracing his particular brand of reckless impetuosity along the arc of the period's chronopolitics than it does with revealing how his unfathomable character—that designation, as we'll see, is a paraphrase of Melville—gestures toward some prospects for the present this book has thus far only partially explored, prospects that possess the latent potential, albeit with no guarantees, to counteract the dangers and fears that made prudence, the same prudence that so perturbed Paul Jones, seem the only reasonable political disposition in the 1850s. These prospects point toward the generative, even the world-building potential of acting rashly—or analogously, of writing presently. Such possibilities, I'll argue in this section, reside in part in what George Herbert Mead calls "the social nature of the present."[65] For Mead, sociality is the result of what he terms "emergence." Because in the present something is always happening, emergence or novelty—or what Ahab might call "the living act, the undoubted deed"—necessitates processes of readjustment. "Nature takes on new characters with the appearance of life," Mead says, "or the stellar system takes on new characters with the loss of mass by the collapse of atoms through the processes that go on within a star. There is an adjustment to this new situation."[66] Sociality resides not in the new conditions created by emergence, but in the transition from the old to the new state, in what Mead calls "the process of readjustment." (Note the echoes here, of Emerson's claim in "Self-Reliance" that "power...resides in the moment of transition from a past to a new state.") Hence Mead's definition of sociality as the "capacity of being several things at once."[67]

Such a conception of the present as a social process of readjustment helps to account for Israel's protean, improvisatory character—figured, most evidently, in his many changes of clothing—and his capacity for adapting (adjusting) to ever-new situations, to being "dropped...hither and thither."[68] Melville illustrates Israel's fluidity most strikingly in the rich chapter on sociability called "The Shuttle," which I consider at length in the next section. But the crisis of (homo) social belonging that chapter dramatizes takes on added significance when considered in relation to Paul Jones, whom Melville casts as the harbinger of some undisclosed future. The waggish depiction of Jones revisits and revises Melville's handling of sociability in *Moby-Dick*, especially with regard to forms of intimate attachment among men. And so, with the entrance of Jones, the temporal preoccupations of *Israel Potter*, as well as my reading of that interest, take something of a queer turn, as the novel's formal investment in undoing conventional uses of narrative anticipation, its embrace of historiographical directionlessness, joins with its ethical investment in anticipating, in the sense both of presentiment and expectation, new modes of being and affiliation not yet in existence but flickering just over the horizon of articulacy.

By arguing for Jones as a queer figure, I mean to make no claims about what today we would call his sexual identity—although he is certainly sexualized, engaging in "by-play" with the "pretty chambermaids" at Franklin's quarters, "throwing a passing arm round" them as he passes by them, "kissing them resoundingly." Following Jack Halberstam, I mean instead that Jones participates in the kinds of "willfully eccentric modes of being" that mark queer existence, the "nonnormative logics and organizations of community, sexual identity, embodiment, and activity in space and time."[69] Indeed, Jones cuts an outlandish figure, marked by a number of humorous contradictions. Upon his first appearance in the novel—he has come to complain to Benjamin Franklin about the naval commission he has been given—Melville devotes a paragraph to describing his peculiar character. A "small, elastic, swarthy man, with an aspect of a disinherited Indian Chief in European clothes," he evinces an "unvanquishable enthusiasm...couched in his savage, self-possessed eye."[70] Dressed "elegantly," he "carried himself with a rustic, barbaric jauntiness, strangely dashed with a superinduced touch of the Parisian *salon*." And despite what appears to be an "atmosphere of proud friendlessness and scornful isolation invest[ing] him," there is also "a bit of the poet as well as the outlaw in him," the latter, perhaps, indicated by the "cool solemnity of intrepidity...on his lip."[71] It's hard to know what to make of such a strange assemblage of characteristics, such a hodgepodge of habiliment, temper, and trait; there is really nothing else quite like him. Indian and European, savage and elegant, barbaric and civilized, rustic and sophisticated, poet and outlaw, Melville associates Jones with different nations, different attitudes, and different stages of historical development—that is, with several disparate things at once. Israel himself, upon first meeting Jones, thinks to himself, "seldom before had he seen such a being."[72] Indeed, Jones conjoins, confounds, or otherwise defies ordinary categories of understanding, whether they be temporal, moral, or national. He combines the barbarism of earlier stages of human development with the sophistication of modernity. He may be "a knave, or a hero, or a union of both." And although fighting for the American cause he claims no national affiliation but declares himself "a citizen and sailor of the universe."[73]

Both of them not dissimilarly unsettled, Jones and Israel soon form a kind of Queequeg/Ishmael bond, with the swarthy, part-savage Jones cast in the role of the former. Quite explicitly, the chapter subsequent to Jones's arrival in the novel, titled "Paul Jones in a Reverie," combines, restages, and reworks the optics and, to a degree, the erotics of Chapters 3 and 4 of *Moby-Dick*, where Ishmael and Queequeg meet (at "The Spouter Inn") and then share an intimate night together as bedfellows (in "The Counterpane").[74] But while Jones and Israel share a room together, at the insistence of Franklin, they do not, like Queequeg and Ishmael, share a bed—a fact that is not for a lack of trying on Israel's part. "Why not sleep together?" he asks Jones, "see, it is a big bed. Or perhaps you don't fancy your bedfellow, Captain?" Israel, unlike Ishmael, appears to harbor no initial trepidation at the prospect of sharing a bed with an exotic stranger. But Jones, unlike Queequeg, does, offering this rather obscure reply:

> "When, before the mast, I first sailed out of Whitehaven to Norway," said Paul, coolly, "I had for hammock-mate a full-blooded Congo. We had a white blanket spread in our hammock. Every time I turned in I found the Congo's black wool worked in with the white worsted. By the end of the voyage the blanket was of a pepper-and-salt look, like an old man's turning head. So it's not because I am notional at all, but because I don't care to, my lad."[75]

There will be no bridegroom clasp in this bed. Still, the exact purport of this cryptic anecdote and its Bartlebian declaration is not altogether clear. Jones reveals that he himself has, at one point, played Ishmael to another's Queequeg—in his case, a "full-blooded Congo." But the significance of his description of the intermixing of their two blankets, which allude to the counterpane in *Moby-Dick*, is rather elusive. Metaphorically, of course, it might seem to suggest, as Ian Maloney has observed, that while Jones did once share a hammock with a Congo, he nevertheless has a certain distaste for racial mixing—for the intermingling of "black wool" with "white worsted" and perhaps even the degradation of the latter by the former.[76] Yet Jones's concluding statement does not necessarily seem (or at least not clearly so) to support such an explanation. The story of the blended blankets might just as well serve to illustrate his degree of comfort with such arrangements. Or, given Jones's rather fastidious penchant for finery, perhaps his concern over black wool worked into his own white worsted is merely aesthetic. Either way, the question seems to turn on the meaning of the term "notional." What does it mean for Jones to say that he isn't notional? Is it that he is not in possession of certain notions or ideas? And if so, what ideas? The idea that people of different races or of the same gender ought not to share beds? Or does Jones mean to say that he is not prone to "fanciful speculation," is not one who holds "speculative views."[77] And if so, what speculative views does he profess not to hold? Is Jones being deliberately evasive, perhaps even coy? Or maybe, we're to take his last statement quite literally: he's just not in the mood.

Whatever the case, Israel accepts this response to his invitation and retires to bed. But the pacing of Jones about the room, "wrapped in Indian meditations," makes it impossible for Israel to sleep. So he takes instead to eyeing Jones, "furtively." After a moment, as Israel watches, Jones catches a "glimpse" of himself in the mirror:

> He paused, grimly regarding it, while a dash of pleased coxcombry seemed to mingle with the otherwise savage satisfaction expressed in his face. But the latter predominated. Soon, rolling up his sleeve, with a queer wild smile, Paul lifted his right arm, and stood thus for an interval, eyeing its image in the glass. From where he lay, Israel could not see that side of the arm presented to the mirror, but he saw its reflection, and started at perceiving there, framed in the carved and

gilded wood, certain large intertwisted cyphers covering the whole inside of
the arm, so far as exposed, with mysterious tatooings. The design was wholly
unlike the fanciful figures of anchors, hearts, and cables, sometimes decorating
small portions of seamen's bodies. It was a sort of tattooing such as is seen only
on thorough-bred savages—deep blue, elaborate, labyrinthine, cabalistic. Israel
remembered having beheld, on one of his early voyages, something similar on the
arm of a New Zealand warrior, once met, fresh from battle, in his native village.[78]

The intricate optics of this intriguing passage merge together two scenes from
"The Spouter Inn" chapter of *Moby-Dick*: the first, the scene in which, to borrow
Christopher Looby's splendid description, Ishamel "gazes at himself in the mirror
while playing dress-up in Queequeg's damp, odorous, shaggy, and suggestively
configured clothing;" the second scene, occurring just shortly after, when Ishmael
lies in bed "trying," as Geoffrey Sanborn describes the scene "to decide whether
Queequeg," having just entered the room, "is a tattooed white man or an abomina-
ble cannibal."[79] Yet the updated rendering of these scenes in *Israel Potter* entails a
series of departures and inversions, not easy to sort, from the scenes in *Moby-Dick*.
In the first scene from *Moby-Dick* I have mentioned, Ishmael, apprehensive about
the roommate he has not yet met, finds himself looking through the absent
Queequeg's personal effects. At one point, he happens across a garment that looks
to Ishmael like a "doormat" with a hole cut into it. Ishmael tries it on. But catching
a look at himself in the glass, he is so startled that he gets "out of it in such a hurry
that I gave myself a kink in the neck." In *Israel Potter*, the situation is even more
involved. For one thing, Jones, the so-called savage, is the dressed-up figure who
espies himself in the mirror. But it's not altogether clear what constitutes Jones's
"true" identity and what is merely costume. Is it that his "European clothes,"
their ruffles and laces and "Parisian rings" are adornments that cover and hide the
real savage beneath? Or is he, a white British subject after all, simply "dressed" in
cannibal drag?

Jones's response to his own mirrored reflection—not at all like Israel's glimpse
of himself in Queequeg's shaggy skin—seems to support the former supposition.
Rather than shrinking back, shocked at encountering a phantasmagorical image of
himself, Jones seems to indulge in his own reflection, expressing both "pleased
coxcombry" and "savage satisfaction." He then lets slip "a queer wild smile" as he
rolls back the ruffled sleeve of his shirt to peer more closely—and evidently self-
satisfyingly—at the "cabalistic" cyphers decorating his skin. The smile and the gesture here reinforce the predominance of savagery over coxcombry; the peeling
back of the shirt implies a kind of revelation, the disclosure of a secret, perhaps
more authentic, self. Yet this gesture is complicated by the fact that Israel is watching Jones—or more precisely, watching Jones watch himself (indeed, Israel can
only see Jones's tattooed arm reflected in the mirror, the same way that Jones sees it).
Meanwhile it is entirely possible that Jones is likewise watching Israel watch. It may
even be that he is performing for Israel—not just indulging in a self-kept secret,
but revealing it, intimately though indirectly, to the peeping Israel, just as Melville
has him reveal it to the reader.

In this way, the scene significantly revises the second scene in "The Spouter Inn" when Israel gets his first look at Queequeg. There, Ishmael watches Queequeg furtively from the bed also, registering with alarm and bewilderment the marks on the other man's skin. But there, it is a direct, one-way gaze, in which Ishmael slowly learns how to see Queequeg aright, learns, in Sanborn's formulation, "to advance from inauthentic sight to authentic insight."[80] But the recursivity of the scene Melville orchestrates in *Israel Potter* bespeaks a more dynamic, multilayered inter-subjective encounter, one in which each subject not only looks, but is aware of being looked at, so that each subject gazes and mirrors back to the other—in this case, quite literally—the other's gaze. The dynamic resembles Mead's well-known conception of a "social self," a self that is not the precondition for a social encoun-ter but the product of it. Like Charles Horton Cooley's "looking glass self" (obvi-ously resonant in this context), which influenced Mead's theory, Mead conceives the self as emerging from a social process in which one adopts the attitude of another toward oneself; that is, in which one sees oneself from the perspective of another.[81] In *Israel Potter*, this process is nicely figured by the mirror, in which Jones views his own tattooed arm, symbol of his secret savage identity, in the same way that Israel does, reflected back at him. Jones *literally* sees himself as Israel does. In turn, Jones's self-disclosure also mirrors back to Israel Israel's own secret savagery. Similarly, assuming that Jones can see Israel (the text suggests that "Paul thought himself unwatched," but it is just as likely that he is mistaken or that Israel *thinks* Paul thinks himself unwatched, and hence views Paul's behavior in terms of how Israel might behave if he himself thought himself unwatched). Likewise, Jones, too, would see Israel only as a reflection in the mirror. In which case, Israel mirrors back to Jones Jones's self-disclosure, a disclosure meant for Israel.

"Paul Jones in a Reverie" thus reads backward toward *Moby-Dick*'s similarly recursive, mutually constituting relationship between Queequeg and Ishmael. Queequeg, we might recall, is explicitly aligned with a heroic American Revolu-tionary figure. Prefiguring Paul Jones, "George Washington cannibalistically developed" anachronistically posits savage cannibalism as a state of advancement. Complementarily, Ishmael is eventually aligned with primitive savagery. "I myself am a savage," he says at one point, "owing no allegiance but to the King of the Cannibals." Yet "Paul Jones in a Reverie" also reads forward toward latent possibili-ties swallowed up in *Moby-Dick* by the vortex of the Pequod's sinking; Queequeg dies, but America "may yet be the Paul Jones of nations." After Jones reveals what lies beneath his "laced coat-sleeve," on the surface of his body—the "labyrinthine, cabalistic" tattooings—he re-covers his arm and "glance[s] ironically" at his hand "now half muffled in ruffles, and ornamented with several Parisian rings." Then, he returns to pacing about the room "while a gleam of the consciousness of possess-ing a character as yet unfathomed … irradiated his cold, white brow."[82] Here, then, is one more of the novel's many anticipations. But this time, it is an entirely *un*knowing foreshadowing. That is, in this case "as yet" does not refer to some moment later in the text when Paul's character will be fathomed by way of some revelation. Indeed, we've just witnessed the revelation of Paul's secret: his "cabalistic" tattoos. But their meaning, like the meaning of Queequeg's tattoos or like "the mystic-marked whale," remain "undecipherable," beyond present understanding, their true depth still not measured, still "as yet."[83] I but put this arm before you, Melville seems to have Paul say, read it if you can.

In the absence of some later narrative disclosure, one that fulfills the promise of its foreshadowing, what the novel offers in this instance is a flickering apprehension of some future mode of being—queer and wild—yet to come. Indeed, queer and wild might well describe the novel's foreshadowing here insofar as it fails to adhere to the conventional temporal logic of prolepsis—which anticipates but, sooner or later, one way or another, *arrives*. This asynchrony is brought into relief in the chapter's penultimate paragraph:

> So at midnight, the heart of the metropolis of modern civilization was secretly trod by this jaunty barbarian in broadcloth; a sort of prophetical ghost, glimmering in anticipation upon the advent of those tragic scenes of the French Revolution which levelled the exquisite refinement of Paris with the blood-thirsty ferocity of Borneo; showing that broaches and finger-rings, not less than nose-rings and tattooing, are tokens of the primeval savageness which ever slumbers in human kind, civilised or uncivilised.[84]

The allusion to the French Revolution itself points in two directions at once: in the Revolutionary world of the novel's setting, it points ahead toward the Reign of Terror and, therefore, marks Jones, who combines in his person "exquisite refinement" and "blood-thirsty ferocity," as a Jacobin. But in the narrator's (or Melville's) present, the French Revolution, as an historical event, lies in the past. At the same time, the routine likening of radical abolitionists like Garrison to "Jacobins" demonstrates the degree to which the violence of the French Revolution continued to haunt many Americans. Hence, Melville's description of Jones as a "prophetical ghost," a forerunner of the "tragic scenes" in France; Jones has returned as a specter to predict, perhaps, the American future. This might well align Jones with John Brown, whom Melville also understood in terms of portent. Except in this case, the outcome or end to which Jones might well portend or prophesy remains beyond present apprehension.

Melville's Queer Future?

Prophecy, of course, is the classic form of prolepsis. Prophecy knows and thus foretells the future. But this is a queer sort of prophesying—perhaps akin to what Carla Freccero has termed "*a prolepsis of queer*"—not only because its fulfillment remains an open question (what, after all, does Jones herald? and how would we know if it even arrived?), but also because it is not unidirectional; it looks backward, to the dead, at the same time that it looks forward to the future, whatever or wherever that future might be.[85] So here we have yet another example of the novel's investment in the irregular movements of time, its commitment to the nonteleological course of history—what we might call its "hither and thither" historiography—a disruption of straightforward linearity that resonates especially with some of the asynchronous experiences and nonnormative temporal modes brought into visibility by queer studies: feeling backward, growing sideways, temporal drag, spectrality.[86] And while *Israel Potter* is not a queer novel in the sense that is centrally concerned with matters pertaining to gender and sexuality or physical and intimate attachment and desire (which is not to say that it is not wholly *un*concerned with such things either, for the novel evinces plenty of characteristically Melvillean moments of ribaldry and sly suggestiveness[87]), it *is* queer in the sense that is very much invested in questions of (homo)social belonging, modes of affiliation not assimilable to accepted social categories, and to ways of being that are "as yet unfathomable." The scholarship on queer temporalities, including vital debates about futurity and (anti)sociality, can help explain that investment.

Nowhere is this interest more evident than in the relationship between Paul Jones and Israel—their missed opportunity in the bedroom notwithstanding. After all, Jones and Israel are associated in other ways in the novel, as Jones "flits and re-flits like a crimson thread" across "the blue jean career of Israel."[88] Michael Paul Rogin observes that Jones "disappears" after Melville's lengthy and vivid account of the famous naval battle between Jones's ship the *Bonhomme Richard* and the British *Serapis*. But the spirit of Jones remains, the "friendlessness" and "isolation" that seem to invest him, his ghostliness, and above all, the portentous "as yet" he embodies all return in the chapter that immediately follows called "The Shuttle." By a fluke during an encounter with another British ship, Israel soon finds himself again in the hands of the enemy. Except in this case, owing to the peculiar circumstances of his transfer from one ship to the other by way of an overly hasty leap upon an errant spanker boom, no one on the British ship observes Israel's chance arrival on board. With no other means to ensure his safety, Israel decides to try to pass himself off as one of the British sailors. Thus ensues a comical, but philosophically suggestive episode in which Israel attempts to convince everyone aboard the ship that he belongs there. Affecting "the utmost sociability," Israel attempts to claim affiliation with several of the ship's various bands: the maintopmen, the sheet-anchor-men, the forecastlemen, the holders, and, finally, the waisters, "the vilest caste of an armed ship's company; mere dregs and settlings—sea-Pariahs."[89] However, he is continually rebuffed and rejected; "no social circle would receive him." Thus finding himself alone, "black-balled out of every club," Israel takes to "promiscuously circulating," making various "offers of intimacy" but still finding himself "successively repulsed as before."[90] Eventually, representatives of the various bands inform one another of having been "molested by a vagabond claiming fraternity," at which point Israel is collared by the master-at-arms and presented to the officer-on-deck for interrogation.

The ensuing scene recalls Rip Van Winkle's dislocation upon his return from his long sleep in the mountains, his alienation from the social body, his interrogation at the hands of the villagers, and eventually, his reintegration into the community.[91] "Who the deuce *are* you?" asks the officer of the deck, "Where did you come from? What's your business? Where are you stationed? What's your name? Who are you, any way? How did you get here? and Where are you going?"[92] Read allegorically, this passage comments upon the novel's own unsettling of the orderly movement of history, as the officer attempts to identify Israel by assembling the materials of a coherent narrative, with a clear origin ("Where did you come from?") and telos ("Where are you going?"). But ironically, this is one moment in the novel where Israel, who repeatedly tells and re-tells his story (in a novel that is itself a retelling of a telling of a story) does *not* give another account of himself. Instead, Israel continues to insist that he is just another member of the crew "going to my regular duty." In response, the officer exclaims, "He's out of all reason; out of all men's knowledge and memories!"—another meta-comment that states, succinctly, the terms of the novel's critique of monumental history's erasure of ordinary soldiers like Israel Potter from national memory. Indeed, Israel himself, adopting the name "Peter Perkins," laments that "all hands seem to be against me; none of them willing to remember me."[93]

But here I am less concerned with rehearsing how "The Shuttle" participates in the novel's sustained critique of nationalist history's exclusions than I am in the chapter's meditation on social identity and social belonging, which critics have likewise viewed almost uniformly in terms of critique. That is, most readers regard "The Shuttle" as, at best, comic pathos, or at worst, tragedy.[94] Whether attributed to Melville's own artistic failure, to impoverished national myths, to the hypocrisy of the Revolution's so-called heroes, or to the disintegration of the individual occasioned by modernity and the capitalist marketplace, a kind of doleful concern for Israel's loss or lack of identity, his "inability to develop a cohesive self," has been a persistent theme in readings of the novel.[95] And not without good reason. Failing to extract from Israel anything resembling the truth about his identity or about his sudden appearance aboard the ship, the exasperated officer finally commands the master-at-arms to take him away. "But where am I to take him?" asks the officer, "He don't seem to belong anywhere, sir." The officer responds (twice) only with a nonplussed "out of sight," at which point the master-at-arms turns to Israel: " 'Come along, then, my ghost,' said the master-at-arms. And, collaring the phantom, he led it hither and thither, not knowing exactly what to do with it." Eventually, the captain emerges from below deck and asks the master-at-arms "To what end do you lead that man about?" and he receives the ambiguous reply, "To no end in the world, sir. I keep leading him about because he has no final destination."[96]

Certainly the image here of alienated purposelessness, of disaffiliated aimlessness might well seem desolate. But what if we regard this ghostliness, this desultory movement, and this state of unbelonging not as a condition to be lamented, but as one of possibility? One might, for instance, view Israel's various expulsions from shipboard communities as an opportunity to embrace the radical antirelationality promoted by one compelling strain of queer theory.[97] The ship's various "bands" might thus be seen to represent a whole host of conventional social arrangements, whose stability is threatened less by the prospect of assimilating Israel than by the fact of his "promiscuous circulation." Rather than lamenting Israel's failed attempts to "palm himself off upon decent society," such a reading might instead celebrate his disturbance of ordinary forms of belonging, relinquish the dream of achieving or even of desiring anything like a coherent identity, reject the future that might guarantee such wholeness, and embrace instead the heedless now—like Paul Jones in all of *his* "proud friendlessness and scornful isolation." Such a reading is not without its appeal. Yet while it may gesture in that direction, antisociality is ultimately not the route "The Shuttle" endorses. Indeed, as it turns out, it is Israel's "general sociability" that "served in the end, to turn in his favor the suspicious hearts of the mariners." This "general sociability," concomitant to promiscuous circulation, I take to be anti-identitarian but not antisocial. It is akin to what Tim Dean, in his critique of queer antirelationality, describes as a Deleuzian "becoming— a ceaseless movement of being that is not coordinated by teleology and that never results in anything resembling an identity."[98] This is an apt description, I think, of Israel's "devious wanderings" with "no final destination," though rather than Deleuze, I might draw upon Mead's (related) conception of sociality as arising out of a state of *transition*, as generated by continual processes of readjustment. "Nothing is more promiscuously sociable," Dean says, "more intent on hooking up, than that part of our being separate from selfhood...beyond the normative coordinates of selfhood lies an orgy of connection that no regime can regulate."[99] "The Shuttle" nicely illustrates the point: Israel's lack of identity, his unsettled state and directionlessness, by the end beckon toward new social formations, new modes of belonging "as yet unfathomed."[100]

"The Shuttle's" figure for this aimless state of promiscuous, anti-identitarian unbelonging is the ghost. "Come along, my ghost," says the master-at-arms before leading the "phantom" "hither and thither." Paul Jones, too, we should recall, is associated more than once with spectrality. Along the Irish coast, for instance, he glides "like an invisible ghost." Nor is "The Shuttle" the only time Israel is likened to a ghost. Earlier in the novel, entombed behind a wall in Squire Woodcock's mansion, Israel makes his escape by pretending to be the ghost of the dead Squire. Later, as he "wandered and wandered" the city of London, he becomes yet another of that city's countless "uninvoked ghosts."[101] And in the novel's final chapter, Israel is explicitly described as a revenant, in another scene that alludes to "Rip Van Winkle." Finally, back in America after his "fifty years" of wandering, Israel returns with his son to his birthplace along the Housatonic, "but the exile's presence in these old mountain townships proved less a return than a resurrection," for "none knew him nor could recall having heard of him."[102] Israel goes to visit his father's old home, but finds the region transformed and the old house burned down. Gazing upon a decaying woodpile, the very "type...of for ever arrested intentions, and a long life still rotting in early mishap," Israel, like Rip, doubts the reality of time's passage:

> "Do I dream?" mused the bewildered old man, "or what is this vision that comes to me, of a cold, cloudy morning, long, long ago, and I heaving yon elbowed log against the beech, then a sapling? Nay, nay; I can not be so old."[103]

At which point his son, taking the role of the master-at-arms in "The Shuttle," says, "'Come away, father, from this dismal damp wood'...and led him forth," the two of them "blindly ranging to and fro."

Of course, "Rip Van Winkle," as Carolyn Dinshaw reminds us, is also a ghost story, a fact she leverages to reveal the story's queer potential, its rendering of the "unsettling, marvelous, fearsome asynchrony of life that the hold of classically scientific time-as-measurement would lead us to discount."[104] Dinshaw thus joins a number of other queer scholars who have explored what Carla Freccero calls "queer spectrality." Like the revolutionary soldiers of Whitman's "A Boston Ballad" or Garrison's resurrected dead, appalled by the benumbed citizenry of the present, ghosts can figure, as Dinshaw puts it, "unfinished business" as well as "anxious exclusions from the present—unheard voices, unacknowledged bodies, foreclosed potentials."[105] The critique of revolutionary history Melville advances in *Israel Potter* has long been read as a bleak acknowledgment of those exclusions and erasures. But what I have tried to suggest is that the novel also recognizes, if only glancingly, certain "foreclosed potentials." It briefly imagines, in the persons of those "prophetical ghost[s]" Paul Jones and Israel, the conditions of a more hopeful future—a future that will come to pass only if, paradoxically, we can let go of trying to determine or dictate what its terms might be. "Spectrality," Freccero argues, "counters the teleological drive of heteroreproductive futurity."[106] *Israel Potter* similarly counters the teleological drive of U.S. history and in doing so, joins with a host of other reckless, hasty, heedless, hurried, impatient, rash, impetuous, dangerous figures in antebellum U.S. culture, urgently alive to *now*, and ready to contend with all possible futures.

Ultimately, Melville was too much of a skeptic to embrace the heedless impetuosity of his charismatic heroes Paul Jones and Ahab, however much, temperamentally speaking, he might have identified with their particular brand of reckless immediatism—at least partly anyway—and however much he, too, wished not to be confined or bound by conventional social arrangements or known ways of being. Yet those same dispositions, or something very much like them, seem to have appealed to Melville as an artist as well; the unruliness of so much of his fiction reveals, perhaps, the formal possibilities of intrepidity also. Yet notwithstanding some visionary moments, Melville couldn't, finally, see his way out of the darkness that comes with not knowing. In *Israel Potter*, this may be because the novel's narrator has decided that he—of necessity—must follow Israel, even into heartbreaking, penurious wandering. At the same time, "The Shuttle" flirts, if only briefly, with another more sanguine possibility: a disposition adopted by William

James in an anecdote that Mead liked to tell about James and Josiah Royce out sight-seeing in a city. The prudent Royce checks schedules and time-tables, planning and gathering information about where they are going so that he can inform James about which cars they'll take to ensure that in the end they will arrive at their desired location. When they get to a junction where they have to change cars, James gets on the wrong car. Royce corrects him, telling him that that car is headed to a different point. To which James replies, "Yes, that's where I wanted to go."[107]

Coda

#STAYWOKE

Although the archive of materials I have explored in this study was drawn primarily from the first half of the nineteenth century, I consider the social turbulence of the second decade of the twenty-first century, culminating in the presidency of Donald Trump, to be the historical context within which my readings have taken place: state-sanctioned violence against African Americans, the visible resurgence of violent white nationalism, the growth of new protest movements like Black Lives Matter, the renaming of buildings commemorating white supremacists on college campuses, and debates over the removal of Confederate flags, statues, and other Lost Cause iconography from state capitols and other public spaces across the country.

I drafted the bulk of this manuscript against this backdrop, a series of events that brings into sharp relief some of the temporalities of our present-day politics. This brief slice of twenty-first century history is marked by belated or long overdue recognitions, by revealing the fiction of historical progress, by the slow pace or deferral of racial justice, by hesitation and delay, by the renewed visibility of the nation's racist past. Or, more affirmatively, it is marked by impatience, by restlessness, by waking, by arousal, by impulsiveness, by action in the living present, by mobilization, by spontaneous collective responses to what Martin Luther King, Jr. called "the fierce urgenc[ies] of now." Black Lives Matter; counter-protests in Charlottesville, Virginia; ordinary citizens holding their elected representatives accountable (impolitely); and calling white supremacy by its name—these are the new immediatisms, the newly reinvigorated sites and scenes of romantic presentism. The slogan for this twenty-first century politics of impatience is the phrase "Stay Woke," which gained traction as a hashtag employed by Black Lives Matter activists. To be "woke" is to possess a certain form of social consciousness, an awareness of historically constituted structural racism and still-operative present-day systems of black oppression.[1]

Although *wokeness* has a longer history in the African American vernacular tradition, dating at least back to black artists in the early 1960s[2]—the current usage of the phrase "Stay Woke" derives from a 2008 song performed by the musical artist Erykah Badu called "Master Teacher," which appears on the first of Badu's two *New Amerykah* albums, *New Amerykah, Part One (4th World War).* The chrono-political roots of Stay Woke are evident in Badu's association with Afrofuturism. A movement and cultural style that gained prominence in the 1990s among black musicians, artists, science fiction writers, and cultural critics, Afrofuturism cultivates a temporal aesthetics that resonates in certain ways with the kinds of asynchronous experiences of historical being this book has explored. Blending and refashioning the tropes of techno culture with the products of African diasporic cultures, Afrofuturism "creat[es] temporal complications and anachronistic episodes that disturb the linear time of progress," and develops "a temporal orientation that seems to contradict discourses of the future predicated on either ignoring the past or rendering it as staid and stagnant."[3] In these terms, one might read the conclusion of Frederick Douglass's Fourth of July address, for instance, in a kind of proto-Afrofuturist key, as he speculates upon a future transformed by the technologies of his own day, imagining the transmission of information ("intelligence") "over and under the sea" by "wind, steam, and lightning," its "chartered agents." Because of these advancements, Douglass concludes speculatively, anticipating the laying of the transatlantic telegraphic cable (which wouldn't begin to be constructed until two years later), "Space is comparatively annihilated," he says, "thoughts expressed on one side of the Atlantic are distinctly heard on the other."[4]

Of course, in other crucial ways, the futural disposition that characterizes Afrofuturist art was unavailable to antebellum writers like Douglass. I have in mind here not just the advent of digital culture—which etherized and rendered even more instantaneous the transmission of intelligence Douglass already saw on the horizon in 1852—but also the limitations imposed upon Douglass's proleptic vision by the then-present fact of slavery. From that vantage, Douglass could imagine emancipation, but the possibilities for postemancipation modes of African American being or alternative national configurations in a more distant future remained shrouded in mist and clouds. Or put differently, largely unavailable to antebellum writers like Douglass were "disembodied, identity-free" forms of "radical black subjectivity" of the sort that twenty-first century Afrofuturists like Badu seek to reconcile, as Marlo David has argued, with the "embodied, identity-specific past and present."[5] That process of reconciliation, an historiographical project, is evident in *New Amerykah* in both the album's "neo-soul" sound, which draws upon both older (soul, funk) and newer (hip hop, fusion) musical forms and in the striking visual grammar of its art.[6] Echoing the visual style of 1960s era psychedelic art, the cover of *New Amerykah, Part One* features a portrait of Badu, her fists thrust forward just below her chin with the album's title emblazoned on large, blinged-out hip-hop inspired knuckle rings. Two-thirds of the portrait is taken up by Badu's afro, loose ringlets of which spell out her name at the top of the image. The rest contains dozens of individual gold icons, encompassing more than two hundred years of African American history—the chains of slavery, the scales of justice, open books, a factory, the U.S. Capitol building, Black Power fists, a boom box, abusive cops, a DJ's turntable, drug paraphernalia, and much more. Badu's afro, itself a signifier of earlier eras (and right now[7]), thus becomes a kind of alternative visual historiography whose principle might be described as *afro-organization*. That is, the image pointedly refuses to present the historical experience of African Americans in terms of chronology, cause and effect, or a conventional linear timeline. Which is not to say its various elements are presented randomly; the image has its gatherings, symmetries, and repetitions. The cover convenes the past and present together in a dense, crowded, nonhierarchical assemblage in which elements touch and overlap, jostle and collide, their movement as much centrifugal as centripetal. This imagining of history as clutter is inextricable from Badu's vision of the future. In "Master Teacher," for example, she sings that she is "in search of something new," "a beautiful world" of racial liberation. But that world, "hard to find," is as yet available only in "dreams," which suggest both sleep and futurity and provide yet another way of reading the album's cover art: as a visual rendering of the projections of Badu's mind. At the same time, the song's refrain, the phrase "I stay woke," registers the imperative to remain vigilant, mindful of the past and cognizant of present-day conditions.[8]

This book has revealed another, somewhat unlikely, genealogy of #StayWoke, locating it within an antebellum U.S. historical sensibility that shares with Afrofuturism both a resistance to conventional understandings of historical time and a commitment to racial justice. Surprisingly, two of the era's best-known and most popular literary productions—"Rip Van Winkle" and Longfellow's "A Psalm for Life"—constitute early versions of #StayWoke. Rip, as Martin Luther King, Jr. reminds us, slept through the revolution. And "A Psalm for Life," you might recall, begins:

> Tell me not, in mournful numbers
> That Life is but an empty dream!
> For the soul is dead that slumbers,
> And things are not what they seem.

Both of these texts, I have shown, resonated powerfully for black activists and writers, from the delegates of the 1841 black suffrage convention to James McCune Smith and Frederick Douglass to Martin Luther King, Jr. African American writers and activists thus played a pivotal role in activating those texts' political potential.[9] They resonated, too, for white abolitionists and romantic thinkers like Garrison, Emerson, Whitman, and John Brown—all of whom perceived the sleepy insensibility of their fellow citizens, the need to rouse them from their slumber, and to spur them to action. Thus, the story of romantic presentism might thus be seen in part as a story about cross-racial allyship. In her important and compelling new history of abolition *The Slave's Cause*, Manisha Sinha describes the tradition of "interracial immediatism," demonstrating how "black protest" and "instances of slave rebellion...shaped immediate abolition."[10] My account supplements Sinha's by revealing some of the ways in which black leaders (and readers) taught white writers (and their readers) about the ethical value and political potential of their own work.

Mindful of the leadership role that young black women—master teachers—have played in present-day struggles for social justice like the Black Lives Matter movement, we should, therefore, foreground in this genealogy, this prehistory of #StayWoke, the voices of African American women writers in the antebellum period like Maria Stewart and Frances Ellen Watkins Harper, both of whom also sought to reanimate torpid bodies, to wake their neighbors. In 1831, for instance, Garrison published Stewart's pamphlet "Religion and the Pure Principles of Morality," an impassioned entreaty directed specifically toward her fellow African Americans, particularly toward other black women.[11] It's not hard to see why Stewart's essay appealed to Garrison. In it, Stewart displays the heightened affective state, the felt sense of being alive to present exigencies, that typified Garrison's own rhetorical posture and, more broadly, the inflamed disposition of romantic presentists:

> I am sensible of my ignorance; but such knowledge as God has give to me, I impart to you. I am sensible of former prejudices; but it is high time for prejudices and animosities to cease from among us. I am sensible of exposing myself to calumny and reproach; but shall I, for fear of feeble man, who shall die, hold my peace? Shall I, for fear of scoffs and frowns, refrain my tongue? Ah no! I speak as one that must give an account at the awful bar of God; I speak as a dying mortal to dying mortals. O, ye daughters of Africa, awake! Awake! Arise! No longer sleep nor slumber, but distinguish yourselves.[12]

Emphasizing through anaphora her "sensible" state, Stewart appeals, in an urgent present tense ("I am," "I speak"), to the living dead and the somnolent, calling for their resurrection ("arise!") and their arousal ("awake!"). Like other immediatists—whether nineteenth-century abolitionists or twenty-first-century Black Lives Matter activists—she is also impatient of change, tired of waiting, and unwilling, to recall King once again, to passively expect that time will itself bring about social justice. "It is high time," she insists in a sentence that sounds as urgent today as it did nearly two hundred years ago, "for prejudices and animosities to cease from among us."

Better known than Stewart, but no less ardent, Frances Harper likewise associated with romantic presentists and gave expression to their animating principles. Her poetry appeared in *The Liberator*, and Garrison wrote the preface to her 1855 *Poems on Miscellaneous Subjects*. She participated in the Underground Railroad and befriended John and Mary Brown, supporting Mary after her husband's prosecution and writing to Brown while he was in prison, casting him, as Emerson and Thoreau did, as a Christian martyr.[13] Harper communed with these romantics in other ways as well. In 1866, she published a poem about harnessing present moments—an effort she likens to literary production—called "To-day Is a King in Disguise." It concludes,

The truly wise are they who know
The unheralded step of this king;
Who count each hour with its weal or woe
A sacred and solemn thing.
Who write on the desk of the passing hour
Some record to be borne above;
Who endow the moments with living power
And transcribe them with deeds of love.[14]

Harper's poem draws its inspiration, and its title, from Emerson's 1841 "Lecture on the Times." "To-day is a king in disguise," Emerson says there, "To-day always looks mean to the thoughtless, in the face of an uniform experience, that all good and great and happy actions are made up precisely of these blank todays. Let us not be so deceived. Let us unmask the king as he passes."[15]

One of Harper's most famous poems, "Bury Me in a Free Land," sounds other immediatist themes. Specifically, it offers a variation of the Garrisonian contrast between the dead past and the living present in its imagining of an undead future that perturbs the poem's implicit lifeless present—so much so that the poet, in a series of future conditionals, insists upon remaining awake even in death. The poem was first published in the Ohio newspaper the *Anti-Slavery Bugle* in November 1858. It was reprinted in *The Liberator* the following month and has been republished and anthologized frequently ever since. Lydia Maria Child, for example, printed it, along with a few other poems by Harper, in her 1865 anthology *The Freedman's Book*, and Harper included it in her *Poems* in 1871. The poem begins with the speaker anticipating her own death: "Make me a grave where'er you will," she says, so long as it is "not in a land where men are slaves."[16] Then, in a series of quatrains, she lists the conditions that would prevent any lasting peace:

I could not rest if around my grave
I heard the steps of a trembling slave;
His shadow above my silent tomb
Would make it a place of fearful gloom.
I could not rest if I heard the tread
Of a coffle gang to the shambles led,
And the mother's shriek of wild despair
Rise like a curse on the trembling air.
I could not sleep if I saw the lash
Drinking her blood at each fearful gash,
And I saw her babes torn from her breast,
Like trembling doves from their parent nest.[17]

Experiencing, from the grave, the sounds and sights of slavery—the footsteps of a runaway slave a coffle, the whipping of a slave mother and her shrieks as she is separated from her children—the speaker imagines death as a state of quickly intensifying sensibility. The living world, the above ground world, by contrast, mainly signals lifelessness: ghostly shadows, sites of carnage, despair, blood. The only sign of life in the world of the ostensibly living is "trembling," a term repeated in each of these stanzas and attributed, variously, to persons (the slave), the atmosphere (air), and the creatures of nature (doves). But to the extent that trembling—an involuntary somatic response associated with apprehension—is a sign of life, it too suggests a nearness to death, whether in the form of frightful, perhaps even murderous, things near at hand or of disease.

In the movement of the poem, the repetition of trembling also marks the escalation of the now-dead speaker's affective state, as she too begins to quiver:

> I'd shudder and start if I heard the bay
> Of bloodhounds seizing their human prey,
> And I heard the captive plead in vain
> As they bound afresh his galling chain.
> If I saw young girls from their mother's arms
> Bartered and sold for their youthful charms,
> My eye would flash with a mournful flame,
> My death-paled cheek grow red with shame.[18]

Here the speaker moves from passively registering slavery's atrocities (seeing and hearing) to physically responding to them through a series of spontaneous bodily sensations: a shudder, a start, flashing eyes, and reddened cheeks. With these images, the poem mirrors back to its readers—its *sensible* readers—the very responses their reading of the poem, with its terrifying images of cruelty (preying upon runaways and rape) is meant to induce. Harper deploys a similar strategy, even more explicitly, in "The Slave Mother," which proceeds by way of a series of interrogations of the poem's implied bystanders: "Heard you that shriek?" the poem begins. "Bury Me in a Free Land" likewise works as a kind of thermometer, taking its readers' temperatures. Do they, too, find themselves aroused, rekindled, on the verge of combustibility? Or are they deadened to such scenes of brutality?

This moment, the poem's test as to whether its living readers are more or less alive than its proleptically dead speaker, marks the poem's climax, as the final two stanzas state instead the conditions of potential restfulness:

> I would sleep, dear friends, where bloated might
> Can rob no man of his dearest right;
> My rest shall be calm in any grave
> Where none can call his brother a slave.
> I ask no monument, proud and high,
> To arrest the gaze of the passers-by;
> All that my yearning spirit craves,
> Is bury me not in a land of slaves.[19]

In the final stanza, the speaker returns from the projected future—returns from the dead—back to the present whereupon the poem invokes national frameworks and, thereby, takes a sort of historical turn. The last stanza considers how the speaker might be commemorated after death, rejecting those forms of historical memory associated with the national body: "proud and high" monuments. Monumentalizing, she implies, brings with it its own sort of insensibility insofar as it "arrest[s]" one's "gaze." Of course, "arrest" here denotes the capturing of one's attention. But it also connotes stasis, the cessation of movement—in contrast to the inflamed, flashing eye of the earlier stanza, the bodily signs of potential action. In a different context, Dana Luciano, in a penetrating reading of Harper's poem "The Slave Auction," aligns Harper with the "countermonumental" tradition, which challenges the "death and fixity" (in Lewis Mumford's phrase) of monumentalism.[20] The latter, Luciano demonstrates, "induces...kinds of forgetting, circumscribing the limits of critical engagement with the past by transmitting a completed account of its significance."[21] But Harper, like her contemporaries Douglass and Melville, works to "counter the monumental erasure of certain perspectives on the nation."[22] "Bury Me in a Free Land" performs a similar, though not identical, kind of work in its concluding projection of a future moment in time in which the nation cultivates a relationship to the past that is less concerned with preservation or even remembrance than with justice.[23] This urgent claim constitutes Harper's own oblique reference to and modification of "A Psalm for Life." Harper resequences the poem's famous stanza, to which I have returned so frequently throughout the preceding chapters:

> Trust no Future, howe'er pleasant!
> Let the dead Past bury its dead!
> Act,—act in the living Present!
> Heart within, and God o'erhead!

For Harper, as for Whitman in "A Boston Ballad" and Thoreau in "A Plea for Captain John Brown," action in the living present—the elimination of slavery, striving toward racial justice, staying woke—becomes the *precondition* for burying the dead.

So Harper's poem helps make clear that staying woke, even in its earliest iterations, is not just an affective state; it is also an imperative to act.[24] In our own day, spontaneous protests, organized marches, political petitioning, and sundry confrontations with the legacies and ongoing manifestations of white supremacy (checking one's privilege, ascending a flag pole to tear down the stars and bars, witnessing police interactions with people of color, spontaneously tearing down a cheap Confederate statue, and punching a neo-Nazi) all constitute forms of wokeness. Not surprisingly, the forces of gradualism, of lethargy and delay, have responded to those provocations in familiar ways: by insisting upon sober deliberation, by seeking to temper or delegitimize passion and rage with pleas for civility, by counseling patience, by stoking fears, by making false equivalencies, and with endless deferrals.[25] This more moderate disposition, wary of intensified affective states, distrustful of spontaneity, and leery of sudden change seeks to evade or avoid *now*, the heat of the present moment. Its appeals are to the past or at least to a certain attitude toward the past, one that has more in common with the monumental impulse than with countermonumentalism. Interestingly enough, that circumspection toward *now* has revealed itself, during recent debates over historical monuments and other public forms of remembrance and commemoration, in a curious renaissance of pious warnings about the dangers of presentism.

Those warnings have been a distinct feature, most especially, of movements on college campuses and elsewhere to rename buildings and to remove statues, flags, or other iconography commemorating white supremacy in public spaces, movements intertwined with the resurgent activism generated by Black Lives Matter, and other new forms of social activism. Perhaps the most prominent example of this came from the remarks in October 2017 by President Trump's chief of staff, former General John Kelly, when asked about debates over Confederate monuments following violent protests in Charlottesville, Virginia, several weeks before. "I think we make a mistake," Kelly said "when we take what is today accepted as right and wrong and go back 100, 200, 300 years or more and say what those, you know, what Christopher Columbus did was wrong. You know, 500 years later, it's inconceivable to me that you would take what we think now and apply it back then."[26]

Nor have concerns about presentism been confined to the public political sphere; rather, they echo similar claims taking place in academic contexts. In February 2017, for instance, Yale University announced that it would change the name of Calhoun College, one of its residential colleges, named for the aggressively proslavery South Carolina statesman John C. Calhoun, who graduate from Yale in 1804. Yale's president endorsed the decision only tepidly, remarking during the announcement that "We have a strong presumption against renaming buildings on this campus....I have been concerned all along and remain concerned that we don't do things that erase history. So renamings are going to be exceptional."[27] In fact, the news reversed a decision made less than a year earlier when the university announced that it would *not* yield to pressure from student groups and others to change the name. At that time, Salovey expressed concern "that eliminating the name Calhoun would reduce the likelihood that the legacy of slavery would be more likely to be taught" and warned of the dangers of "changing history because it offends us, because we don't like it." He continued, taking note of the nation's "history of slavery and racism":

> Erasing Calhoun's name from a much-beloved residential college risks masking this past, downplaying the lasting effects of slavery, and substituting a false and misleading narrative, albeit one that might allow us to feel complacent or, even, self-congratulatory.[28]

The notion that the fate of historical knowledge somehow rests on preserving certain commemorations (like building names) is a rhetorical mainstay of debates of this sort. For instance, in an essay on renaming movements that appeared in *Perspectives on History*, the publication of the American Historical Association, the historian David Lowenthal called it "fanatical folly to erase or hide a disconcerting past."[29] Similarly, in the *New York Review of Books*, the law professor David Cole called it a "sideshow" to "airbrush disturbing facts about our past."[30] Similar handwringing over erasing, effacing, obliterating, or otherwise sanitizing U.S. history can be found in countless editorials, letters to the editor, and online forum comments across the country and the Internet.

Indeed, during a similar episode back in 2010—which may well have established the template for how such renaming controversies proceed—when the literary scholar Christopher Hanlon proposed changing the name of a residence hall on the campus of Eastern Illinois University named for the slavery-abetting Illinois Senator Stephen Douglas, Hanlon was routinely accused of attempting to erase history. "One senior professor of history," Hanlon writes in his account of the debate, "made a written statement indicating that my proposal reminded him of the Taliban destroying statues of the Buddha or the practice of ancient Romans in defacing the images of defamed leaders. Another professor of history described, in a listserv discussion, her own scholarship on medieval anti-Semitic graffiti, pointing out that though she herself is not an anti-Semite, she would never advocate the erasure of such medieval artifacts."[31] Eventually, Hanlon recounts, the university's student senate passed a resolution opposing the name change, "citing the importance of not erasing local history." Of course, no one is apt to argue in favor of erasing history. The problem, however, is that this persistent, almost reflexive, charge makes little sense. For one thing, removing a name from a building or memorial does not erase anyone from history; that should seem obvious. It's hard to believe, for instance, that removing Calhoun's name from a building on the Yale campus is going to preclude teachers and historians of Andrew Jackson's presidency, the Nullification Crisis, or southern defenses of slavery from speaking and writing and teaching about Calhoun's role in those important historical affairs. No one is calling for a moratorium on books written about Calhoun, a ban on the publication of his writings and statements, or his elimination from history textbooks. For another, if anything, debates of this sort, rather than erasing history, tend to render it even *more* visible, to lend it a vitality and material urgency in the public sphere that—let's be honest—is ordinarily quite rare in our culture. After all, it requires historical *knowledge* to produce an argument about why John C. Calhoun is an historical figure unworthy of commemoration at one of the nation's most venerable educational institutions, just as it requires—or ought to require—historical knowledge to defend Calhoun's legacy and, therefore, his worthiness for such an honorific. But as Hanlon learned, the charge of historical erasure—levied, paradoxically, by those who profess to want to *promote* historical knowledge—functions as "a kind of slogan, rather than an impetus for further exploration." And, finally, those who accuse name-change activists of "masking the past" tend to obscure (or simply ignore) the later historical contexts in which so many commemorations ought to be understood. Calhoun College, for instance, was founded (and named) in 1932, in a post-Reconstruction, pre-Civil Rights era at an institution with very few minority students and faculty where the decision to honor a white supremacist was met, presumably, with little or no objection from the campus community. What about *that* history? Hanlon makes a similar point when he describes the circumstances surrounding the original naming of Douglas Hall in the 1950s—a story that is quite frankly rather chilling.[32]

But what interests me more than unfounded fears of historical erasure is the kind of concern Salovey expresses when he worries that changing the name of Calhoun College risks "substituting a false and misleading narrative, albeit one that might allow us to feel complacent or, even, self-congratulatory."[33] By self-congratulatory, presumably Salovey means adopting a posture toward the past that condescends to it, that issues from our own secure sense that we have overcome the prejudices that plagued someone like Calhoun. The implication, of course, is that such a view fails to appreciate the past "on its own terms," that, in the present instance, it fails to properly understand Calhoun in the context of—that is, according to the terms and values of—Calhoun's own time. In other words, like John Kelly, Salovey invokes the specter of presentism.[34] In doing so, he echoes other presidents, historians, and editorialists who have weighed in on similar controversies elsewhere across the country. Soon after Yale announced the name change, for example, the writer Joshua Jelly-Schapiro, in the *New York Review of Books*, expressed his approval of Salovey's statement of concern over erasing history, writing that Salovey's "words affirmed a principle—that we can't judge the past by standards of the present—sacred to historians."[35] Similarly, when in 2015 the University of Maryland announced that it would change the name of its football stadium, which was named after the twentieth-century segregationist Harry Clifton Byrd, President Wallace Loh also announced a five-year moratorium on the renaming of other buildings (a rather curious gesture of deferral the purpose of which isn't altogether clear). "History is not about the past," Loh asserted, somewhat illogically, "It concerns today's debates about the past. We must be wary of 'presentism'—judging historical figures based on contemporary moral standards. It is unfair to fault them for not transcending the values of their time, even when we no longer subscribe to those values."[36]

Conservative commentators, in particular, have seemed especially eager to relive their undergraduate historiographical methods courses and have likewise waved this banner of methodological rigor. At the website libertarianism.org, in 2015, Jason Kuznicki provided an extended lesson on the follies of presentism, which he equates with political correctness. "A dedicated classical liberal scholar," he declares, "would embarrass [the new presentists], not with hurtful words, but with the depth of his or her knowledge. While they pick at their feelings, let us be in the archives."[37] The same year, Paul Bartow (a doctoral student in history) wrote an article for the American Enterprise Institute warning, as the headline put it, of "the growing threat of presentism," which he claims is also a "threat" to "the preservation of the past...to free speech" and "to proper historical understanding."[38] Writing for the Hoover Institution in 2016, David Davenport and Gordon Lloyd describe presentism as a kind of virus—"malware" in their terms—which they associate not only with Herbert Butterfield but with the French Revolution![39] And in an especially indignant fulmination published in *USA Today*, the political scientist Ross Baker denounces presentism on the grounds that "it is ignorant of context and erects impossibly high obstacles to which virtually no major figure can measure up."[40]

To hear all of these defenders of historiographical virtue tell it, no one in the nineteenth century was woke.[41] The implication—or sometimes the explicit suggestion—is that we must refrain from judging figures from the past by current standards because those standards are always going to be unfair; historical personages will always, invariably, fail to live up to them. The irony of this view is that those who espouse it wind up indicting themselves for the very transgression they mean to police. That is, what makes presentism "complacent" and "self-congratulatory" or as Baker describes it, "smug" in its own "highmindedness," is the assumption that the present is more advanced than—and, therefore, morally superior to—the past. But it's the antipresentists that operate under this assumption of historical progress, not those whom they seek to criticize. That's what the dichotomy between "modern standards" and the "values of their time" presumes in the first place. But in fact, it is precisely the *persistence* of objectionable views into the present, the *presence* of the not-really past, that presentists reveal. Today's presentist-activists aren't smugly reveling in our era's moral superiority; they're critiquing its moral failures. Their critics completely miss this point. Thus, to call attention to why we might not want to bestow upon John Calhoun or Stephen Douglas the honor of naming cherished sites and institutions after them points out the complacency of those who are otherwise not likely to give those honorifics a second thought, who prefer to imagine that the past is simply past, sometimes ugly, sometimes "complicated," to be sure, but safely, unthreateningly behind us. Not here, not now.

Another way to put this is to say that the antipresentists—historicists, of a sort—totalize the present by assuming a universality of "contemporary moral standards." Yet recent history—the present-day historical contexts I described above—has clearly taught us that certain moral standards are quite plainly *not* universally shared. The same holds true of the antipresentist, contextualists' view of the past. When they insist that historical figures are best judged "in context," according to the "values of their time," one can't help but wonder which standards, *whose* standards? After all, the worthiness of John Calhoun for commemoration, for instance, was far from a foregone conclusion in the nineteenth century; certainly, he did not represent a set of values or moral standards that were universally—nor even predominantly—accepted during his lifetime. Frederick Douglass, for instance, described Calhoun as the "prince of tyrants."[42] "He positively makes his boast," Douglass said acridly, of the "disgraceful fact" of being a slave owner, "and assigns it as a reason why he should be listened to as a man of consequence—a person of great importance."[43] Elsewhere, Douglass rendered this final judgment: "No man of the nation has left a broader or a blacker mark on the politics of the nation, than he."[44] Or consider Garrison's *Liberator*, which upon Calhoun's death in 1850, ran a brief two-paragraph notice. "At least, three millions of slaves, six hundred thousand free people of color, and their posterity," the announcement reads," together with the friends of freedom universally, have no cause to bewail his exit. His memory shall rot, or be remembered by future generations only to be execrated for his tyrannical and impious principles."[45] In other words, it's not hard to demonstrate (with just a little time spent in the archives!) that the advocates for removing Calhoun's name from Yale's residential college are judging him according to the moral standards of *his* time, as much as of our own.

All of which is to say that among the things that ought to be consigned to history's dustbin, regarded as relics of a past we no longer wish to inhabit, is the "sacred" principle that presentism is antihistorical, unhistorical, irresponsible, smug, unmindful of the past, or a methodological or ethical error. Indeed, if anything, a half century of historical methodology that cautions against rendering moral judgments upon the figures of the past out of fear of committing an historiographical transgression has conspired with an earlier century's systematic silencing of oppressed groups, marginalized peoples, and dissenters to obscure history, to give the false impression that systems of oppression like slavery were simply the result of an earlier period's almost universally accepted "moral standards," rather than the exercise of power on the part of a specific and identifiable portion of the population. Douglass made a version of this point quite powerfully more than a century and a half ago in his Fourth of July address, "Must I argue the wrongfulness of slavery?" Douglass asks, incredulously:

> Is that a question for Republicans? Is it to be settled by the rules of logic and argumentation, as a matter beset with great difficulty, involving a doubtful application of the principle of justice, hard to be understood? How should I look to-day, in the presence of Americans, dividing, and subdividing a discourse, to show that men have a natural right to freedom? speaking of it relatively and positively, negatively and affirmatively. To do so, would be to make myself ridiculous, and to offer an insult to your understanding. There is not a man beneath the canopy of heaven that does not know that slavery is wrong for him.[46]

Not a man beneath the canopy of heaven. Which era's moral standards does Douglass apply here? How does it advance historical knowledge, how does it help us remember the past, and, more importantly—to bear in mind Frances Harper's dictate—how does it advance social justice to pretend that John Calhoun was a good faith interlocutor in the debate over black freedom, that he was simply, through no fault of his own, unable to transcend his era's values? In response to that point, Frederick Douglass calls bullshit.

Like Douglass, I want to make my point bluntly: the methodological injunction against presentism in the historical profession and in literary historicism has unwittingly helped to sustain and prolong white supremacy in the United States. It has taught us to value monuments, "proud and high," over right, knowledge over experience, and has itself contributed to the very kinds of erasures of history it claims to want to prevent. All of which is not to say that renaming a residential college or a football stadium will end white supremacy—a point made ad nauseum by those who oppose such measures. As the historian James Cobb put it in his meditation on the renaming debate in *Time* magazine, "Anyone who expects that merely scouring the taint of slavery from the faces of a variety of American institutions and edifices moves us toward a definitive resolution of so intricate and complex a historical dilemma would do well to heed the words of a former bondsman recounted in Edward Baptist's on slavery and American capitalism, for they are truly reacting to a story whose 'half has never been told.' "[47] But of course, remarks like this are disingenuous: *nobody* expects any such thing. At the same time, this is not to say that such gestures are merely symbolic. They are instead incitements, challenges, provocations. They ask us to consider and declare *which* moral values— regardless of which era those values are said to "belong" to—we wish to promote through our public memorials. To respond with recourse to abstract historiographical principles, historical inaccuracies, and bromides about fidelity to historical context, is not a way of taking on that challenge, it's an evasion of it.

Thus if the arguments and readings produced in these pages have themselves sometimes run afoul of historicist orthodoxies and normative historiographical assumptions and practices, the impetus for those departures has not been a disrespect toward history nor a sense that when literary scholars went historical we took a wrong turn. To the contrary: I feel strongly that we're not yet done with history—but not done precisely *because*, not despite, of the history that we inhabit. When Garrison—or Longfellow or Emerson or Frances Harper or Martin Luther King—extols the living present over the dead past, he doesn't turn away from history as such, only history that is calcified, fossilized, beyond reanimation. These writers and activists understood that only in the ever-present now can we raise the dead.[48]

{ ENDNOTES }

Introduction

1. Garrison, William Lloyd, *The Liberator* (Mar. 6, 1857): 39.

2. Garrison, "To the Public," *The Liberator* (Jan. 1, 1831): 1.

3. Garrison, "The Dead Past and the Living Present," Eunice McIntosh Merrill Collection of William Lloyd Garrison Papers (MS 73–01, Box 3, FF1), Wichita State University Libraries Special Collections, Wichita, KS. I am grateful to Lorraine Madway, curator and archivist at Wichita State University for assistance in obtaining the Garrison manuscript. For Garrison's Emersonian echoes, see "Self-Reliance": "Speak your latent conviction, and it shall be the universal sense; for the inmost in due time becomes the outmost—and our first thought is rendered back to us by the trumpets of the Last Judgment. Familiar as the voice of the mind is to each, the highest merit we ascribe to Moses, Plato, and Milton is, that they set at naught books and traditions, and spoke not what men but what they thought" (see *CW*, Vol. II: 27); and *Nature*: "The foregoing generations beheld God and nature face to face; we, through their eyes. Why should not we also enjoy an original relation to the universe? Why should not we have a poetry and philosophy of insight and not of tradition, and a religion by revelation to us, and not the history of theirs? Embosomed for a season in nature, whose floods of life stream around and through us, and invite us by the powers they supply, to action proportioned to nature, why should we grope among the dry bones of the past, or put the living generation into masquerade out of its faded wardrobe?" (see *CW*, Vol. I: 7).

4. Wright, Henry C., *The Living Present and the Dead Past: or, God Made Manifest and Useful in Living Men and Women as He Was in Jesus* (Boston, MA: Bela Marsh, 1865): 11.

5. Douglass, Frederic, "What to the Slave Is the Fourth of July? An Address Delivered in Rochester, New York, on 5 July 1852," in *The Frederick Douglass Papers, Series One: Speeches, Debates and Interviews, Vol. 2: 1847–54.* John Blassingame, Ed. (New Haven, CT: Yale UP, 1982): 366.

6. Longfellow, Henry Wadsworth, *Poems and Other Writings* (New York: Library of America, 2000), 4.

7. Frederick Douglass to Elizabeth Pease, July 6, 1846, in *The Frederick Douglass Papers, Series Three: Correspondence, Vol. 2: 1847–54*, Ed. John McKivigan (New Haven, CT: Yale UP, 2009): 141.

8. "Free Soil Movement—Buffalo Convention. This Grand Movement," *The North Star* (Aug. 21, 1848).

9. "The Nomination—The Past—The Present—The Duty," *The National Era* (Aug. 24, 1848): 134.

10. "Proceedings of the New York State Convention," The Colored American (Sept. 11, 1841): 109.

11. See, respectively, Wendell, Barrett, *A Literary History of America* (New York: Charles Scribner's Sons, 1905): 387; Brooks, Cleanth, and Robert Penn Warren, *Understanding*

Poetry (New York: Henry Holt, 1947): ix; "Longfellow in the Aftermath of Modernism," in *The Columbia History of American Poetry*, Jay Parini, Ed. (New York: Columbia UP, 1993): 79; Buell, Lawrence, "The Literary Significance of the Unitarian Movement," in *The American Renaissance*, Harold Bloom, Ed. (New York: Chelsea House, 2004): 250; Spiller, Robert, Ed., *Literary History of the United States* (New York: Macmillan, 1953).

12. Of course, Longfellow it seems is always being reconsidered. See *Henry W. Longfellow Reconsidered: A Symposium* (Hartford: Transcendental Books, 1970); Calhoun, Charles C., *Longfellow: A Rediscovered Life* (Boston: Beacon Press, 2004); Irmasher, Christopher, *Longfellow Redux* (Champaign: U of Illinois P, 2008); Irmasher, Christoph, and Robert Arbour, Eds., *Reconsidering Longfellow* (Teaneck, NJ: Fairleigh Dickinson UP, 2014).

13. Gruesz, Kirsten Silva, "Feeling for the Fireside: Longfellow, Lynch, and the Topography of Poetic Power," in *Sentimental Men: Masculinity and the Politics of Affect in American Culture*, Mary Chapman and Glenn Hendler, Eds. (Berkeley: U of California P, 1999): 49.

14. Anderson, Jill, "'Be Up and Doing': Henry Wadsworth Longfellow and Poetic Labor," *Journal of American Studies* 37:1 (Apr. 2003): 1–15. See also, along similar lines, Haralson, Eric L., "Mars in Petticoats: Longfellow and Sentimental Masculinity," *Nineteenth-Century Literature* 51:3 (Dec. 1996): 327–56; Gartner, Matthew, "Becoming Longfellow: Work, Manhood, and Poetry," *American Literature* 72:1 (Mar. 2000): 59–86; Peck, David R., "'Let Us, Then, Be Up and Doing,'" *ANQ* 16:3 (Summer 2003): 30–5.

15. Hawthorne, Nathaniel, *Life of Franklin Pierce* (Boston: Ticknor, Reed, and Fields, 1852): 111–13. Additionally, in the hallmark gesture of the gradualists, Hawthorne points out that "the good" sought by antislavery agitators is, "at best, a contingency" and might well lead to "the aggravated injury of those whose condition it aimed to ameliorate." The "statesman of practical sagacity," by contrast, "demands to feel his firm grasp upon a better reality before he quits the one already gained". For another representative specimen of the gradualist view, here is T. R. Sullivan in his *Letters Against the Immediate Abolition of Slavery* (Boston: Hilliar, Gray and Co., 1835): 45—"He, by whose providence slavery was permitted to begin in this land three hundred years ago, will, in his own due time end it, if such be his will."

16. Elisa Tamarkin identifies another important site of nineteenth-century presentism— one that this book does not take up—in daily newspapers, the speed of which produced in the reading public a certain impatience that, in Tamarkin's interesting account, put pressure on the period's literature. See Tamarkin, Elisa, "Literature and the News" in *The Oxford Handbook of Nineteenth-Century American Literature*, Russ Castronovo, Ed. (New York: Oxford UP, 2012): 309–26.

17. My understanding of historical experience has been informed by Ankersmit, Frank, *Sublime Historical Experience* (Stanford, CA: Stanford UP, 2005); and Martin Jay's vast survey *Songs of Experience: Modern American and European Variations on a Universal Theme* (Berkeley: U of California P, 2005). For an important and provocative treatment of experience in antebellum American literature, one that displaces experiences from the domain of the individual subject, see Davis, Theo, *Formalism, Experience and the Making of American Literature in the Nineteenth Century* (New York: Cambridge UP, 2010).

18. I suspect that most readers of this book could generate their own extensive lists of scholarly works that have performed this work. For a useful shorthand, one might simply cite the work attributed to the "New Americanists." Two influential collections might be

said to typify this work: *Ideology and Classic American Literature*, Sacvan Bercovitch and Myra Jehlen, Eds. (New York: Cambridge UP, 1987); and Donald Pease, Ed., *Revisionist Interventions into the Americanist Canon* (Durham, NC: Duke UP, 1994).

19. Coincidentally, Brown was hanged only four days after Irving died, a fact that did not go unnoticed at the time. For more on this, see my essay "Historicism" in *Time and Literature*, Thomas Allen, Ed. (Cambridge: Cambridge UP, 2018): 180–92.

20. On stadialist theory, see also Smith, Henry Nash, *Virgin Land: The American West as Symbol and Myth* (Cambridge, MA: Harvard UP, 1957); Miller, Angela L., *The Empire of the Eye: Landscape Representation and American Cultural Politics*, 1825–1875 (Ithaca, NY: Cornel UP, 1996); Allen, Thomas M., *A Republic in Time: Temporality and Imagination in Nineteenth-Century America* (Chapel Hill: U of North Carolina P, 2008).

21. There are, of course, many different historicist practices, not all of them coincident with the historical turn in Americanist scholarship. In fact, Roy Harvey Pearce published his book *Historicism Once More* in 1969. Nor has all historicist criticism understood Frederic Jameson's injunction in *The Political Unconscious* to "always historicize!" in precisely the same way. But while distinctions can be (and have been) made between, say, first generation New Historicism—itself comprised of a number of different strains, like the New Americanist criticism, British Renaissance new historicism, and the work associated with the founding of the journal *Representations* at Berkeley—the canon revisionism and recovery of minority and women writers that began to flourish in the 1970s, and the extensive body of more recent scholarship that simply takes contextualization for granted, I'm using the term *historicism* as a shorthand for a set of assumptions broadly shared by all of these historicisms, assumptions I explore in greater detail, especially, in Chapters 1 and 2. For a range of critical responses, including one of my own, to historicist practices, see *The Limits of Literary Historicism*, Allen Dunn and Thomas Haddox, Eds. (Knoxville: U of Tennessee P, 2012).

22. Emerson, Ralph Waldo, *Collected Works*, Vol. VI, 99; Frederick Douglass, *Frederick Douglass Papers, Series 1, Vol. 3*; Melville, *Pierre; or the Ambiguities* (Evanston, IL: Northwestern UP, 1971): 8. Thoreau, *Journals, Vol. 2 159*.

23. Fisher, David Hackett, *Historians' Fallacies: Toward a Logic of Historical Thought* (New York: Harper Perennial, 1970): 135–42.

24. See Felski, Rita, "Context Stinks!," in which she describes "context as a kind of box or container in which individual texts are encased and held fast." *New Literary History* 42:4 (Autumn 2011): 577.

25. Rohy, Valerie, *Anachronism and Its Others: Sexuality, Race, Temporality* (Albany, NY: SUNY UP, 2009): 126.

26. Ibid, 577: "Historicism serves as the functional equivalent of cultural relativism, quarantining difference, denying relatedness, and suspending—or less kindly, evading—the question of why past texts still matter and how they speak to us now."

27. For more on historicism's entanglements with presentism, see Fleissner, Jennifer, "Is Feminism a Historicism," *Tulsa Studies in Women's Literature* 21:1 (Spring 2002): 45–66; and "Historicism Blues," *American Literary History* 25:4 (Winter 2015): 699–717.

28. Rohy, *Anachronism* 129.

29. Fleissner, "Historicism Blues," *American Literary History* 25: 4: 702.

30. On this point, see Fleissner, "Is Feminism and Historian?" 49, and Felski's description of the hermeneutics of suspicion: "The critic probes for meanings inaccessible to authors

as well as ordinary readers, and exposes the text's complicity in social conditions that it seeks to deny or disavow. Context, as the ampler, more expansive reference point, will invariably trump the claims of the individual text, knowing it far better than it can ever know itself," in "Context Stinks!" 574. I make a similar point in "Prospects for the Present," *American Literary History* 26:4 (Winter 2014): 837. Also relevant here is Jonathan Ree's mordant "The Vanity of Historicism," *New Literary History* 22 (1981): 970–71. More recently, Lloyd Pratt in a penetrating essay draws upon Jacques Ranciere's notion of an "equality of intelligences" in search of an alternative to "intellectual work on the past [that] takes for granted the superiority of the current critic's knowledge when measured against knowledge generated in the past. 'If only they knew then what we know now,' in other words, represents a pernicious manifestation of a position that rejects the equality of intelligences across time." See Pratt, "Stranger History," *J19* 1:1 (Spring 2013): 155.

31. My attempt to avoid such an historical posture has much in common with Lloyd Pratt's assumption, by way of Jacques Rancierre, of an "equality of intelligences" across periods. See *The Strangers Book: The Human of African American Literature* (Philadelphia: U of Pennsylvania P, 2016): 92–6.

32. Noting that the historical turn took Jameson's "always historicize!" in two divergent directions (the first of which, I might add, has been the path generally taken by Americanists): "always historicize in relation either to a moment (that is, always synchronize!) or to a transition (always diachronize!)," Jonathan Gil Harris suggests that critics have failed to recognize how Jameson also called on critics to "polychronize" in *Untimely Matter in the Time of Shakespeare* (Philadelphia: U of Pennsylvania P, 2009): 10.

33. Hawkes, Terence, *Shakespeare in the Present* (London, Routledge, 2002); Grady, Hugh, and Terence Hawkes, Eds. *Presentist Shakespeares* (London: Routledge, 2007); Gajowski, Evelyn, *Presentism, Gender, and Sexuality in Shakespeare* (London: Palgrave Macmillan, 2009); O'Rourke, James, *Retheorizing Shakespeare through Presentist Readings* (London: Routledge, 2012); and Cary DiPietro and Hugh Grady, Eds., *Shakespeare and the Urgency of Now* (London: Palgrave Macmillan, 2013).

34. Garber, Marjorie, *A Manifesto for Literary Studies* (Seattle: U of Washington P, 2004): 180.

35. Barrish, Phillip, *White Liberal Identity, Literary Pedagogy, and Classic American Realism* (Columbus: The Ohio State UP, 2005): 18–19.

36. Castronovo, Russ, "Death to the American Renaissance: History, Heidegger, Poe," *ESQ: A Journal of the American Renaissance* 49 (2003): 181.

37. Dawes, James, "Abolition and Activism: The Present Uses of Literary Criticism" in *The Oxford Handbook of Nineteenth-Century American Literature*, Ed. Russ Castronovo (New York: Oxford, 2012): 360. For other iterations of presentist or otherwise antihistoricist reading practices, see Dimock, Wai Chee, *Through Other Continents: American Literature Across Deep Time* (Princeton: Princeton UP, 2008) and "Crowdsourcing History: Tony Kushner, and Steven Spielberg Update the Civil War," *American Literary History* 25 (Winter 2013): 896–914; Loughran, Trish, "Reading in the Present Tense: Benito Cereno and the Time of Reading" in *American Literature's Aesthetic Dimensions*, Cindy Weinstein and Christopher Looby, Eds. (New York: Columbia UP, 2012); and Judith Halberstam on "perverse presentism" in *Female Masculinity* (Durham, NC: Duke UP, 1998): 45–74. For a survey of some varieties of presentist reading practices, see also Insko, Jeffrey, "Prospects for the Present," *American Literary History* 26 (Dec. 2014): 836–48. For an historian's defense

of presentism, see Hull, David L., "In Defense of Presentism," *History and Theory* 18 (Feb. 1979): 1–15.

38. For a survey of the various forms of this exhaustion see *The Limits of Literary Historicism*, Allen Dunn and Thomas F. Haddox, Eds. (Knoxville: U of Tennessee P, 2011).

39. Here I would include the various "strategies of presentism" explored by the recently formed V21 Collective in British Victorian Studies. See *Victorian Studies* (Autumn 2016): 87–126; and the V21 special issue on "Presentism, Form, and the Future of History," Anna Kornbluh and Benjamin Morgan, Eds., *b2o: an online journal* (Oct. 2016): http://www. boundary2.org/b2o-v21-special-issue/. Accessed June 14, 2018.

40. See Dimock, *Through Other Continents* (Princeton, NJ: Princeton UP, 2008); O'Malley, Michael, *Keeping Watch: A History of American Time* (New York: Viking Penguin, 1990); Smith, Mark M., *Mastered By the Clock: Time, Slavery, and Freedom in the American South* (Chapel Hill: U of North Carolina P, 1997); Luciano, Dana, *Arranging Grief: Sacred Time and the Body in Nineteenth-Century America* (New York: NYU P, 2007); Allen, Thomas M., *A Republic in Time: Temporality and Imagination in Nineteenth-Century America* (Chapel Hill: U of North Carolina P, 2008); Pratt, Lloyd, *Archives of American Time: Literature and Modernity in the Nineteenth Century.* (Philadelphia: U of Pennsylvania P, 2010); English, Daylanne, *Each Hour Redeem: Time and Justice in African American Literature* (Minneapolis: U of Minnesota P, 2013); Marrs, Cody, *Nineteenth-Century American Literature and the Long Civil War* (New York: Cambridge UP, 2015); Weinstein, Cindy, *Time, Tense, and American Literature: When is Now?* (New York: Cambridge UP, 2015); Laski, Gregory, *Untimely Democracy: The Politics of Progress After Slavery* (New York: Oxford UP, 2017); and Sizemore, Michelle, *American Enchantment: Rituals of the People in the Post-Revolutionary World* (New York: Oxford UP, 2017). In Chapter 3, I also engage James R. Guthrie's *Above Time: Emerson's and Thoreau's Temporal Revolutions* (Columbia: U of Missouri P, 2001). Also worth mentioning is John F. Lynen's often insightful, but now largely forgotten, *The Design of the Present: Essays on Time and Form in American Literature* (New Haven, CT: Yale UP, 1969).

41. In addition to the works listed above, my thinking about time owes a deep debt to the extraordinary and varied work on queer temporalities produced during the past decade or so. See, most especially, Freeman, Elizabeth, *Time Binds: Queer Temporalities, Queer Histories* (Durham, NC: Duke UP, 2010); Edelman, Lee, *No Future: Queer Theory and the Death Drive* (Durham, NC: Duke UP, 2004); Halberstam, Jack, *In a Queer Time and Place: Transgender Bodies, Subcultural Lives* (New York: NYU P, 2005); Muñoz, José Esteban, *Cruising Utopia: The Then and There of Queer Futurity* (New York: NYU P, 2009); Snediker, Michael, *Queer Optimism: Lyric Personhood and Other Felicitous Persuasions* (Minneapolis: U of Minnesota P, 2008); Love, Heather, *Feeling Backward: Loss and the Politics of Queer History* (Cambridge: Harvard UP, 2007); Dinshaw, Carolyn, *How Soon is Now? Medieval Texts, Amateur Readers, and the Queerness of Time* (Durham, NC: Duke UP, 2012); and Coviello, Peter, *Tomorrow's Parties: Sex and the Untimely in Nineteenth-Century American Literature* (New York: NYU P, 2013).

42. Stein, Jordan Alexander, "American Literary History and Queer Temporalities," *American Literary History* 25:4 (Winter 2013): 863.

43. Ibid, 866.

44. Weinstein, Cindy, *Time, Tense, and American Literature: When is Now?* (Cambridge: Cambridge UP, 2015).

45. Ibid, 3.

46. Dinshaw, Carolyn, *How Soon is Now? Medieval Texts, Amateur Readers, and the Queerness of Time* (Durham, NC: Duke UP, 2012): 53.

47. Ibid, 4.

48. Ibid, 7.

49. Ibid, 170.

50. Like Rifkin, Michelle Wright also draws upon advances in post-Einsteinian space-time in *Physics of Blackness: Beyond the Middle Passage Epistemology* (Minneapolis: U of Minnesota P, 2015). I draw upon Wright's considerable insights in Chapter 4.

51. In fact, my readings might also provide a framework adaptable to or generative as a point of departure for examinations of Native American writings of the antebellum period.

52. Weinstein, *Time, Tense* 7.

53. Freeman, *Time Binds* xvii.

54. Coviello, *Tomorrow's Parties* 18.

55. Best, Stephen, and Sharon Marcus, "Surface Reading: An Introduction," *Representations* 108 (2009): 10.

56. Nietzsche, Friedrich, *Untimely Meditations*, Daniel Breazeale, Ed. (Cambridge: Cambridge UP, 1997): 77.

57. Ibid, 77.

58. Ibid, 62.

59. For a helpful gloss on Nietzche's "untimely," see Gil Harris, *Untimely Matter* 11–13.

60. Ankersmit, "Sublime Historical" 170.

61. Ibid: "Where we have narrative, experience is impossible; and experience excludes narrative," 172.

62. Rifkin is a notable exception. See *Beyond Settler Time* 1–48.

63. Felski aptly describes Benjamin as "the patronizing saint of all those wary of periodizing schemes" (see "Context Stinks!" 576). Barrish, Dinshaw, Luciano, and Pratt all cite Benjamin. See also Thomas, Brook, *The New Historicism and Other Old-Fashioned Topics* (Princeton: Princeton UP, 1991); Chakrabarty, Dipesh, *Provincializing Europe: Postcolonial Thought and Historical Difference* (Princeton: Princeton UP, 2000).

64. Benjamin's "Theses on the Philosophy of History" turn away from historicism's focus on the past as it was and toward the present as a site of transformative potential. In thesis five, for instance, Benjamin states "For every image of the past that is not recognized by the present as one of its own concerns threatens to disappear irretrievably." Although equally crowded and full, Benjamin's present, unlike Mead's, is arrested. In his sixteenth thesis, he says, that the "historical materialist cannot do without the notion of a present which is not a transition, but in which time stands still and has come to a stop. For this notion defines the present in which he himself is writing history. Historicism gives the 'eternal' image of the past historical materialism supplies a unique experience with the past."—See Benjamin, Walter, *Illuminations*, Hannah Arendt, Ed. (New York: Schocken Books, 1968): 255, 262. For more on Benjamin and the present, see Brown, Wendy, *Edgework: Critical Essays on Knowledge and Politics* (Princeton, NJ: Princeton U, 2005): 11–14.

65. Mead published only a handful of articles over the course of his career. Following his death in 1931, his former students compiled and edited his unpublished writings and lecture notes into four volumes: *The Philosophy of the Present* (1932); *Mind, Self, and Society* (1934); *Movements of Thought in the Nineteenth Century* (1936); and *The Philosophy of the Act*

(1938). *The Philosophy of the Present* is drawn from Mead's Carus Lectures delivered to the American Philosophical Society in Berkeley in 1930.

66. Dinshaw provides a succinct gloss of Aristotle's and Aquinas's grappling with temporal experience (see 7–16).

67. For affinities between Mead and Husserl, neither of whom directly engaged the other's work, see Joas, Hans, *G. H. Mead: A Contemporary Re-examination of His Thought* (Cambridge, MA: MIT P, 1997): 64–89; Seeburger, Francis F., and David D. Franks, "Husserl's Phenomenology and Meadian Theory," *The Sociological Quarterly* 19 (Spring 1978): 345–47. On Mead and the phenomenological tradition in philosophy, see Rosenthal, Sandra B., and Patrick L. Bourgeois, *Pragmatism and Phenomenology: A Philosophic Encounter* (Amsterdam: B.R. Gruner, 1980); *Mead and Merleau-Ponty: Toward a Common Vision* (Albany: SUNY P, 1991). For a helpful account of the present in the phenomenological tradition, see Couzens Hoy, David, *The Time of Our Lives: A Critical History of Temporality* (Cambridge, MA: MIT P, 2009): 41–94.

68. Husserl, Edmund, *On the Phenomenology of the Consciousness of Internal Time (1893–1917)*, J. B. Brough, trans. (Dordecht: Kluwer, 1990). The string of beads metaphor is from William James in "The Perception of Time," citing James Mill: "If the constitution of consciousness were that of a string of bead-like sensations and images, all separate, 'we never could have any knowledge except that of the present instant. The moment each of our sensations ceased it would be gone for ever'." See James, *The Principles of Psychology*, Vol. I (New York: Henry Holt, 1890): 605. Compare James's beads to Benjamin's, somewhat differently inflected, in the "Theses on the Philosophy of History" 263: "Historicism contents itself with establishing a causal connection between various moments in history. But no fact that is a cause is for that very reason historical. It became historical posthumously, as it were, through events that may be separated from it by thousands of years. A historian who takes this as his point of departure stops telling the sequence of events like the beads of a rosary."

69. "What is, for me, the present moment?" Henri Bergson asks:

The essence of time is that it goes by; time already gone by is the past, and we call the present the instant in which it goes by. But there can be no question here of a mathematical instant. No doubt there is an ideal present—a pure conception, the indivisible limit which separates past from future. But the real, concrete, live present—that of which I speak when I speak of my present perception—that present necessarily occupies a duration.

Matter and Memory (New York: Macmillan, 1913): 176.

70. As Mead puts it in his own account of Bergson, "What is characteristic of the melody is the fact that the note which you are hearing and singing extends on, endures into later notes. It is a relationship between the different notes that makes up the melody. Mead, George Herbert, *Movements of Thought in the Nineteenth Century* (Chicago: U of Chicago P, 1936): 297, 148.

71. Ibid, 298.

72. James likened Bergson's thinking about time to a second Copernican revolution. See James, William, *A Pluralistic Universe* (Cambridge, MA: Harvard UP, 1977): 101–24.

73. James, William, *Principles of Psychology* 606.

74. Ibid, 608.

75. Ibid, 609.

76. James, *A Pluralistic Universe* 104. Drawing upon various psychological experiments, James concludes that the temporal extent of the specious present is limited to less than a minute. Such a limit is important for James because it allows him to distinguish between the experience of duration and the function of memory. As James puts it, "to remember a thing as past, the notion of 'past' should be one of our 'ideas.'" But James's interest in the perception of time involves asking a more fundamental question, how do things (objects of perception and memory) "get their pastness? What is our original of the experience of pastness from whence we get the meaning of the term?" The answer is that pastness derives from what James earlier in *The Principles* has called "the stream of thought": the sensation of the present continually slipping out of our grasp into the past, "the constant feeling *sui generis* of pastness, to which every one of our experiences in turn falls a prey." In order for an object or fact to be an object or fact of memory, it must be "thought as in the past"; it must be "conceived, not perceived." That is, it must be "by a name or other symbol or certain concrete events, associated therewithal." See *The Principles of Psychology* 650.

77. My account of Bergson is informed by Hoy and, of course, by Deleuze, Gilles, *Bergsonism* (Cambridge, MA: Zone Books, 1990).

78. Bergson, *Matter and Memory* 194.

79. Mead, *Movements* 303.

80. Indeed, the former actually prevents contact with the latter. Bergson says:

> To call up the past in the form of an image, we must be able to withdraw ourselves from the action of the moment, we must have the power to value the useless, we must have the will to dream. Man alone is capable of such an effort. But even in him the past to which he returns is fugitive, ever on the point of escaping him, as though his backward turning memory were thwarted by the other, more natural, memory, of which the forward movement bears him on to action and to life.

Matter and Memory 94.

81. Mead, George Herbert, *The Philosophy of the Present*, Ed. A. E. Murphy (The Open Court Company, 1932): 35.

82. Ibid, 58.

83. Ibid, 58.

84. Mead, *The Philosophy of the Act*, C. W. Morris, et al., Eds. (University of Chicago 1938): 616.

85. Mead, *The Philosophy of the Present* 41.

86. Note on *Prehistory of Posthistoricism*, Greenblatt.

87. Mead, *The Philosophy of the Present*.

88. Mead, *The Philosophy of the Act* 65.

89. See, analogously, Ankersmit, *Sublime Historical Experience*.

90. Mead, *The Philosophy of the Present* 46.

91. Ibid, 3.

92. To a certain degree, I am picking up on the unelaborated insight with which the historian David Brion Davis concludes his influential essay on immediatism more than fifty years ago:

> It falls beyond the scope of the present essay to show how immediatism itself became institutionalized as a rigid test of faith, and how it served as a medium for attacking all rival institutions that limited individual freedom or defined standards

of thought and conduct. It is enough to suggest that immediatism, while latent in early antislavery thought, was part of a larger reaction against a type of mind that tended to think of history in terms of linear time and logical categories, and that emphasized the importance of self-interest, expediency, moderation, and planning in accordance with economic and social laws. Immediatism shared with the romantic frame of mind a hostility to all dualisms of thought and feeling, an allegiance to both emotional sympathy and abstract principle, an assumption that mind can rise above self-interest, and a belief that ideas, when held with sufficient intensity, can be transformed into irresistible moral action.

It seems remarkable that no one has pursued this observation before now: see "The Emergence of Immediatism" 230.

93. Fanuzzi, Robert, *Abolition's Public Sphere* (Minneapolis: U of Minnesota P, 2003): xvi–xvii. Fanuzzi is virtually alone in examining the temporality of abolition, but, curiously, takes little interest in immediatism. Trish Loughran challenges Fanuzzi's thesis, arguing for abolition as a spatial rather than temporal practice: see *The Republic in Print: Print Culture in the Age of U.S. Nation Building, 1770–1870* (New York: Columbia UP, 2007): 303–62. The historiography of immediatism is vast, but rarely if ever concerned with immediatism's conceptions of time and history (whether implicit or implicit). Davis, David Brion, "The Emergence of Immediatism in British and American Antislavery Thought," *Mississippi Valley Historical Review* 49 (Sep. 1962): 209–30 is full of unexplored insight and remains the most important account of immediatism's rise. See also Hawkins, Hugh, Ed, *The Abolitionists: Immediatism and the Question of Means* (Boston: D.C. Heath, 1964); Pease, William H., and Jane H. Pease, "Antislavery Ambivalence: Immediatism, Expediency, Race," *American Quarterly* 17 (Winter, 1965): 682–95; Loveland, Anne C., "Evangelicalism and 'Immediate Emancipation' in American Antislavery Thought," *Journal of Southern History* 32 (May 1966): 172–88; Kraditor, Aileen, *Means and Ends in American Abolitionism. Garrison and His Critics on Strategy and Tactics* (New York: Vintage, 1962); Friedman, Lawrence Jacob, *Gregarious Saints: Self and Community in American Abolitionism, 1830–1870* (New York: Cambridge UP, 1982); Henry Mayer, *All on Fire: William Lloyd Garrison and the Abolition of Slavery* (New York: W.W. Norton, 1998); and Goodman, Paul, *Of One Blood: Abolitionism and the Origins of Racial Equality* (Berkeley: U of California P, 2000). And as I discuss in more detail in Chapter 4, Frederick Douglass adopted the role of historian of immediatism.

94. Relatedly, see Fanuzzi on "Garrison's Persecution Complex" 13–21.

95. Garrison, "The Dead Past and the Living Present."

96. On Everett's "Character of Washington" Tour, see Reid, Ronald F., *Edward Everett: Unionist Orator* (Westport, CT: Greenwood Press, 1990): 80–106.

97. On the Hayne debate, see Remini, Robert V., *Daniel Webster: The Man and His Time* (New York: W.W. Norton, 1997): 312–31; and Smith, Craig R., *Daniel Webster and the Oratory of Civil Religion* (Columbia: U of Missouri P, 2005): 109–19.

98. See also Martha Schoolman, who similarly finds "that abolitionists ended up discovering in the unpredictable path of revolutionary violence the only possible end to slavery that they could in good conscience endorse." *Abolitionist Geographies* (Minneapolis: U of Minnesota P, 2014): 19.

99. Douglass, Frederick, *Selected Speeches and Writings*, Philip S. Foner, Ed. (Chicago: Lawrence Hill Books, 1999): 367. I take up Douglass's and Melville's deployment of thunder and lightning imagery toward presentist ends in more detail in Chapters 4 and 5.

Chapter 1

1. See Robert Berkhofer, who argues that "temporal succession is fundamental to the ordering of" historian's data:

What makes chronology work in historical practice is the assumption of the order or sequence of time that measures both succession and duration. Thus a historic event embraces a specific span of time while simultaneously being before, during, or after other events at the same or different times. Historic time is both singular for the moment of dating and continuous for measuring duration. The irreversibility of historic time allows assumptions about causality, contingency, irrelevance and anachronism.

Beyond the Great Story: History as Text and Discourse, (Cambridge, MA: Belknap Press of Harvard UP, 1995): 109–10.

2. These quotations are drawn from, respectively, Spiller, Robert, Ed., *Literary History of the United States*, 2nd ed. (New York: Macmillan, 1953): 242; Springer, Haskell, "Washington Irving and the Knickerbocker Group," *Columbia Literary History of the United States*, Emory Elliot, Ed. (New York: Columbia UP, 1988): 239; Gilmore, Michael, "Washington Irving," *The Cambridge History of American Literature*, Sacvan Bercovitch, Ed. (Cambridge: Cambridge UP, 1994): 661. Gilmore registers some ambivalence toward this prevailing view, remarking that Irving was "nonetheless an innovator who established American writing on a new footing as a viable profession" (661).

3. Irving, Washington, *History, Tales, and Sketches, The Sketch Book | A History of New York | Salmagundi | Letters of Jonathan Oldstyle, Gent*, James Tuttleton, Ed. (Library of America): 380. This and all subsequent page references refer to the Library of America reprint (1983), which follows the original edition of 1809. Irving published revised editions of the *History* at several points during his career. For extended commentary on its publication history and Irving's revisions, see Black and Black, *The Complete Works of Washington Irving*. Most critics agree that Irving's later revisions robbed the original of its potency.

4. Irving, *History, Tales, and Sketches* 380.

5. Ibid, 662, 380, 381, respectively.

6. Ibid, 381.

7. Williams, Stanley T., *The Life of Washington Irving, Vol. 1* (New York: Oxford UP, 1935): xiii.

8. Greene, Thomas, "History and Anachronism," *The Vulnerable Text: Essays on Renaissance Literature*, Thomas M. Greene, Ed. (New York: Columbia UP, 1986): 233.

9. Martin Roth, for instance, begins his study of Irving by claiming, "Irving's bequest to the major writers of nineteenth-century American literature is deeper and more meaningful than it is generally supposed to be." Hence, the "subject of Irving's relationship to that richer literature would obviously provide my anticipated audience with a book more pertinent to the announced interests of American literary study," *Comedy and America: The Lost World of Washington Irving* (Port Washington, NY: Kennikat Press, 1976): ix. Such deference to the later masters is evident, too, in Jeffrey Rubin-Dorsky's study. Irving, Rubin-Dorsky claims, "was not an 'original' writer in the way we might apply the term" to later writers. Yet at times, he did "ventur[e] into the underside of the American psyche before Poe, Hawthorne, and Melville would stake it out as their particular terrain," *Adrift in the Old World: The Psychological Pilgrimmage of Washington Irving* (Chicago: U of Chicago P, 1988): xiv, xviii. Even the very best of Irving's critics, William Hedges, cites

approvingly Harry Levin's suggestion that "there are tinges of shadow in the allegedly lighthearted Irving that ultimately relate him to the darker aspects of Hawthorne, Poe, and Melville" and asserts that the "transition to [the American Renaissance] must be a central concern in any detailed examination of Irving's career," *Washington Irving: An American Study, 1802–32* (Baltimore, MD: Johns Hopkins UP, 1965): 15. The question of Irving's relation to the American Renaissance authors is also implicit in the title of and the essays collected in *The Old and New World Romanticism of Washington Irving*, edited by Brodwin. See, for instance, Hedges's introduction, where he refers to Irving as a "half-way figure," *The Old and New World Romanticism of Washington Irving* (New York: Greenwood Press, 1986): 4.

10. Indeed, over the past decade, in particular, there has been a flurry of interest in Irving, mostly devoted to "contextualizing" his works. See Traister, Bryce, "The Wandering Bachelor: Irving, Masculinity, and Authorship," *American Literature* 74:1 (Mar. 2002): 112. For compelling treatments of Irving in relation to U.S. imperialism and manifest destiny, see, especially, McLamore, Richard V., "The Dutchman in the Attic: Claiming an Inheritance in The Sketch Book of Geoffrey Crayon," *American Literature* 72:1 (Mar. 2000): 31–57; and LeMenager, Stephanie, "Trading Stories: Washington Irving and the Global West," *American Literary History* 15:4 (Winter 2003): 683–708. Irving has also attracted considerable interest among queer theorists and critics interested in conceptions of masculine selfhood. See Warner, Michael, "Irving's Posterity," *ELH* 67 (2000): 773–99; Anthony, David, "'Gone Distracted': 'Sleepy Hollow,' Gothic Masculinity, and the Panic of 1819," *Early American Literature* 40:1 (2005): 111–44; and Greven, David, "Troubling Our Heads about Ichabod: 'The Legend of Sleepy Hollow,' Classic American Literature, and the Sexual Politics of Homosocial Brotherhood," *American Quarterly* 56:1 (Mar. 2004): 83–110.

11. Anthony, "Gone Distracted" 112. Warner, "Irving's Posterity" 776–7. See also Traister, who argues that bachelorhood in the early republic was, in part, a discourse of nostalgia for lost freedom.

12. Hazlitt, William, *The Spirit of the Age* (London: H. Colburn, 1825): 421.

13. Hutcheon, Linda, "Historiographic Metafiction Parody and the Intertextuality of History," *Intertextuality and Contemporary American Fiction*. P. O'Donnell and Robert Con Davis, Eds. (Baltimore, MD: Johns Hopkins UP, 1989): 3–32.

14. See Pratt, *Archives of American Time*, esp. Ch. 2.

15. Despite this assessment, Hedges's remains the most extensive exploration of Irving's "attitudes toward historiography," "Knickerbocker, Bolingbroke, and the Fiction of History," *Journal of the History of Ideas* 20 (1959): 318; and *Washington Irving: An American Study*. In addition, in his introduction to *The Old and New World Romanticism of Washington Irving*, Hedges says, "I think we have not yet learned how to respond to Irving's mock-history because we have been trying too hard to grasp what it means" (see 8). Implicit in my argument is that, strangely, it may have taken the poststructuralist challenges to history in the wake of the historical turn to teach us how to respond to Irving's historiographical critique. See also Gilmore, who asserts that in *A History of New York*, "laughter and confusion deflate history's authority as the realm of truth," "Washington Irving" 661. And Lloyd Daigrepont notes, briefly, Irving's rejection of history as a "coherent process," "Rip Van Winkle and the Gnostic Vision of History," *Clio* 15 (Fall 1985): 48.

16. See esp. White, Hayden, *Tropics of Discourse: Essays in Cultural Criticism* (Baltimore, MD: Johns Hopkins UP, 1985).

17. See Black, Michael L., "Political Satire in Knickerbocker's History," *The Knickerbocker Tradition: Washington Irving's New York*, Andrew B. Myers, Ed. (Tarrytown, NY: Sleepy

Hollow Restorations, 1974): 80–1; and Irving, Washington, *Diedrich Knickerbocker's A History of New York, by Washington Irving*, Stanley T. Williams and Tremaine McDowell, Eds. (New York: Harcourt Brace, 1927).

18. See Gilmore, "Washington Irving" 664–7, who views this fact as Irving's "conservative challenge to the emerging liberal consensus."

19. Irving, *A History of New York* (New York: G.P. Putnam's, 1848): 11. Precisely which works of "pedantic lore" Irving had it in mind to burlesque remains largely a matter of conjecture, though his documented sources provide several clues. For a discussion of those sources, and the seventeenth and eighteenth-century historians Irving parodies, see Williams and McDowell, in Irving, to whom much of the following account is indebted. See also Burstein, who locates the "genesis" of the work in a response to Samuel L. Mitchill's 1807 *Picture of New York* 70.

20. In his study of Revolutionary histories, *The Politics of History*, Arthur H. Shaffer notes that there was a "hiatus, chronological as well as political or ideological" between the colonial historians and the generation of historians born in the three decades before the revolution. He invokes "Rip Van Winkle" to describe the effects of this hiatus on history writing in the United States. "Having reawakened," Shaffer writes, "in a changed world after a sleep of more than twenty years, American historical writing changed profoundly. The Revolution shattered the colonial frame of reference and created a new perspective; it transformed a colonial into a national psychology." See *The Politics of History: Writing the History of the American Revolution, 1783–1815* (Chicago: Precedent Publishing, 1975): 8.

21. The most extended discussion of Irving's adaptation of such satires and burlesques is found in Roth *Comedy and America*. See also Williams and McDowell, in Irving, and Hedges, *An American Study*.

22. Calcott, George, *History in the United States, 1800–1860* (Baltimore, MD: Johns Hopkins UP, 1970): 113.

23. Irving, *History, Tales, and Sketches* 377.

24. Ibid, 381, 437, 452.

25. See Calcott, *History* 121–50; and Shaffer, *The History* 34.

26. Irving, *History, Tales, and Sketches* 379.

27. Ibid, 449, 451, 476, 581, 642, and 595, respectively.

28. See Van Tassel, David, *Recording America's Past: An Interpretation of the Development of Historical Studies in America, 1607–1884* (Chicago: U of Chicago P, 1960): 103–10.

29. Calcott, *History* 35–45. Shaffer adds, "the United States led the world in the development of archival techniques and the establishment of repositories" of historical materials—*The History* 33.

30. Trumbull, Benjamin, *A Complete History of Connecticut, Civil and Ecclesiastical* (New Haven: Maltby, Goldsmith and Co., 1818): 8.

31. Irving, *History, Tales, and Sketches* 377, 379, 381, respectively.

32. Ibid, 387.

33. Ibid, 391.

34. See, for instance, Black, Michael L. and Nancy, "Introduction," *The Complete Works of Washington Irving, v. 7*, Michael L. and Nancy Black, Eds. (Boston: Twayne Publishers, 1984); Black, Michael L., "Political Satire in Knickerbocker's History," *The Knickerbocker Tradition: Washington Irving's New York*, Andrew B Myers, Ed. (Tarrytown, NY: Sleepy Hollow Restorations, 1974): 64–87; Weatherspoon Bowden, Mary, "Knickerbocker's History

and the 'Enlightened' Men of New York," *American Literature* 47 (May 1975): 159–72; Ferguson, Robert A., *Law and Letters in American Literature* (Cambridge, MA: Harvard UP, 1984); Burstein, Andrew, *The Original Knickerbocker: The Life of Washington Irving* (New York: Basic Books, 2007).

35. Shafffer, *The History* 37.

36. Cohen, *The Revolutionary Histories* 15.

37. Civic and political leaders in the colonies had long recognized the importance of an educated populace and saw instruction in history as integral to the project of creating good republican citizens. As George Calcott has noted, Benjamin Franklin as early as 1749 was insisting in his Proposals Relating to the Education of Youth in Pensilvania [sic] that for children, "History be made a constant Part of their Reading"—*History* 56. In 1779, Thomas Jefferson's Diffusion of Knowledge Bill made Virginia the first state to require the instruction of American history in its public schools. But emphasis on instruction in history became even more imperative in the years after the War for Independence as a crucial means of inculcating the citizenry on the republican principles informing the Revolutionary cause. Jefferson along with such prominent Americans as Benjamin Rush, David Ramsay, and John Adams insisted strongly on the need for versions of the history of the Revolution from the American point of view. These calls were answered not just by accounts of the Revolution, like David Ramsay's *The History of the American Revolution* (1789) and Mercy Otis Warren's *History of the Rise, Progress and Termination of the American Revolution* (1805), but by filiopietistic biographies of heroes of the war, like Mason Locke Weems's notorious *Life of Washington* (1800) and William Wirt's biography, *Patrick Henry* (1817).

38. Carpenter, Stephen, "History," *The Monthly Register and Review of the United States*, I (1806): 21.

39. Ibid, 3.

40. Ibid, 3.

41. Irving, *History, Tales, and Sketches* 502–3.

42. Ibid, 580.

43. Ibid, 581.

44. Ibid, 552.

45. Ibid, 553.

46. Ibid, 721.

47. Ibid, 722.

48. Irving's "Author's Apology" prefatory to the 1848 edition portrays the original work as merely "a temporary jeu d'esprit" (see Ibid, 11), the production of a "young and inexperienced writer" who made "presumptuous trespasses into the sacred, though neglected, region of history" and was met with "deserved rebuke from men of soberer minds" (see Ibid, 12). He now wishes his readers will receive it with "good-humored indulgence" and that it will be "thumbed and chuckled over by the family fireside" (see Ibid, 14).

49. The chain of causes—or what Irving here calls the "chain of effects"—was also a familiar trope among early American historians. Beginning, in effect, with Independence, nationalist historians, as Lester Cohen argues, "impose[d] on events a single-minded linearity that attempts to account for its end-point," *The Revolutionary Histories: Contemporary Narratives of the American Revolution* (Ithaca, NY: Cornell UP, 1980): 97. David Ramsay, for example, claimed that the battle won by the Americans at Bennington, Vermont, "was the first in a grand chain of causes, which finally drew down ruin on the whole royal army."

Similarly, Mercy Otis Warren, echoing Knickerbocker's insistence on the "necessity" of demonstrating the formation of the globe, argued that historians' "circumstantial detail of lesser events, when antecedent to the convulsions of empire, and national revolution, are not only excusable, but necessary" (qtd. in Cohen, *The Revolutionary Histories* 97). Warren might just as well be referring to the Dutch action at Fort Casimir as to the events at Lexington. After all, using the "chain-of-causes metaphor," Cohen points out, "the historian could portray virtually any event, no matter how trivial, as the first link in a long series of consequences"—*The Revolutionary Histories* 98.

50. Cohen, *The Revolutionary Histories* 391.

51. Brown, Charles Brockden, "Annals of Europe and America," *The American Register, or General Repository of History, Politics, & Science, V. I* (Philadelphia: C & A Conrad & Co., 1807): 3.

52. In fact, Brown proves at least as surprisingly "postmodern" as Irving. New historicists might be interested, for instance, to read Brown's essay "On Anecdotes," where he argues compellingly for the use of the seemingly trivial, the insignificant, and the out-of-the-way in the writing of histories. "History itself," Brown insists, "derives some of its most agreeable instructions from a skillful introduction of anecdotes. We should not now dwell with anxiety on a dull chronicle of the reigns of monarchs; a parish register might prove more interesting." See Brown, Charles Brockden, "On Anecdotes," *Literary Magazine and American Register* (Jan. 1806): 37. Similarly, readers of Hayden White might take interest in Brown's essay "Historical Characters are False Representations of Nature" (1806), in which he argues that "The historian is a sculptor, who, though he displays a correct semblance of nature, is not less solicitous of displaying the miracles of his art," "Historical Characters are False Representations of Nature," *Literary Magazine and American Register* (Feb. 1806): 113. For more detailed treatment of Brown's theories of history, see Kamrath, Mark L., "Charles Brockden Brown and the 'Art of the Historian': An Essay Concerning (Post)Modern Historical Understanding," *Journal of the Early Republic* 21 (Summer 2001): 231–60.

53. Irving, *History, Tales, and Sketches* 397–8.

54. Ibid, 402.

55. Ibid, 419.

56. Christopher Looby, for instance, has argued convincingly that in the History "the necessary metalepsis of historiographical reconstruction was brilliantly parodied," *Voicing America: Language, Literary Form, and the Origins of the United States* (Chicago: Chicago UP, 1996): 90. He provides an illuminating discussion of how "Knickerbocker reasoned from present facts to necessary preconditions," and demonstrates Irving's "recognition that historical necessity was an illusion of retrospection" (see 96–7). Similarly, Hedges notes that Irving learned from Lord Bolingbroke that "the past is to a certain extent a function of the interests of the present" (see 326). Or as Looby puts it, Knickerbocker narrates his history as if "what happens—what happened—was an effect of his writing," "collapsing the time of his writing and the time of the historical event" so that "past historical events [are presented as] the direct objects of present-tense verbs": *Voicing America* 91, 93, respectively.

57. Irving, *History, Tales, and Sketches* 643.

58. Ibid, 643–4.

59. Looby does not pursue the point. Instead, he cites these instances of Knickerbocker's "performative retrodiction" (see *Voicing America* 92), as examples supporting his more general claim that the American nation was created as an effect of linguistic utterance.

In this, he is in basic agreement with Martin Roth, who has argued that Knickerbocker effects "a new beginning" for America through an act of "artistic creation" (see *Comedy and America* 172).

60. Robert Ferguson argues that the History "is the first American book to question the civic vision of the founding fathers" (see 30). Gilmore also takes note of Irving's attempt to mock puffed-up patriotic histories, asserting that the History set about "toppling history from its cultural preeminence." But, ultimately, Gilmore is in agreement with Roth that he did so in order to "clear the way for American Romanticism" by "free[ing] the imagination to invent its own version of the world" (see "Washington Irving" 665). By contrast, I am suggesting that we need not look at Irving through the later Romanticist frame. Rather, Irving demonstrates that all histories invent their own versions of the world; history and imaginative freedom are in no way at odds.

61. Looby, *Voicing America* 91.

62. Irving, *History, Tales, and Sketches* 398.

63. Ibid, 385.

64. Ibid, 413.

65. Ibid, 399.

66. Montrose, Louis, "The Poetics and Politics of Culture," *The New Historicism*, H. Aram Veesei, Ed. (New York: Routledge, 1989): 17

67. Hence, "the signifier 'context,'" as Christopher Lane puts it in a recent critique, "promises interpretive leverage and revelation." See, "The Poverty of Context," *PMLA* 118 (May 2003): 451. For other recent critiques of new historicist assumptions about time and context in addition to Lane, see Dimock, Wai-Chee, "Non-Newtonian Time: Robert Lowell, Roman History, and Vietnam War," *American Literature* 74 (Dec. 2002): 911–31; Garber, Marjorie, *Quotation Marks* (New York: Routledge, 2003); Castronovo; and my own "Anachronistic Imaginings: *Hope Leslie's* Challenge to Historicism," *American Literary History* 16:2 (2004): 179–207. Garber for instance, argues that "New Historicism tried to avoid or complicate causality; it preferred terms like resonance, circulation, poetics, and social energy. But through its very avoidances, this strategy whetted the appetite for causation. To put it another way, New Historicism began by reading history as a text, but it created, despite its best efforts, a desire for history as a ground. In the wake of postmodernism and the general questioning of foundations, a longing to find causality—the priority of history, history as explanation—seems to have come back to literary study even more strongly than before," 178.

68. Irving, *History, Tales, and Sketches* 404.

69. Ibid.

70. Christopher Lane argues, "critics use a literary work's publication to initiate—and sometimes to authorize—a set of lateral cultural comparisons, based on events that might have influenced the writer in question. The difficulty of verifying influence—centrally important to traditional historians—proves secondary, for new historicists, to what the comparison enables." See Lane, "The Poverty of Context," *PMLA* (2003): 452–3.

71. Dimock, "*Non-Newtonian Time*" 916.

72. Irving, *History, Tales, and Sketches* 647.

73. Ibid, 648.

74. Until quite recently, the temporal dimension of "Rip Van Winkle" received comparatively little extended treatment. The most extended consideration of the theme of time in "Rip Van Winkle" are Young, Philip, "Fallen From Time: The Mythic Rip Van Winkle,"

Kenyon Review 22 (1960): 556–69; Walter Shear, "Time in 'Rip Van Winkle' and 'The Legend of Sleepy Hollow'," *Midwest Quarterly* 17 (1976): 158–72; Lynen, John F., *The Design of the Present: Essays on Time and Form in American Literature* (New Haven, CT: Yale UP, 1969); and Warner. Yet each of them, in different ways, suggests that in the story, Rip seeks to somehow escape time and history. By contrast, Pratt, Dinshaw, and Sizemore all view the story's complex web of temporalities as its central feature. Sizemore, for instance, reads it as a tale of "temporal convergence." Similarly, Pratt shows how "traditional and modern forms of time overlay each other" in the tale. And Carolyn Dinshaw describes it as a story of "temporal asynchrony" in *How Soon is Now? Medieval Texts, Amateur Readers, and the Queerness of Time* (Durham, NC: Duke UP, 2012): 135.

75. For a recent notable exception, see Blakemore, Steven, "Family Resemblances: The Texts and Contexts of 'Rip Van Winkle'": *Early American Literature* 35 (2000): 187–212.

76. Readings of "Rip Van Winkle" have long neglected its complex, layered framing device. Notable exceptions are Douglas R. Anderson, "Freedom's Lullaby: Rip Van Winkle and the Framings of Self-Deception," *ESQ: A Journal of the American Renaissance* 46 (200): 255–83; Blakemore; Warner, and Ferguson, Robert, "Rip Van Winkle and the Generational Divide in American Culture," *Early American Literature* 40 (Nov. 2005): 111–44.

77. Irving, *History, Tales, and Sketches* 767.

78. Ibid, 767.

79. Ibid, 784.

80. Ibid, 378.

81. Ibid, 783–4.

82. Burstein suggests that Irving's discussion of Indian and European rights to the land in Book I of the History "may be the only indication in any of his writings that [Irving] was a lawyer," *The Original Knickerbocker* 74. I am suggesting that "Rip Van Winkle" may well be another such indication.

83. Calcott, *History* 126.

84. Irving, *History, Tales, and Sketches* 1058.

85. Ibid, 1087.

86. Ibid, 1088.

87. Ibid, 303.

88. Ibid, 303.

89. Ibid, 648–9.

90. Ibid, 668.

91. Ibid, 774.

92. Ibid, 775.

93. Ibid, 775.

94. Ibid, 776.

95. Ibid, 779.

96. Ibid, 779.

97. These phrases are, respectively, Ferguson, "Generational Divide" 541; and Dinshaw, *How Soon is Now?* 114.

98. Dinshaw, *How Soon is Now?* 137.

99. Ibid.

100. Looby calls this "the allegorization of historical process as semiotic substitution," remarking that these substitutions, while different, also constitute a "repetition: the new face of George Washington was the same old face of George III": *Voicing America* 95.

101. Sizemore, Michelle R., "'Changing by Enchantment': Temporal Convergence, Early National Comparison's, and Washington Irving's *Sketchbook*," *Studies in American Fiction* 40 (2013): 172.

102. Irving, *History, Tales, and Sketches* 778.

103. Ibid, 778.

104. Ibid, 778.

105. Ibid, 779.

106. Ibid, 779.

107. Ibid, 782.

108. Ibid, 784.

109. Ibid, 783.

110. The final irony of "Rip Van Winkle" is that Rip, the unreliable narrator, ultimately becomes the village historian. At the end of the story, he "took his place once more at the inn door and was reverenced as one of the patriarchs of the village and a chronicle of the 'old times' before the war" (see 40).

111. The phrase is adapted from Castronovo, "Anachronistic Imaginings" 190.

112. Garber, *Quotation Marks* 180.

113. See Pratt, *Archives of American Time* 62; and Sizemore, "'Changing by Enchantment'" 176, respectively.

114. For instance, *Freedom's Journal* published Irving's sketch "Ellen" in 1827. See "Ellen," *Freedom's Journal* (Oct. 5, 1827): 117. An item in in the same paper in 1829 cites Irving's *Life and Voyages of Christopher Columbus* on the origins of slavery in the western world. See "Slavery," *Freedom's Journal* (Feb. 14, 1829): 359. *Frederick Douglass's Paper* ran items on Irving's health and his fall from a horse in 1854 and 1855, respectively. See *Frederick Douglass's Paper* (Feb. 27, 1854) and (May 11, 1855). On Irving's politics and support from Fremont, see "Slavery Despotism," *The National Era* (Sept. 10, 1857).

115. "Letter from Communipaw," *Frederick Douglass's Paper* (Mar. 18, 1852).

116. Fagan, Benjamin "'Feebler than the Original': Translation and Early Black Nationalism," *Transnational American Studies*, Udo J. Hebel, Ed. (Heidelberg: Universitätsverlag Winter, 2012): 236.

117. North Carolina was nicknamed the "Rip Van Winkle state" for maintaining outdated economic policies, making the state appear to be sound asleep, missing out on the modern progress going on all around it.

118. "Colonization," *The Liberator* (June 26, 1847).

119. "Mr. Webster's Compromise Speech," *The Liberator* (Mar. 29, 1850).

120. "Better Be a Dumb Bell," *The Liberator* (Feb. 29, 1856): 34.

121. "Delusions of the President," *The Liberator* (Jan. 15, 1858): 12.

122. "Boston Flunkeyism," *The Liberator* (July 16, 1858): 116.

123. King first delivered the address, in much abbreviated form, at the Morehouse College Commencement in 1959. See *The Papers of Martin Luther King, Jr. Vol. 5*, Clayborne Carson, Ed. (Berkeley: U of California P): 219–26. I am relying here on the version transcribed at the Oberlin College Archives. See http://www.oberlin.edu/external/EOG/BlackHistoryMonth/MLK/MLKmainpage.html.

124. In addition to attributed quotations from the poetry of Bryant and Lowell, King also draws indirectly on Parker for what would eventually become one of King's better-known quotations: "Yes, we shall overcome because the arc of the moral universe is long, but it bends toward justice." King condensed this passage from a sermon Parker delivered

in 1853 titled "Justice and the Conscience": "Look at the facts of the world. You see a continual and progressive triumph of the right. I do not pretend to understand the moral universe; the arc is a long one, my eye reaches but a little ways; I cannot calculate the curve and complete the figure by the experience of sight; I can divine it by conscience. And from what I see I am sure it bends toward justice." See Parker, Theodore, *Ten Sermons of Religion* (Boston: Crosby, Nichols, and Company, 1853): 84–5.

125. As cause for hope, Douglass turns toward "the tendencies of the age." He says, "[n]ations do not now stand in the same relation to each other that they did ages ago. No nation can now shut itself up from the surrounding world and trot round in the same old path of its fathers without interference." What's more, "The arm of commerce has borne away the gates of the strong city. Intelligence is penetrating the darkest corners of the globe. It makes its pathway over and under the sea, as well as on the earth. Wind, steam, and lightning are its chartered agents. Oceans no longer divide, but link nations together. From Boston to London is now a holiday excursion. Space is comparatively annihilated—Thoughts expressed on one side of the Atlantic are distinctly heard on the other," Douglass, Frederick, "What to the Slave Is the Fourth of July? An Address Delivered in Rochester, New York, on 5 July 1852," in *The Frederick Douglass Papers, Series One: Speeches, Debates and Interviews, Vol. 2: 1847–54,* John Blassingame, Ed. (New Haven, CT: Yale UP, 1982): 387. Compare to King, in which mainly highways and jets replace trains and telegraphs: "Modern man, through his scientific genius, has been able to dwarf distance and place time in chains. Yes, we've been able to carve highways through the stratosphere, and our jet planes have compressed into minutes distances that once took weeks and months. This is a small world from a geographical point of view. What we are facing today is the fact that through our scientific and technological genius we've made of this world a neighborhood." Web. http://www.oberlin.edu/external/EOG/BlackHistoryMonth/MLK/MLKmainpage.html. Accessed June 11, 2018.

126. In King's conclusion he says, "we will be able to transform the jangling discords of our nation into a beautiful symphony of brotherhood, and speed up the day when, in the words of the prophet Amos, "Justice will roll down like waters; and righteousness like a mighty stream" and "we will speed up that great day when the American Dream will be a reality." Ibid.

127. See Douglass, "Letter from Communipaw," *Frederick Douglass's Paper* (Mar. 18, 1852).

Chapter 2

1. George Dekker, in *The American Historical Romance* (Cambridge: Cambridge UP, 1987): 112–31, views Irving's signal contribution as his archetypal rendering of the conflict between the Dutch New York and the Yankee settlers.

2. On nationalist pedagogy, see Allen, Thomas, *A Republic in Time: Temporality and Imagination in Nineteenth-Century America* (Chapel Hill: U of North Carolina P, 2008): 31–46.

3. Yet this mode of history writing has a great deal in common with what Linda Hutcheon has identified as postmodern "historiographic metafiction" in *A Poetics of Postmodernism: History, Theory, Fiction* (New York: Routledge, 1988). Among the novels Hutcheon identifies with the genre is E.L. Doctorow's *Ragtime*, which Cyrus K. Patell, perceptively, aligns with *A History of New York*, as both novels "challenge our conventional notions of what constitutes historical fiction"; see *Cosmopolitanism and the Literary Imagination* (New York: Palgrave Macmillan, 2015): 46.

4. For critical histories of each, see Damon-Bach, Lucinda and Victorian Clements, Eds., *Catharine Maria Sedgwick: Critical Perspectives* (Boston: Northeastern UP, 2003); Watts, Edward, and David J. Carlson, Eds., *John Neal and Nineteenth-Century American Literature and Culture* (Lewisberg, PA: Bucknell UP, 2011).

5. See Gould, Philip, *Covenant and Republic: Historical Romance and the Politics of Puritanism* (Cambridge: Cambridge UP, 1996): 92, 204.

6. Pratt, *Archives of American Time* 80.

7. Temporal studies has done much to reveal the oppositional force of *Hope Leslie*. See Insko, Jeffrey, "Anachronistic Imaginings"; Pratt, Lloyd, *Archives of American Time: Literature and Modernity in the Nineteenth Century* (Philadelphia: U of Pennsylvania P, 2010); and Luciano, Dana. *Arranging Grief: Sacred Time and the Body in Nineteenth-Century America* (New York: NYU P, 2007): 170. For a slightly different, but compatible reading, see Hankins, Laurel. "The Voice of Nature: *Hope Leslie* and Early American Romanticism," *Legacy* 31 (2014): 160–82.

8. Sedgwick, Catharine Maria, *Hope Leslie, or Early Times in the Massachusetts* (New York: Penguin Books, 1998): 309.

9. Luciano, in an apt neologism, says that Magawisca here "*pre-bespeaks* the rhetoric of the American Revolution." Luciano's welcome reading focuses upon Magawisca's "melancholy voice" as "the key to the novel's reimagination of historical time": see *Arranging Grief* 102.

10. See Sedgwick, Catharine Maria, "*Hope Leslie*: The Crisis between Ethical Political Action and US Literary Nationalism in the New Republic," *American Transcendental Quarterly* 12 (1998): 297, 302, 340. Such "nativizing" may be one of the text's key themes. In an interesting reading, Mary Karafalis has suggested that Magawisca functions as a "host" for the novel's Puritan heroine Hope; thus "Hope's absorption of autochthonous traces links her to the New World." See Karafalis, Maria, "Catharine Maria Sedgwick's *Hope Leslie*: The Crisis between Ethical Political Action and US Literary Nationalism in the New Republic," *American Transcendental Quarterly* (Dec. 1998): 339.

11. Walter, Benjamin, "Between Ethical Politica," *Illuminations*, Hannah Arendt, Ed., and Harry Zohn, trans. (New York: Schocken Books, 1969): 263.

12. Gustavus Stadler remarks that "When Magawisca anachronistically alludes to Patrick Henry…she becomes not simply heroic, but more specifically an embodied voice in the young United States' discourse of nation-founding." See "Magawisca's Body of Knowledge: Nation-Building in Hope Leslie," *The Yale Journal of Criticism* 12.1 (1999): 51. Sandra A. Zagarell views "the echo of Patrick Henry's words" as part of the novel's extended critique of "Puritan gynophobia" and its articulation of a "different concept of liberty." See "Expanding 'America': Lydia Sigourney''s Sketch of Connecticut, Catharine Sedgwick's *Hope Leslie*," *Tulsa Studies in Womens Literature* 6 (1987): 238–9. And Suzanne Gossett and Barbara Ann Bardes argue that Magawisca's defiance "allow[s] Sedgwick to question the legitimacy of a political authority which excludes certain groups in the population. See "Women and Political Power in the Republic: Two Early American Novels," *Legacy* 2 (1985): 23. My reading differs from each of these, however, in that what interests me is the complex "historicity" of this moment, rather than its implications for the politics of Sedgwick's day. In other words, I mean to explore not the meaning of the anachronistic reference (its Revolutionary origins, its early national resonances), but the meanings of the anachronism itself. Luciano and Pratt are exceptions to this strain of criticism.

13. For present purposes, I am following the definition of historicism provided by F. R. Ankersmit: "the view that we should conceive of history as consisting of a series of epochs each possessing its own individuality." See "Experience, Transcendentalism and the Limits of Interpretation," *Proceedings of History and the Limits of Interpretation: A Symposium*. Rice University, Mar. 16, 1996. Web. http://www.ruf.rice.edu/~culture/papers/Ankersmit. html. Accessed June 11, 2018. In referring to historicism among Americanist literary scholars, I mean, in a broad sense, works of literary criticism and literary history that, implicitly or explicitly, participate in what has come to be known as the "return to history," works that seek, in other words, to explain the relations between literary texts and the "individuality" of a particular epoch or historical moment. This includes, but is not limited to, the "new historicism." Americanist literary scholarship, in particular, has taken up the "historicist" cause with especial fervency. And while I recognize the extraordinary diversity of critical practices (and the variety of historicisms practiced) among Americanists—what Sacvan Bercovitch has famously called "dissensus"—I also agree with Bercovitch that what unites a great deal of the most important work in American literary studies in recent decades is an historicist orientation. As he puts it in his introduction to the Cambridge Literary History of the United States:

> "...the emphasis on history as the vehicle of critical revision...is the emphasis, too, of our critical moment. At no time in literary studies has awareness of history—or more accurately, theorizing about history—been more acute and pervasive. It is hardly too much to say that what joins all the special interests in the field, all factions in our current critical dissensus, is an overriding interest in history: as the ground and texture of ideas, metaphors, and myths; as the substance of the texts we read and the spirit in which we interpret them.

Bercovitch, Sacvan, "Introduction," *The Cambridge History of American Literature* (New York: Cambridge UP, 1994): 4. What I am questioning and what *Hope Leslie* along with a host of other antebellum texts—not all of them "historical fictions"—challenges is a fundamental assumption of this emphasis on history: the conception of time as "a series of epochs each possessing its own individuality." For a useful general discussion of the "historical turn" in literary criticism, see Simpson, David, "Literary Criticism and the Return to 'History,'" *Critical Inquiry* 14 (Summer 1998): 721–47. On the new historicism, see especially Veeser, H. Aram, *The New Historicism* (New York: Routledge, 1989); and Thomas, Brook, *The New Historicism and Other Old-Fashioned Topics* (Princeton: Princeton UP, 1991). The historicist hold on Americanist scholarship is perhaps best reflected by Duke UP's "New Americanist" series, published under the general editorship of Donald Pease. The essay that spawned that series is Pease's "New Americanists: Revisionist Interventions into the Americanist Canon." For an important dissent from the orthodoxy that claims today's critics have a greater interest in history than earlier generations (especially the New Critical generation), see Levin, David, "American Historicisms Old and New," *American Literary History* 6 (Fall 1994): 527–38, a review of the historicist collection *The New American Studies: Essays from Representations*, Philip Fisher, Ed. (Berkeley: U of California Press, 1991).

14. Dekker's definition of historical fiction is capacious. He asks, "For a fiction to qualify as "historical" what more can be required than that the leading or (more to the point) determinative social and psychological traits it represents clearly belong to a period historically distinct from our own?" *American Historical Romance* 14. I would, however—as my essay will make clear—take issue with the phrase "clearly belong." Nina Baym describes

historical fiction as those works that "bring in notable historical personages or important historical events to make a historical point, and give the imagined story a shape that is significantly determined by the time and place of its setting." See *American Women Writers and the Work of History, 1790–1860* (New Brunswick, NJ: Rutgers UP, 1995): 153. *Hope Leslie* complicates both of these definitions through the multiplicity of both its temporal and discursive settings.

15. Benjamin, "Philosophthe Philosophy of History" 263.

16. See, respectively, Douglass, Ann, *The Feminization of American Culture* (New York: Farrar, Strauss, and Giroux, 1977): 185; and Buell, Lawrence, *New England Literary Culture from Renaissance through Revolution.* (Cambridge: Cambridge UP, 1986): 242.

17. Following Mary Kelley's lead in her fine introduction to the Rutgers UP re-print of *Hope Leslie*, Cheri Louise Ross, Carol J. Singley, and Dana D. Nelson all use the phrase "alternative history." See Kelley, Mary, "Introduction," *Hope Leslie, or Early Times in the Massachusetts* (New Brunswick: Rutgers UP, 1987); Ross, Cheri Louise, "(Re)Writing the Frontier Romance: Catharine Maria Sedgwick's Hope Leslie," *CLA Journal* 39 (1996): 325, 332; Singley, Carol J., "Catharine Maria Sedgwick's Hope Leslie: Radical Frontier Romance," *Desert, Garden, Margin, Range: Literature on the American Frontier*, Eric Heyne, Ed. (New York: Twayne, 1992): 115; and Nelson, Dana, "Sympathy as Strategy in Sedgwick's Hope Leslie," *The Culture of Sentiment: Race, Gender, and Sentimentality in Nineteenth-Century America*, Shirley Samuels, Ed. (New York: Oxford UP, 1992): 202. T. Gregory Garvey asserts that the novel "revises the history of Puritan New England" in "Risking Reprisal: Catharine Sedgwick's Hope Leslie and the Legitimation of Public Action by Women," *American Transcendental Quarterly* 8 (1994): 290. Lucy Maddox calls it a "self-consciously feminist revision of male-transmitted history." See *Removals: Nineteenth-Century American Literature and the Politics of Indian Affairs* (New York: Oxford UP, 1991): 103. And Sandra A. Zagarell argues that "the novel challenges the official history of original settlements": "Expanding America" 235. Among these commentators, Nelson offers the most detailed reading of the text's handling of history, which she views as dialogic: "Sympathy as Strategy 195–7. Only Nina Baym dissents from this view, arguing that Sedgwick's revisionism "is only lukewarm": *American Women Writers* 158.

18. Gould, Philip, "Catharine Sedgwick's 'Recital' of the Pequot War," *American Literature* 66 (1994): 641–2. 642.

19. Ibid, 644.

20. Ibid, 644.

21. Ibid, 644, 653.

22. This point is made more explicitly in Gould's book-length study of historical romances of New England, in which is included an expanded version of his article on *Hope Leslie*). There he suggests that "recent admirers of Sedgwick...often inscribe their own language and values onto" the novel [italics original]. See *Covenant and Republic* (New York: Cambridge, 1996): 93.

23. Berkhofer, Robert F., *Beyond the Great Story: History as Text and Discourse* (Cambridge, MA: Belknap Press of Harvard UP, 1995): 32.

24. Hence the critique of presentism, in which the projection of modern-day political interests is submitted to the censure of disinterested historicism, actually often creates, in a kind of boomerang effect, the very problem it is meant to forestall. For instance, soon after exposing the present-minded interests of earlier scholars, Gould concedes that his own contextualizing approach has been influenced (and, I hasten to add, granted critical

legitimacy) by the new historicism: *Covenant and Republic* 7–9. But doesn't that mean that his readings, too, are determined by inscribing a certain set of current critical values onto the texts of the past: the historicist insistence on what constitutes a text's "proper context"? That is, Gould's reading also simply confirms the premise with which he set out. Moreover, by assuming that to inscribe one's own "language and values" onto a text is to "decontextualize" it, he implies that the present somehow cannot supply a context, as if "context" only resides in history understood as the distant past. Thus in his reading Gould simultaneously makes a case for the presentism of Sedgwick's text (it is an expression of the early republic), critiques the presentism of others (insofar as they inscribe their own language and values) and engages in a presentist discourse himself (a version of the new historicism).

25. I mean to call attention here only to the frequency with which appeals to context are preceded by the definite article, as in Donald Pease's well-known "new historicist return of the repressed context," or possessive pronouns (its, their), as in Wai-chee Dimock's concise formulation: "the text and its context are in every case inseparable, the latter … encompassing [the former] and permeating it as the condition of its textuality." See, respectively," Pease, Donald, "New Americanists: Revisionist Interventions into the Americanist Canon," *Revisionary Interventions Into the Americanist Canon*, Donald Pease, Ed. (Durham: Duke UP, 1994): 35; and Dimock, Wai-chee, *Empire for Liberty: Melville and the Poetics of Individualism* (Princeton: Princeton UP, 1989): 5. My concerns about this historicist procedure are also intended to echo those of Judith Fetterley, who has questioned its "strategic usefulness for changing the evaluation of nineteenth-century American women writers." Citing Jane Tompkins's important and influential historicist work, *Sensational Designs*, Fetterley asks,

> Might Tompkins's emphasis on the distance between the culture that produced, for example, The Wide, Wide World and the culture we inhabit, on the gulf between the aesthetics that produced a text of "trifles" and the aesthetics that modernists have taught us to value, in fact have the effect of making this literature seem at once uninteresting and inaccessible to contemporary readers? of suggesting that the power of these texts cannot be realized by anyone less than thoroughly conversant with certain aspects of nineteenth-century American culture, indeed by anyone not of the nineteenth century, and thus of drawing a line around these texts—that was then, this is now—that effectively seals them off from the contemporary?

While I share Fetterley's reservations about readings that seek to recover past contexts, I would add that this potential problem is not confined only to nineteenth-century American women writers. My argument supplements Fetterley's in that my analysis of *Hope Leslie* is intended to bring out its "thematic significance for readers of our own day": the novel speaks directly to the widespread interest in history among Americanist literary scholars. See Fetterley, "Commentary: Nineteenth-Century American Women Writers and the Politics of Recovery," *American Literary History* 6 (Fall 1994): 606. Further, I suggest that the problems presented by historicism involve not only its means of evaluating texts, but, more fundamentally, the conception of history that underwrites it: namely, the privileging of a text's moment of production over and above its moments of reception.

26. For another version of this point, see Rohy, who notes, "historical alterity is a recent invention, the conviction that past ages are noncontinuous with modernity is a hallmark of modernity": *Anachronism and Its Others* 129.

27. In *Beyond Settler Time*, Mark Rifkin, identifies yet another (related) way in which conceptions of the present can subsume difference. The synchronic method of what he calls

"European historicism" relies on the notion of a shared present, one characterized by simultaneity in time, coevalness. "The supposedly objective givenness of simultaneity, of an unmediated mutual now, depends upon a historicist conception of time as an unfolding universal line of development." Such a view of "a shared present overrides the possibility for conceptualizing discrepant temporal formations." See Rifkin, *Beyond Settler Time: Temporal Sovereignty and Indigenous Self-Determination* (Durham, NC: Duke UP, 2017): 19.

28. See Berkhofer, *Beyond the Great Story* 106: "historians assume the otherness of past times: the longer ago they are, the more the then and there differ from the here and now."

29. A recognition of the present as replete with disparate temporalities, not all of them reducible to settler colonial frames of reference, is central to Rifkin's notion of "temporal sovereignty."

30. Sedgwick, *Hope Leslie* 3.

31. Ibid.

32. See Kammen, Michael, *A Season of Youth: The American Revolution and the Historical Imagination* (New York: Knopf, 1978): 243.

33. Ibid, 248.

34. Ibid, 249. Kammen also provides a brief but excellent discussion of the importance of "character" in the nineteenth-century historical imagination; see esp. 248–51. For a discussion of "national character" as a racial discourse in nineteenth-century history writing, see Calcott, *History in the United States*, 166–71. Gould concentrates his reading on the related term "virtue" to show how Sedgwick revises that term's gendered meanings: "Recital" 62–8.

35. Sedgwick, *Hope Leslie* 3.

36. See, for example, Gould, *Covenant and Republic* 9–12, 81–9; and Buell, *New England Literary Culture* 208–11.

37. Sedgwick, *Hope Leslie* 4.

38. On this point, I am in agreement with both Gould and Nelson. However, for Gould this raises the issue of "Sedgwick's intentions. He argues, "the gendered meanings of republicanism during this era…make it difficult for one to believe that Sedgwick stood so theoretically detached from Magawisca's account": *Covenant and Republic* 84. Of course, I also agree that Sedgwick's intentions are "open to debate," though my reading of both the theoretical self-consciousness of the preface and the narrator's running meta-commentary throughout the novel reveals a much greater detachment (on the part of the narrator, at any rate) from the narrative proper than Gould allows.

39. Sedgwick, *Hope Leslie* 3.

40. Gould discusses the historiographic controversy surrounding the Pequot War at length. See esp. *Covenant and Republic* 64–77.

41. Not surprisingly, Magawisca's retelling of the Puritan attack on the Pequots figures prominently in many readings of the novel. See, for example, Gould, *Covenant and Republic*; Zagarell, "Expanding America" 234–5; Kelley, "Introduction" xxxii; Ross "(Re)writing" 325–7; and Nelson, "Sympathy as Strategy" 195–7. See also Baym, *American Women Writers* 158, who compares Sedgwick's attempt to narrate history from the Indian point of view unfavorably to Washington Irving's essay, "Philip of Pokanoket."

42. White, Hayden V., *Metahistory: The Historical Imagination in Nineteenth-Century Europe* (Baltimore: Johns Hopkins UP, 1973): 7.

43. For a discussion of the formalism of new historicists, see Thomas, *The New Historicism* 42–4. By contrast, Mary Poovey has recently questioned whether "close reading [still]

constitutes an appropriate interpretive tool" for the kinds of historicist and cultural studies readings that characterize much of the work in literary studies. See Poovey, Mary, "Beyond the Current Impasse in Literary Studies," *American Literary History* 11:2 (Summer 1999): 368. Judith Fetterley, on the other hand, has persuasively argued for the continued value of older methodologies like close reading. See her " 'My Sister! My Sister!': The Rhetoric of Catharine Sedgwick's Hope Leslie," *American Literature* 70 (1998): 492. It should be evident from my reading that I am in agreement with Fetterley.

44. Margaret Higonnet mentions that Sedgwick's "many metanarrative interventions disrupt" the story, but does not pursue this metanarrative in any detail: see "Comparative Reading: Catharine M. Sedgwick's Hope Leslie," *Legacy* 15 (1998): 20. Mary Kelley ("Introduction") also takes note of several instances of direct address to the reader, but attributes these to Sedgwick, rather than to the novel's narrator. Only Dana D. Nelson treats the narrator's discourse in an extended way, arguing persuasively that the novel's many "textual apologies" and "narrative asides" form a "subversive political commentary on the patriarchal assumptions of both the Puritans and her contemporary male audience": "Sympathy as Strategy" 193–4. Since my own essay, "Anachronistic Imaginings" first appeared in 2004, other readers have attended generatively to the novel's mode of narration. In addition to Luciano, see Pratt, who examines the "strategy of narratorial interpellation that defines the work as a whole," in *Archives of American Time* 101, and Hankins, who argues that "Sedgwick's sarcastic narrator is her primary method for challenging the generic expectations of Romantic historiography," in "Voice of Nature" 167. Hankins's reading departs from mine, however, in its suggestion that the novel advances a cyclical view of history to critique progressive nationalist histories.

45. Pratt reads these moments as Sedgwick's mode of keeping time: "Unwilling to let a single hour go uncounted," he writes, "Sedgwick resets her narrative clock after nearly every chapter break": *Archives of American Time* 104.

46. Sedgwick, *Hope Leslie* 126. The poor quality of women's education and the submissiveness of women in marriage are the two issues in Sedgwick's published and unpublished writings for which she reserved her most caustic remarks. In her unpublished autobiography she writes, matter of factly, " 'Education' in the common sense I had next to none," and later, more bitterly: "What would the children now, who are steeped to the lips in 'ologies,' think of a girl of eight spending a whole summer working a wretched sampler which was not even a tolerable specimen of the species." See Kelley, Mary, Ed., *The Power of Her Sympathy: The Autobiography and Journal of Catharine Maria Sedgwick* (Boston: Massachusetts Historical Society, 1993): 74. In her conduct manual *Means and Ends; or Self-Training* (Boston: Marsh, Capen, Lyon and Webb, 1840): 19, written for young girls, Sedgwick wrote even more frankly, and with barely contained venom, about women's education, linking it explicitly to the inequalities of marriage:

> Women by their defective educations have been left helpless and dependent on men for support and protection. This has been the most effective cause of those marriages (the curse of woman, and man too,) without affection on the one side and respect on the other. Be sure to be so educated that you can have an independent pursuit … then marriage will not be essential to your usefulness, respectability, or happiness.

The point here, however, is not to attribute the narrative intrusions to the "author," the historical Catharine Sedgwick; rather, the point is only that, knowing the author, it should come as no surprise that she would imbue her narrator with something approximating her own acerbic wit.

47. Sedgwick, *Hope Leslie* 160.

48. Ibid, 149.

49. Several readers have commented on the novel's pattern of imprisonment. Fetterley, for instance, argues, "Sedgwick manages to keep Hope out of jail, both literally and figuratively": "My Sister!" 501. Obviously, I disagree.

50. Following the section on Mrs. Winthrop, the narrator echoes this language in another meta-commentary, this time taking on male literary authority: As she begins to describe the Governor's mansion, she adopts her typically self-deprecatory tone. "The mighty master of fiction," she notes, referring to Sir Walter Scott, "has but to wave the wand of his office, to present the past to his readers, with all the vividness of the present." Juxtaposed with her description of the Winthrops' marriage, this passage, too, should be read as ironic. That is, the narrator's "obedience" to a "master" is meant to echo the description of Mrs. Winthrop's relation to her husband, just as "following" Scott "at an immeasurable distance" resonates with the Governor "leading" his wife like a horse. Scott, the "mighty master" is constructed as Governor Winthrop's surrogate, while the narrator, "in obedience," is reduced to the status of the Governor's wife. Intriguingly, this play perhaps suggests that although, like most nineteenth-century Americans, Sedgwick admired Scott and read his work with interest, she was also keenly aware, even at this early stage in the development of American literature, of the gender politics of literary production. Nelson ventures that these asides, ostensibly deferent, "might" be "less sincere than calculatingly rhetorical": "Sympathy as Strategy" 194. I would state this more strongly: more than just a mollifying rhetorical stance toward male authority, they are subversive of it.

51. Ibid, 151.

52. Irving, *History, Tales, and Sketches* 783.

53. Sedgwick, *Hope Leslie* 6. For a more extended discussion of how the novel "defines liberty from a woman's perspective," see Zagarell, "Expanding America" 238–9.

54. The phrase is from Anderson, Benedict, *Imagined Communities: Reflections on the Origin and Spread of Nationalism* (New York: Verso: 1991): 33. A wholly intended implication of my argument here is that the "linkages" that historicists make between text and context are, like Anderson's communities, "imagined."

55. Sedgwick, *Hope Leslie* 127.

56. Pratt, *Archives of American Time* 91, 94.

57. Bell, Michael D., "History and Romance Convention in Catharine Sedgwick's *Hope Leslie*," *American Quarterly* 22 (1970): 218.

58. Zagarell, for instance, asserts that the novel "refuses to see history as a matter of progression or regression," a statement with which I wholeheartedly agree. I don't agree, however, when she further asserts that "it pays little attention to the movement of history at all": "Expanding America" 236. To the contrary, the narrator's commentary, I am arguing, is deeply concerned with historical movement, historical time: it proffers anachronism as an alternative to the progress/regress binary.

59. Sedgwick, *Hope Leslie* 164.

60. Ibid, 15.

61. See Bell, "History and Romance" 214. For more on the tradition of romantic historiography, see Levin, *History as Romantic Art*, which I discuss briefly in my introductory chapter.

62. Sedgwick, *Hope Leslie* 16.

63. Anderson, *Imagined Communities* 33.

64. My description of the narrator's news here is meant to echo Anderson's argument about the function of the newspaper in *Imagined Communities*. Anderson writes that the emergence of print culture, and the newspaper in particular, served as a "source of imagined linkage" for the nation, a ritual of "simultaneous consumption ('imagining')": *Imagined Communities* 33, 35. The paradox of the newspaper is that it takes place privately, "in the lair of the skull," yet knowing that millions of others participate in the same ritual at the same time makes of it a communal activity. What for Anderson makes the newspaper such a powerful figure for imagining a community is that it is an "extreme form" of the novel: *Imagined Communities* 34. Both constitute a "complex gloss upon the word 'meanwhile'": *Imagined Communities* 25. That is, when reading a novel the reader is privy to the actions of characters who may never meet, but whose acts are nevertheless "performed at the same cloaked, calendrical time." For instance, while we watch the movements of our protagonist Hope, we also know, though we don't see it, that somewhere at the same time, her sister Faith goes about her own business. The newspaper replicates this process on a much larger scale. In any paper on any given day will be grouped together, arbitrarily, events and incidents from all over the world that bear no other relation to one another save "calendrical coincidence": *Imagined Communities* 33. So if an event that occurs in say, Mali (to use Anderson's own example) is reported one day followed by a long period of time in which Mali does not appear in the news, "readers do not for a moment imagine that Mali has disappeared or that famine has wiped out all its citizens. The novelistic format of the newspaper assures them that somewhere out there the 'character' Mali moves along quietly, awaiting its next reappearance in the plot": *Imagined Communities* 33. For a useful discussion of Anderson and novelistic time, see Culler, Jonathan, "Anderson and the Novel," *diacritics* 29:4 (Winter 1999): 20–39.

65. Sedgwick, *Hope Leslie* 58.

66. Gould notes that both Everell and the reader are "seduced" by Magawisca's narrative: *Covenant and Republic* 653. Thus, "The power of historical narrative, the text suggests, lies inevitably along an axis of imaginative feeling between author and reader": *Covenant and Republic* 654. But again, as I have shown, such moments of emotional seduction are precisely the ones the narrator often interrupts; the narrator draws readers' attention, in other words, to their own experience of having been seduced.

67. Ibid, 75.

68. I take up this process of becoming, which I align especially with Emerson and George Herbert Mead in more detail in Chapters 4 and 5. My sense of the present as the (temporal) site of such becoming also resonates with Rifkin's interest in "persistent Indigenous becoming": *Beyond Settler Time* 5.

69. Thomas, *The New Historicism* 32.

70. Sedgwick, *Hope Leslie* 237.

71. See Fetterley, "My Sister!" 504; Arch, Stephen Carl, "Romancing the Puritans: American Historical Fiction in the 1820s," *Esq-A Journal of the American Renaissance* 39 (1993): 118; Singley, "Radical Frontier Romance" 121; Ford, Douglas, "Inscribing the 'Impartial Observer' in Sedgwick's Hope Leslie," *Legacy* 14 (1997): 84.

72. Sedgwick, *Hope Leslie* 240.

73. Ibid, 4.

74. Ibid, 239.

75. Ibid.

76. Karcher, "Introduction," in Sedgwick *Hope Leslie*, xxiii.

77. Sedgwick, *Hope Leslie* 253.

78. Hope's heart (see Ibid, 124, 189) and Governor Winthrop (see, Ibid, 245, 310).

79. Karcher helpfully notes that "from the first to the last chapters," the narrator "shares narrative authority with her characters" ("Introduction" xxxii–xxxiii), through both direct (narrative) discourse and its incorporation of the epistolary form.

80. On this point, see Pratt's description of "revolutionary messianic time," which also brings the past and the future into the present at a moment that "provides the opportunity for the distribution of pure and equal justice": *Archives of American Time* 112.

81. Sedgwick, *Hope Leslie* 349, 359, 349.

82. The first of these quotations is from Neal's *Wandering Recollections of a Somewhat Busy Life: An Autobiography* (Boston: Roberts Brothers, 1869): 224; the others appear in Neal's "American Writers," *Blackwood's Edinburgh Magazine* (1825): 197.

83. See Pratt, *Archives of American Time* 106–8.

84. See Poe, Edgar Allan, "Marginalia," *Southern Literary Messenger* V. 15 (May 1849): 294. See also Bain, Robert A., "Introduction," *Seventy-Six: "Our Country!—Right or Wrong,"* 2 vols, 1823; reprint (Bainbridge, NY: York Mail-Print, 1971): xvi.

85. Neal, John, "Neal, John,oth dire*Blackwoodhn,Print, 19 Magazine* (1825): 197.

86. Despite Neal's own view of the book, *Seventy-Six* has received very little critical attention. It merits only passing mention, for instance, in Dekker's *The American Historical Romance* and in Michael Kammen's chapter on the historical romance in his wide-ranging study of the persistence of the Revolution in American cultural memory, *A Season of Youth*. Donald Ringe, in an essay on "The American Revolution in American Romance," devotes more detailed attention to the novel, but only to conclude that "As a sustained work of historical fiction…*Seventy-Six* is a failure" that "has little if anything to say about the American Revolution." In Ringe's view, Neal fails where James Fenimore Cooper and other historical romancers—John Pendleton Kennedy and William Gilmore Simms in particular— succeeded by not recognizing that in a work of historical fiction "the historical and nonhistorical parts had to be integrated in such a way as to reveal the meaning and significance of the entire action." See Ringe, Donald, "The American Revolution in American Romance," *American Literature* 49 (Nov. 1977): 354. Unlike the works of Cooper, Kennedy, and Simms—and, I would add, Catharine Maria Sedgwick in her later novel *The Linwoods* (1835)—*Seventy-Six* "makes no attempt to unite its disparate strains." In fact, ultimately "the war is simply dropped and attention is focused on the absurd posturing of a Byronic character and the girl he loves": Ringe, "The American Revolution" 354. More recently, Joseph J. Letter has provided an implied corrective to Ringe's view, arguing for important continuities between Neal's historical romance of the revolution and Cooper's novel *The Spy*. Viewing both novels as engaged in what he calls "past presentism," Letter makes a compelling case for reading *Seventy-Six* within the context of Congressional debates, following the War of 1812, over pensions for Revolutionary War veterans, debates that reflected a broader cultural concern in the 1820s and expressed in a number of historical romances of the Revolution for the figure of the "suffering soldier." The pension debates, Letter shows, "exposed a discursive conflict, a contest between official histories of the Revolution and the popular stories of common soldiers preserved mostly through oral traditions." See Letter, Joseph J., "Past Presentisms: Suffering Soldiers, Benjaminian Ruins, and the Discursive Foundations of Early U.S. Historical Novels," *American Literature* 82 (Mar. 2010): 30. Participating in this conflict, *Seventy-Six* calls into question dominant U.S. narratives of historical progress insofar as it "challenges official histories of the Revolution

and draws attention to the present nation's failure to acknowledge the suffering at its historical core": Letter 36. Thus—although Letter does not mention it—the novel's original subtitle, "Our Country!—Right or Wrong," comes to sound less like an expression of nationalistic passion than an ironic critique emphasizing that which the nation has gotten "wrong."

87. Ringe, "The American Revolution" 359.

88. Ibid, 358.

89. Thus for Letter, Ringe would seem to err in treating the Revolutionary period as the locus of the novel's historicity, when in fact the novel's chief concern is the cultural present of its writing and publication. Within this latter context, Letter does indeed reveal how the "historical and nonhistorical" elements of the text are "integrated." As an "allegory of Revolutionary origins": "Past Presentisms": 46. Letter asserts that the (exceedingly convoluted) "familial plot supplements rather than displaces the Revolution," presenting a narrative in which "family personifies nation": see 46–7.

90. For an excellent reading of Neal's *Rachel Dyer*, quite different from my own, in terms of experience, see Davis, Theo, *Formalism, Experience, and the Making of American Literature in Nineteenth-Century America* (Cambridge: Cambridge UP, 2007), esp. Chapter 1.

91. See, for example, Lease, Benjamin, "Yankee Poetics: John Neal's Theory of Poetry and Fiction," *American Literature* (Jan. 1953): 505–19.

92. Neal, "American Writers" 426.

93. Neal, John, *Wandering Recollections of a Somewhat Busy Life: An Autobiography* (Boston: Roberts Brothers, 1869): 197.

94. Neal, *Seventy-Six* II 243.

95. Ibid, v; to Oadleyxes 1869 refer to? Somewhat Busy Life: An Autobiographyineteenth-Century America; his adleyxes 1869 refe," his ad; his adleyxes 1869 refer to? Somewh," his adl; the adleyxes 1869 refer to? So brain," the adle; and late in the novel, the So brain Busy Life: An Autobiographyinete," and lat.

96. Ibid, I: 119, 150, 187, 223; v. II, 134; I: 210; II: 54.

97. Ibid, e.g., v. I: 98, 133, 159, 169; v. II: 19, 22, 31.

98. Ibid, I: 132.

99. Ibid, I: 138.

100. Ibid, I: 176.

101. Ibid, I: 249.

102. Ibid I: 251.

103. Ibid.

104. Ibid, II: 73.

105. Ibid.

106. Ibid, II: 242.

107. Ibid, II: 242–3.

108. Ibid, II: 242.

109. According to David Levin, a similar devotion to "interest"—to "energy…vigor, flesh-and-blood action, stirring movement" and "the illusion of participation" informed the approach to history taken up by the romantic historians Bancroft, Prescott, Motley, and Parkman: *History as Romantic Art* 12. For Levin, this demonstrates the historians' debt to literary art (and to a lesser extent, painting). But Neal's devotion to "interest," I argue, is even more radical, so thoroughgoing, in fact, that it is ultimately at odds with artistic representation.

110. Neal, *Wandering Recollections* 173.

111. Ibid, 5.

112. Ibid, 5.

113. Ibid, 224.

114. Neal, "American Writers" 169.

115. Neal, John, *The Down-Easters*, vol. II (New York: Harper & Bros., 1833): 110.

116. The question, in Hayden White's words, of whether "the world really present[s] itself to perception in the form of well-made stories with central subjects, proper beginnings, middles, and ends, and coherence" has long been a topic of vigorous historiographical debate. White, Arthur C. Danto, and Louis O. Mink have argued that narrative does not inhere in experience. To cite Mink's well-known formulation, "stories are not lived, but told." By contrast, David Carr argues, "narrative structure pervades our very experience of time and social existence, independently of our contemplating the past as historians." For some more recent interventions in the debate, see Berkhofer, Robert, *Beyond the Great Story: History as Text and Discourse* (Cambridge: Harvard UP, 1997), and Ankersmit, Frank, "Truth in History and Literature," *Narrative* 18:1 (Jan. 2010): 29–50. See White, Hayden, "The Value of Narrativity in the Representation of Reality," *Critical Inquiry* 7:1 (Autumn 1980): 27; Danto, Arthur C., *Narration and Knowledge* (New York: Columbia UP, 1985); Mink, Louis O., *Historical Understanding* (Ithaca, NY: Cornell UP, 1987): 60; and Carr, David, *Time, Narrative, and History* (Bloomington: Indiana UP, 1991): 9.

117. Neal, *Seventy-Six*, I: 13.

118. Ibid, I: 14.

119. Ibid, I: 15.

120. Ibid, I: 16.

121. Ibid, I:15.

122. Ibid, I: 16.

123. Emerson, Ralph Waldo, "Concord Hymn," *Collected Poems and Translations* (New York: Library of America, 1994): 125.

124. Ibid.

125. Neal, *Seventy-Six* I: 247–8.

126. Castronovo, Russ, *Fathering the Nation: American Genealogies of Slavery and Freedom* (Berkeley: U of California P, 1996): 109.

127. Ibid, 130.

128. Neal, *Seventy-Six* I; 17.

129. Luciano, *Arranging Grief* 170.

130. Ibid, 181.

131. Ibid, 183.

132. Neal, *Seventy-Six* I: 95.

133. My account here is once again informed by the analysis of temporal experience provided by Mead in *The Philosophy of the Present* (New York: Prometheus Books, 2002), as well as his essay, "The Nature of the Past," In the latter, Mead writes, for instance,

The memory of the unexpected appearance of a supposedly far distant friend, or the memory of an earthquake can never recover the peculiar tang of the experience. I remember that there was a break which is now connected with just the phases of the experience which were unconnected. We recall the joy or the terror, but it is over against a background of a continuum whose discontinuity has been healed.

Something was going on—the rising anger of a titan or the adjustment of the earth's internal pressures which resulted in that which was unexpected, but this was not the original experience, when there was no connection between the events before the occurrence and the sudden emergence.

See Mead, George Herbert. *Selected Writings*, Andrew J. Heck, Ed. (Chicago: U of Chicago P, 1964): 350.

134. Neal, *Seventy-Six* II: 230.

135. Ibid, II: 231.

136. Ibid, II: 232.

137. For more on the importance of the distinction between intellect and emotion in Neal's aesthetic theory, see Lease, Benjamin, "Yankee Poetics: John Neal's Theory of Poetry and Fiction," *American Literature* (Jan. 1953): 505–19.

138. Neal, *Seventy-Six* I: 14.

139. For romantic historian's investments in notions of historical progress, see Levin, *History as Romantic Art* 24–45.

140. See Woods Weierman, Karen, "'A Slave Story I Began and Abandoned': Sedgwick's Antislavery Manuscript," *Catharine Maria Sedgwick: Critical Perspectives*, Lucinda Damon-Back and Victoria Clements, Eds. (Boston: Northeastern UP, 2003): 122–40.

141. Neal, "American Writers" 152, 177.

142. Garrison and Neal had quarreled passionately over Garrison's criticisms of Neal's *American Writers* series and would skirmish again at various points over the years. See, for example, Brennan, Denis, *The Making of an Abolitionist: William Lloyd Garrison's Path to Publishing The Liberator* (Jefferson, NC: McFarland & Co, 2014): 50–1, 71–5.

143. The premise of Sedgwick's rather tone-deaf essay "The Slave and the Slave-owner" is that it is better to be the former than the latter. On the other hand, the essay does speak the language of immediatist abolitionism in its penultimate paragraph:

The slave-owner... hears the fearful threatenings of the gathering storm. He knows it must come,—to him fatally. It is only a question of time!

See *Autographs for Freedom* (Boston: John P. Jewett and Co., 1853): 27. This "question of time" is the central subject of Chapters 3 and 4.

144. *The Liberator*, Mar. 26, 1831.

145. Magawisca, (Sarah Forten), "The Abuse of Liberty," *The Liberator*, Mar. 26, 1831, 50.

Chapter 3

1. See, respectively, Porte, Joel, Ed., *Emerson in His Journals* (Cambridge, MA: Harvard UP, 1984): 152 and Bosco, Ronald A., and Joel Myerson, Eds., *Ralph Waldo Emerson: The Major Prose* (Cambridge, MA: Harvard UP, 2015): 526.

2. Spiller, Robert E., and Wallace E. Williams, Eds., *The Early Lectures of Ralph Waldo Emerson, v. III* (Cambridge, MA: Belknap Press, 1972): 250. For an earlier iteration of the phrase in his journal in October, 1837, see Emerson, Ralph Waldo, *Emerson in His Journals*, Joel Porte, Ed. (Cambridge, Harvard UP, 1984): 72.

3. Emerson, Ralph Waldo, *The Conduct of Life* (Boston: Ticknor and Fields, 1860): 863.

4. One could go on. In "Quotation and Originality," for instance, Emerson writes, "The Past is for us; but the sole terms on which it can become ours are its subordination to the Present." See *The Collected Works of Ralph Waldo Emerson: Vol. VIII, Letters and Social*

Aims (Cambridge: Belknap Press, 2010): 107. Eduardo Cadava takes such comments as "the beginning articulations of a protocol for reading Emerson" in his *Emerson and the Climates of History* (Stanford: Stanford UP, 1997): 5.

5. A long tradition of Emerson criticism, inaugurated by Stephen Whicher, has also seen Emerson as detached from history insofar as that term designates the social and political world of his own time: see, most especially, *Freedom and Fate: An Inner Life of Ralph Waldo Emerson* (Philadelphia: U of Pennsylvania P, 1953). Other important works in this vein include Anderson, Quentin, *The Imperial Self: An Essay in American Literary and Cultural History* (New York: Knopf, 1971), and Poirier, Richard, *A World Elsewhere: The Place of Style in American Literature* (Madison: U of Wisconsin P, 1985). A great deal of work, beginning with Len Gougeon's *Virtue's Hero: Emerson, Antislavery, and Reform* (Athens: U of Georgia P, 1990), has long since effectively challenged the Whicher thesis. For a representative sampling of the work that has followed, see the essays collected in Garvey, T. Gregory, Ed., *The Emerson Dilemma: Essays on Emerson and Social Reform* (Athens: U of Georgia P, 2001); and Levine, Alan M., and Daniel S. Malachuk, Eds. *A Political Companion to Ralph Waldo Emerson* (Lexington: U of Kentucky P, 2011).

6. See Gougeon, Len, and Joel Myerson, Eds. "Fortune of the Republic," *Emerson's Antislavery Writings* (New Haven, CT: Yale UP, 1995): 141.

7. Those exceptions include Dolan, Neal, *Emerson's Liberalism* (Madison: U of Wisconsin P, 2009); Cadava, *Emerson and the Climates of History*; Richardson, Robert D. "Emerson and History," *Emerson: Prospect and Retrospect*, Joel Porte, Ed. (Cambridge, MA: Harvard UP, 1982); Van Cromphout, Gustaaf, "Emerson and the Dialectics of History," *PMLA* 91 (1976): 54–64; and, more recently, Allen, Thomas, *A Republic in Time: Temporality and Social Imagination in Nineteenth-Century America* (Chapel Hill: U of North Carolina P, 2008). Allen attends generatively to Emerson's temporal investments but focuses mainly on his engagement of deep time. But Allen's attention to the importance of present moments in "Self-Reliance" corresponds in some ways to my reading of Emerson's conception of history. Also influential to my understanding of Emerson's proto-pragmatist and presentist conception of history is Friedl, Herwig, "Thinking America: Emerson and Dewey," *Negotiations of America's National Identity*, Roland Hagenbuchle and Josef Rabb, Eds. (Tubingen, Germany: Stauffenberg, 2000): 131–57.

8. Dolan, *Emerson's Liberalism* 9.

9. Ibid, 10.

10. Buell, Lawrence, *Emerson* (Cambridge, MA: Harvard UP, 2004): 332.

11. Lee, Maurice, *Slavery, Philosophy, and American Literature, 1830–60* (Cambridge: Cambridge UP, 2005): 166. See also Robinson, David, *Emerson and the Conduct of Life: Pragmatism and Ethical Purpose in the Later Works* (Cambridge: Cambridge UP, 1993); and von Frank, Albert J., *The Trials of Anthony Burns: Freedom and Slavery in Emerson's Boston* (Cambridge, MA: Harvard UP, 1998).

12. See Gougeon, Len, "Emerson's Abolition Conversion," *The Emerson Dilemma: Essays on Emerson and Social Reform*, T. Gregory Garvey, Ed. (Athens: U of Georgia P, 2000): 170–96.

13. Christopher Hanlon similarly notes that critical attempts "to 'reconcile' Emersonian transcendentalism with his abolitionism ... tend to lean upon chronological narratives of development." But in his groundbreaking reading of Emerson as a composite thinker, Hanlon demonstrates convincingly how "later ... materials draw forth communal conceptions of memory and intellection that seem suddenly if retroactively nascent in the earlier works." This antichronological method of reading Emerson runs parallel to mine. See Hanlon,

Christopher, *Emerson's Memory Loss: Originality, Communality, and the Late Style* (New York: Oxford UP, 2018).

14. Lee, *Slavery, Philosophy, and American Literature* 178.

15. This famous phrase is from Martin Luther King, Jr.'s "I Have a Dream Speech." See *I Have a Dream and Other Speeches that Changed the World* (New York: HarperOne, 2003): 103.

16. *Emerson in His Journals* 407. I am grateful to Christopher Hanlon for directing me to this entry.

17. Emerson, Ralph Waldo, *Emerson's Antislavery Writings*, Len Gougeon and Joel Myerson, Eds. (New Haven: Yale UP, 1994): 49.

18. *The Liberator* reprinted a notice from the Worcester *Christian Citizen*, which reported,

> Mr. Emerson was too unwell to speak, but on being called on, said he felt it his duty to make some sort of a response to the call. Unaccustomed as he is to addressing mass meetings of the people *extempore*, he seemed to find much difficulty in getting his ideas into proper clothing of words. Several times he looked up into the sky and far off into the woods and fields, as if for help in his difficult and unaccustomed task; but the ideas only seemed to put on more fantastic airs in the scholar's brain, and, saving a remark or two the audience only caught a glimpse of what he was striving to express.   (Aug. 17, 1849): 33

19. Emerson, *Antislavery Writings* 53. Subsequent quotations will be cited in the text. When this speech was reprinted in Edward Emerson's 1904 *Complete Works*, he included a stanza from Emerson's 1863 poem "Voluntaries" as an epigraph, which says of "the eternal rights: "They reach no term, they never sleep," 178.

20. Emerson, *Antislavery Writings* 54.

21. Ibid, 66.

22. Ibid, 66.

23. Ibid, 67. For more on Emerson's relation to Webster, see Cadava, *Emerson and the Climates of History* 91–148.

24. The Bosco, Ronald A., and Joel Myerson, Eds., *Later Lectures of Ralph Waldo Emerson, 1843–71, Vol. I.* (Athens: U of Georgia P, 2001): 272. This passage is not included in the version reprinted in *Antislavery Writings*.

25. Channing, *Slavery* (Boston: J. Munroe and Company, 1835): 139, 154, 159. For more on Channing, see Schoolman, "Emerson's Doctrine of Hatred."

26. Ibid, 22.

27. Beecher, Catharine, *An Essay on Slavery and Abolitionism, with Reference to the Duty of American Females* (Philadelphia: H. Perkins, 1837): 83–4.

28. Ibid, 93.

29. Ibid, 47–8, 86. In the course of the essay, Beecher mentions probabilities roughly a dozen times.

30. For a version of this point, see, for example, Albert J. von Frank and Larry J. Reynolds who ask in defense of the actions of John Brown:

> Why is it not a moral crime to sit around and wait for someone else to abolish slavery? If I am my brother's keeper, what is my duty as to those who threaten my brother with a permanently ongoing existential annihilation? What prudence and calculation must I engage before I can act without dishonor?

See "Emerson, John Brown, and Transcendentalism: A Colloquy," *South Central Review* (Summer 2011): 38.

31. *Antislavery Writings* 61. Emerson recorded a version of this passage in his journal:

It is vain to charge the abolitionists with the new stringency of slavery in the South. Blame a ball for rebounding; or a gun for kicking; blame the air for rushing into where a vacuum is made; or blame the boiler for exploding under the pressure of steam. These things are laws of the world water freezes at 32 & boils at 212, & when a man sees reason justice is outraged she revolts anger begins.

See Emerson, *The Poetry Notebooks of Ralph Waldo Emerson*. Orth, Ralph H., Albert J. von Frank, Linda Allardt, and David W. Hill, Eds. (Columbia: U of Missouri Press, 1986): 310.

32. Emerson, *Antislavery Writings* 61.

33. Ibid.

34. Grimké, Angelina, *Letters to Catherine E. Beecher: In Reply to An Essay on Slavery and Abolitionism, addressed to A. E. Grimké* (Boston: printed by Isaac Knapp, 1838): 55.

35. Grimké, *Letters to Catherine E. Beecher* 56.

36. Emerson, *Antislavery Writings* 67.

37. Ibid.

38. "Fumbling" is Russ Castronovo's term. See *Necro Citizenship: Death, Eroticism, and the Public Sphere in the Nineteenth-Century United States* (Durham, NC: Duke UP, 2001): 33. "Hesitation" is Hugh Egan's term in "'On Freedom': Emerson, Douglass, and the Self-Reliant Slave," *ESQ: A Journal of the American Renaissance* 60 (2014): 185. Egan casts Frederick Douglass as Emerson's interlocutor in the poem. A better candidate might have been William H. Seward, whose contribution to Griffiths's earlier *Autographs for Freedom*, (mis)titled "Be Up and Doing" counsels "moderation and benevolence" as opposed to "retaliation and fanaticism." "Whenever the public shall be prepared," Seward continues, "and the public conscience shall demand the abolition of slavery, the way to do it will open before us." Seward, in other words, counsels patience—which is very much at odds with both Emerson and the Longfellow poem from where he takes his title. See *Autographs for Freedom by Harriet Beecher Stowe and Thirty-Five Other Eminent Writers*. Julia Griffiths, Ed. (London: S. Low an J. Cassell, 1853): 10. Also of note is Gougeon's brief discussion of "On Freedom," *Virtue's Hero* 189–90.

39. For example, following Edward Emerson's statement that the poem reflected his father's "feeling that no muse would help should he attack in song African Slavery," Len Gougeon describes the poem as Emerson's "apologia" for not being able to commit himself to writing "propagandistic poetry in support of slavery": *Virtue's Hero* 190. Hugh Egan, in a more extended reading, views the poem as an expression of Emerson's "misgivings" and "equivocations," seeing in it "a fascinating, if tortured, attempt to marry transcendental principle to single-issue politics": "'On Freedom'" 185.

40. The final version of the poem titled only "Freedom" uncouples the original final couplet, inserting another couplet between the two lines (and also alters the final line, changing "rashly" to "rush"):

> Freedom's secret wilt though know?—
> Counsel not with flesh and blood;
> Loiter not for cloak or food;
> Right thou feelest, rush to do.

See von Frank, Albert J., Ed., *Ralph Waldo Emerson: The Major Poetry* (Cambridge, MA: Harvard UP, 2015): 167.

41. Castronovo, *Necro-Citizenship* 51.

42. Ibid.

43. Ibid.

44. The question of who (or what?) speaks the final line is, admittedly, ambiguous. Spirit begins to speak in line 5. But in the poem's original printing there is no closed quote. However, the later version clarifies this by closing the quotation at the end of the final line.

45. John Carlos Rowe is perhaps Emerson's most strident critic in terms of the latter's failure to integrate his thought with his political commitments. See Rowe, John Carlos, *At Emerson's Tomb: The Politics of Classic American Literature* (New York: Columbia UP, 1997). See also Wolfe, Carey, "Alone with America: Cavell, Emerson, and the Politics of Individualism," *New Literary History* 25 (1994): 137–57.

46. Emerson, second Fugitive Slave Law speech 86.

47. Emerson, *Antislavery Writings* 86.

48. Ibid, 87.

49. Dickinson, Emily, *The Poems of Emily Dickinson*, Vol. 1, R.W. Franklin, Ed. (Cambridge: Belknap Press, 1998): 808.

50. Emerson, *Antislavery Writings* 87.

51. Emerson, "Experience" in *The Collected Works of Ralph Waldo Emerson Vol. III* (Cambridge: Belknap Press, 1983): 37.

52. Beecher, *Essay on Slavery and Abolition* 40.

53. Emerson, "Experience" 35.

54. Ibid, 35.

55. Ibid, 39, 40.

56. Ibid, 37.

57. Lee, *Slavery, Philosophy, and American Literature* 180. See also Pease, Donald E., "'Experience,' Antislavery, and the Crisis of Emersoniasm," *boundary 2* (Summer 2007): 71–103. Glancingly, Stanley Cavell also notes the coincidence of "Experience" and Emerson's first public foray into the politics of slavery. See *Emerson's Transcendental Etudes* (Stanford: Stanford UP, 2003): 196.

58. Garrison, Lloyd, *The Liberator* (Jan. 1, 1831): 1.

59. Whitman, Walt, *Leaves of Grass* (Brooklyn, 1855): 89.

60. Adjusting subjectivity "to fit nationalist imperatives," Castronovo maintains that the nation exerts a "necrophilic will to equalize citizens as quiescent bodies beyond the sensuous touches of historical material existence." The state "long[s] for people dressed up in the unremarkable off the rack garb of generic personhood": *Necro Citizenship* 6.

61. Castronovo, *Necro Citizenship* 54, 13.

62. For numerous examples, see Trodd, Zoe, and John Stauffer, Eds., *The Tribunal: Responses to John Brown and the Harpers Ferry Raid* (Cambridge, MA: Harvard UP, 2012). "Reckless": 168, 172, 185, 237, 309, 362, 380. Charles Eliot Norton describes Brown as "a man born out of time" whose "chief fault seems to have been impatience": qtd.in Trodd and Stauffer, *The Tribunal* 185–6.

63. Thoreau, "A Plea for Captain John Brown," *Thoreau: Political Writings*, Nancy L. Rosenblum, Ed. (Cambridge: Cambridge UP, 1996): 137.

64. Thoreau, *Walden and Civil Disobedience* (New York: Penguin, 1984): 134.

65. Thoreau, "A Plea" 144.

66. Ibid, 144.

67. Ibid, 144.

68. Ibid, 148.

69. Ibid, 154.

70. Ibid, 154.

71. Emerson, "Experience" 29.

72. Thoreau, "A Plea" 154.

73. Ibid.

74. On the temporality of the newspaper see, famously, Anderson, Benedict, *Imagined Communities: Reflections on the Origin and Spread of Nationalism* (New York: Verso: 1991).

75. Tamarkin, Elisa, "Literature and the News" *The Oxford Handbook to Nineteenth-Century American Literature*, Russ Castronovo, Ed. (New York: Oxford UP, 2012): 309–26, and "Losing Perspective in the Age of News," which begins with Emerson's "Experience," *PMLA* 125 (Jan. 2010): 192–200.

76. Thoreau, *Walden and Civil Disobedience* 75.

77. Thoreau, "A Plea" 154.

78. Ibid, 145.

79. Tamarkin, Elisa, "Literature and the News" 318; 310, 311; 310, respectively. For scholarship on Garrison and print culture, see Fanuzzi, *Abolition's Public Sphere*; Loughran, Trish, *The Republic in Print: Print Culture in the Age of U.S. Nation Building, 1770–1870* (New York: Columbia, UP, 2007); and De Lombard, Jeannine, *Slavery on Trial: Law, Abolitionism, and Print Culture* (Chapel Hill: U of North Carolina Press, 2007).

80. Ibid, 311.

81. Qtd. in Tamarkin, "Literature and the News" 33.

82. Ibid, 314.

83. Ibid, 314.

84. Thoreau, "A Plea" 138.

85. In his 1859 speech on Brown, Emerson likewise emphasized the old man's link to the Puritans. He joins that perfect Puritan faith which brought his fifth ancestor to Plymouth Rock with his grandfather's ardor in the Revolution," Emerson said. "He believes in two articles,—two instruments, shall I say?—the Golden Rule and the Declaration of Independence; and he used this expression in conversation here concerning them, "Better that a whole generation of men, women and children should pass away by a violent death than that one word of either should be violated in this country": *Antislavery Writings* 118.

86. Thoreau, "A Plea" 157.

87. Ibid.

88. Emerson, "Experience" 49. Lee notes that this sentence is a remnant from Emerson's earlier lecture series on "The Times." See *Slavery, Philosophy, and American Literature* 185.

89. Emerson, "Experience" 48.

90. Ibid, 42.

91. Ibid, 39.

92. Ibid, 49.

93. Ibid, 27.

94. Ibid, 27.

95. In her canonical essay on "Experience," Sharon Cameron describes one view of the essay's movement as a turn from mourning a "lack of binding—of temporal moments to each other" to a celebration of "the force of *un*binding; [Emerson] celebrates the primacy of

the present moment, dissociated from all other moments." For reasons remote from my immediate concerns, Cameron challenges this reading. What interests me about Cameron's observation instead, in addition to her recognition of the crucial temporal component of Emerson's essay, is her misapprehension of the present moment, which duplicates Emerson's misunderstanding of the present at the essay's start. See *Impersonality: Seven Essays* (Chicago: U of Chicago P, 2007): 63.

96. Ibid, 39.

97. Ibid, 39.

98. Dolan, *Emerson's Liberalism* 158.

99. Ibid, 158.

100. Ibid, 40, 41.

101. See, respectively, Van Cromphout (dialectics), Buell, Lawrence, and Finseth, Ian, "Emerson, Cosmopolitanism, and Antislavery Politics," *American Literature* 77 (2005): 729–60 (evolutionary theory); and Dolan (Whig interpretation).

102. King used the phrase frequently. See, for example, *A Testament of Hope: The Essential Writings of Martin Luther King, Jr,* James Washington, Ed. (San Francisco: Harper & Row, 1986):141, 207, 230, 277.

103. Dolan, *Emerson's Liberalism* 32.

104. *Prose Works, v. II,* 13. My argument here for Emerson's investments in change and impermanence resonates with and has profited from Arsić, Branka, *On Leaving: A Reading in Emerson* (Cambridge, MA: Harvard UP, 2010).

105. Guthrie, James, *Above Time: Emerson's and Thoreau's Temporal Revolutions* (Columbia: U of Missouri P, 2001): 105.

106. Emerson, *Antislavery Writings* 33.

107. Ibid, 119.

108. Emerson, "Experience" 49.

109. This may seem a tendentious claim in the wake of an influential reading such as John Carlos Rowe's, which argues that "Emerson's political writings from 1844 to 1863" demonstrate that he suffered from what can only be described as a form of "intellectual schizophrenia" so entirely "incompatible" were his "transcendentalism and political activism": *At Emerson's Tomb* 21. Yet Rowe reduces Emersonian transcendentalism almost exclusively to a single feature, his radical individualism, disregarding other important elements of Emerson's transcendentalist thought. The picture looks somewhat different when viewed through the lens of Emerson's transcendental presentism, which, I am suggesting, informed his heterodox view of history.

110. Respectively, Lee, *Slavery, Philosophy, and American Literature* 179; and Rowe, *At Emerson's Tomb* 26. Gougeon, by contrast, describes the address as "militant and confrontational." Martha Schoolman, in what is to my mind the most perceptive treatment of the address, argues that it "retell[s] the history of emancipation thus far as a black as well as a white story, and one that embodies as it describes the complex relationship between abolitionism and the enslaved." See Schoolman, Martha, *Abolitionist Geographies* (Minneapolis: U of Minnesota Press, 2014): 85.

111. The latter of these essays, on the "Individual," provided material for both "History" and "Self-Reliance," demonstrating the close link for Emerson between those two concepts.

112. See, for example, Robert Spiller: "the whole trend of his thought... was to cut loose from the past as the past in order to emphasize the timeless present. In the usual meaning of the term as in some sense dealing with the chronological past, Emerson's initial

philosophy of history was antihistorical." Spiller, *The Early Lectures of Ralph Waldo Emerson,* *vol. II,* Stephen E. Whicher, Robert E. Spiller, and Wallace E. Williams, Eds. (Cambridge: Belknap Press, 1964): 1.

113. Ibid, 8.

114. Emerson, "History," in *The Collected Works of Ralph Waldo Emerson Vol. II* (Cambridge: Belknap Press, 1983): 3.

115. Ibid, 4.

116. Ibid, 5.

117. Ibid, 5.

118. Ibid, 6.

119. Ibid, 6.

120. Ibid, 7.

121. Ibid, 7.

122. Ibid, 22.

123. Ibid, 15.

124. Emerson, *Antislavery Writings* 22.

125. Ibid, 26.

126. Beecher, *Essay on Slavery and Abolition* 85, 86.

127. Dolan, *Emerson's Liberalism* 220.

128. Emerson, *Antislavery Writings* 9.

129. The distinction here is compatible with Schoolman's reading of the address as committed to the spatialized abolitionist dialectic between "*doing* and *omitting to do,*" that is, between the reality of black slave resistance in the south and white refusal to uphold the system in the north. For Schoolman, Emerson enters "the space of abolitionism not by claiming the right that he does not have to be at the center of the fight for freedom, but rather by refusing to stand in its way": *Abolitionist Geographies* 85.

130. Emerson, *Antislavery Writings* 10.

131. Ibid, 10.

132. Emerson, "History" 22.

133. Emerson, *Antislavery Writings* 19, 26.

134. Emerson, *Antislavery Writings* 37.

135. Emerson, "History" 4.

136. Emerson, *Antislavery Writings* 9.

137. Ibid, 10.

138. Ibid, 13, 14, 21, 22.

139. Ibid, 23.

140. Ibid, 24.

141. Ibid, 25.

142. Schoolman, Martha, "Emerson's Doctrine of Hatred," *Arizona Quarterly* 63 (Summer 2007): 13.

143. Schoolman, "Emerson's Doctrine of Hatred" 15.

144. Ibid, 31.

145. Ibid, 14.

146. Emerson, *Antislavery Writings* 28.

147. Ibid, 29.

148. Ibid, 31–2.

149. Ibid, 31.

150. See Finseth, "Emerson, Cosmopolitanism, and Antislavery Politics" 735 ("biological determinism"), and for "disturbing," Dassow Walls, Laura. *Emerson's Life in Science: The Culture of Truth* (Ithaca: Cornell UP, 2003): 165.

151. On romantic racialism, see Frederickson, George, *The Black Image in the White Mind: The Debate on Afro-American Character and Destiny, 1817–1914* (Middletown, CT: Wesleyan UP, 1971): 97–129.

152. See, for example, Grimké, who was scathingly critical of what she called the "half-way principles" of Clarkson and Wilberforce. After British abolition of the slave trade in 1806, Grimké asks:

> What were British philanthropists doing for the emancipation of the slaves for the next twenty years? Nothing at all; and it was the voice of Elizabeth Heyrick which first awakened them from their dream of *gradualism* to an understanding of the simple doctrine of immediate emancipation; but even though they saw the injustice and inefficiency of *their own* views, yet several years elapsed before they had the courage to promulgate hers.   (emphasis original)

See *Letters to Catherine E. Beecher* 16–17.

153. Emerson, *Antislavery Writings* 31.

154. O'Brien, Colleen, *Race, Romance, and Rebellion: Literatures of the Americas in the Nineteenth Century* (Charlottesville: U of Virginia P, 2013).

155. Charles's lecture is perhaps as forceful, trenchant, and forward-looking a public pronouncement on immediatism as any that appeared in the 1830s. Although we have no record of Waldo's response to his brother's lecture, it's unlikely, given their close relationship, that he wouldn't have read it or that the two of them wouldn't have discussed its assertions. Indeed, Charles's lecture forms an important touchstone for portions of Waldo's West Indies address specifically, and, more generally, for his attitude toward immediatism, both philosophical and political. West Indian emancipation and the Haitian Revolution play a significant role in Charles's lecture, but neither the history of slavery nor of antislavery constitute his primary concern. Rather, "our business," he says in a phrase that Frederick Douglass would later make famous (and that I take up in the Chapter 4), "is not with the past, but the present." Expressing the impatience that typified immediatism, Charles argues that emancipation "is the wisest expedient in a pressing emergency." The bulk of the lecture is devoted to unraveling the specious arguments of those who object to immediate emancipation. Charles gives voice to those arguments late in the speech, in terms we've encountered before in this chapter:

> …the cry is this subject is of a delicate nature—not rashly to be meddled with. You are tossing fire about in a magazine of powder. The effect of your doctrine & discussions is to excite the slaves; & for fear of this the masters pass laws more & more severe—& the condition of the negroes is the worse for all you do.

In 1851, Waldo would call such arguments absurd. In 1835, Charles took pains to address and assuage these and other speculative fears held and promulgated by slaveholders and antislavery gradualists alike. Yet Charles does not disavow charges of rashness and agitation, even though, unlike his brother in "Circles," he does not court and look forward to the prospect of upheaval. Instead, he seeks to demonstrate its unlikelihood. He recognizes the uncertainties of a postemancipation future that so bedevil the public mind: "the friends of emancipation," he says "feel a tenderness in calling upon their fellow citizens to make an experiment wholly untried, with the possibility of a highly disastrous issue." But he also insists that those calling for emancipation have for that very reason "undertaken to furnish evidence of its practicability & safety." Evidence of that conduct is provided by the example of freed former slaves in various locations in the southern hemisphere, most especially following the revolution in Haiti and emancipation in the West Indies. In the latter case, for instance, Charles presents the same scenes of calm, nonviolent, "innocent & decent rejoicing" that Waldo describes in his 1844 West Indies address. The manuscript, dated April 29, 1835 (MS AM 82.6) is housed at the Houghton Library, Harvard.

156. Emerson, "Experience" 40.

157. Emerson, "Circles," *The Collected Works of Ralph Waldo Emerson Vol. II* (Cambridge: Belknap Press, 1983): 181.

158. Ibid, 179.

159. Ibid, 180.

160. Ibid, 189.

161. Ibid, 186.

162. Ibid, 186.

163. Emerson, "Prudence," *Collected Works, Vol. 2*, 136.

164. Ibid, 131.

165. Ibid, 131.

166. Ibid, 131, 141.

167. Emerson, "Circles" 186.

168. Ibid, 187.

169. Ibid, 190.

170. Ibid, 187.

171. Emerson, "Self-Reliance" 33.

172. Of course, for many gradualists and antiabolitionists, slave insurrection and the French Revolution are virtually synonymous. Immediatists were routinely likened to Jacobins. For more on this point, see Chapter 5.

173. Emerson, "Circles" 189.

174. Emerson, *Antislavery Writings* 95.

175. Ibid, 96.

176. Emerson, "Circles" (respectively), 180, 181, 181, 184, 189.

177. Ibid, 189.

178. Emerson, "Self-Reliance" 40.

179. See Cadava, *Emerson and the Climates of History* 2–3.

180. Mead, *The Philosophy of the Present* 35.

181. Ibid, 107.

182. Emerson, "Circles" 225.

183. Ibid, 236.

184. Mead, *The Philosophy of the Present* 73.

185. Compare to Van Cromphout: "only in the mind of the present could the past achieve existential reality...he regarded the past as a creation of the present, as a product of the retrospectively creative force of the mind of the present."

186. Mead, *The Philosophy of the Present* 52.

187. "The Nature of the Past," *Essays in Honor of John Dewey*, John Coss, Ed. (New York: Henry Holt & Co., 1929): 242.

188. Emerson, "Circles" 180.

189. Ibid, 184.
190. Ibid, 190.
191. Mead, *The Philosophy of the Present* 50.
192. Emerson, "Circles" 189.

Chapter 4

1. Douglass, Frederick, *My Bondage and My Freedom, 1855. Autobiographies* (New York: Library of America, 1994): 148.

2. Bromell, Nick, "'A Voice from the Enslaved': The Origins of Frederick Douglass's Political Philosophy of Democracy," *American Literary History* 23 (Winter 2011): 699.

3. Luciano, Dana, *Arranging Grief: Sacred Time and the Body in Nineteenth-Century America* (New York: NYU P, 2007): 186.

4. My account that follows of the complex relationship toward a hoped-for future Douglass developed in some ways aligns with certain elements of that important recent strain of African-American thought gathered under the name of Afro-pessimism. I have in mind, for instance, Jared Sexton's description of the temporal-historical dimension of "black optimism": "We want to think about what makes New World slavery what it is in order to pursue that future anteriority which, being both within it and irreducible to it, will have unmade it, and that anterior futurity which always already unmakes it." See Sexton, "The Social Life of Social Death: On Afro-Pessimism and Black Optimism," *InTensions* (Fall/Winer 2011): 17. See also Sexton's "Ante-Anti-Blackness: Afterthoughts," *Lateral* (Spring 2012): online; Wilderson III, Frank B., *Red, White, and Black: Cinema and the Structure of U.S. Antagonisms.* (Durham, NC: Duke UP, 2012); Moten, Fred, "Blackness and Nothingness (Mysticism in the Flesh)," *South Atlantic Quarterly* 112 (Fall 2013): 737–80.

5. For a discussion of Douglass's complex relationships to chance and providence, see Lee, Maurice, *Uncertain Chances: Science, Skepticism, and Belief in Nineteenth-Century American Literature* (New York: Oxford UP, 2012): 89–119. For a qualified response to Lee, see Hickman, Jared, "Douglass Unbound," *Nineteenth-Century Literature* 68 (Fall 2014): 323–62.

6. Of course, post-Civil War conditions, notably Reconstruction and the "nadir" of race relations that followed Reconstruction, significantly altered Douglass's thinking about time, history, and hope. For a powerful reading of this later phase of Douglass's career that tracks "his emergent consciousness of the political potency of nonprogressive modes of time" as he attempts to com[e] to terms with recursivity and stasis": see Laski, Gregory, *Untimely Democracy: The Politics of Progress After Slavery* (New York: Oxford UP, 2017): 62–92.

7. Douglass, Frederick, *My Bondage and My Freedom* (New York: Miller, Orton, and Mulligan, 1855): 273.

8. Rohy, *Anachronism and Its Others* 23.

9. "Farewell to the British People: An Address Delivered in London, England, on 30 March 1847," *The Fredrick Douglass Papers, Series One; Speeches, Debates, and Interviews, Vol. 2: 1847–54.* John W. Blassingame, Ed. (New Haven: Yale UP, 1982): 32.

10. On Douglass's Christian millennialism, see John Stauffer, *The Black Hearts of Men* (Cambridge, MA: Harvard UP, 2001).

11. By calling it wishful thinking I mean to distinguish Douglass's historiography from the long African-American prophetic tradition. Although Douglass was clearly influenced

by this tradition, the orientation that Douglass adopts toward the future that I attempt to sketch out here is not a matter of prophesying. For an excellent recent account of black prophetic thought, see Christopher Z. Hobson, *The Mount of Vision: African American Prophetic Tradition, 1800–1950* (London: Oxford UP, 2012).

12. Douglass, Frederick, "What of the Night," *Selected Speeches and Writings*. Philip S. Foner and Yuval Taylor, Eds. (Chicago: Lawrence Hill Books, 1999): 97.

13. Douglass, Frederick, "Rights of Women," *The North Star*, July 28, 1848.

14. Douglass, "What of the Night" 97.

15. Ibid.

16. Douglass, "The Revolution of 1848," in *Selected Speeches and Writings* 105.

17. Ibid.

18. Marrs, Cody, "Frederick Douglass in 1848," *American Literature* 85 (September 2013): 450.

19. Douglass, "Addressed to the Colored People of the United States," in *Selected Speeches and Writings* 118.

20. Ibid, 118.

21. Ibid, 118.

22. Ibid, 118.

23. Ibid, 119.

24. One is reminded here again of Emerson's "Self-Reliance": "the soul becomes," which I discuss in Chapter 3.

25. Bromell, "'A Voice from the Enslaved'" 712. See also Crane, Gregg D., *Race, Citizenship, and Law in American Literature* (Cambridge: Cambridge UP, 2002): 87–130.

26. Bromell, "'A Voice from the Enslaved'" 715.

27. Douglass, "The Destiny of Colored Americans," *Selected Speeches and Writings* 148.

28. Douglass, *The Heroic Slave*, in *Selected Speeches and Writings* 220.

29. Douglass, *The Heroic Slave* 221.

30. David Walker and Martin Delany similarly figured the transformations wrought by black revolutionary action. In Walker's *Appeal*, he writes, "This country is as much ours as it is the whites, whether they will admit it now or not, they will see and believe it bye and bye...Their prejudices will be obliged to fall like lightning to the ground, in succeeding generations...I hope the residue of the coloured people, will stand still and see the salvation of God, and the miracle which he will work for our delivery...." See Walker, David, "An Appeal in Four Articles," (1830) *Classic Black Nationalism: From the American Revolution to Marcus Garvey*. Wilson J. Moses, Ed. (New York: NYU Press, 1996): 88. And early in *Blake*, Delany's hero describes his insurrectionary plans thusly: "So simple is it that the trees of the forest or an orchard illustrate it...tobacco, rice, or cotton, the whistling of the wind, rustling of the leaves, flashing of lightning, roaring of thunder, and running of streams all keep it constantly before their eyes and in their memory, so that they can't forget it if they would." Delany, Martin, *Blake, or the Huts of America* (Boston: Beacon Press, 1970): 39.

31. Shamir, Millette, *Inexpressible Privacy: The Interior Life of Antebellum American Literature* (Philadelphia: U of Pennsylvania P): 135.

32. Beecher Stowe, Harriet, *Uncle Tom's Cabin; or, Life Among the Lowly* (New York: Library of America, 1982): 212–13.

33. Dickinson, Emily, *The Poems of Emily Dickinson*, Thomas H. Johnson, Ed. (Cambridge: Belknap Press, 1951): 792.

34. I have Christopher Hanlon to thank for directing me to Dickinson here.

35. Douglass, "What to the Slave," in *Selected Speeches and Writings* 196.

36. Emerson, Ralph Waldo, "Address to the Citizens of Concord on the Fugitive Slave Law, 3 May, 1851," *Emerson's Antislavery Writings*, Len Gougeon and Joel Myerson, Eds. (New Haven: Yale UP, 1995): 55.

37. Ibid. For other treatments of the rhetoric of powerful natural occurrences in relation to slavery and especially slave rebellion, see Cadava, Eduardo, *Emerson and the Climates of History* (Stanford, CA: Stanford UP, 1997); Montesinos Sale, Maggie, *The Slumbering Volcano: American Slave Ship Revolts and the Production of Rebellious Masculinity* (Durham: Duke UP, 1997): 146–72; Gleason, William, "Volcanoes and Meteors: Douglass, Melville, and the Poetics of Insurrection," *Frederick Douglass and Herman Melville: Essays in Relation* (Chapel Hill: UNC P, 2008): 119; Fuller, Randall, *From Battlefields Rising: How the Civil War Transformed American Literature* (New York: Oxford UP, 2011): 5–12; Armstrong, Tim, *The Logic of Slavery: Debt, Technology, and Pain in American Literature* (Cambridge: Cambridge UP, 2012): 173–204.

38. See Stauffer, John, "Melville, Slavery, and the American Dilemma," *A Companion to Herman Melville*. Wyn Kelley, Ed. (London: Blackwell, 2006): 225.

39. Melville, Herman, *Mardi; and a Voyage Thither* (New York: Library of America, 1982): 1189.

40. Levine, Robert S., *Conspiracy and Romance: Studies in Brockden Brown, Cooper, Hawthorne, and Melville* (Cambridge: Cambridge UP, 1989): 187.

41. Melville, Herman, *Typee, Omoo, Mardi* (New York: Library of America, 1982): 1192.

42. On Calhoun as Ahab-like monomaniac see Stauffer, "Melville, Slavery, and the American Dilemma," and Alan Heimert, who (allegorically speaking) notes that Ahab could just as likely be Garrison: "*Moby-Dick* and American Political Symbolism," *American Quarterly* 15 (Winter 1963): 498–534. See also Rogin, Michael Paul, *Subversive Genealogy: The Politics and Art of Herman Melville* (Berkeley: U of California P, 1979): 102–51. The most detailed allegorical reading of *Moby-Dick* likening Ahab to Garrison is Weathers, Willie T., "Moby-Dick and the Nineteenth-Century Scene," *Texas Studies in Literature and Language* (Winter 1960): 477–501. Weathers gathers intriguing historical evidence for the connection, though he does not take up Garrison's immediatism. He is also rather disapproving of Garrison, in keeping with many mid-twentieth-century assessments.

43. Melville, Herman, *Moby-Dick; or The Whale* (Evanston, IL: Northwestern-Newberry, 1988): 508.

44. For fascinating discussions of foundlings and orphanage in *Moby-Dick* in the context of literary nationalism, see Coviello, Peter, *Intimacy in America: Dreams of Affiliation in Antebellum Literature* (Minneapolis: U of Minnesota P, 2005): 91–126; Bersani, Leo, "Incomparable America," *The Culture of Redemption* (Cambridge, MA: Harvard UP, 1990): 136–54.

45. Luciano, *Arranging Grief* 179–80.

46. Etymologically, "unregenerate" has its origin in the Latin verb "regenirare: to reproduce," later taken to mean spiritually reborn. Comparatively speaking, recent readers of *Moby-Dick* have largely avoided "The Candles"—perhaps for good reason. Notable exceptions include Leverenz, David, *Manhood and the American Renaissance* (Ithaca: Cornell UP, 1989): 279–306; and Casarino, Cesare, *Modernity at Sea: Melville, Marx, Conrad in Crisis* (Minneapolis: U of Minnesota P, 2002): 128–33.

47. Melville, *Moby-Dick* 164.

48. Stauffer, "Melville, Slavery, and the American Dilemma" 229.

49. Luciano and Cody Marrs have each analyzed how in that speech and elsewhere, Douglass embraces a "now-time" that "reactualize[s]" the Revolution or "extract[s] from the nation's revolutionary history a latent temporality of rebellion." See Luciano, *Arranging Grief* 186, and Marrs "Frederick Douglass in 1848" 467, respectively. The term "now-time" that each deploys (see Luciano, *Arranging Grief* 186, 1871; and Marrs, "Frederick Douglass in 1848" 450) derives from Walter Benjamin's concept *Jettzeit*, which in his *Theses on the Philosophy of History* he contrasts with the "empty, homogeneous time" of conventional historicizing. *Jetztzeit* disrupts conventional distinctions between past and present. For Benjamin it is a form of messianic time, associated with political action and justice in the present. In this, it resonates with Douglass's immediatism.

50. Douglass, Frederick, "What to the Slave Is the Fourth of July? An Address Delivered in Rochester, New York, on 5 July 1852," *The Fredrick Douglass Papers, Series One; Speeches, Debates, and Interviews.* Vol. 2: 1847–54. John W. Blassingame, Ed. (New Haven: Yale UP, 1982): 366.

51. Luciano, *Arranging Grief* 185.

52. Ibid, 187.

53. Longfellow, Henry Wadsworth, *Poems and Other Writings* (New York: Library of America, 2000): 4.

54. See Bromell, "'A Voice from the Enslaved'" 714–17.

55. Douglass, "What to the Slave?" 369.

56. The fact that Douglass's presentism emerges from his engagements with the past distinguishes it sharply, I think, from the "strategic presentism" that Daylanne English locates in her fascinating discussion of the Black Arts and Black Power movements of the 1960 and 1970s, especially with regard to the "Dasein group" of poets. But as English employs the term, "presentism" signifies a contemporaneity that verges on the unhistorical. See English, *Each Hour Redeem: Time and Justice in African American Literature* (Minneapolis: U of Minnesota P, 2013): 103–28.

57. Douglass, Frederick, "The Present Condition and Future Prospects of the Negro People," *Selected Speeches and Writings,* 256.

58. Ibid.

59. On Douglass's attraction to probabilistic thinking, see Lee, Maurice, *Uncertain Chances: Science, Skepticism, and Belief in Nineteenth-Century American Literature* (New York: Oxford UP, 2012): 89–119.

60. Douglass's break with Garrison and change of mind on the Constitutionality of slavery has understandably attracted a great deal of critical attention. In addition to Bromell, see Crane, *Race, Citizenship, and Law* 104–30; Martin, Waldo E., *The Mind of Frederick Douglass* (Chapel Hill: UNC P, 1984): 23–48; McFeely, William S., *Frederick Douglass* (New York: W.W. Norton, 1993): 169–73; Garvey, Gregory T., "Frederick Douglas's Change of Opinion on the U.S. Constitution: Abolitionism and the 'Elements of Moral Power'," *American Transcendental Quarterly* 9 (Sept. 1995): 229–43; Dorsey, Peter A., "Becoming the Other: The Mimesis of Metaphor in Douglass's *My Bondage and My Freedom*," *PMLA* 111 (May 1996): 435–50; Mills, Charles W., "Whose Fourth of July? Frederick Douglass and 'Original Intent'," *Frederick Douglass: A Critical Reader*, Bill E. Lawson and Frank M. Kirkland, Eds. (Oxford: Blackwell, 1999): 100–42; Blight, David W., *Frederick Douglass's Civil War: Keeping Faith in Jubilee* (Baton Rouge: LSU P, 1999): 30–5; Montás, Roosevelt,

"Meaning and Transcendence: Melville, Douglass, and the Anxiety of Interpretation,"
Leviathan (June 2008): 69–83; Moses, Wilson J., "'The Ever-Present Now': Frederick
Douglass's Pragmatic Constitutionalism," *Journal of African American History* 99 (Winter-
Spring 2014): 71–88.

61. Marrs, "Frederick Douglass in 1848" 466.

62. Douglass, Frederick, "To Gerrit Smith," *Selected Speeches and Writings* 171.

63. Ibid.

64. Douglass, Frederick, "Change of Opinion Announced," *Selected Speeches and
Writings* 174.

65. Douglass, Frederick, "Speeches and Writings", *Selected Speeches and Writings* 129.

66. Ibid.

67. Ibid.

68. Ellis, Cristin, "Amoral Abolitionism: Frederick Douglass and the Environmental
Case Against Slavery," *American Literature* 86 (June 2014): 294.

69. Ibid.

70. For a related version of this point, see Robert S. Levine, who argues that "[Gerrit]
Smith's political abolitionism legitimized and encouraged social action that was more
pragmatically grounded than Garrison's moral-suasion immediatism": *Frederick Douglass,
Martin Delany, and the Politics of Representative Identity* (Chapel Hill: U of North Carolina
P, 1997): 72.

71. Douglass's embrace of a historically minded presentism somewhat unsettles
Daylanne English's otherwise elegant distinction between strategies of anachronism and
strategies of presentism in the African American literary tradition. It adds an additional
dimension, too, to her description of the temporal concerns in early African American
Literature. See *Each Hour Redeem*.

72. Douglass, *My Bondage and My Freedom* 446.

73. On Douglass's arch tone in this speech, see also Lee, Maurice, *Slavery, Philosophy,
and American Literature* (Cambridge: Cambridge UP, 2005): 125–6; although he appears not
to hear Douglass's bitter irony quite as overtly as I do.

74. Douglass, "The Anti-Slavery Movement," *Selected Speeches and Writings* 314.

75. Ibid, 313.

76. Ibid, 315.

77. Oxford English Dictionary. For a grim reworking of this formula—the new as a
repetition—see Douglass's 1865 speech "The Need for Continuing Antislavery Work," where
he anticipates slavery's immediate future forebodingly: "all of us had better wait and see
what new form this old monster will assume," he says, in what new skin this old snake will
come forth next," in *Selected Speeches and Writings* 578.

78. Douglass here provides an early iteration of the kind of "multidimensional." Blackness
that Michelle Wright identifies in her reading of James Baldwin. Within "Epiphenomenal
time"—the now—subjectivity "involves a potentially endless set of negotiations." Rather
than "being moved down a line through cause and effect as in a strictly linear interpellation,
the Subject in the moment is variously informed by a variety of external and internal
stimuli…that also can intersect with one another." See Wright, Michelle M., *The Physics of
Blackness: Beyond the Middle Passage Epistemology* (Minneapolis: U of Minnesota P, 2015): 116.

79. Mead, George Herbert, *The Philosophy of the Present*, A. E. Murphy, Ed. (The Open
Court Company, 1932): 58.

80. The best account of Douglass's fluid sense of his own personal narrative over the course of his lifelong autobiographical project is Levine, Robert S., *The Lives of Frederick Douglass* (Cambridge: Harvard UP, 2016). My reading of Douglass's self-fashioning here is also informed by Stepto, Robert B., "Narration, Authentication, and Authorial Control in Frederick Douglass's Narrative of 1845," *African American Autobiography: A Collection of Critical Essays*, William L. Andrews, Ed. (Englewood Cliffs, NJ: Prentice Hall, 1993; Stone, Albert E., "Identity and Art in Frederick Douglass's Narrative," *College Language Association Journal* 17 (1973): 192–213; Gibson, Donald B., "Reconciling Public and Private in Frederick Douglass's Narrative," *American Literature* 57 (Dec. 1985): 549–69; Leverenz, David, "Frederick Douglass's Self-Refashioning," *Criticism: A Quarterly for Literature and the Arts* 29.3 (1987): 341–70; Gates, Henry Louis, *Figures in Black: Words, Signs, and the "Racial" Self.* (New York: Oxford UP, 1987); Goddu, Teresa A., and Craig V. Smith, "Scenes of Writing in Frederick Douglass's Narrative: Autobiography and the Creation of Self," *The Southern Review* 25.4 (1989): 822–40.

81. Andrews, William, *To Tell a Free Story: The First Century of Afro-American Autobiography* (Champaign: U of Illinois P, 1986): 214–39.

82. Mead,George Herbert, *The Philosophy of the Act*, Charles W. Morris, Ed. (Chicago: U of Chicago P): 149.

83. Ibid, 161.

84. Ibid, 161.

85. Ibid, 160.

86. Douglass, *My Bondage* 137.

87. See Pratt, Lloyd, " 'I Am a Stranger with Thee': Frederick Douglass and Recognition after 1845," *American Literature* 85 (2013): 247–72; and Smith, Mark M., *Mastered By the Clock: Time, Slavery, and Freedom in the American South* (Chapel Hill: U of North Carolina P, 1997)—both of whom discuss slavery's multiple temporalities.

88. Douglass, "The Anti-Slavery Movement" 328.

89. Douglass, "The Present Condition and Future Prospects of the Negro," *Selected Speeches and Writings* 256.

90. Douglass, *My Bondage* 170.

91. Ibid, 221.

92. Douglass, "Present Condition" 256.

93. Later in the speech, Douglass leans on "while" again, this time to indicate a contrast:

> There is nothing in the present aspect of the anti-slavery question which should drive us into the extravagance and nonsense of advocating a dissolution of the American Union as a means of overthrowing slavery, or freeing the North from the malign influence of slavery upon the morals of the Northern people. While the press is at liberty, and speech is free, and the ballot-box is open to the people of the sixteen free States; while the slaveholders are but four hundred thousand in number, and we are fourteen millions; while the mental and moral power of the nation is with us; while we are really the strong and they are the weak, it would look worse than cowardly to retreat from the Union.

94. Douglass, "The Dred Scott Decision," *Selected Speeches and Writings* 345.

95. Ibid, 346.

96. Ibid, 346.

97. Ibid, 346.

98. Ibid, 346.

99. Ibid, 346.

100. Ibid, 347.

101. Ibid, 347.

102. Ibid, 347.

103. Ibid, 349.

104. Ibid, 349.

105. Gleason, "Volcanoes and Meteors" 114.

106. On the portability of the psalm form, generally, and "A Psalm of Life," in particular, I am indebted to Virginia Jackson and her unpublished conference paper "Before Modernism," delivered at the C19 conference in Chapel Hill, North Carolina, in 2014. Alexander Pope's "An Essay on Criticism" famously describes the laggard pace of the Alexandrine couplet: "A needless Alexandrine ends the song,/That, like a wounded snake, drags its slow length along."

107. Qtd. in English, *Each Hour Redeem* 111.

108. English links the poem's "presentist, global" politics to the Dasein poets and to the black musical currents of the period. She does not note the allusion to Longfellow, which I would suggest links Baraka's poem to a much longer—and more racially complicated— literary history.

109. Douglass, Redeem, and Writings" 351.

110. Ibid, 353.

111. Qtd. in "The Dred Scott Decision," 355.

112. Ibid, 354.

113. See also 204, "What to the Slave is the Fourth of July?": "I hold that every American citizen has a right to form an opinion of the Constitution, and to propagate that opinion, and to use all honorable means to make his opinion the prevailing one."

114. See Dinshaw, Carolyn, *How Soon is Now? Medieval Texts, Amateur Readers, and the Queerness of Time* (Durham, NC: Duke UP, 2012): 24—"amateurism is bricolage, bringing whatever can be found, whatever works, to the activity." "Amateur readings, participating in nonmodern ways of apprehending time, can help us to contemplate different ways of being, knowing, and world making."

115. Douglass, "The Dred Scott Decision" 355.

116. Ibid.

117. Wald, Priscilla, *Constituting Americans: Cultural Anxiety and Narrative Form* (Durham: Duke UP, 1995): 14–105. Also on the question of citizenship, see Goldberg, Shari, *Quiet Testimony: A Theory of Witnessing from Nineteenth-Century American Literature* (New York: Fordham UP, 2013): 57–86.

118. See Pratt's marvelous, "'I Am a Stranger with Thee'" 247–72. Douglass here also provides a vivid illustration of what Wright describes as "the multifarious dimensions of Blackness that exist in any one moment, or 'now'," dimensions made visible through the deployment of an Epiphenomenal concept of spacetime" (see *Physics of Blackness* 20).

Chapter 5

1. Melville, Herman, *The Writings of Herman Melville, Israel Potter: His Fifty Years of Exile* (Evanston: Northwestern UP and the Newberry Library, 1982): 57.

2. Ibid, 145.

3. Emerson, Ralph Waldo, *Emerson's Antislavery Writings*, Len Gougeon and Joel Myerson, Eds. (New Haven: Yale UP, 1994): 87.

4. Melville's source text is the 1824 *Life and Remarkable Adventures of Israel Potter*, published and most likely written by Henry Trumbull. For details on Melville's source and his transformations of it, see Chacko, David, and Alexander Kulcsar, "Israel Potter: Genesis of a Legend," *William and Mary Quarterly* 41 (1984): 365–89; see Walter Bezanson's Historical Note to *Israel Potter, His Fifty Years of Exile*. Harrison Hayford, Hershel Parke, and G. Thomas Tanselle, Eds. (Evanston and Chicago: Northwestern UP and The Newberry Library, 1982); Levine, Robert S., "Introduction," *Israel Potter: His Fifty Years of Exile* (New York: Penguin, 2008). On Melville's critique of nationalist history, see especially Castronovo, Russ, *Fathering the Nation: American Genealogies of Slavery and Freedom* (Berkeley: U of California P, 1995); and Bellis, Peter, "Fiction as History as Autobiography," *American Literary History* (1990): 607–26.

5. "Hope, along with its other, fear, are affective structures that can be described as anticipatory." See Muñoz, José Esteban, *Cruising Utopia: The Then and there of Queer Futurity* (New York: NYU P, 2009): 3.

6. See, for instance, Fisher, Marvin, "'The Lightning-Rod Man': Melville's Testament of Rejection." *Studies in Short Fiction* 7 (1970): 433–8; Verdier, Douglas L., "Who Is the Lightning-Rod Man?" *Studies in Short Fiction* 18 (1981): 273–9; Silver, Sean R., "The Temporality of Allegory: Melville's 'The Lightning-Rod Man,'" *Arizona Quarterly* 62 (2006): 1–33.

7. Criticism on "Benito Cereno" is vast. On "The Bell-Tower," see Castronovo, Russ, "Radical Configurations of History in the Era of American Slavery." *American Literature: A Journal of Literary History, Criticism, and Bibliography* 65.3 (1993): 523–47; Wilson, Ivy G., "'no Soul Above': Labor and the 'Law in Art' in Melville's 'the Bell-Tower,'" *Arizona Quarterly: A Journal of American Literature, Culture, and Theory* 63.1 (2007): 27–47; Karcher, Carolyn L., "Melville's 'the Bell-Tower' and 'Benito Cereno': Companion-Pieces on Slavery," *Essays in Literature* 6 (1979): 57–69. On "The Encantadas," see Freeburg, Christopher, *Melville and the Idea of Blackness: Race and Imperialism in Nineteenth-Century America* (Cambridge UP, 2012). On "I and My Chimney," see Emery, Allan Moore, "The Political Significance of Melville's Chimney." *New England Quarterly: A Historical Review of New England Life and Letters* 55.2 (1982): 201–28.

8. Philip Young asks if there is a connection between the lightning rod man and Ahab in "Melville in the Berkshire Bishopric: 'The Lightning-Rod Man," *College Literature* 16 (Fall 1989): 203.

9. Melville, Herman, "The Piazza Tales and Other Prose Pieces, 1839–60," *The Writings of Herman Melville* (Evanston: Northwestern UP and the Newberry Library, 1987): 118.

10. Ibid, 122.

11. Ibid, 124.

12. Ibid, 124.

13. Ibid, 124.

14. Ibid, 124.

15. In an illuminating reading of the story, Joshua Matthews suggests that a contextualized, rather than allegorical, approach best explains this textual oddity. In antebellum America, the promotion and sale of lightning rods not only took place inside people's homes, as in Melville's story, it also, Matthews shows, took place in newspapers and magazines like *Putnam's Monthly*. Thus, in rejecting the salesman's pitch, the narrator also

rejects "the authoritative weight of a commercial print culture's discourse of the lightning rod." Only a fool, one who refuses to adhere to orthodoxy—an infidel—would reject the safety and security the lightning rod offers. Matthews' recovery of print culture and its "lightning rod rhetoric," indeed, provides a key point of historical reference for the story. However, that context need not obviate allegorical readings. To the contrary, I am suggesting, it can also enable them. See "Peddlers of the Rod: Melville's 'The Lightning-Rod Man' and the Antebellum Periodical Market," *Leviathan* 12 (Oct. 2010): 55–70.

16. On abolition and print culture, see, for instance, Fanuzzi, Robert, *Abolition's Public Sphere* (Minneapolis: U of Minnesota P, 2003); DeLombard, Jeannine Marie, *Slavery on Trial: Law, Abolitionism, and Print Culture* (Chapel Hill: U of North Carolina P, 2007); Loughran, Trish, *The Republic in Print: Print Culture in the Age of Nation Building, 1770–1870* (New York: Columbia UP, 2009).

17. Garrison, *The Liberator*, June 21, 1850.

18. Garrison, *The Liberator*, June 17, 1853.

19. Garrison, *The Liberator*, Jan. 15, 1847.

20. Ibid, 122.

21. In the eighteenth and nineteenth centuries, lightning often figured revolution. See, for example, Delbourgo, James, *A Most Amazing Scene of Wonders: Electricity and Enlightenment in Early America* (Cambridge: Harvard UP, 2006); Insko, Jeffrey, "Passing Current: Electricity, Magnetism, and Historical Transmission in *The Linwoods*," *ESQ: A Journal of the American Renaissance* 56 (2010): 293–326.

22. Matthews, "Peddlers of the Rod" 69.

23. Douglass, *Selected Speeches and Writings* 367.

24. In his indispensable biography of Garrison, Henry Mayer recounts Garrison's reply to his friend Samuel May, who counseled Garrison to temper his rhetoric and "keep more cool." "Brother May," Garrison replied, " "I have need to be all on fire, for I have mountains of ice about me to melt." See Mayer, *All on Fire: William Lloyd Garrison and the Abolition of Slavery* (New York: Norton, 1998): 119–20. In the first issue of *The Liberator*, Garrison addressed his ongoing legal troubles: "How do I bear up under my adversities? I answer—like the oak—like the alps—unshaken, storm-proof"—*The Liberator*, Jan. 1, 1831. And in an 1833 letter to his friend, the black abolitionist John Vashon, Garrison wrote "My enemies will find out, by and by, that I am storm-proof." See *The Letters of William Lloyd Garrison*, v. I. Walter M. Merrill, Ed. (Cambridge: Belknap Press, 1971): 267.

25. *Emerson in His Journals*, July 1852, 435. It is perhaps telling that this journal entry is sandwiched between an entry on Franklin Pierce and Daniel Webster, whom Emerson calls "low conspirators," and another on the fugitive slave Thomas Sims.

26. *Letters of William Lloyd Garrison* 62. Garrison also wrote, "How ought I to feel and speak? As a man! as a patriot! as a philanthropist! as a Christian! My soul should be, as it is, on fire. I should thunder—I should lighten." See "Vindication of the Liberator" in *Selections from the Speeches and Writings of William Lloyd Garrison* (Boston: R.F. Walcutt, 1852): 180. It is perhaps also worth noting that in the twentieth-century, Garrison has routinely been described as a "lightning-rod." That metaphor, deployed to describe someone who attracts controversy, seems not to have existed in the nineteenth-century (perhaps because it is built upon a misunderstanding of how lightning rods work). Melville's fiction—*Moby-Dick* and "The Lightning-Rod Man" in particular—might well have played a role in creating the conditions for the metaphor's emergence.

27. Simms, William Gilmore, "'Our Parties and Our Politics': A Southerner's View of the Subject," *Putnam's Monthly Magazine of American Literature, Science, and Art* (Dec. 1854): 633–50.

28. Ibid, 633.

29. Ibid, 663.

30. Ibid, 634–5.

31. Ibid, 635.

32. Ibid, 638.

33. Ibid, 640.

34. Ibid, 647. The similarity with Douglass here is striking enough to suggest that in his Dred Scott address, Douglass is mocking Simms specifically. See my discussion in Chapter 4.

35. Simms, 1852, 435. It is perhaps telling 648.

36. Also of relevance here is Melville's poem "The Coming Storm," which as Christopher Freeburg notes, "embodies a tormenting sense of pause, realizing an abrupt sense of danger [the speaker] is powerless to change." See *Melville and the Idea of Blackness: Race and Imperialism in Nineteenth-Century America* (Cambridge: Cambridge UP, 2012): xiii.

37. Melville, "The Lightning-Rod Man" 122.

38. Gerard Genette notes that even passages of dialogue cannot reflect the speed with which words are spoken or the pauses and dead spaces that characterize any conversation: see *Narrative Discourse: An Essay in Method*, Jane E. Lewin, trans. (Ithaca, NY: Cornell UP, 1980): 87.

39. Bezanson, "Historical Note" 205.

40. See, Higgins, Brian, and Hershel Parker, Eds., *Herman Melville: the Contemporary Reviews* (Cambridge: Cambridge UP, 1995): 463, 457.

41. My reading thus adapts the method of Weinstein's rich and inventive *Time, Tense, and American Literature*.

42. F. O. Matthiessen deemed *Israel Potter* a "failure": see *American Renaissance: Art and Expression in the Age of Emerson and Whitman* (New York: Oxford UP, 1941): 492.

43. Melville, *Israel Potter* 153.

44. Levine, "Introduction" xx.

45. For readings that consider Melville's deviations from his primary source, see Bellis, "Fiction as History"; and Lackey, Kris, "The Two Handles of *Israel Potter*," *College Literature* 21 (Feb. 1994): 32–45.

46. For a reading that considers temporality in *Pierre*, see Weinstein, Cindy, *Family, Kinship, and Sympathy in Nineteenth-Century American Literature* (Cambridge: Cambridge UP, 2004): 159–84.

47. Bellis notes the use of foreshadowing in the novel but does not develop the observation in detail.

48. Melville, *Israel Potter* 6.

49. Ibid, 9.

50. Ibid, 9.

51. Ibid, 10.

52. Ibid, 13.

53. Ibid, 19.

54. Ibid, 15–16.

55. Ibid, 16.

56. Ibid, 31–2.

57. Ibid, 32.

58. Ibid, 84.

59. Genette says this is a nineteenth-century convention.

60. Melville, *Israel Potter* 84.

61. Ibid, 114.

62. Ibid, 120.

63. See, respectively, Keyssar, Alexander, *Melville's Israel Potter: Reflections on the American Dream* (Cambridge: Harvard UP, 1969); Sten, Christopher, *The Weaver God, He Weaves: Melville and the Poetics of the Novel* (Kent, Ohio: Kent State UP, 1996); Lackey, "Two Handles" 39. Matthiessen asserts that Melville "observed in Paul Jones a fascinating but terrible symbol for the American character" (see *American Renaissance* 444), a view echoed in various ways by Dryden, Edgar A., *Monumental Melville: The Formation of a Literary Career* (Stanford: Stanford UP, 2004); Rampersad, Arnold, *Melville's Israel Potter: A Pilgrimage and Progress* (Bowling Green, OH: Bowling Green Popular Press, 1969); Samson, John, *White Lies: Melville's Narratives of Facts* (Ithaca: Cornell UP, 1989); Dilingham, William B., *Melville's Later Novels* (Athens: U of Georgia P, 1986). Karcher says that during the fight with the Serapis, Jones emerges as a "diabolical madman." See Karcher, Carolyn, *Shadow Over the Promised Land: Slavery, Race, and Violence in Melville's America* (Baton Rouge: Louisiana State UP, 1980): 105. For a somewhat different take on Jones, see Anne Roth-Reinhardt's fascinating "John Paul Jones, a New 'Pattern' for America," *Common-Place* 14 (Summer 2014).

64. Melville, *Israel Potter* 120.

65. Mead, *Philosophy of the Present*, A. E. Murphy, Ed. (The Open Court Company, 1932): 47.

66. Ibid, 47.

67. Ibid, 50.

68. On the motif of clothing and disguise in the novel see Temple, Gale, "*Israel Potter*: Sketch Patriotism," *Leviathan* 11 (Mar. 2009): 3–18.

69. Halberstam, Judith, *In a Queer Time and Place: Transgender Bodies, Subcultural Lives* (New York: NYU P, 2005): 6.

70. Melville, *Israel Potter* 56.

71. Ibid, 56.

72. Ibid, 63.

73. This is Melville's adaptation of the historical Jones's declaration, "I profess myself a Citizen of the World, totally unfettered by the little mean distinctions of climate or of country; which diminish the benevolence of the heart, and set bounds to Philanthropy." This statement—or at least its spirit—forms the basis of "The Shuttle" chapter. See *John Paul Jones' Memoir of the American Revolution*, Gerard W. Gewalt, trans. and Ed. (Honolulu: UP of the Pacific, 2001): 91. Karcher reads this free agency of Jones negatively, describing him as "incapable of love." He seems to "represent an America impermeable to human fellowship" (see *Shadow* 106). I am suggesting instead that Jones represents possibilities for fellowship not bound by traditional categories—race, nation, and sexual desire, for example.

74. Karcher calls it "an inverted replay of Ishmael's encounter with Queequeg" (see *Shadow* 106).

75. Melville, *Israel Potter* 62.

76. Maloney, Ian S., *Melville's Monumental Imagination* (New York: Routledge, 2014).

77. Oxford English Dictionary.

78. Melville, *Israel Potter* 63.

79. Looby, Christopher, "Strange Sensations: Sex and Aesthetics in 'The Counterpane,'" *Melville and Aesthetics*. Sam Otter and Geoffrey Sanborn, Eds. (Palgrave 2011): 74; Sanborn, Geoffrey, *The Sign of the Cannibal: Melville and the Making of a Postcolonial Reader* (Durham: Duke UP): 130.

80. Sanborn, *Sign of the Cannibal* 136.

81. See, for instance, Mead's essay "Cooley's Contribution to American Social Thought," *American Journal of Sociology* 35 (Mar. 1930): 693–706.

82. Melville, *Israel Potter* 70.

83. Melville, *Moby-Dick* 306.

84. Melville, *Israel Potter* 63.

85. Freccero, Carla, *Queer/Early/Modern* (Durham, NC, and London: Duke UP, 2006): 2.

86. See, respectively, Love, Heather, *Feeling Backward: Loss and the Politics of Queer History* (Cambridge: Harvard UP, 2007); Stockton, Kathryn Bond, *The Queer Child, Or Growing Sideways in the Twentieth Century* (Durham: Duke UP, 2009); Freeman, Elizabeth, *Time Binds: Queer Temporalities, Queer Histories* (Durham, NC: Duke UP, 2010), and Freccero, *Queer/Early/Modern*.

87. Samson, *White Lies* 196–7.

88. Melville, *Israel Potter* 131.

89. Ibid, 135.

90. Ibid, 136.

91. Melville engaged with "Rip Van Winkle" also in his prose and poetry narrative "Rip Van Winkle's Lilac," published in Melville, Herman, *Weeds and Wildings: Chiefly with a Rose or Two*, Robert Charles Ryan, Ed. (Evanston: Northwestern UP, 1967).

92. Ibid, 137.

93. Ibid, 138.

94. For a notable exception, see Blum, Hester, "Atlantic Trade," *A Companion to Herman Melville*, Wyn Kelley, Ed. (Oxford: Blackwell, 2006): 119. Blum's contextualized reading emphasizes the opportunities for "fluidity of identity and affiliation" and "flexible citizenship" afforded by the Atlantic world in which Israel, like other sailors, circulates.

95. See Samson ("loss of identity"), *White Lies* 200; Maloney ("lack of identity"), *Monumental* 151. Rampersad describes Israel's/Perkins's attempt to pass himself off as a crewmember as a "sacreligious indiscretion" (see *Pilgrimmage and Progress* 104). Keyssar calls "The Shuttle" a "tragedy of human fate" (see *Melville's Israel Potter* 39). Temple asserts that Potter "lose(s) his identity" (see "Sketch Patriotism" 12), which she sees as a result of the "schizophrenic formation of identity under capitalism" (see 13). And as Russell Reising points out, "John Seelye laments that Israel 'becomes many things without becoming anybody,' his 'many identities add up to no identity at all.'" See Reising, *Loose Ends: Closure and Crisis in the American Social Text* (Durham: Duke UP, 1996): 119.

96. Reising, *Loose Ends* 140.

97. On the antisocial thesis in queer studies, see Bersani, Leo, *Homos* (Cambridge: Harvard UP, 1996); Edelamn, Lee, *No Future: Queer Theory and the Death Drive* (Durham: Duke UP, 2004). In 2006, *PMLA* published a forum, "The Antisocial Thesis in Queer Theory" featuring short essays by Robert L. Caserio, Lee Edelman, Judith Halberstam, José Esteban Muñoz, and Tim Dean. *PMLA* 21 (2006): 819–28.

98. Dean,Tim, "The Antisocial Thesis in Queer Theory," *PMLA* 21 (2006), 827–8. *Israel Potter*, I am suggesting, negotiates between the antirelational present and anti-present futurity.

99. Ibid.

100. Compare to Elizabeth Freeman on one strain of queer theory: "Another structure of feeling correlates with the emergent, which [Raymond] Williams defines as the semi-intelligible signs of a production process that has not yet come to dominate. Queer scholars tarry with the emergent in their description of radically anticipatory stances or gestures that have not yet congealed into dominant cultural forms like identity, community, or market niche" (see Freeman, "Introduction" 163).

101. Melville, *Israel Potter* 160.

102. Ibid, 168.

103. Ibid, 169.

104. Dinshaw, *How Soon is Now?* 136.

105. Ibid, 137.

106. Freccero, *Queer/Early/Modern* 195.

107. George Herbert Mead's gloss on the anecdote is as follows: "Can we state the end of our own conduct and the end of creation; can it be stated in exact, definite form if the world is something that is moving on from that which is to that which is not? If that is the nature of reality, can the end toward which movement is to take place be stated in a conceptual form? Certainly we can say that it cannot be stated at any given time." See Mead, *Movements of Thought in the Nineteenth Century* (Chicago: U of Chicago P, 1936): 508.

Coda

1. These systems also participate, intersectionally, in the devaluation of gay, queer, and trans lives; the immiseration of the poor; gender discrimination; and the mistreatment of immigrants. See, for instance, Holland, Sharon, *The Erotic Life of Racism* (Durham, NC: Duke UP, 2012). Holland argues for a recuperation of the black-white binary as a way of coming to grips with other forms of oppression.

2. Holiday, Nicole, "How 'Woke' Fell Asleep," *Oxford Dictionaries Blog*, Nov. 16, 2016. Web. Accessed Mar. 11, 2017.

3. See, respectively, Eshun, Kodwo, "Further Considerations of Afrofuturism," *CR: The New Centennial Review* (Summer 2003): 297; Alondra Nelson, "Introduction: Future Texts," *Social Text* 71 (Summer 2002): 7. In addition to Eshun and Nelson, my understanding of Afrofuturism is informed by David, Marlo, "Afrofuturism and Post-Soul Possibility in Black Popular Music," *African American Review* (Winter 2007): 695–707; Womack, Ytasha L., *Afrofuturism: The World of Black Sci-Fi and Fantasy Culture* (Chicago: Lawrence Hill Books, 2013); Steinskog, Erik, *Afrofuturism and Black Sound Studies: Culture, Technology, and Things to Come* (New York: Palgrave Macmillan, 2018). The term was first used by Mark Dery in "Black to the Future: Interviews with Samuel R. Delany, Greg Tate, and Tricia Rose," *South Atlantic Quarterly* 92 (Fall 1992): 735–78; and in Nelson, respectively.

4. Douglass, Fredrick, "What to the Slave Is the Fourth of July? An Address Delivered in Rochester, New York, on 5 July 1852." *The Fredrick Douglass Papers, Series One; Speeches, Debates, and Interviews. Vol. 2: 1847–54*, Ed. John W. Blassingame (New Haven, CT: Yale UP, 1982). Eshun's description of Afrofuturism as "concerned with the possibilities for intervention within the dimension of the predictive, the projected, the proleptic, the envisioned, the virtual, the anticipatory and the future conditional" (see "Further Considerations"

293) provides a reasonably accurate description of my description of Douglass's historical thought in this book's Chapter 4.

5. See David, "Afrofuturism and Post-Soul Possibility" 697.

6. For another examination of Badu and Afrofuturism, see Peach, Rob, "Toward a New 'Amerykah': Erykah Badu's Black Feminist Politics of Hip-Hop." https://hiphopmatrix. wordpress.com/2015/04/22/toward-a-new-amerykah-erykah-badus-black-feminist-politics-of-hip-hop/ Web. Accessed Apr. 29, 2018.

7. See, for example, Miles, Tiya, "Black Hair's Blockbuster Moment," *New York Times* (Feb. 25, 2018), SR6.

8. For an excellent article that traces the shifting meanings of the phrase, see Pulliam-Moore, Charles, "How 'Woke' Went from Black Activist Watchword to Teen Internet Slang," *Fusion*, Jan. 8, 2016. Web. Accessed Mar. 12, 2017.

9. Consider also the aptly titled anthology of nineteenth-century African American women activists *"We Must Be Up and Doing": A Reader in Early African American Feminisms*, Teresa C. Zackodink, Ed. (New York: Broadview Press, 2010). See also Harriet Jacobs's 1854 letter to Amy Post (which echoes Emerson's wish for sound sleep I discuss in Chapter 3): "I sometimes wish I could fall into a Rip Van Winkle sleep and awake with the blest belief of that little Witch Topsy that I never was born." The letter is quoted in Rohy, who also provides an illuminating discussion of it: *Anachronism and Its Others* 30).

10. Sinha, Manisha, *The Slave's Cause. A History of Abolition* (New Haven: Yale UP, 2016): 195.

11. Frances Smith Foster discusses Stewart's pamphlet in *Written by Herself: Literary Production by African American Women, 1746–1892* (Bloomington: Indiana UP, 1993).

12. Stewart, Maria W., *America's First Black Woman Political Writer: Essays and Speeches*, Marilyn Richardson, Ed. (Bloomington: Indiana UP, 1987): 30.

13. For Harper's work assisting runaway slaves, see Still, William, *The Underground Railroad* (Philadelphia: People's Publishing Company, 1871): 755–80. For Harper's associations with the Browns, see *Discarded Legacy: Politics and Poetics in the Life of Frances E. W. Harper, 1825–1911*, Melba Joyce Boyd, Ed. (Detroit, MI: Wayne State UP, 1994). I am grateful to Michael Stancliff for directing me to Still and for his helpful remarks on my discussion of Harper below. I have benefitted, too, from Stancliff's excellent book, *Frances Ellen Watkins Harper: African American Reform Rhetoric and the Rise of a Modern Nation State* (New York: Routledge, 2011).

14. Smith Foster, Frances, Ed., *A Brighter Day Coming: A Frances Ellen Watkins Harper Reader* (New York: Feminist Press, 1990): 138.

15. Emerson, *Collected Works, v. I, 171*.

16. Smith Foster, *A Brighter Day Coming* 177–8.

17. Graham, Maryemma, Ed., *Complete Poems of Frances E. W. Harper* (New York: Oxford, 1988): 93.

18. Ibid, 93.

19. Ibid, 94.

20. Luciano, *Arranging Grief* 180.

21. Ibid, 174.

22. Ibid, 171.

23. For an example of a contemporary black countermonumental critique, complementary to my reading of Harper, see John Levi Barnard's brilliant reading of Kara Walker's "Sugar Baby" sculpture in the last chapter of his *Empire of Ruin: Black Classicism and American Imperial Culture* (New York: Oxford UP, 2018).

24. Indeed, Harper's commitment to action was evident in her support for John Brown. In 1859, Harper wrote to Aaron Stevens, one of Brown's compatriots, while he awaited execution for his role in the Harpers Ferry raid. She included with her letter, a copy of "Bury Me in a Free Land," perhaps in the hopes that its images of the animated dead (not unlike Thoreau's) would provide Stevens with a measure of comfort or courage. See Boyd, *Discarded Legacy* 51.

25. See, for example, Brooks, David, "The Trouble with Wokeness," *New York Times* (Apr. 7, 2018): A27.

26. Rosenberg, Eli. "John Kelly calls Robert E. Lee an 'honorable man' and says 'lack of compromise' caused the Civil War," *Washington Post*, Oct. 31, 2017. Web. Accessed Nov. 11, 2017.

27. Salovey, Peter, "Decision on the Name of Calhoun College," *Yale University Office of the President*, Feb. 11, 2017. Web. Accessed Feb. 12, 2017.

28. Salovey, Peter, "Decision Residential College Names and 'Master' Title," *Yale University Office of the President*, Apr. 27, 2016. Web. Accessed Feb. 12, 2017.

29. Lowenthal, David, "Facing Up to the Depolorable Past," *Perspectives on History*, May 2016. Web. Accessed Mar. 1, 2017.

30. Cole, David, "The Trouble at Yale," *New York Review of Books* (Jan. 14, 2016).

31. Hanlon, C., "Integrating Stephen Douglas," *Pedagogy* 13 (Fall 2013): 429–52.

32. Hanlon writes:

Eastern's board of trustees approved the names of Douglas Hall and Lincoln Hall in March 1951, in response to a proposal authored by the chair of social sciences, Glen Seymour—a historian whose opinions on Douglas typified the revisionary agendas of midcentury historiography. In his 1929 University of Illinois PhD dissertation on Douglas, Seymour argued that the Civil War was brought about by fringe radicals whose unwillingness to compromise overcame more temperate voices of which Douglas's was an example. In 1961, in fact, Seymour gave an address at the Chicago Civil War Roundtable in which he rehearsed the argument, claiming that the Romantic movement instilled a cultural climate in which novels such as *Uncle Tom's Cabin* as well as "abolitionist oratory…charged with emotion" plunged the nation into war. In such a time of extremism, Seymour opined, "the moderates were lost," and though for all that he was also a product of commonly held notions of negro inferiority, Douglas proved an outlier to a more general hardening of polarities.

Ibid, 435

33. Salovey appears to be quoting a widely circulated essay by former American Historical Association President Lynn Hunt, published in the Association's news magazine *Perspectives on History*: "Presentism," Hunt claims, "at its worst, encourages a kind of moral complacency and self-congratulation." See "Against Presentism," *Perspectives on History* (May 2002). https://www.historians.org/publications-and-directories/perspectives-on-history/may-2002/against-presentism. Web. Accessed Apr. 28, 2018.

34. This is a feature of Hanlon's experience as well (see 442).

35. Jelly-Schapiro, Joshua, "Yale: the History We Can't Erase," *NYR Daily*, Feb. 27, 2017. Web. Accessed Feb. 27, 2017.

36. Loh, Wallace D., "Recommendation on Byrd Stadium Naming," *University of Maryland Office of the President*, Dec. 7, 2015. Web. Accessed Feb. 24, 2017.

37. Kuznicki, Jason, "The New Presentism: Leftist Banality in the Academy," https://www.libertarianism.org, Sept. 29, 2015. Web. Accessed Feb. 24, 2017.

38. Bartow, Paul, "The Growing Threat of Historical Presentism," *AEIdeas*, Dec. 10, 2015. Web. Accessed Feb. 24, 2017.

39. Davenport, David, and Gordon Lloyd, "When College Radicals Obliterate History," *Hoover.org*, Jan. 27, 2016. Web. Accessed Feb. 24, 2017. See also Davenport's, "Presentism: The Dangerous Virus Spreading Across College Campuses," *Forbes*, Dec. 1, 2015. Web. Accessed Feb. 24, 2017.

40. Baker, Ross K., "Democrats Foolishly Purge Heroes," *USA Today*, Aug. 10, 2015. Web. Accessed Feb. 24, 2017.

41. A vivid example of this sort of casual historical erasure was provided by the conservative writer Matt Walsh soon after the Charlottesville rally. Walsh tweeted: "Challenge: name five historical figures from mid 19th century or earlier who wouldn't be considered extremely racist by modern standards." See @mattwalshblog, *Twitter*, Aug. 17, 2017, 11.00 am, /twitter.com/MattWalshBlog/status/898243087545323521.

42. "What of the Night?" in *Frederick Douglass: Selected Speeches and Writings*, Philip S. Foner, Ed. (Chicago: Lawrence Hill Books, 1999): 97.

43. Douglass, "Farewell Speech to the British People," *Selected Speeches and Writings* 60.

44. Douglass, "The Kansas Nebraska Bill," *Selected Speeches and Writings* 302.

45. *The Liberator*, Apr. 5, 1850

46. Douglass, *Selected Speeches and Writings* 196.

47. Cobb, James C., "Cleansing American Culture of Ties to Slavery Will Be Harder Than You Think," *Time*, Mar. 30, 2016. Web. Accessed Mar. 14, 2017.

48. In addition to the foregoing chapter, I mean to allude here also to Sharon Holland's important book *Raising the Dead: Readings of Death and (Black) Subjectivity* (Durham, NC: Duke UP, 2000).

{ INDEX }